# SAVE 50% OFF
## THE COVER PRICE

## IT'S LIKE GETTING 6 ISSUES
# FREE!

**OVER 350+ PAGES PER ISSUE**

This monthly magazine contains 7 of the coolest manga available in the U.S., PLUS anime news, and info about video & card games, toys AND more!

❏ **I want 12 HUGE issues of SHONEN JUMP for only $29.95*!**

**NAME**

**ADDRESS**

**CITY/STATE/ZIP**

**EMAIL ADDRESS**                              **DATE OF BIRTH**

❏ YES, send me via email information, advertising, offers, and promotions related to VIZ Media, SHONEN JUMP, and/or their business partners.

❏ **CHECK ENCLOSED** (payable to SHONEN JUMP)    ❏ **BILL ME LATER**

**CREDIT CARD:**  ❏ Visa  ❏ Mastercard  ~~WITHDRAWN~~

**ACCOUNT NUMBER**                              **EXP. DATE**

**SIGNATURE**

## CLIP&MAIL TO:
SHONEN JUMP Subscriptions Service Dept.
P.O. Box 515
Mount Morris, IL 61054-0515

**P9GNC1**

* Canada price: $41.95 USD, including GST, HST, and QST, US/CAN orders only. Allow 6-8 weeks for delivery.
ONE PIECE © 1997 by Eiichiro Oda/SHUEISHA Inc. BLEACH © 2001 by Tite Kubo/SHUEISHA Inc.
NARUTO © 1999 by Masashi Kishimoto/SHUEISHA Inc.

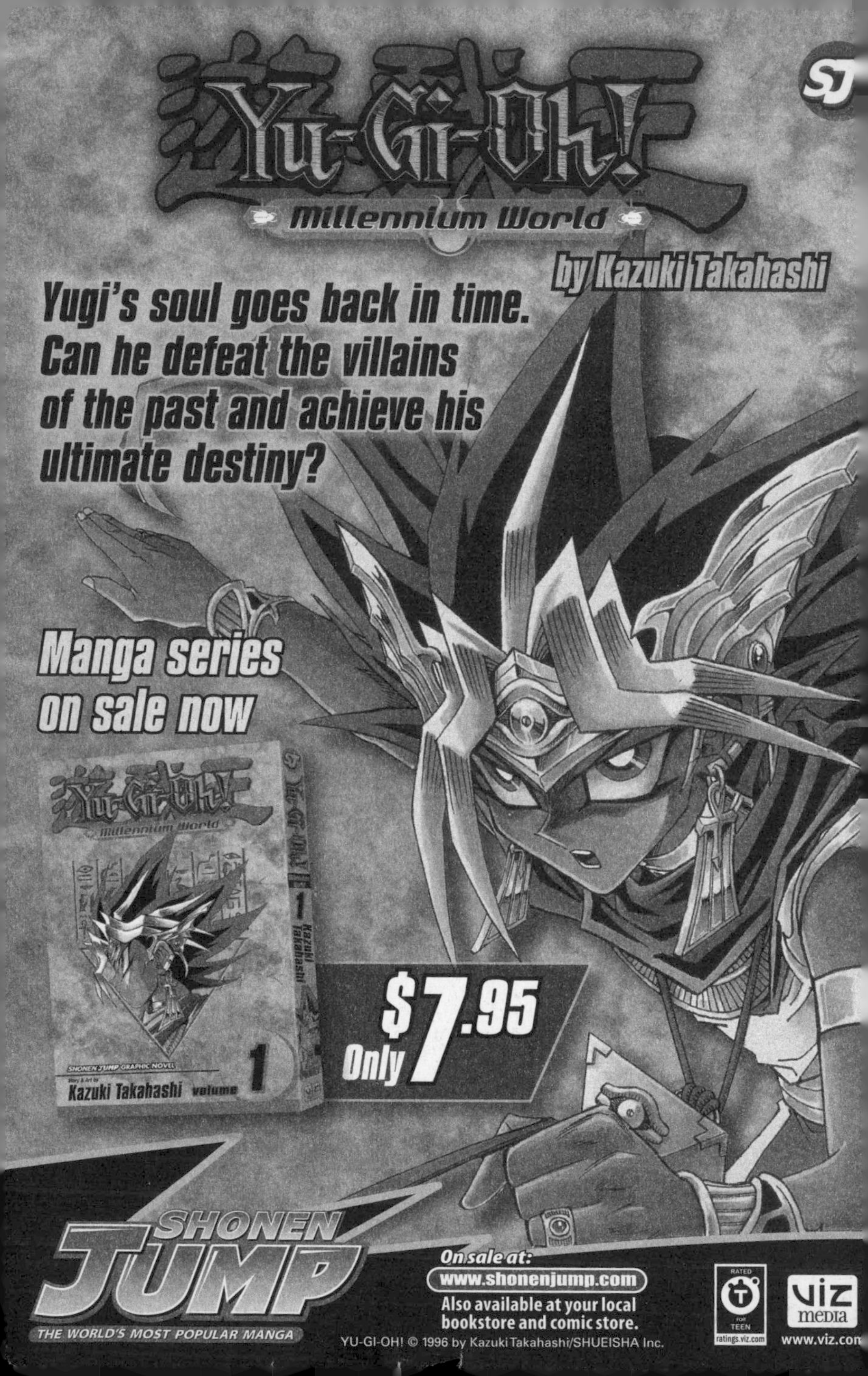

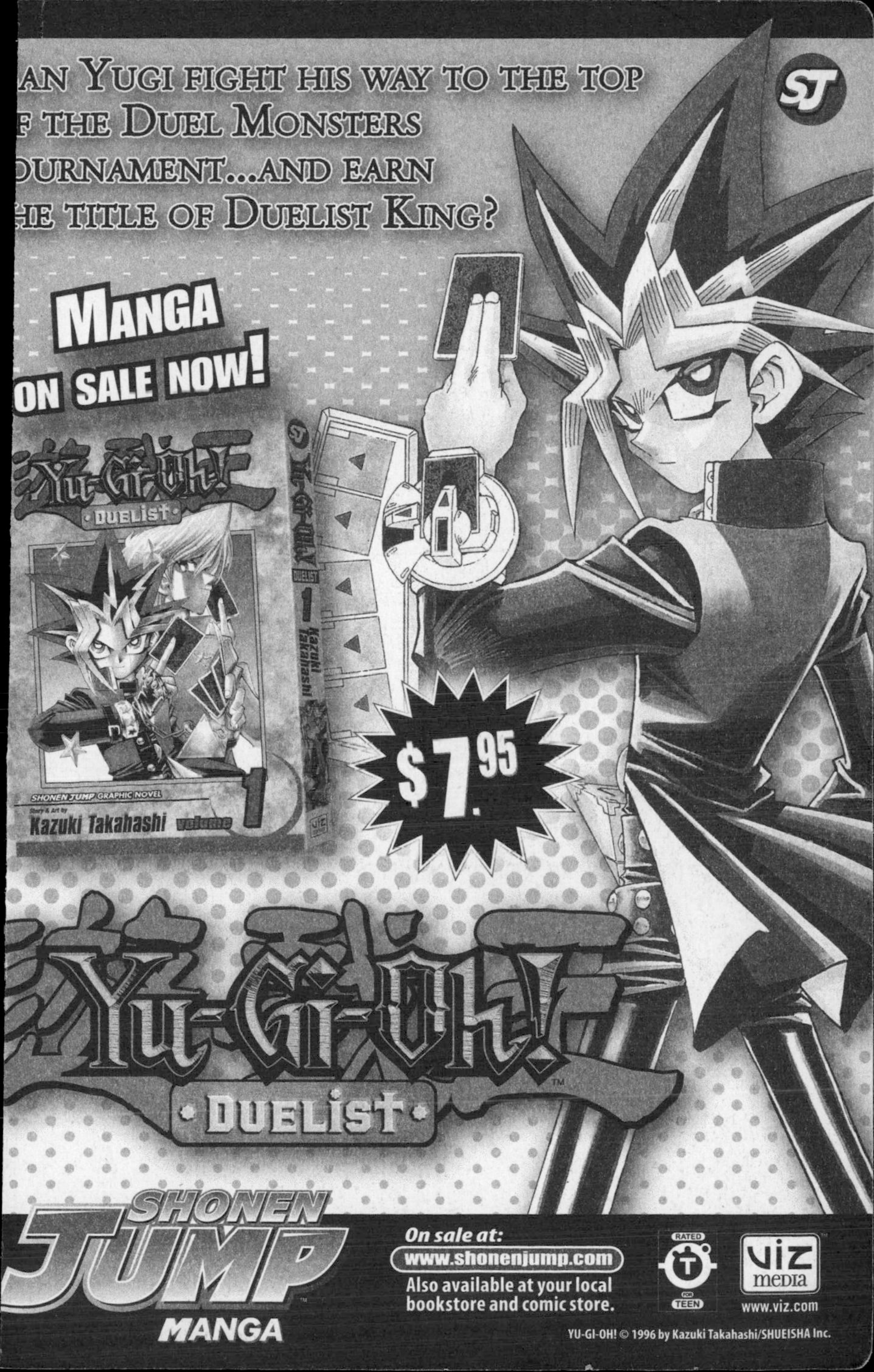
AN YUGI FIGHT HIS WAY TO THE TOP
F THE DUEL MONSTERS
OURNAMENT...AND EARN
HE TITLE OF DUELIST KING?
SJ
MANGA
ON SALE NOW!
Yu-Gi-Oh!
DUELIST
SHONEN JUMP GRAPHIC NOVEL
Story & Art by
Kazuki Takahashi
volume 1
$7.95
Yu-Gi-Oh!™
DUELIST
SHONEN JUMP MANGA
On sale at:
www.shonenjump.com
Also available at your local
bookstore and comic store.
RATED T FOR TEEN
VIZ media
www.viz.com
YU-GI-OH! © 1996 by Kazuki Takahashi/SHUEISHA Inc.

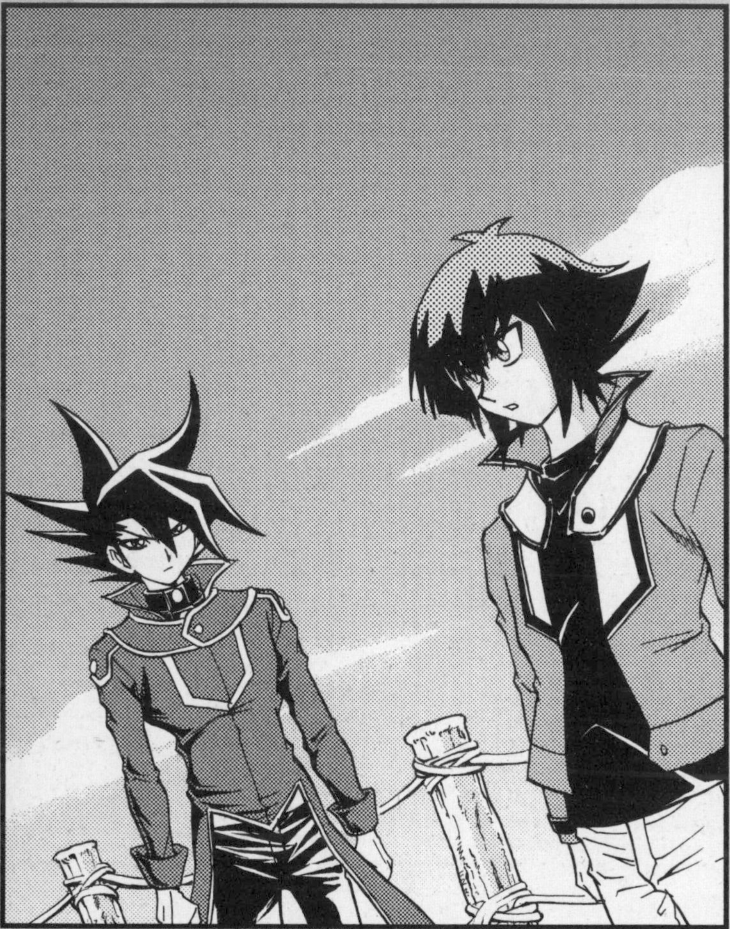

**IN THE NEXT VOLUME...**

James "Crocodile" Cook, one of the four Duelists from America, eagerly challenges Atticus Rhodes to a Duel. Elsewhere, Jaden and Chazz unlock more secrets of their spirit cards, Winged Kuriboh and Light and Darkness Dragon. But their confrontation could lead to a Shadow Game that only one Duelist may survive!

***COMING AUGUST 2011!***

KAZUKI

高橋和希

## KAZUKI TAKAHASHI

*KAZUKI TAKAHASHI*
*YUGI'S 13TH ANNIVERSARY*
*IS COMING UP NEXT YEAR,*
*AND SOME THINK WE SHOULD*
*MAKE A WEBSITE FOR STUDIO*
*DICE TO COMMEMORATE IT.*
*SO WE MIGHT. WE'LL GIVE IT*
*A GOOD TRY.*

## KAZUKI TAKAHASHI

Artist/author Kazuki Takahashi first tried to break into the manga business in 1982, but success eluded him until *Yu-Gi-Oh!* debuted in the Japanese *Weekly Shonen Jump* magazine in 1996. *Yu-Gi-Oh!*'s themes of friendship and fighting, together with Takahashi's weird and imaginative monsters, soon became enormously successful, spawning a real-world card game, video games, and four anime series (two Japanese *Yu-Gi-Oh!* series, *Yu-Gi-Oh! GX* and *Yu-Gi-Oh! 5D's*). A lifelong gamer, Takahashi enjoys Shogi (Japanese chess), Mahjong, card games, and tabletop RPGs, among other games.

## NAOYUKI KAGEYAMA

Naoyuki Kageyama was born April 12, 1969, which makes him an Aries, and is originally from Tokyo, Japan. He is the recipient of an honorable mention for the 1990 *Weekly Shonen Jump* Hop Step Award for his work *Mahou No Trump* (Magic Trump) and started drawing *Yu-Gi-Oh! GX* for *Monthly V Jump* in February 2006. Kageyama is a baseball fan and his favorite team is the Seibu Lions.

影山なおゆき

## NAOYUKI KAGEYAMA

*NAOYUKI KAGEYAMA*
*JADEN, SYRUS, ALEXIS,*
*BASTION, CHAZZ, ZANE,*
*ATTICUS, JOHANN, ADRIAN,*
*JIM, AUSTIN, ASTER...*
*THERE ARE A LOT OF 'EM...*
*WHAT'LL I DO...? ...WELL*
*...JUST AS LONG AS OUR*
*READERS ENJOY IT.*

**YU-GI-OH! GX Volume 6**
**SHONEN JUMP Manga Edition**

ORIGINAL CONCEPT/SUPERVISED BY
KAZUKI TAKAHASHI

STORY AND ART BY
NAOYUKI KAGEYAMA

Translation & English Adaptation/Taylor Engel and Ian Reid, HC Language Solutions
Touch-up Art & Lettering/John Hunt
Designer/Ronnie Casson
Editor/Mike Montesa

Printed in the U.S.A.

Published by VIZ Media, LLC
P.O. Box 77010
San Francisco, CA 94107

10 9 8 7 6 5 4 3 2 1
First printing, March 2011

**PARENTAL ADVISORY**
YU-GI-OH! GX is rated A and is
suitable for readers of all ages.
ratings.viz.com

THE WORLD'S
MOST POPULAR MANGA

www.viz.com

www.shonenjump.com

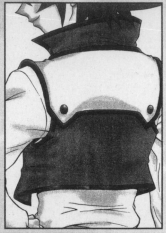

VOLUME
6
The Power
of Kaiser!

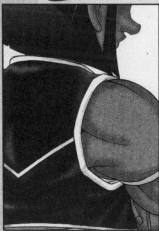

**Story & Art by**
**NAOYUKI**
**KAGEYAMA**

**Original Concept/**
**Supervised by**
**KAZUKI**
**TAKAHASHI**

# THE STORY SO FAR

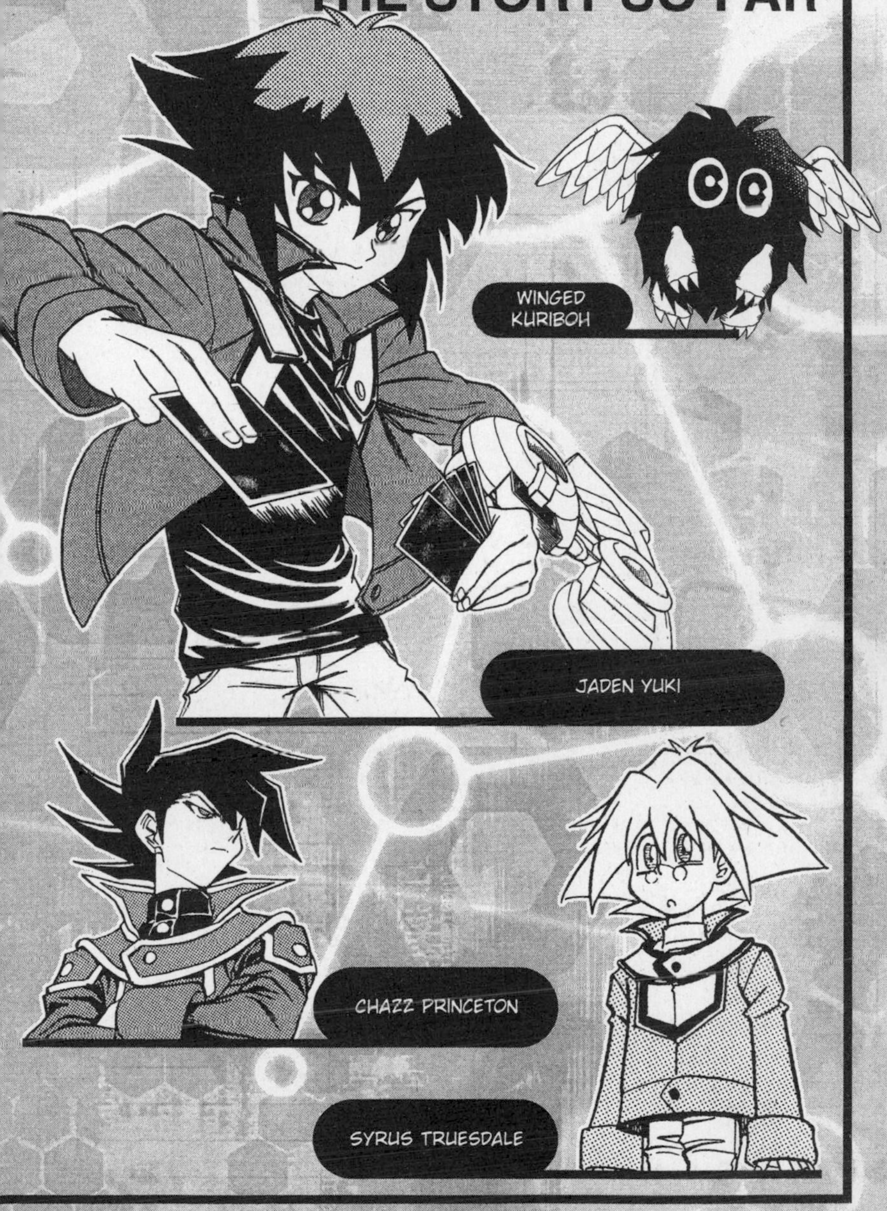
WINGED KURIBOH
JADEN YUKI
CHAZZ PRINCETON
SYRUS TRUESDALE

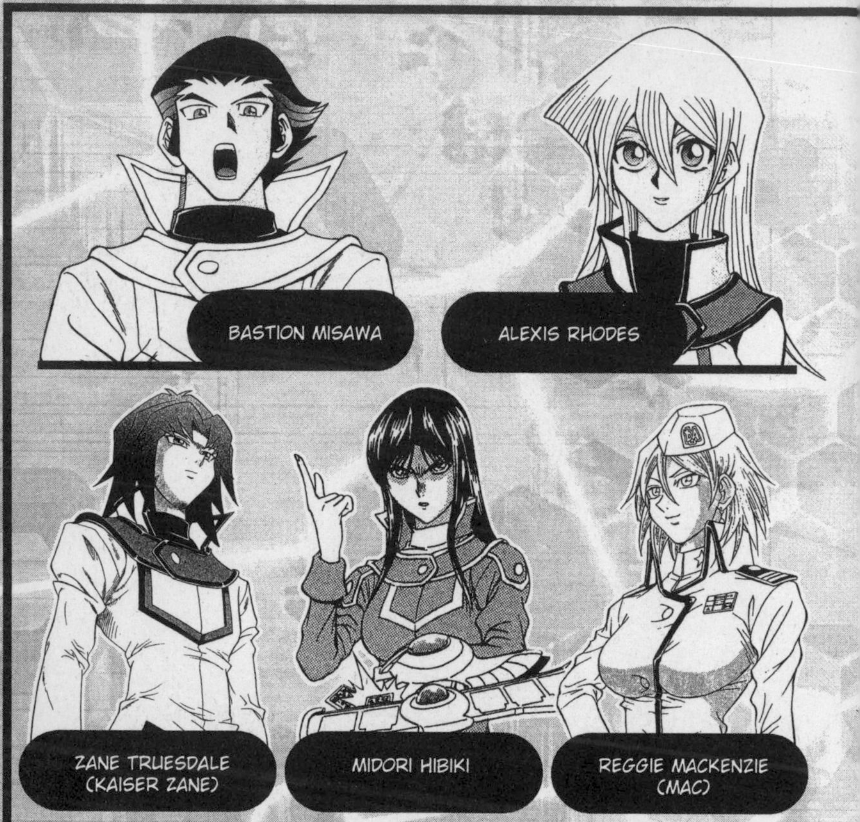
ALEXIS RHODES
BASTION MISAWA
REGGIE MACKENZIE (MAC)
MIDORI HIBIKI
ZANE TRUESDALE (KAISER ZANE)

ON AN ISLAND IN THE SOUTHERN SEA STANDS AN ACADEMY WHERE THE NEXT GENERATION OF DUELISTS IS TRAINED. IT IS CALLED DUEL ACADEMY!

JADEN YUKI LEARNED ABOUT THE EXCITEMENT OF DUELING THROUGH AN ENCOUNTER WITH DUEL WORLD CHAMPION, KOYO HIBIKI. ENTRUSTED WITH HIBIKI'S DECK, JADEN TAKES ON ALL CHALLENGERS AT THE ACADEMY IN ORDER TO BECOME A TRUE DUELIST!

SYRUS'S OLDER BROTHER ZANE, AKA KAISER, HAS RETURNED FROM AMERICA AND A TOURNAMENT IS BEING HELD AT THE ACADEMY TO WIN THE RIGHT TO CHALLENGE HIM. AFTER LOSING A DUEL AGAINST CHAZZ, JADEN IS LED BY WINGED KURIBOH TO WHERE MS. HIBIKI IS FIGHTING A "SHADOW GAME". BUT MS. HIBIKI LOSES TO REGGIE... MEANWHILE, A SPECIAL DUEL BEGINS! CHAZZ HAS TAKEN THE INITIATIVE, SUMMONING THE STRONGEST CARD HE HAS...!

# Volume 6: The Power of Kaiser!

## CONTENTS

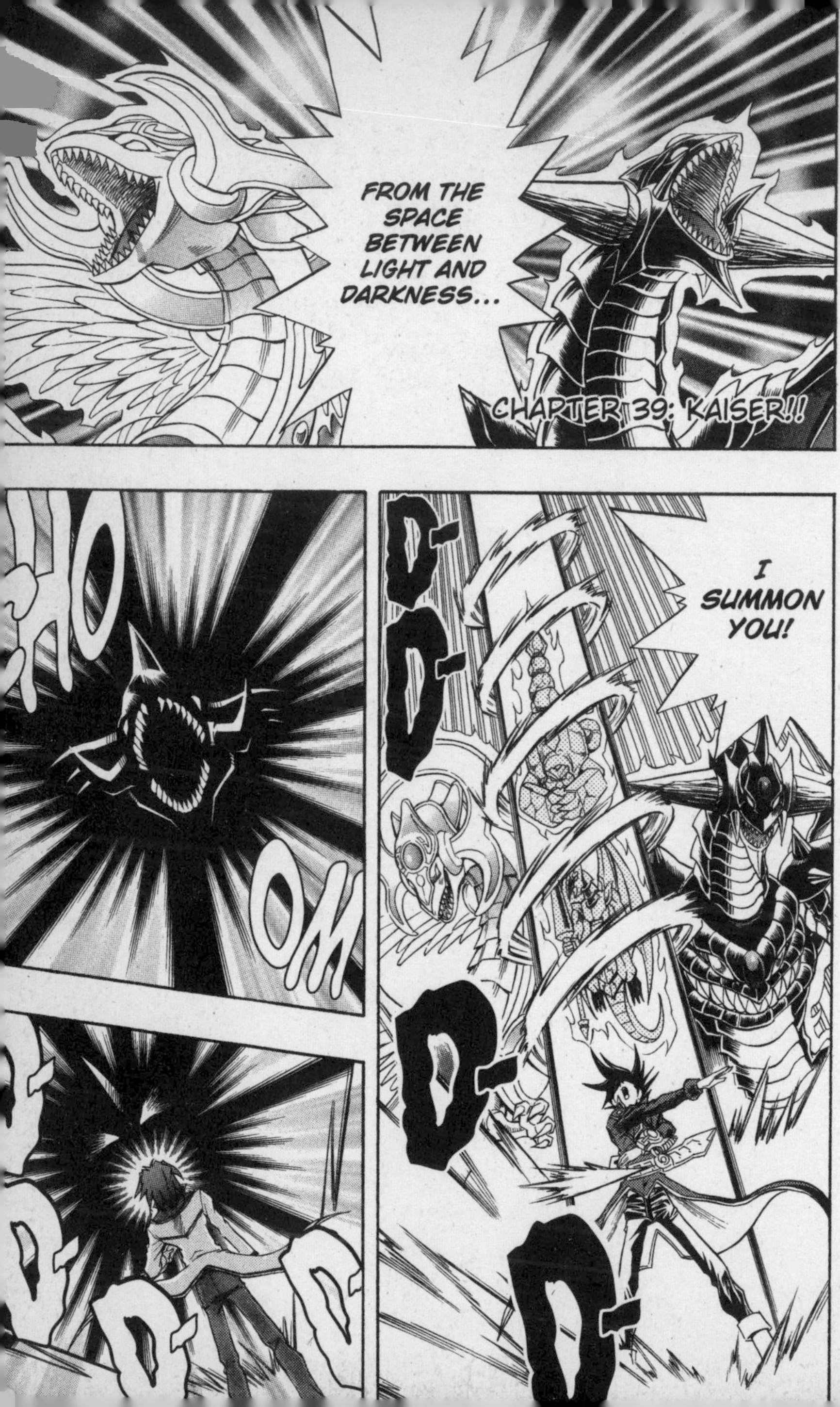
FROM THE SPACE BETWEEN LIGHT AND DARKNESS...
CHAPTER 39: KAISER!!
D- D-
I SUMMON YOU!
D- D-
OM

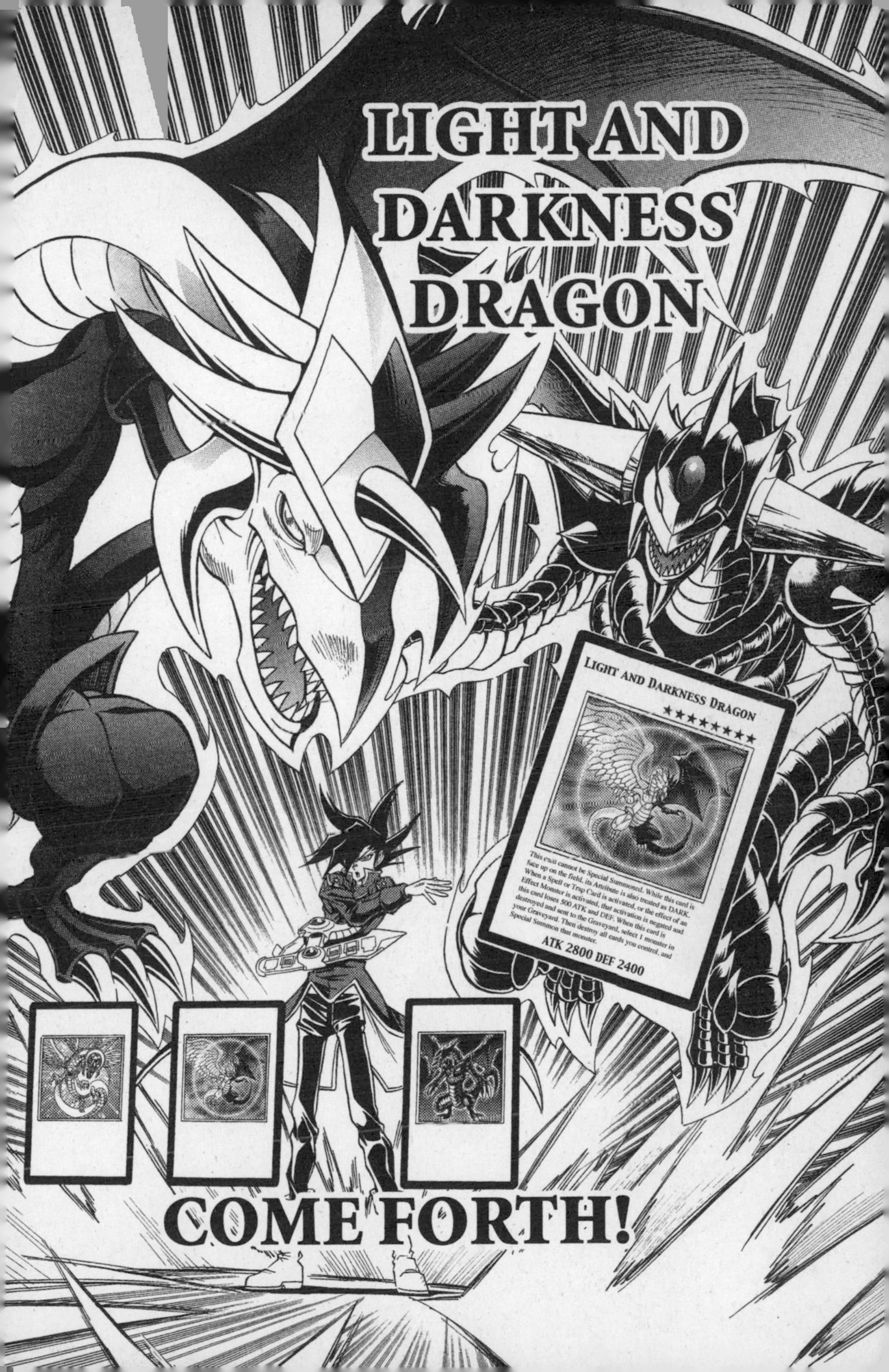
LIGHT AND DARKNESS DRAGON
LIGHT AND DARKNESS DRAGON
★★★★★★★★
This card cannot be Special Summoned. While this card is face up on the field, its Attribute is also treated as DARK. When a Spell or Trap Card is activated, or the effect of an Effect Monster is activated, that activation is negated and this card loses 500 ATK and DEF. When this card is destroyed and sent to the Graveyard, select 1 monster in your Graveyard. Then destroy all cards you control, and Special Summon that monster.
ATK 2800 DEF 2400
COME FORTH!

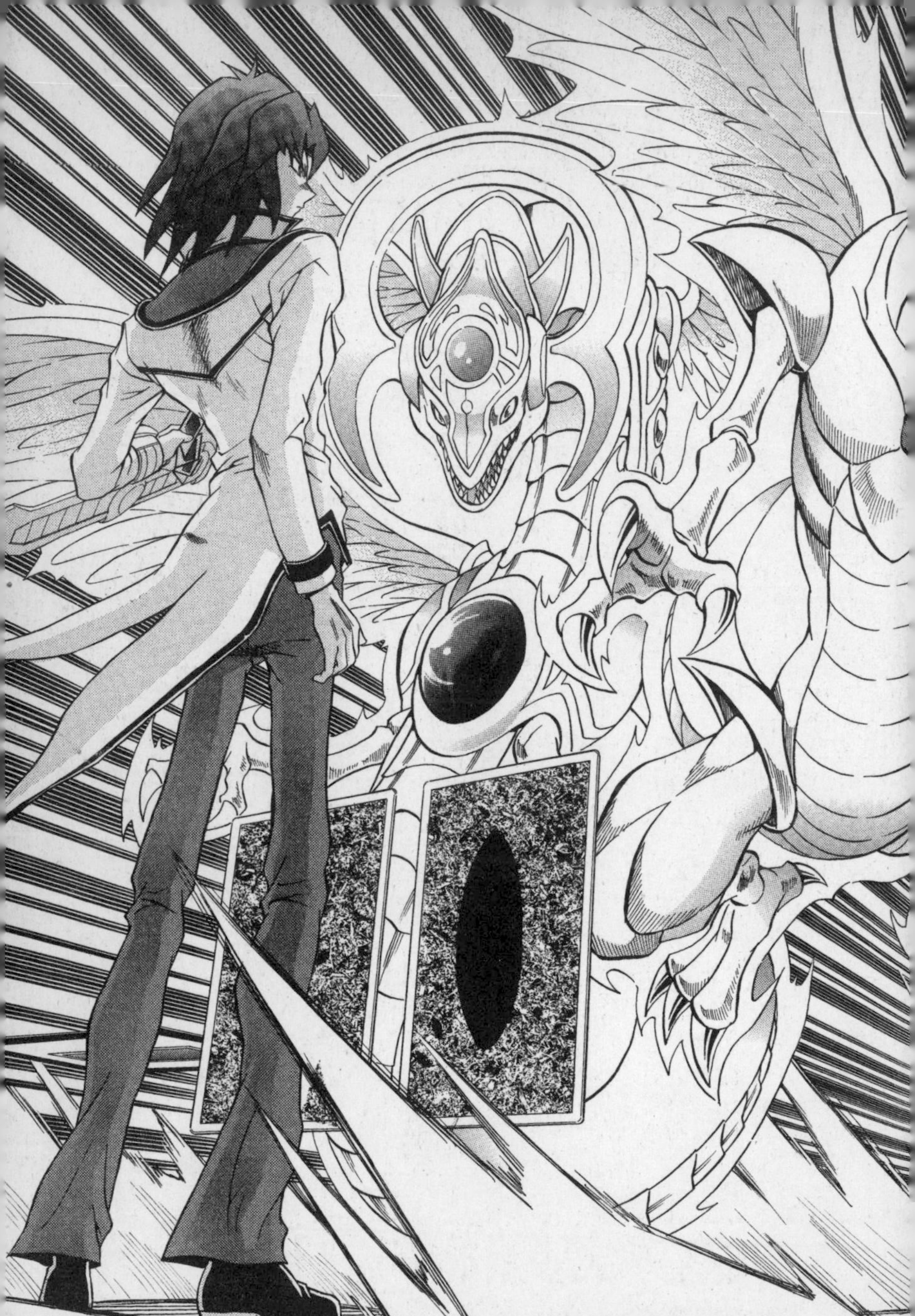

# CHAPTER 39: KAISER!!

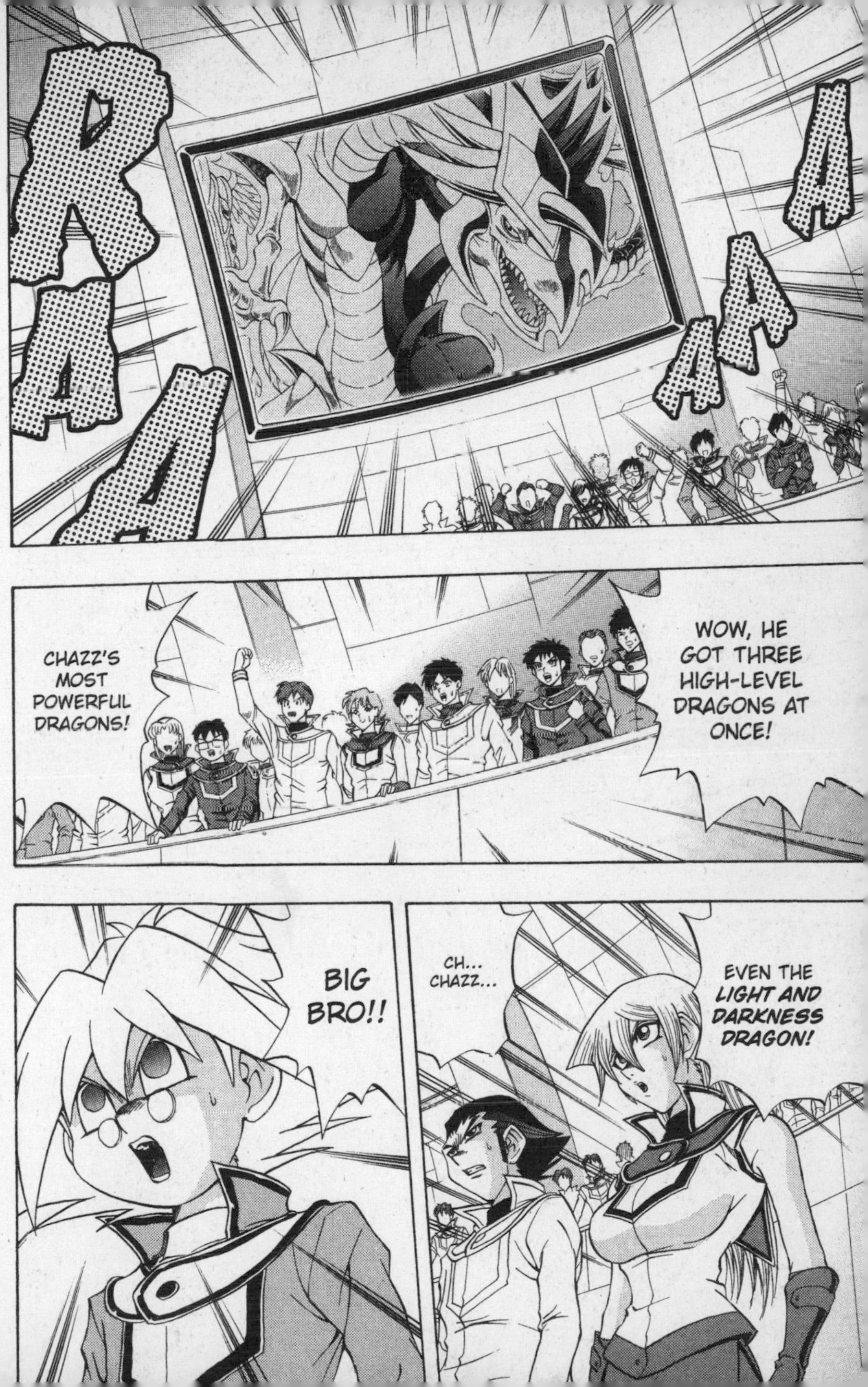
RAAAAAAA
WOW, HE GOT THREE HIGH-LEVEL DRAGONS AT ONCE!
CHAZZ'S MOST POWERFUL DRAGONS!
EVEN THE *LIGHT AND DARKNESS DRAGON!*
CH... CHAZZ...
BIG BRO!!

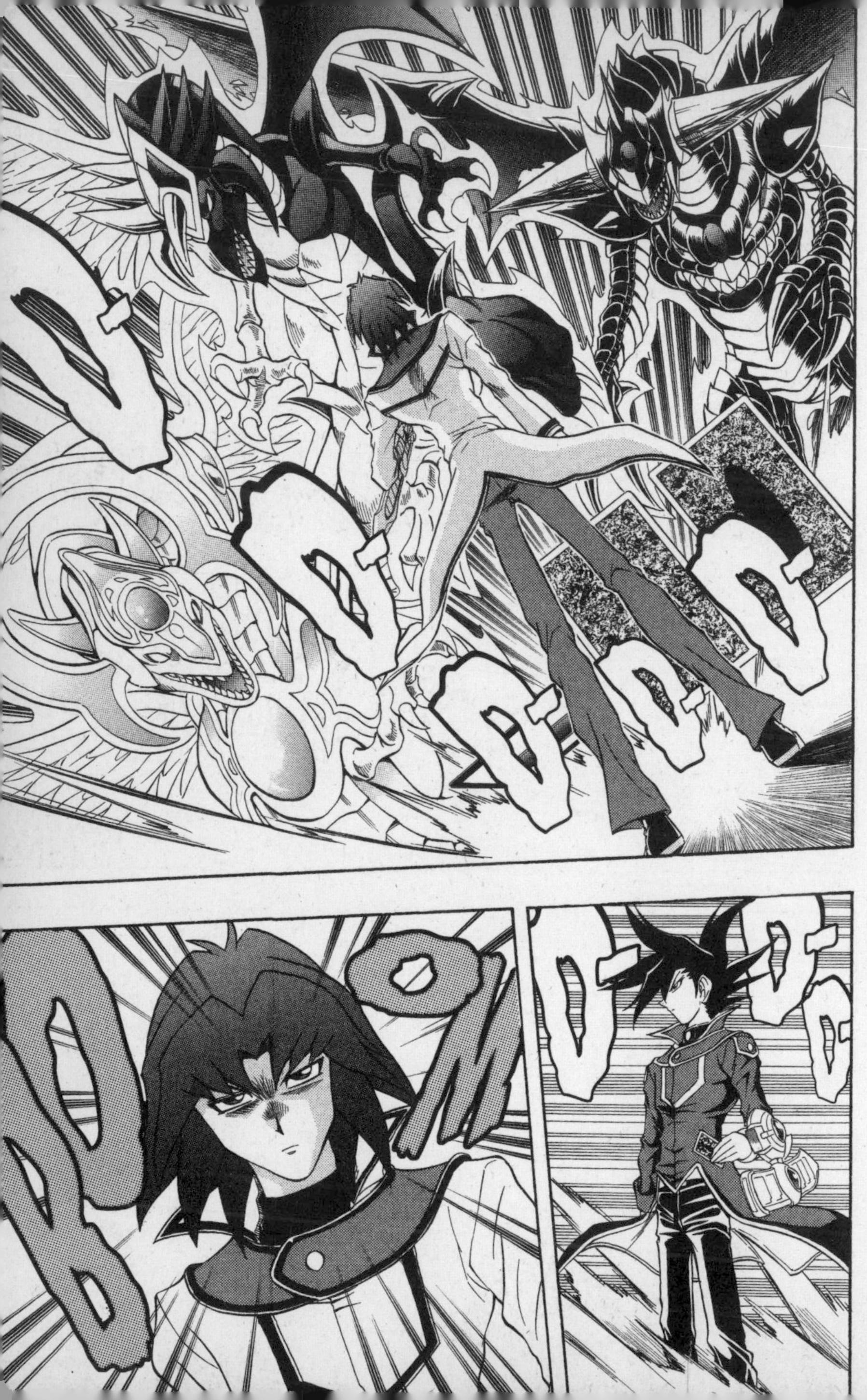

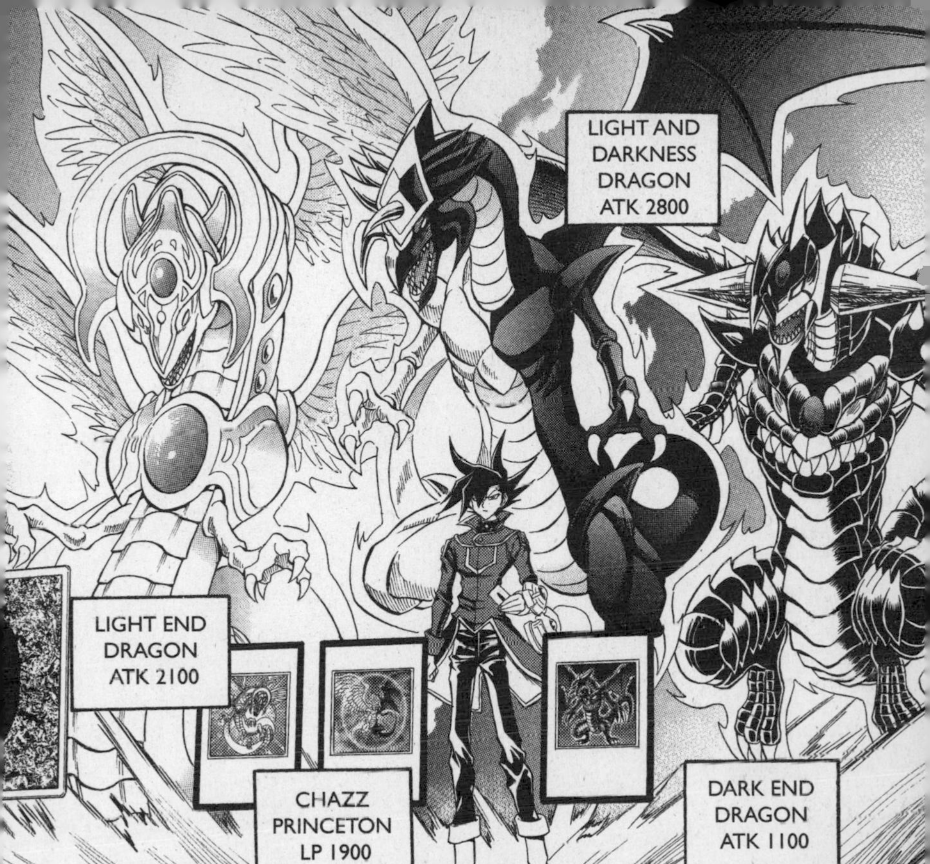
LIGHT AND DARKNESS DRAGON ATK 2800
DARK END DRAGON ATK 1100
CHAZZ PRINCETON LP 1900
LIGHT END DRAGON ATK 2100

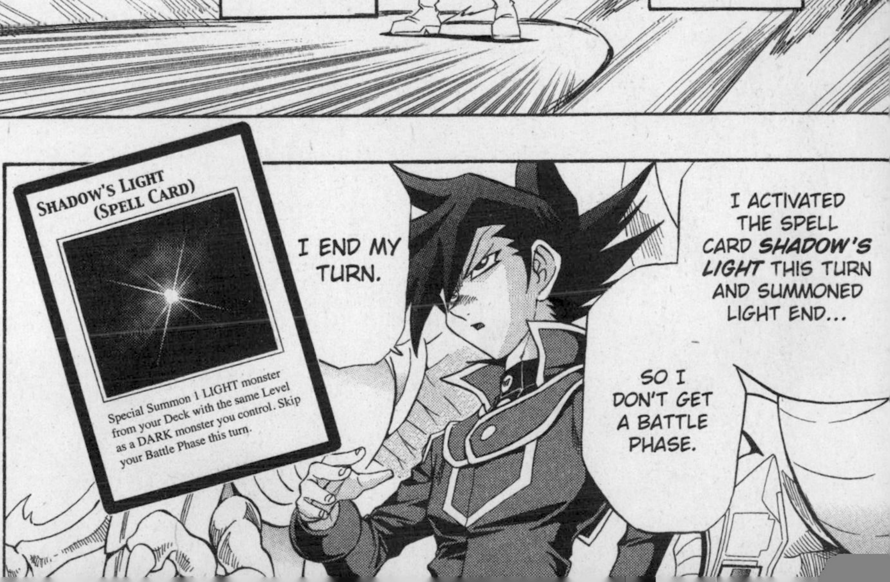
I ACTIVATED THE SPELL CARD ***SHADOW'S LIGHT*** THIS TURN AND SUMMONED LIGHT END...
SO I DON'T GET A BATTLE PHASE.
I END MY TURN.
SHADOW'S LIGHT (SPELL CARD)
Special Summon 1 LIGHT monster from your Deck with the same Level as a DARK monster you control. Skip your Battle Phase this turn.

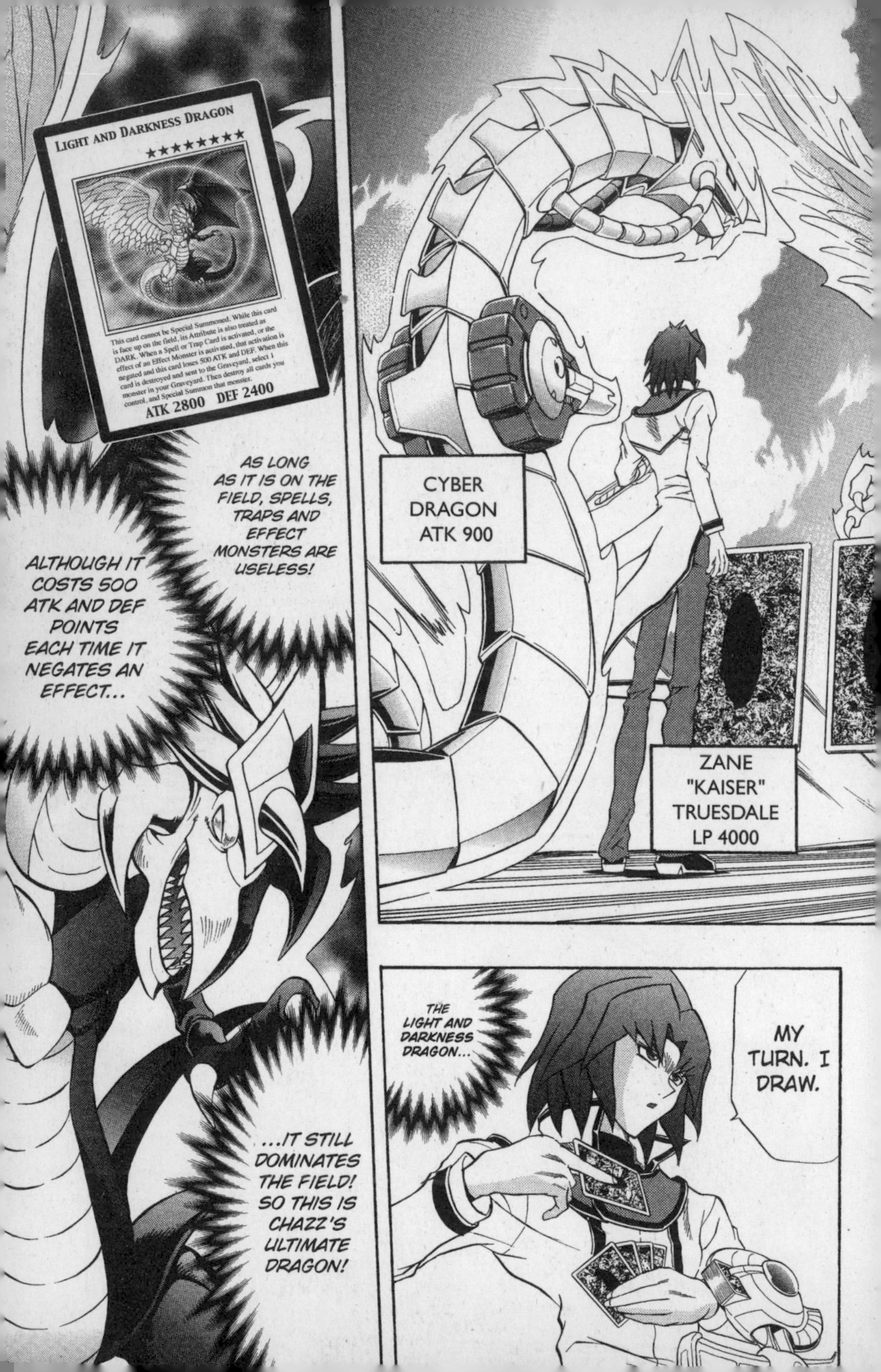
CYBER DRAGON ATK 900
ZANE "KAISER" TRUESDALE LP 4000
MY TURN. I DRAW.
THE LIGHT AND DARKNESS DRAGON...
LIGHT AND DARKNESS DRAGON
This card cannot be Special Summoned. While this card is face up on the field, its Attribute is also treated as DARK. When a Spell or Trap Card is activated, or the effect of an Effect Monster is activated, that activation is negated and this card loses 500 ATK and DEF. When this card is destroyed and sent to the Graveyard, select 1 monster in your Graveyard. Then destroy all cards you control, and Special Summon that monster.
ATK 2800 DEF 2400
AS LONG AS IT IS ON THE FIELD, SPELLS, TRAPS AND EFFECT MONSTERS ARE USELESS!
ALTHOUGH IT COSTS 500 ATK AND DEF POINTS EACH TIME IT NEGATES AN EFFECT...
...IT STILL DOMINATES THE FIELD! SO THIS IS CHAZZ'S ULTIMATE DRAGON!

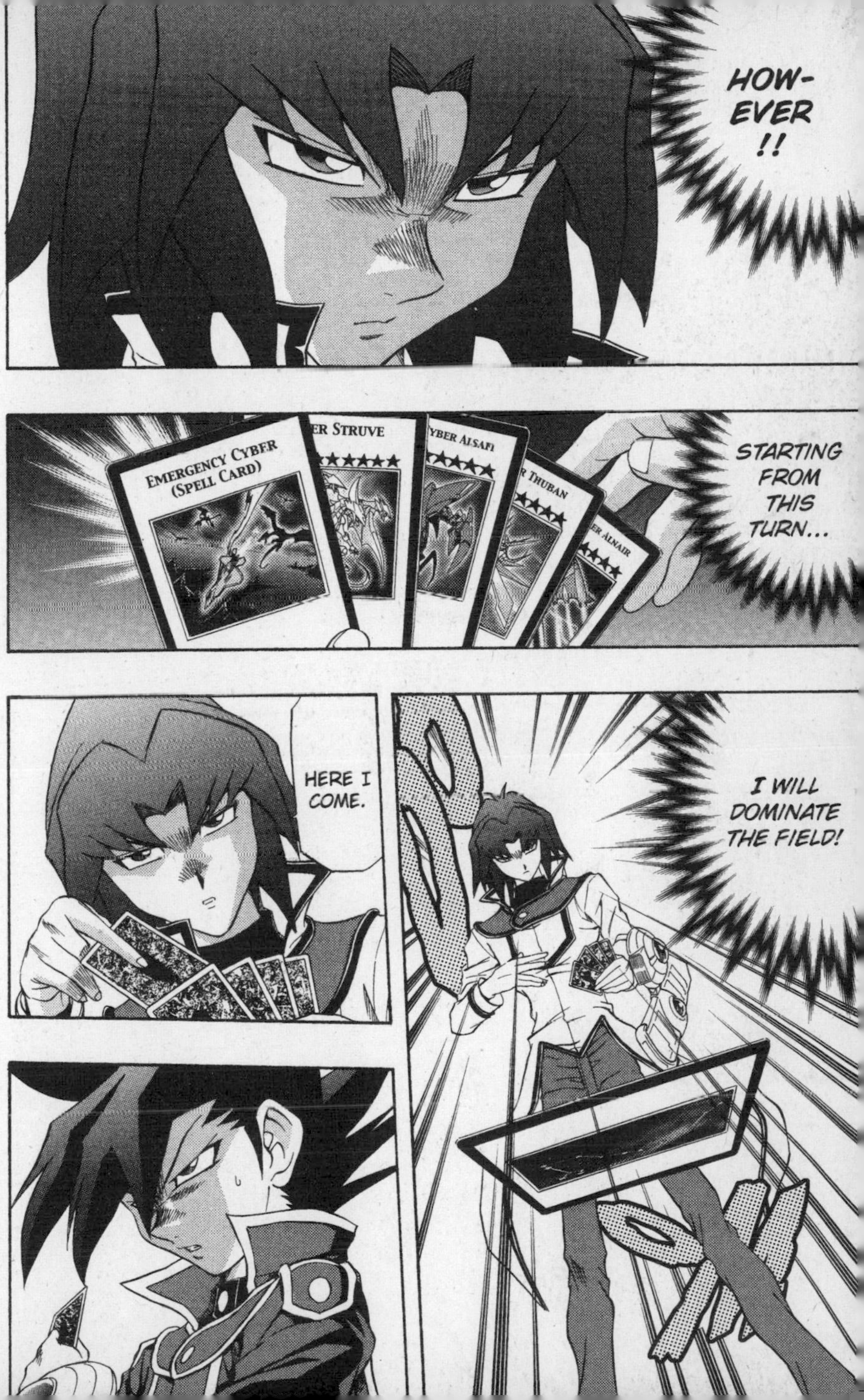
HOW-EVER !!
STARTING FROM THIS TURN...
EMERGENCY CYBER (SPELL CARD)
ER STRUVE
YBER ALSAFI
R THUBAN
ER ALNAIR
I WILL DOMINATE THE FIELD!
HERE I COME.

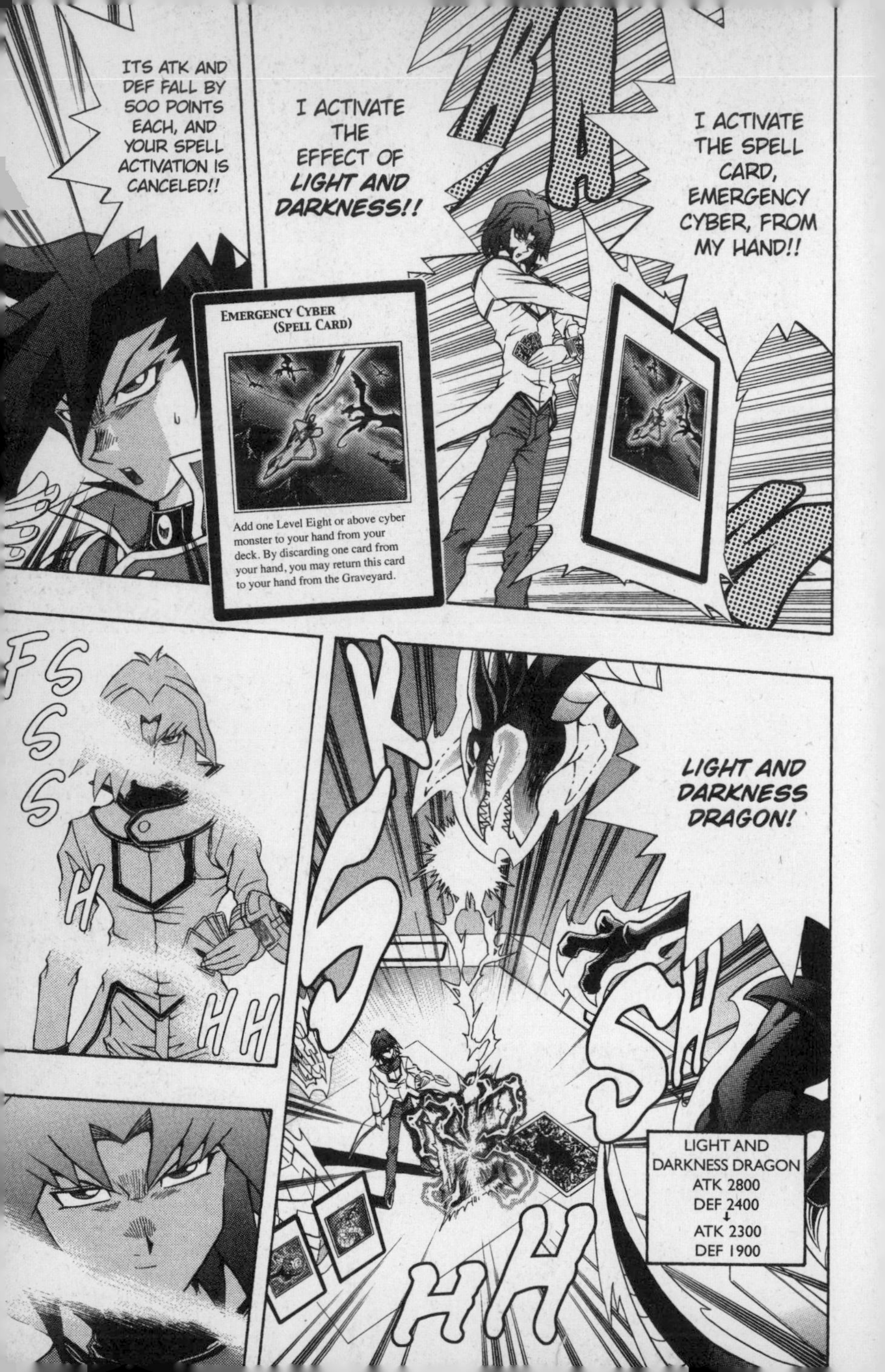

I ACTIVATE THE SPELL CARD, EMERGENCY CYBER, FROM MY HAND!!
EMERGENCY CYBER
(SPELL CARD)
Add one Level Eight or above cyber monster to your hand from your deck. By discarding one card from your hand, you may return this card to your hand from the Graveyard.
I ACTIVATE THE EFFECT OF LIGHT AND DARKNESS!!
ITS ATK AND DEF FALL BY 500 POINTS EACH, AND YOUR SPELL ACTIVATION IS CANCELED!!
LIGHT AND DARKNESS DRAGON!
LIGHT AND DARKNESS DRAGON
ATK 2800
DEF 2400
↓
ATK 2300
DEF 1900
FSSSHHH

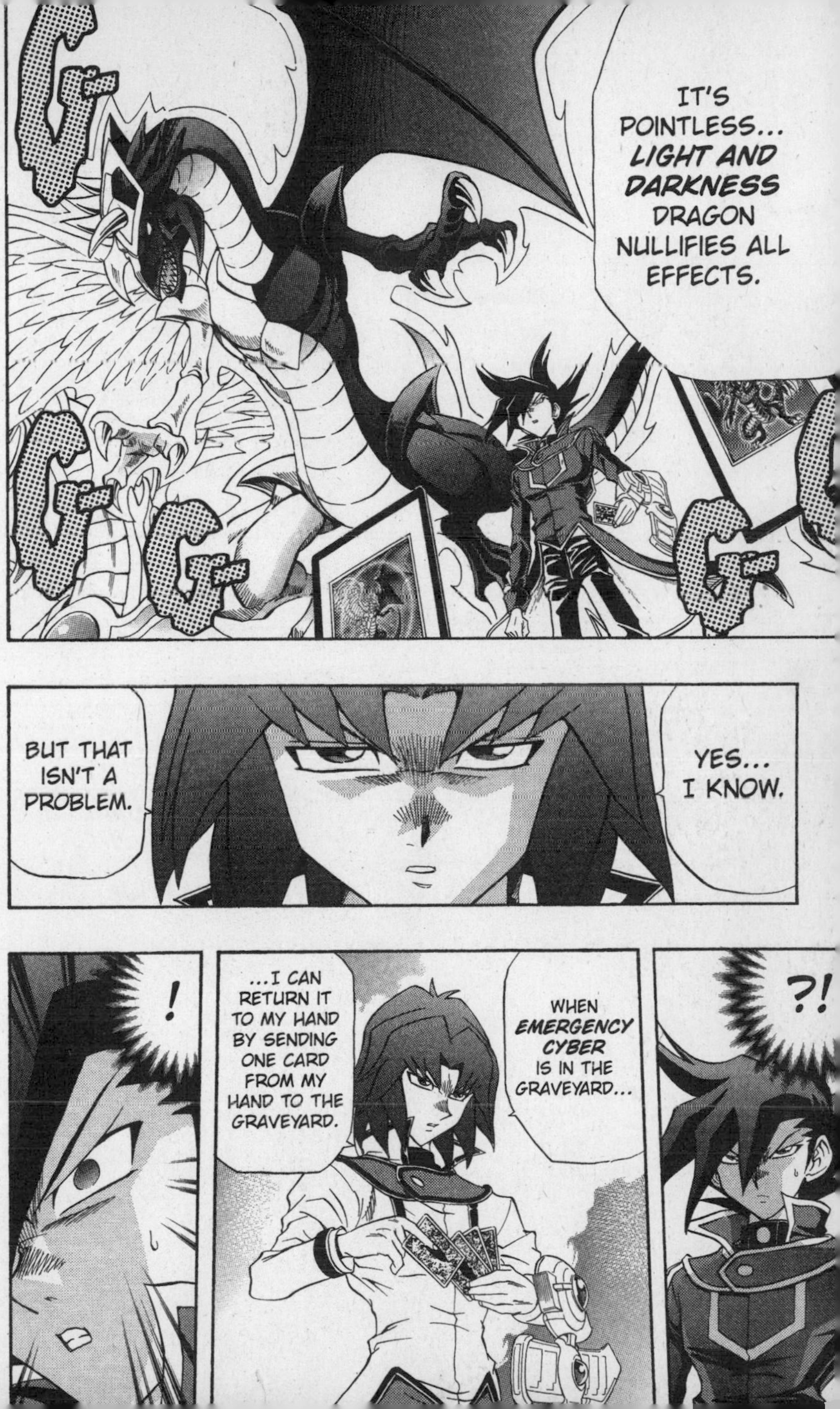
IT'S POINTLESS... *LIGHT AND DARKNESS* DRAGON NULLIFIES ALL EFFECTS.
G-G-G-G-
YES... I KNOW.
BUT THAT ISN'T A PROBLEM.
?!
WHEN *EMERGENCY CYBER* IS IN THE GRAVEYARD...
...I CAN RETURN IT TO MY HAND BY SENDING ONE CARD FROM MY HAND TO THE GRAVEYARD.
!

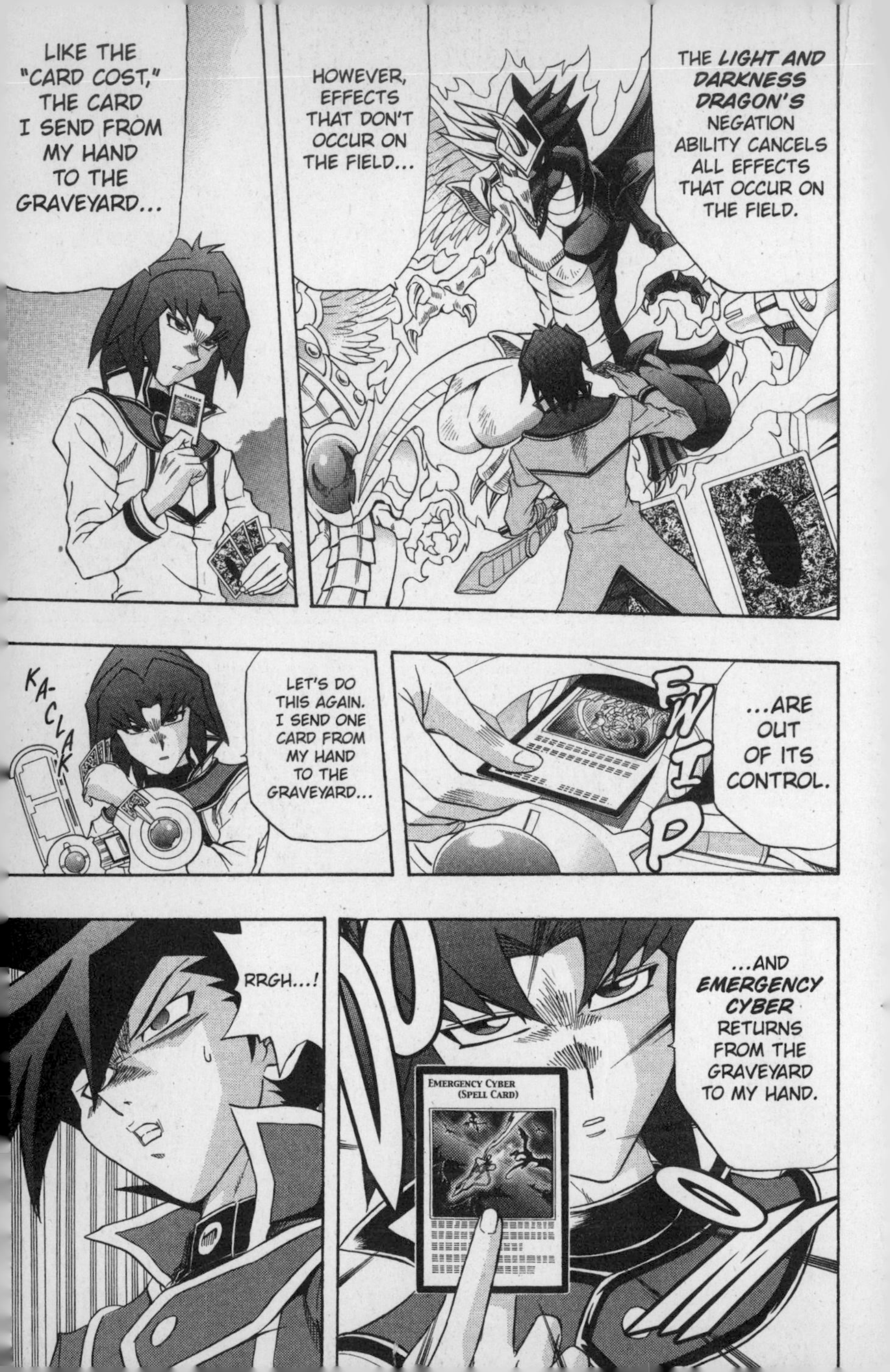
THE LIGHT AND DARKNESS DRAGON'S NEGATION ABILITY CANCELS ALL EFFECTS THAT OCCUR ON THE FIELD.
HOWEVER, EFFECTS THAT DON'T OCCUR ON THE FIELD...
LIKE THE "CARD COST," THE CARD I SEND FROM MY HAND TO THE GRAVEYARD...
FWIP
...ARE OUT OF ITS CONTROL.
LET'S DO THIS AGAIN. I SEND ONE CARD FROM MY HAND TO THE GRAVEYARD...
KA-CLAK
...AND EMERGENCY CYBER RETURNS FROM THE GRAVEYARD TO MY HAND.
EMERGENCY CYBER
(SPELL CARD)
RRGH...!

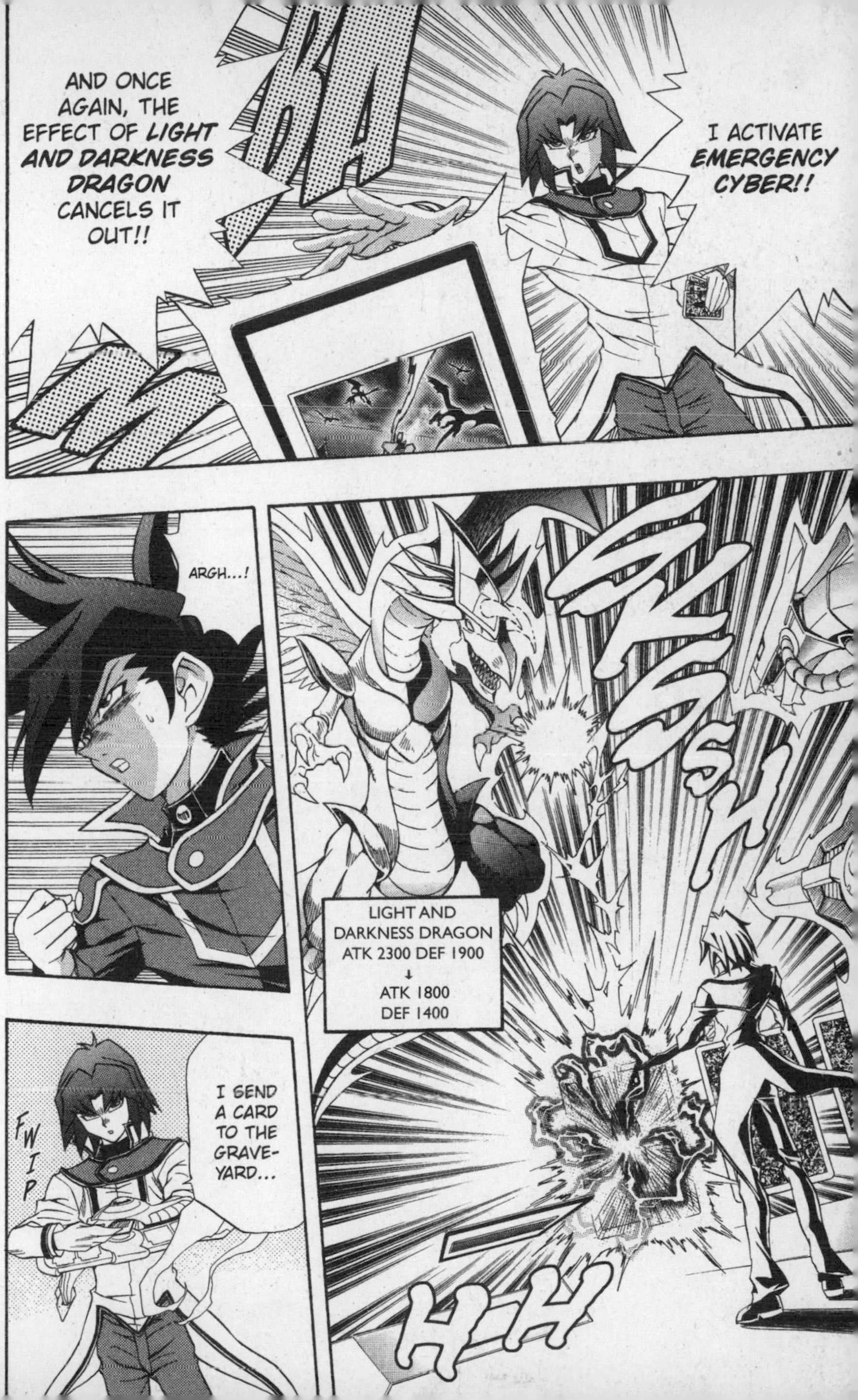
I ACTIVATE EMERGENCY CYBER!!
BA
M
AND ONCE AGAIN, THE EFFECT OF LIGHT AND DARKNESS DRAGON CANCELS IT OUT!!
SWISH
LIGHT AND DARKNESS DRAGON ATK 2300 DEF 1900 ↓ ATK 1800 DEF 1400
H-H
ARGH...!
I SEND A CARD TO THE GRAVE-YARD...
FWIP

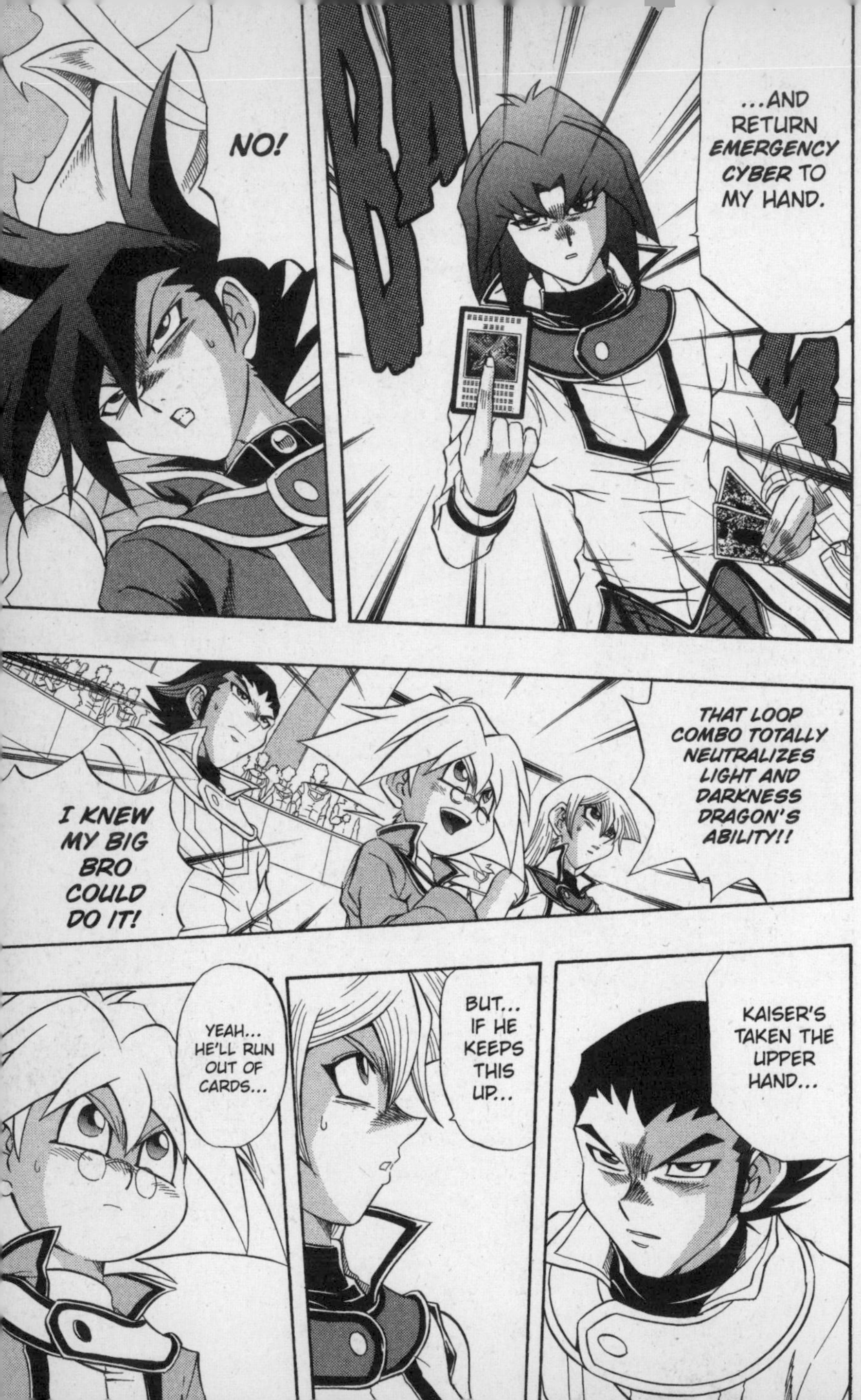
...AND RETURN EMERGENCY CYBER TO MY HAND.
NO!
THAT LOOP COMBO TOTALLY NEUTRALIZES LIGHT AND DARKNESS DRAGON'S ABILITY!!
I KNEW MY BIG BRO COULD DO IT!
KAISER'S TAKEN THE UPPER HAND...
BUT... IF HE KEEPS THIS UP...
YEAH... HE'LL RUN OUT OF CARDS...

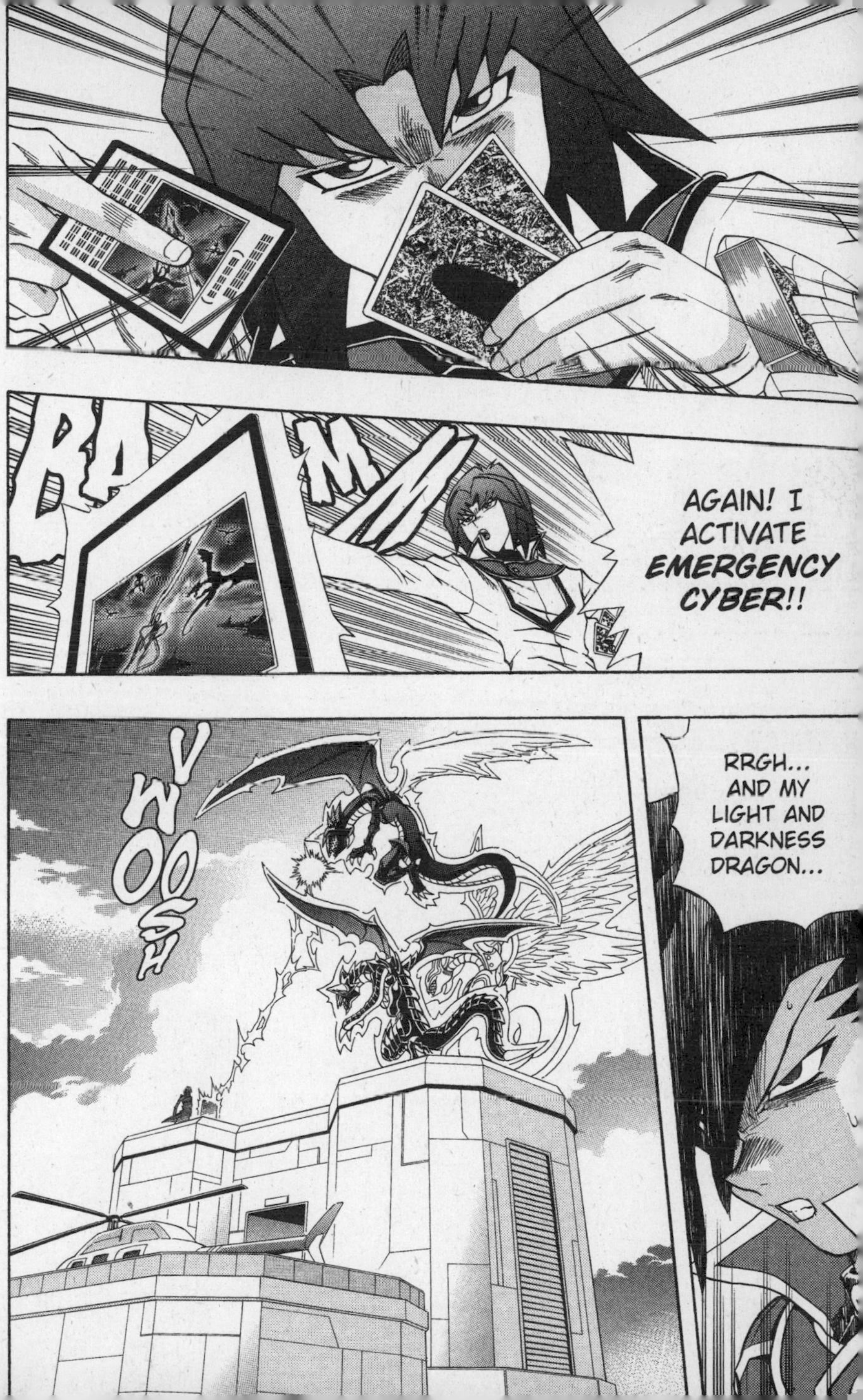
AGAIN! I ACTIVATE EMERGENCY CYBER!!
RRGH... AND MY LIGHT AND DARKNESS DRAGON...
VWOOSH

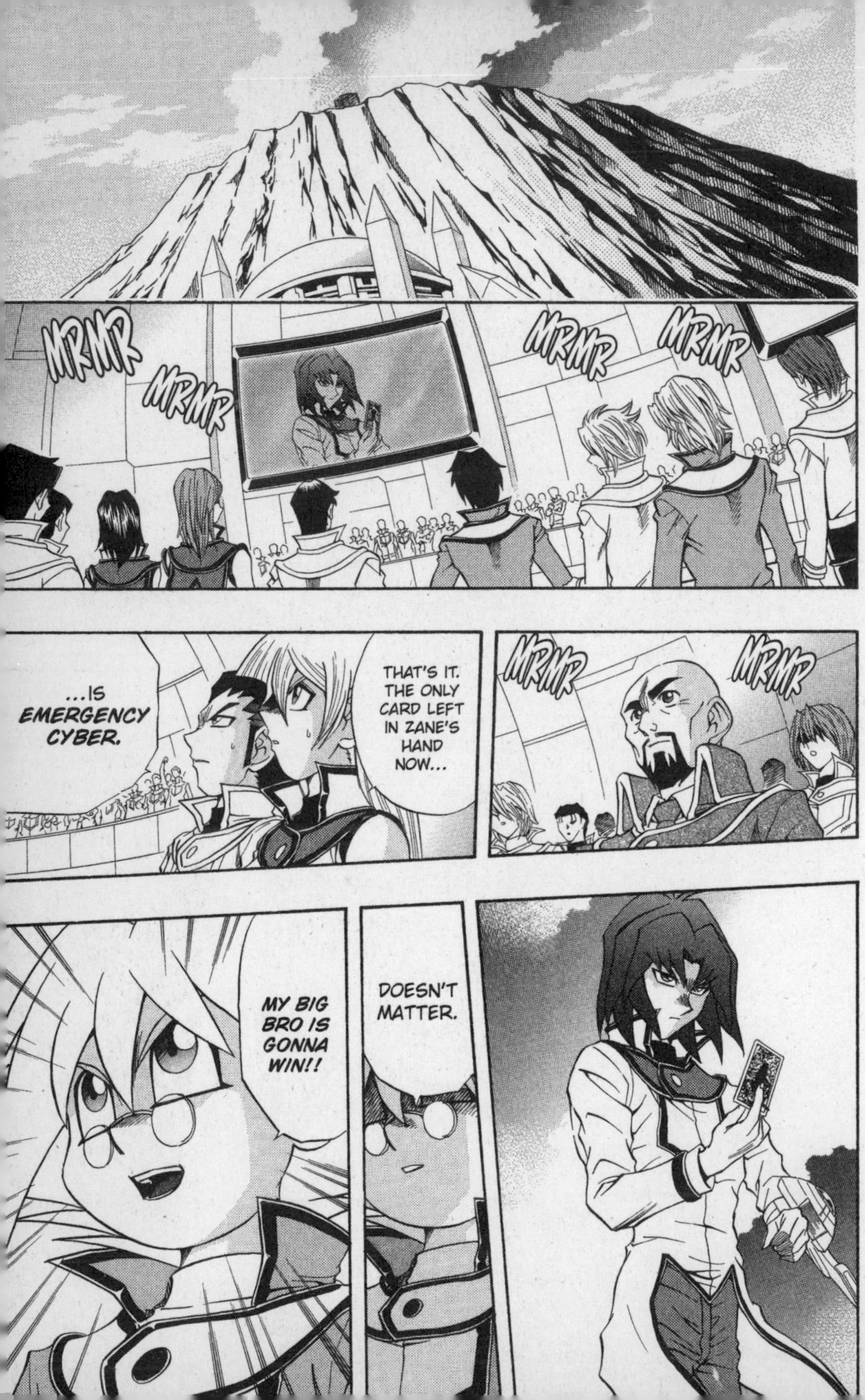
MRMR
MRMR
MRMR
MRMR
MRMR
MRMR
THAT'S IT. THE ONLY CARD LEFT IN ZANE'S HAND NOW...
...IS EMERGENCY CYBER.
DOESN'T MATTER.
MY BIG BRO IS GONNA WIN!!

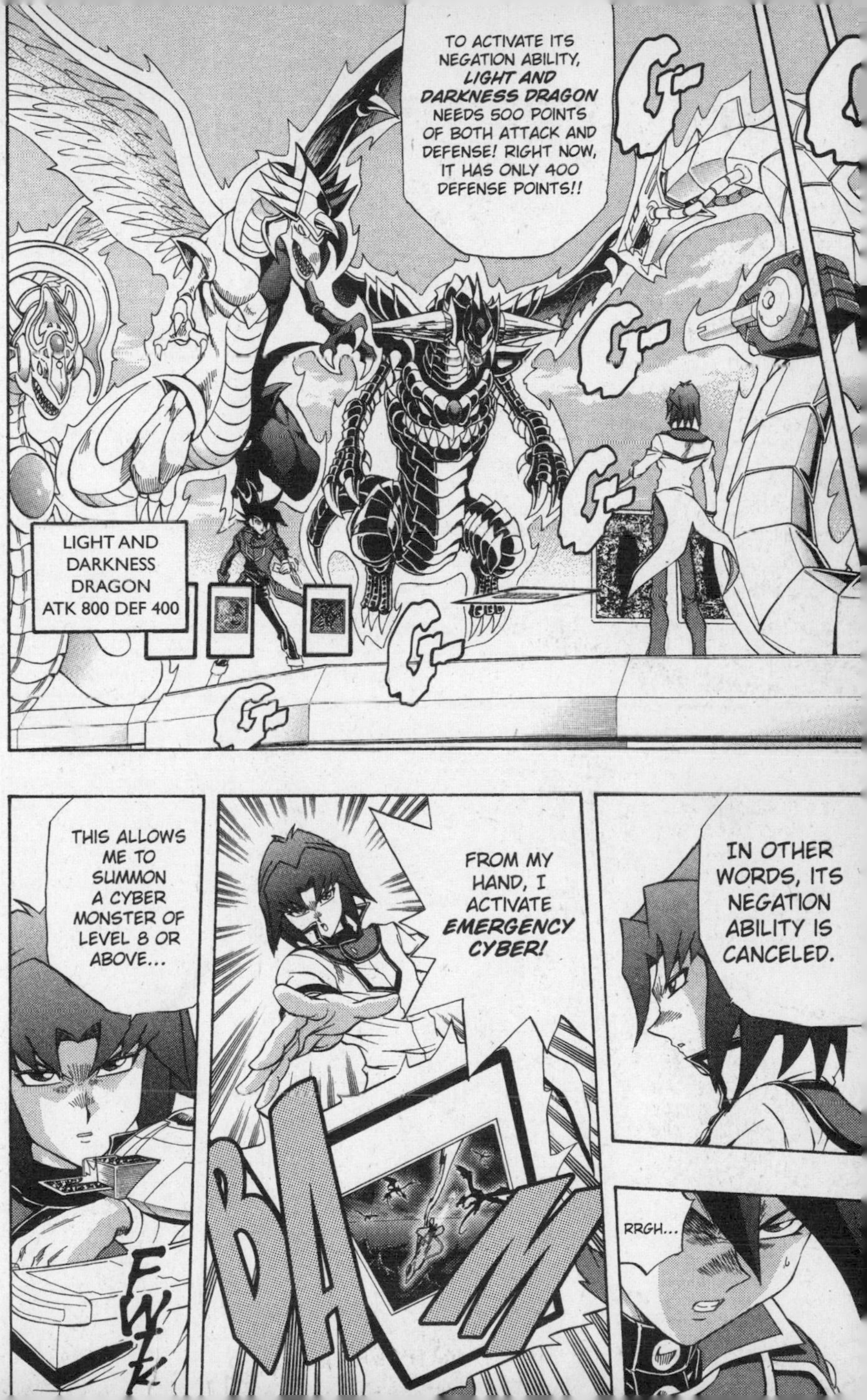

TO ACTIVATE ITS NEGATION ABILITY, *LIGHT AND DARKNESS DRAGON* NEEDS 500 POINTS OF BOTH ATTACK AND DEFENSE! RIGHT NOW, IT HAS ONLY 400 DEFENSE POINTS!!
G-
G-
G-
LIGHT AND DARKNESS DRAGON ATK 800 DEF 400
G-
G-
IN OTHER WORDS, ITS NEGATION ABILITY IS CANCELED.
RRGH...
FROM MY HAND, I ACTIVATE *EMERGENCY CYBER!*
BAM
THIS ALLOWS ME TO SUMMON A CYBER MONSTER OF LEVEL 8 OR ABOVE...
FWK

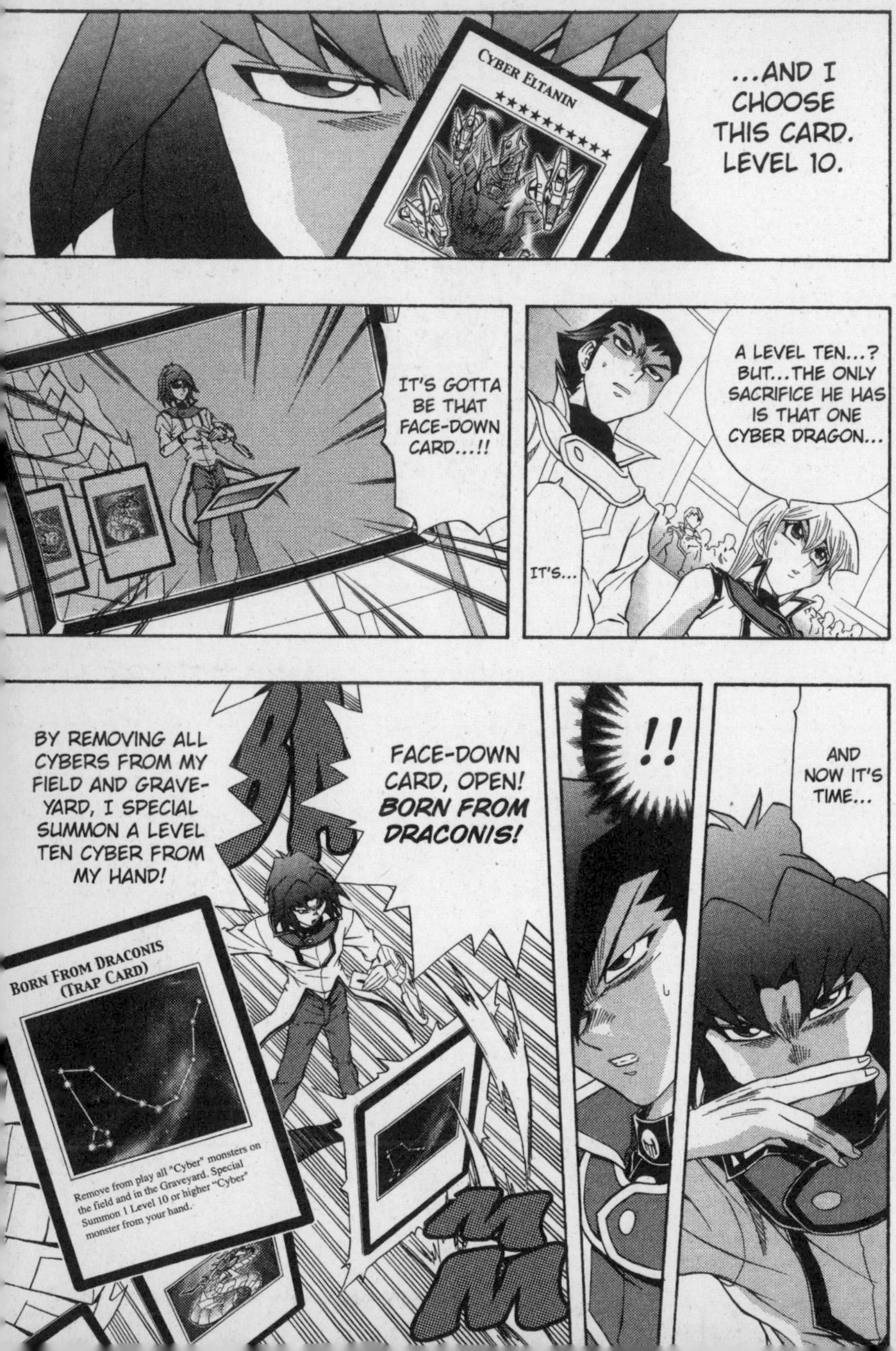
...AND I CHOOSE THIS CARD. LEVEL 10.
CYBER ELTANIN
A LEVEL TEN...? BUT...THE ONLY SACRIFICE HE HAS IS THAT ONE CYBER DRAGON...
IT'S...
IT'S GOTTA BE THAT FACE-DOWN CARD...!!
AND NOW IT'S TIME...
!!
FACE-DOWN CARD, OPEN! BORN FROM DRACONIS!
BY REMOVING ALL CYBERS FROM MY FIELD AND GRAVE-YARD, I SPECIAL SUMMON A LEVEL TEN CYBER FROM MY HAND!
BORN FROM DRACONIS (TRAP CARD)
Remove from play all "Cyber" monsters on the field and in the Graveyard. Special Summon 1 Level 10 or higher "Cyber" monster from your hand.

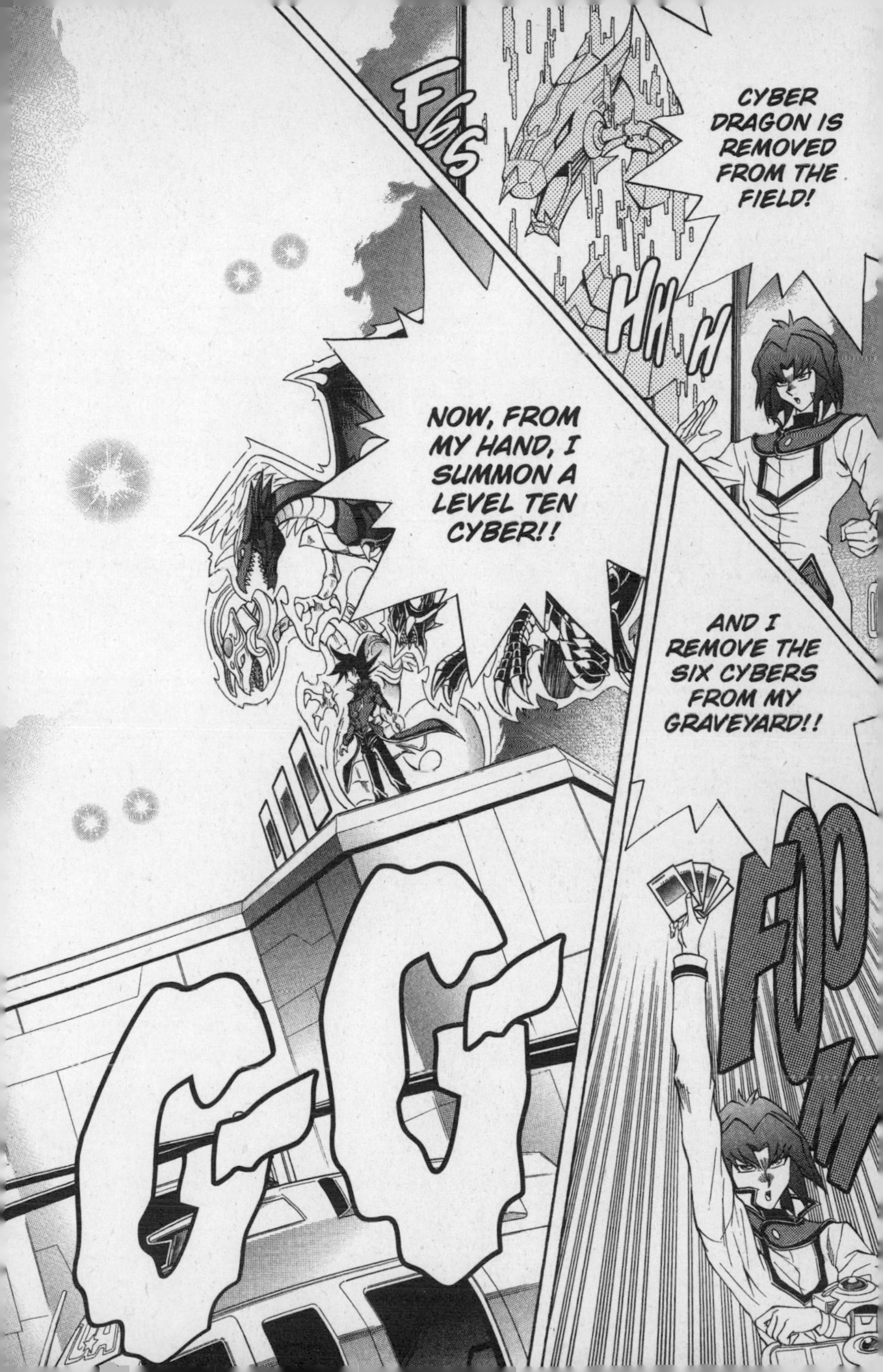
FSS
CYBER DRAGON IS REMOVED FROM THE FIELD!
HHH
AND I REMOVE THE SIX CYBERS FROM MY GRAVEYARD!!
FOOM
NOW, FROM MY HAND, I SUMMON A LEVEL TEN CYBER!!
GG

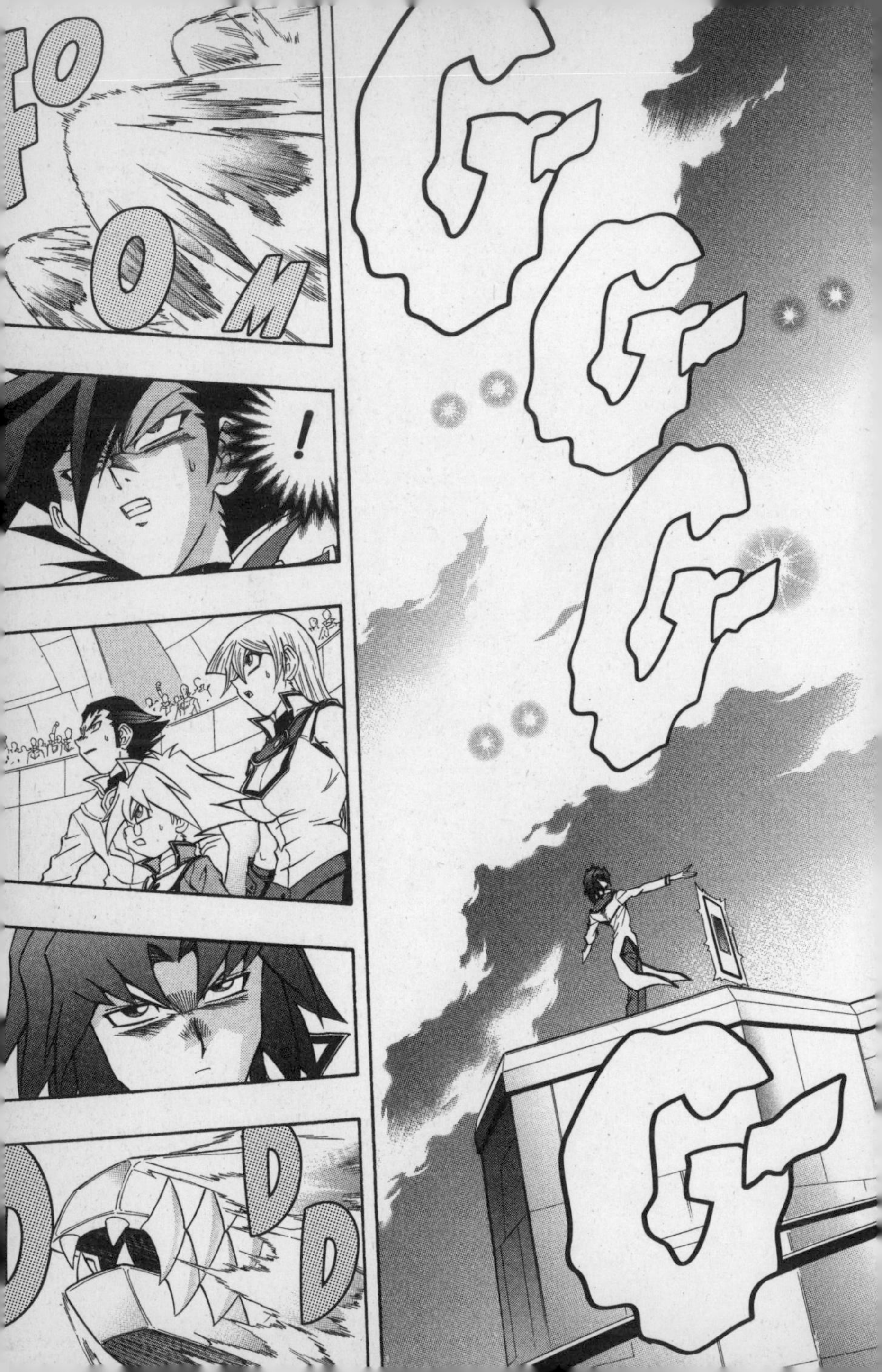
GGGG
FOOM
!
DDDD

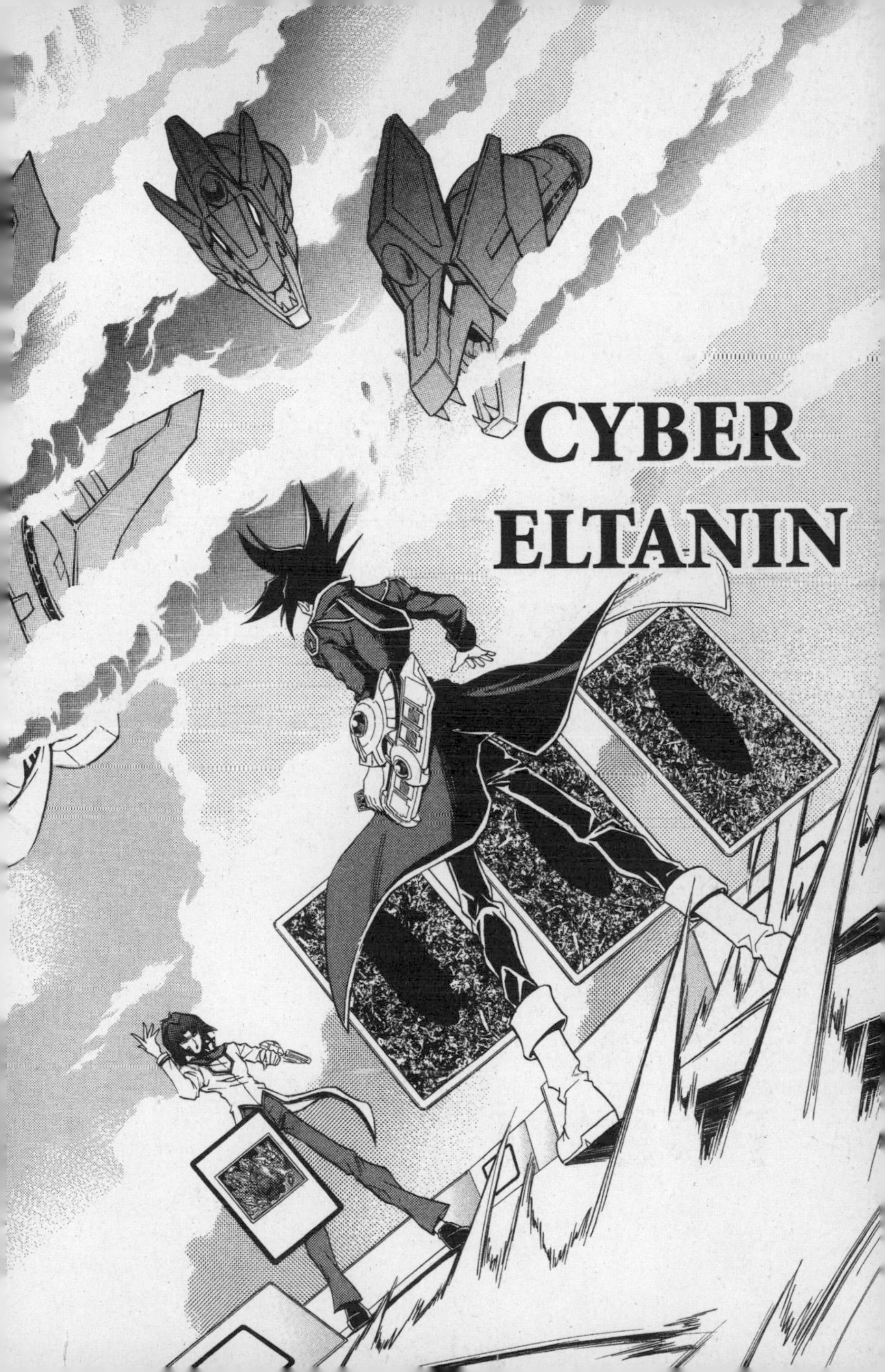
CYBER
ELTANIN

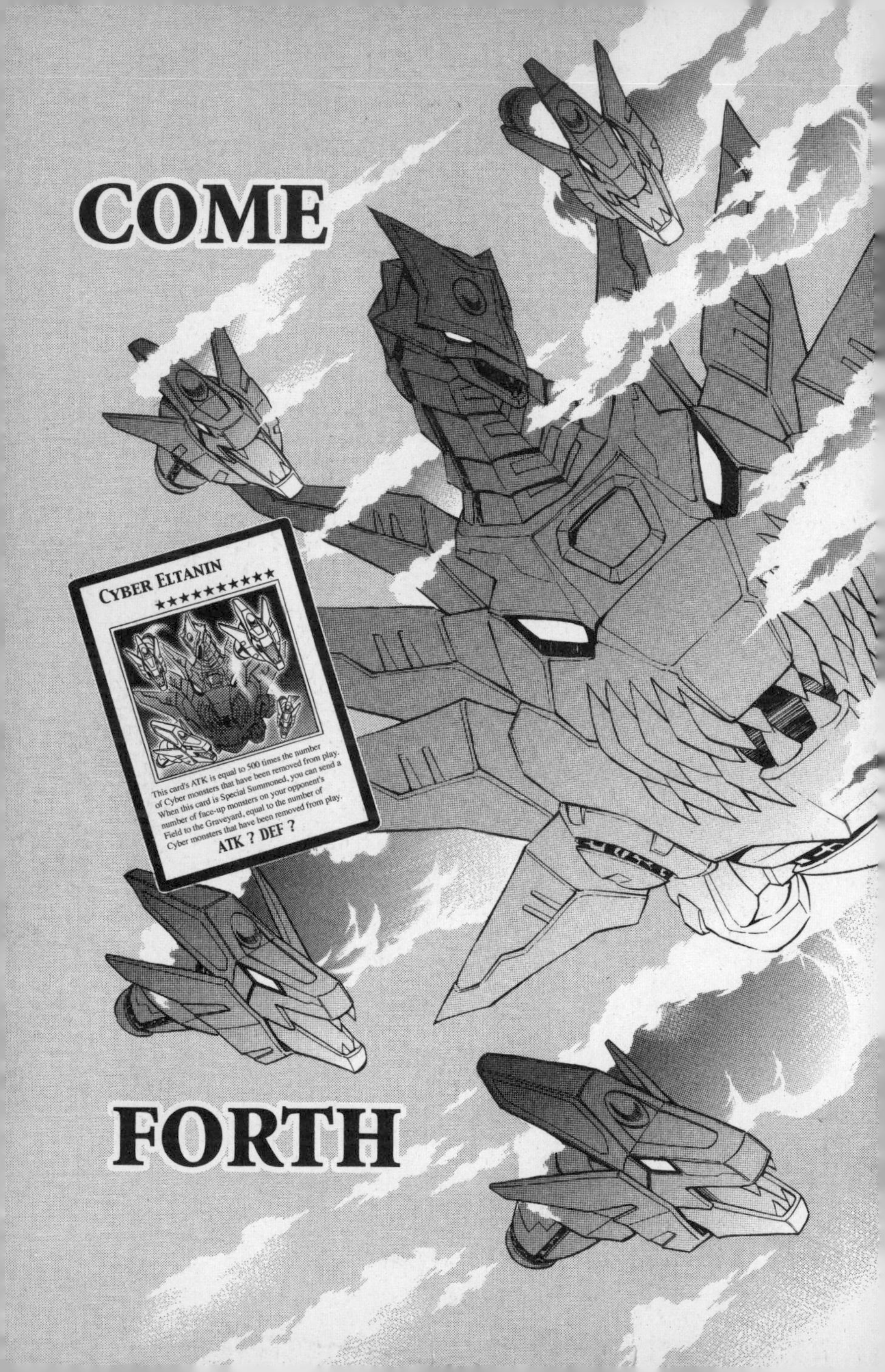
COME
CYBER ELTANIN
★★★★★★★★★★
This card's ATK is equal to 500 times the number of Cyber monsters that have been removed from play. When this card is Special Summoned, you can send a number of face-up monsters on your opponent's Field to the Graveyard, equal to the number of Cyber monsters that have been removed from play.
ATK ? DEF ?
FORTH

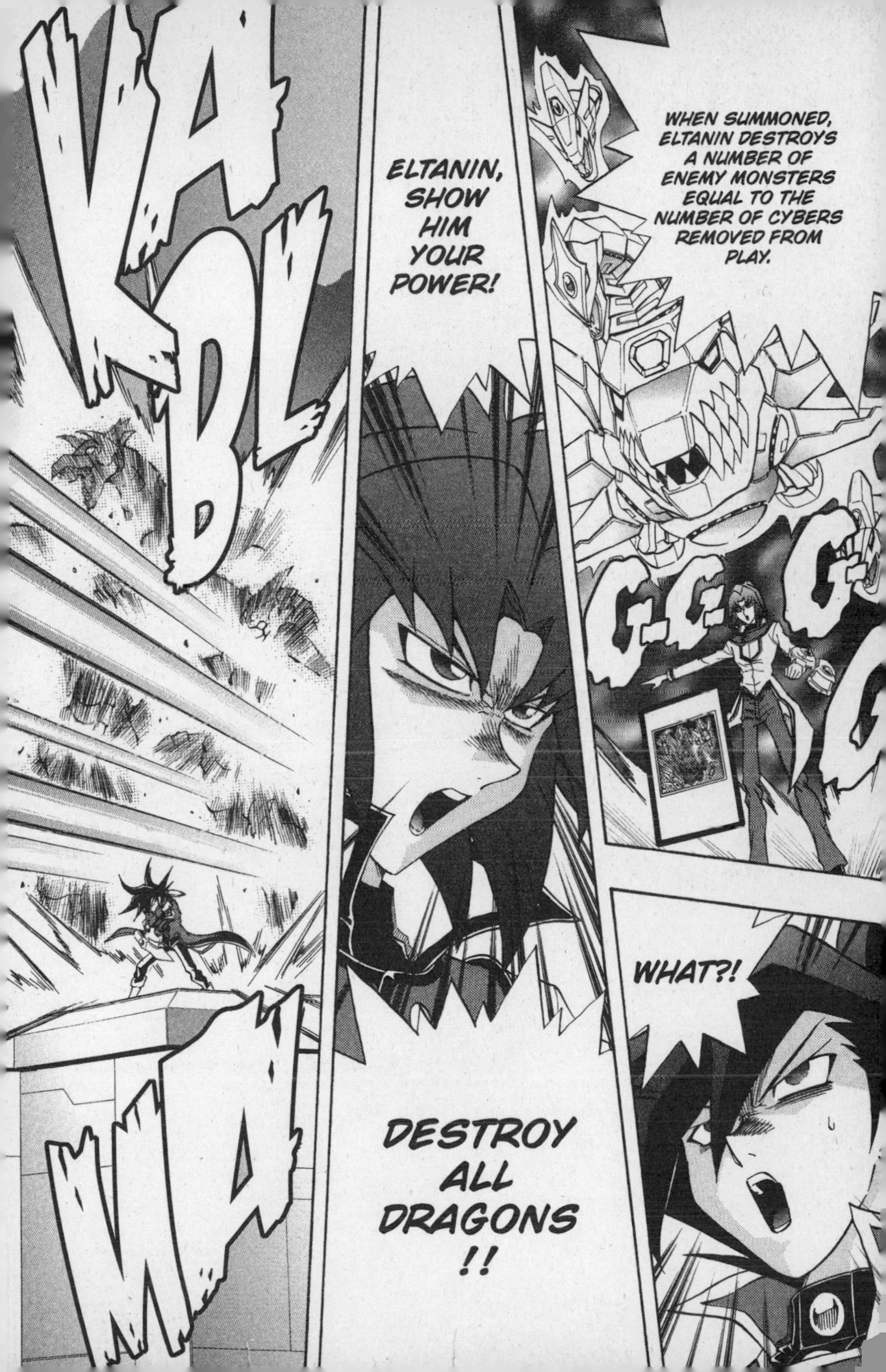
WHEN SUMMONED, ELTANIN DESTROYS A NUMBER OF ENEMY MONSTERS EQUAL TO THE NUMBER OF CYBERS REMOVED FROM PLAY.
WHAT?!
ELTANIN, SHOW HIM YOUR POWER!
DESTROY ALL DRAGONS !!

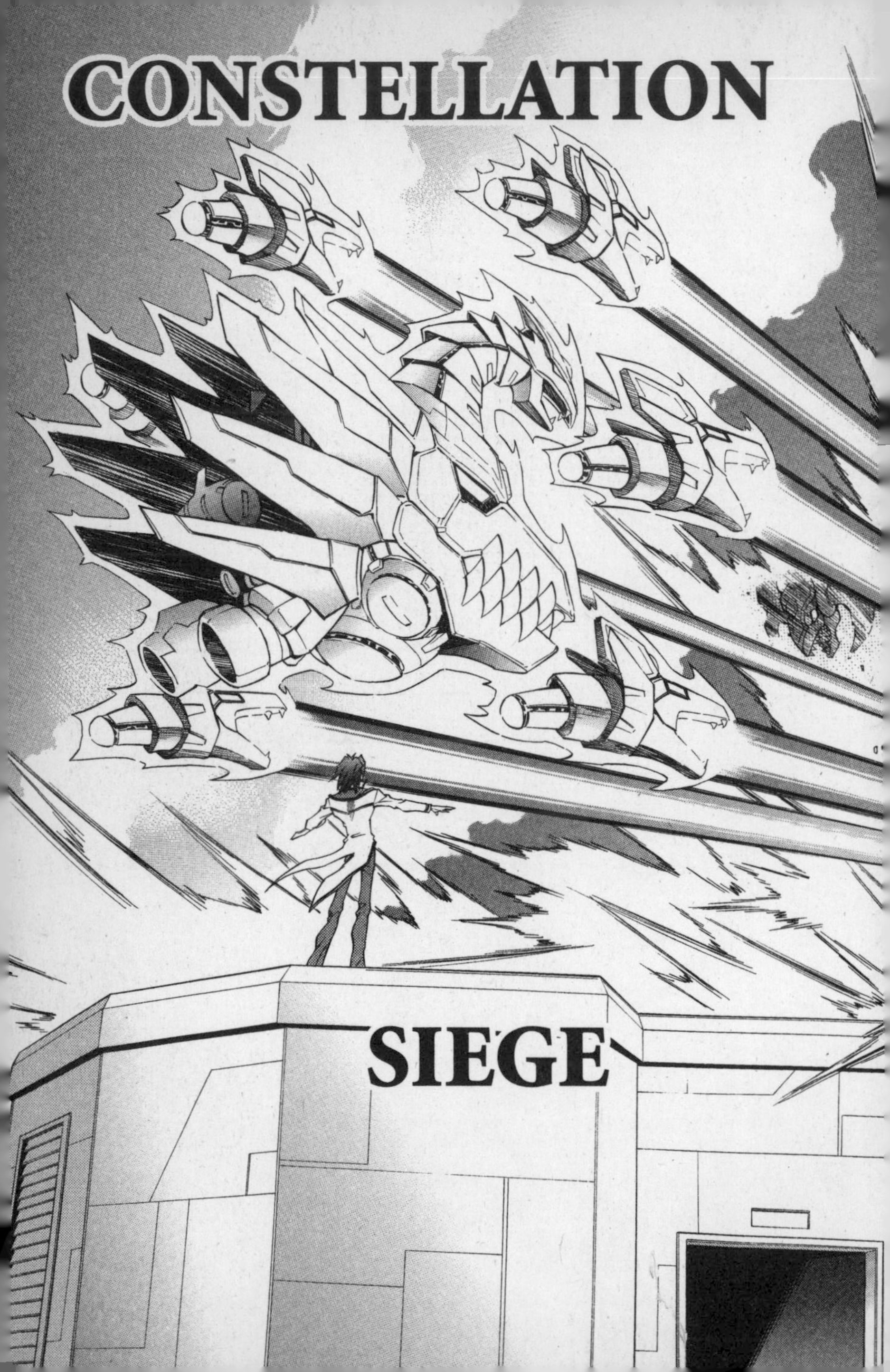
CONSTELLATION
SIEGE

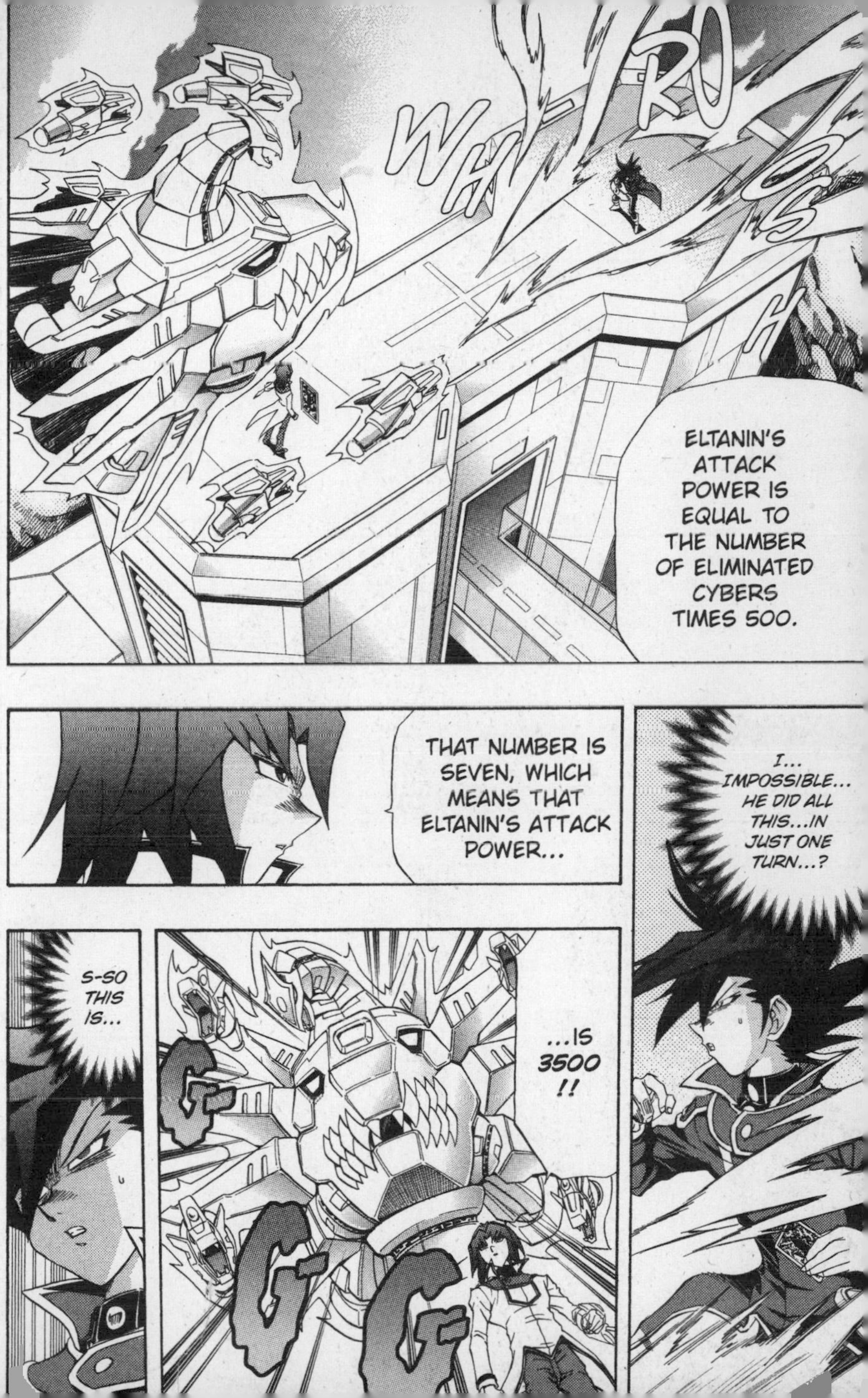
WHI-ROOSH
ELTANIN'S ATTACK POWER IS EQUAL TO THE NUMBER OF ELIMINATED CYBERS TIMES 500.
I... IMPOSSIBLE... HE DID ALL THIS...IN JUST ONE TURN...?
THAT NUMBER IS SEVEN, WHICH MEANS THAT ELTANIN'S ATTACK POWER...
...IS 3500!!
GGG
S-SO THIS IS...

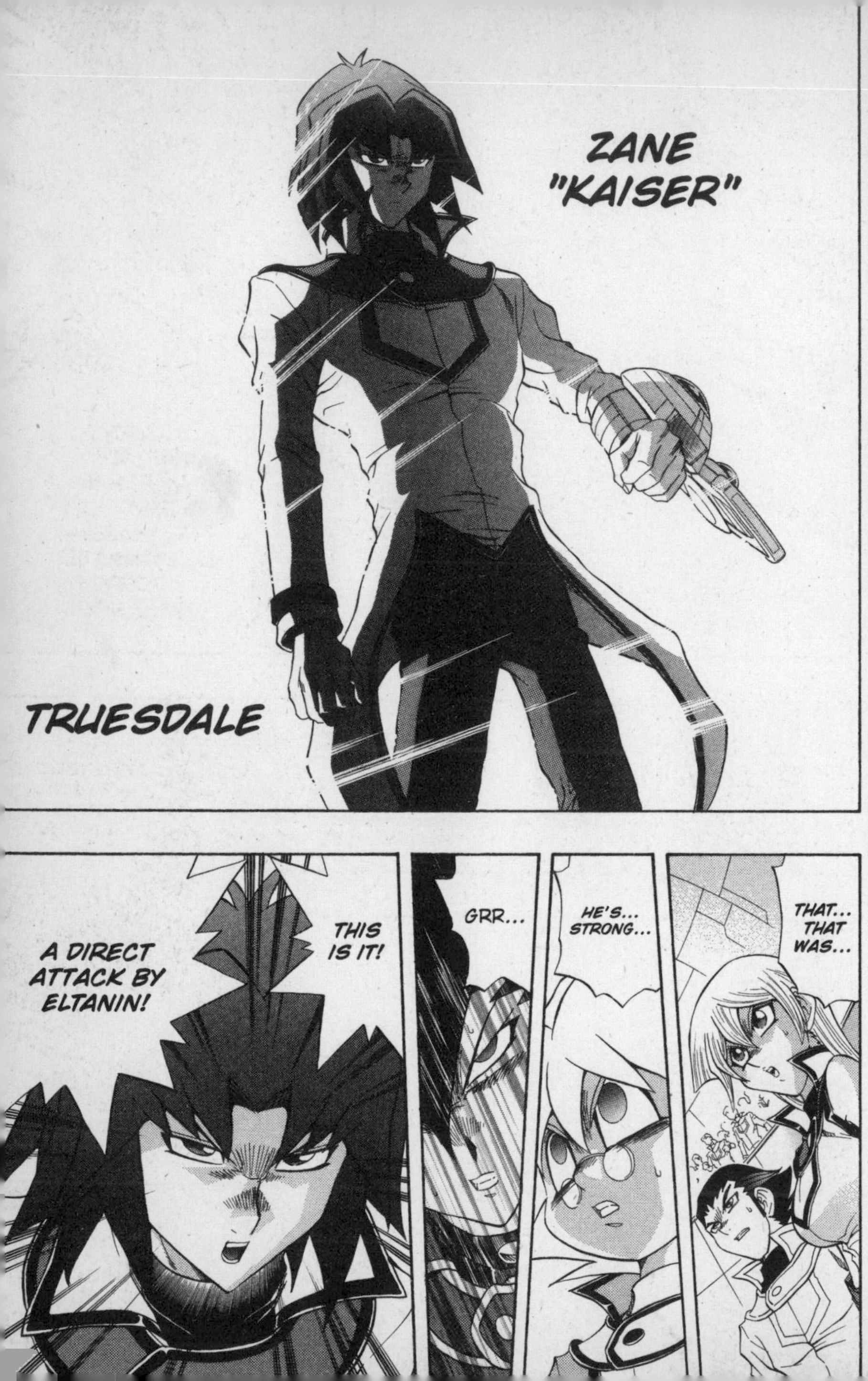
ZANE "KAISER"
TRUESDALE
THAT... THAT WAS...
HE'S... STRONG...
GRR...
THIS IS IT!
A DIRECT ATTACK BY ELTANIN!

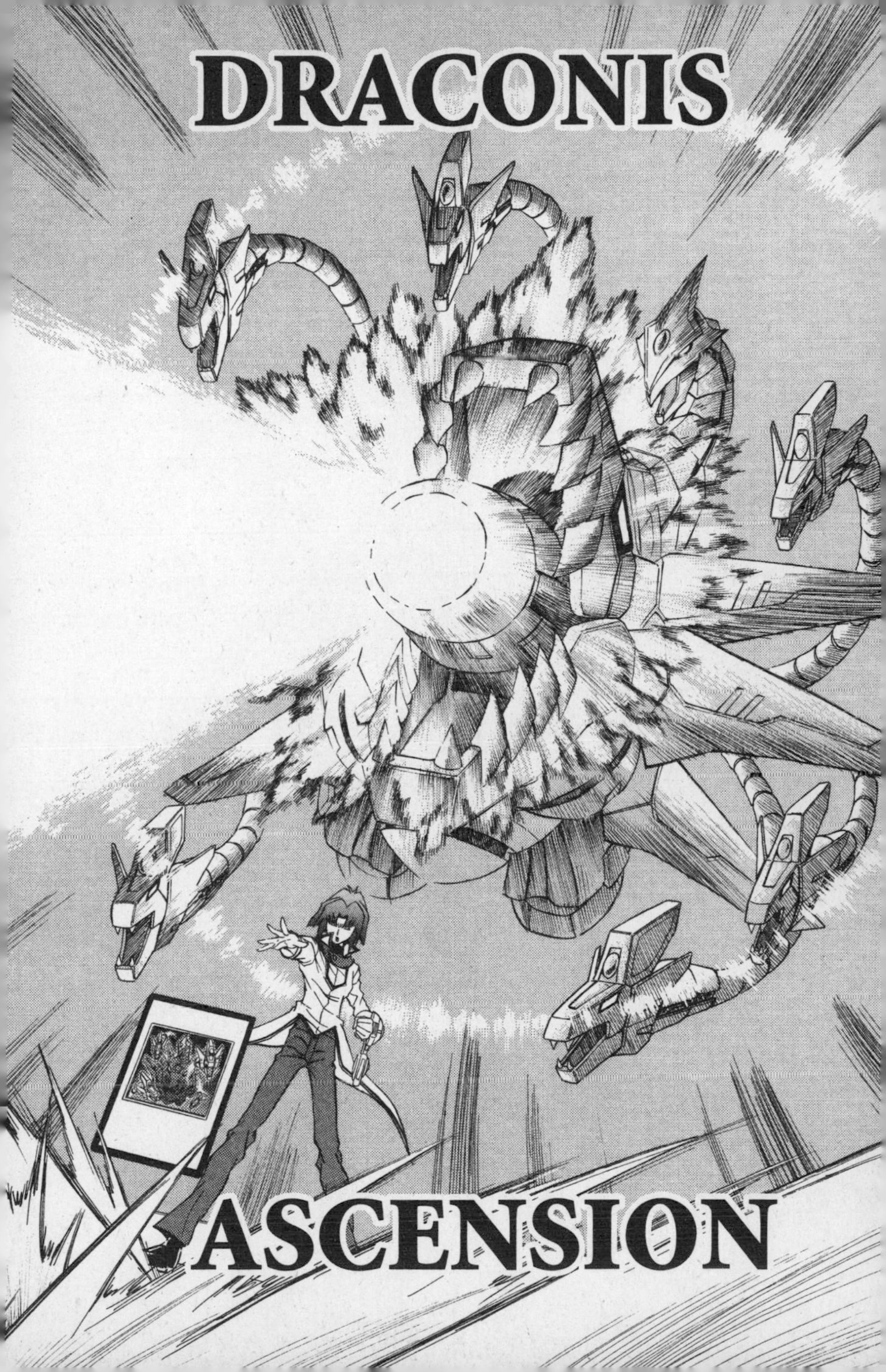
DRACONIS
ASCENSION

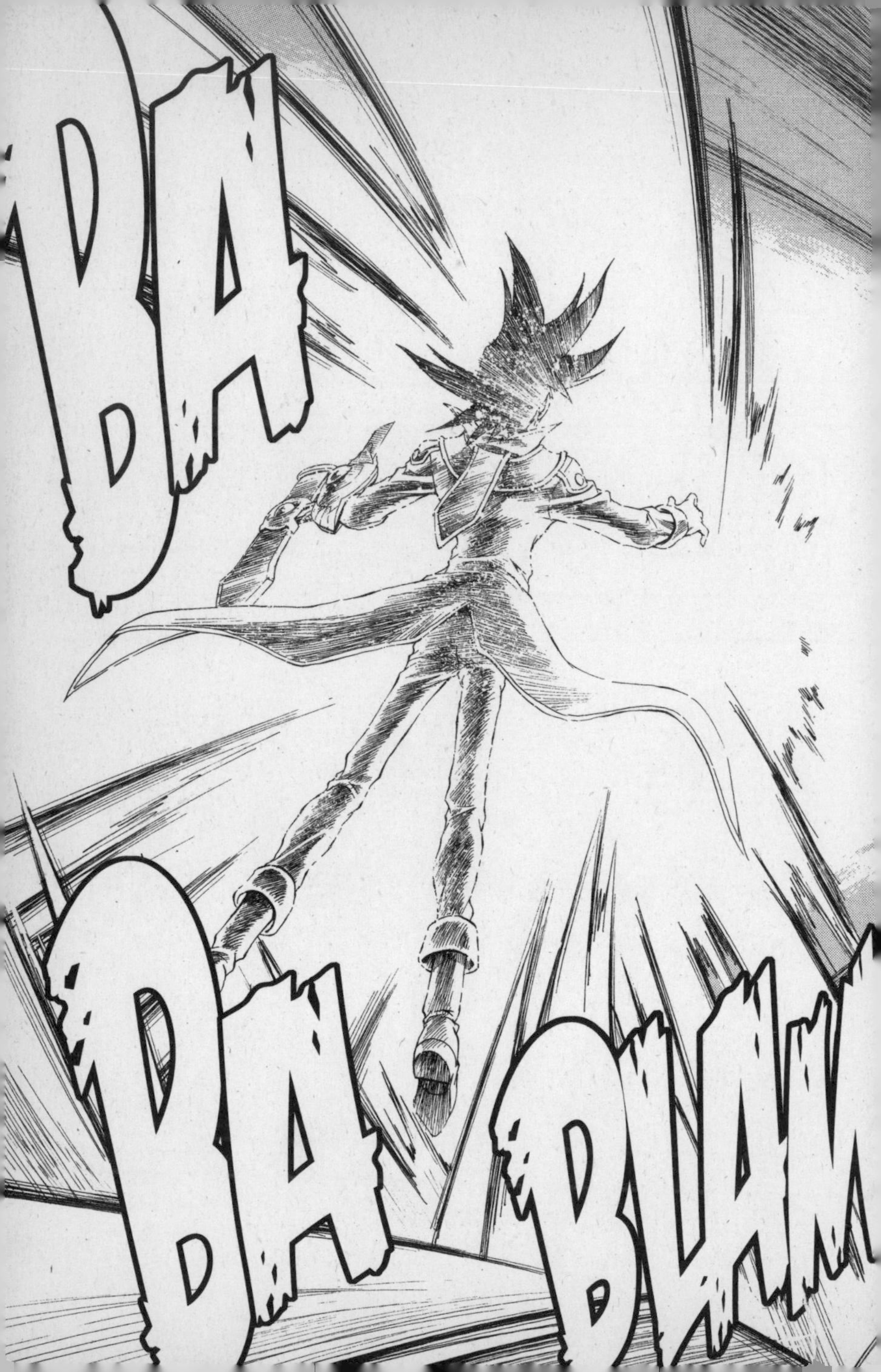
BA
BA
BLAM

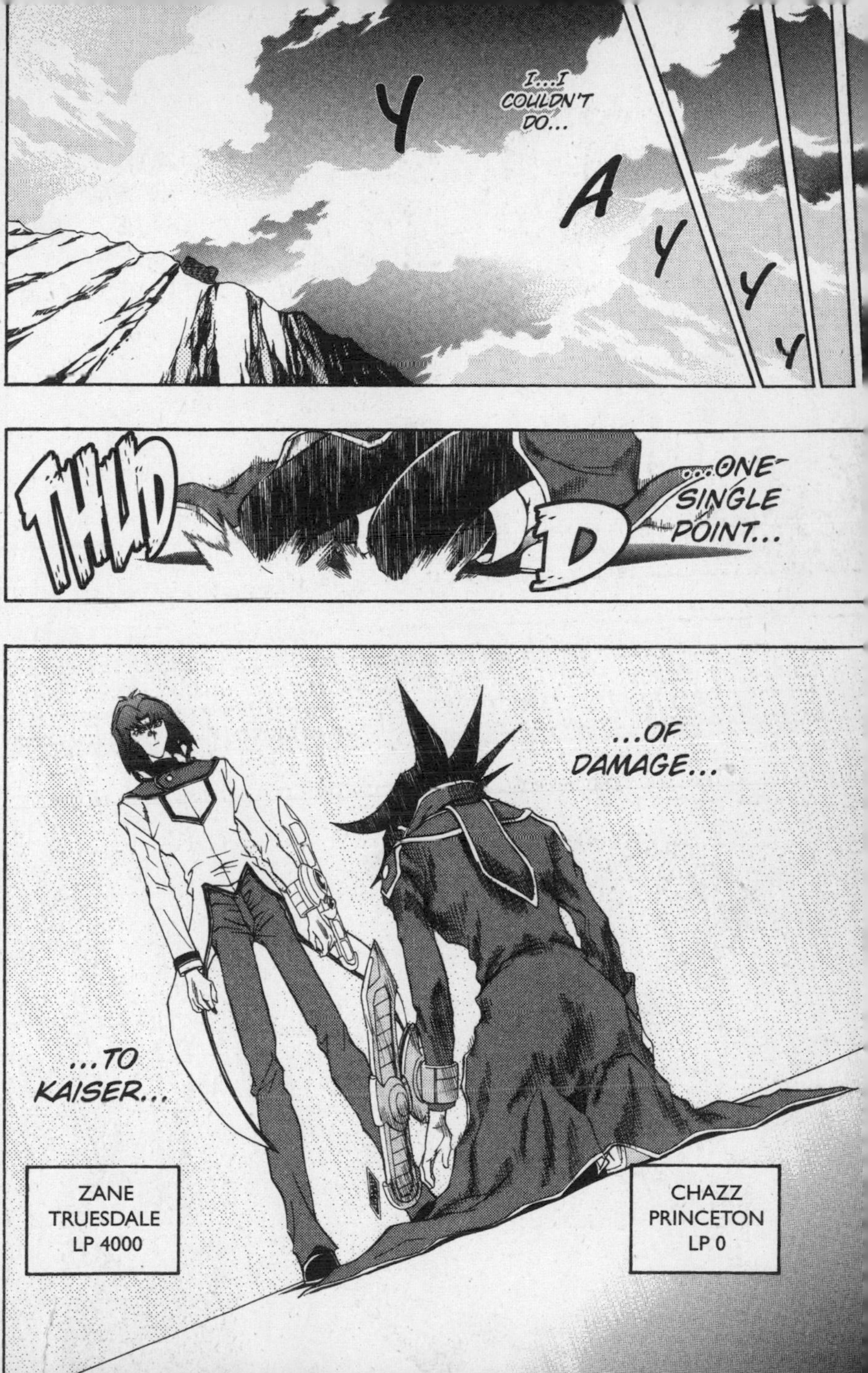
I...I COULDN'T DO...
Y A Y Y Y
...ONE SINGLE POINT...
D
THUD
...OF DAMAGE...
...TO KAISER...
CHAZZ PRINCETON LP 0
ZANE TRUESDALE LP 4000

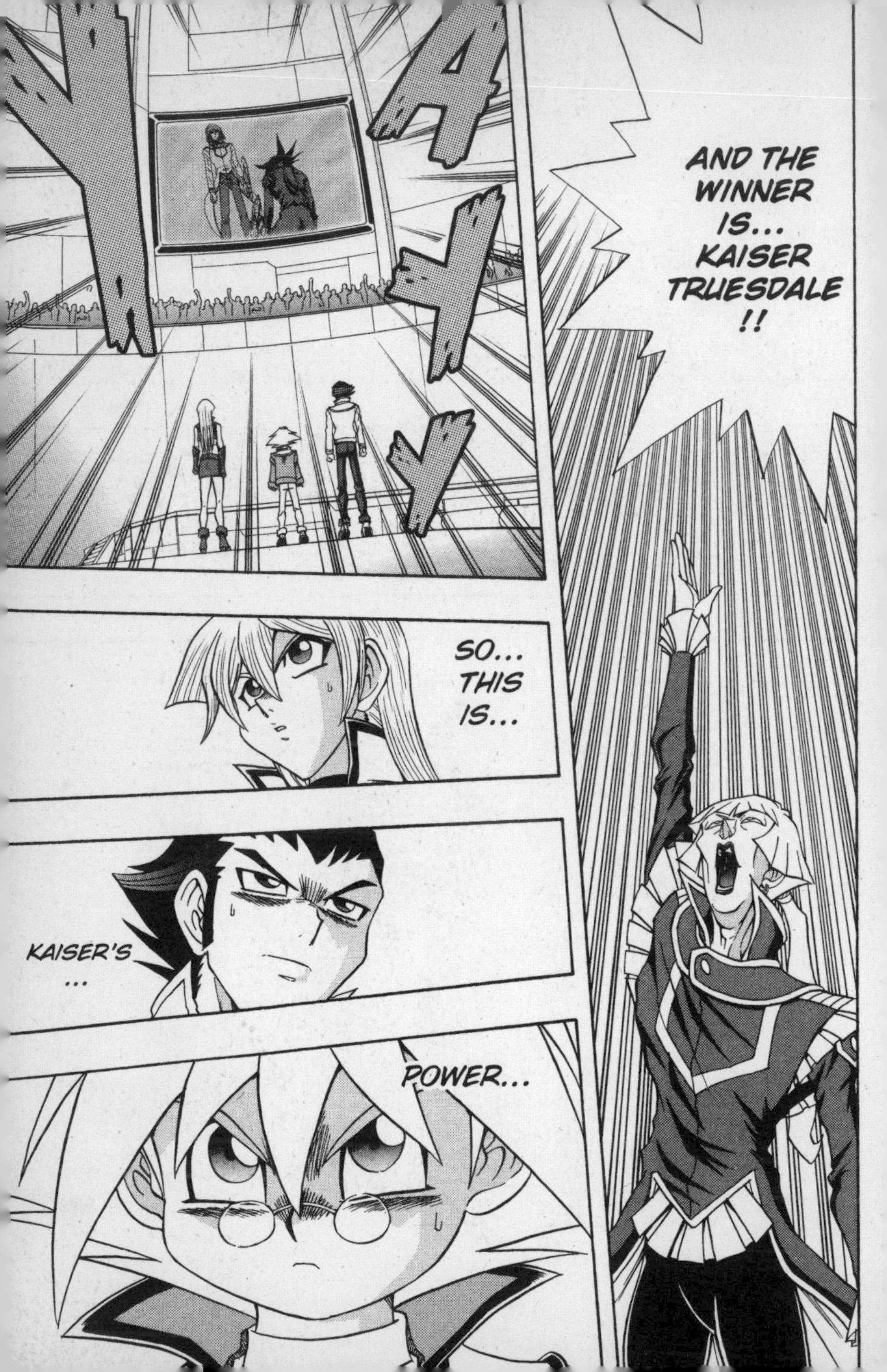
AND THE WINNER IS... KAISER TRUESDALE !!
SO... THIS IS...
KAISER'S ...
POWER...

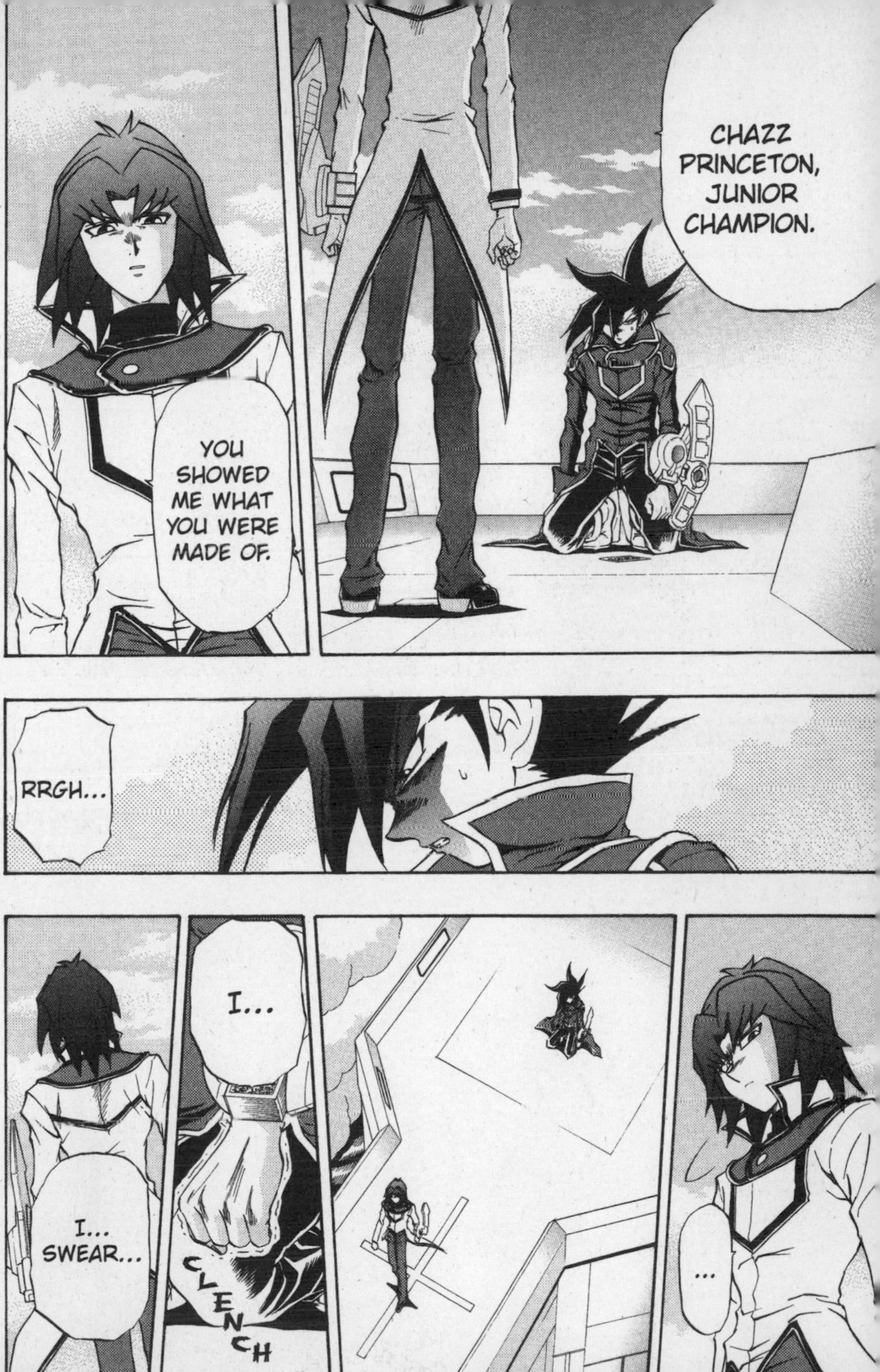
CHAZZ PRINCETON, JUNIOR CHAMPION.
YOU SHOWED ME WHAT YOU WERE MADE OF.
RRGH...
...
I...
CLENCH
I... SWEAR...

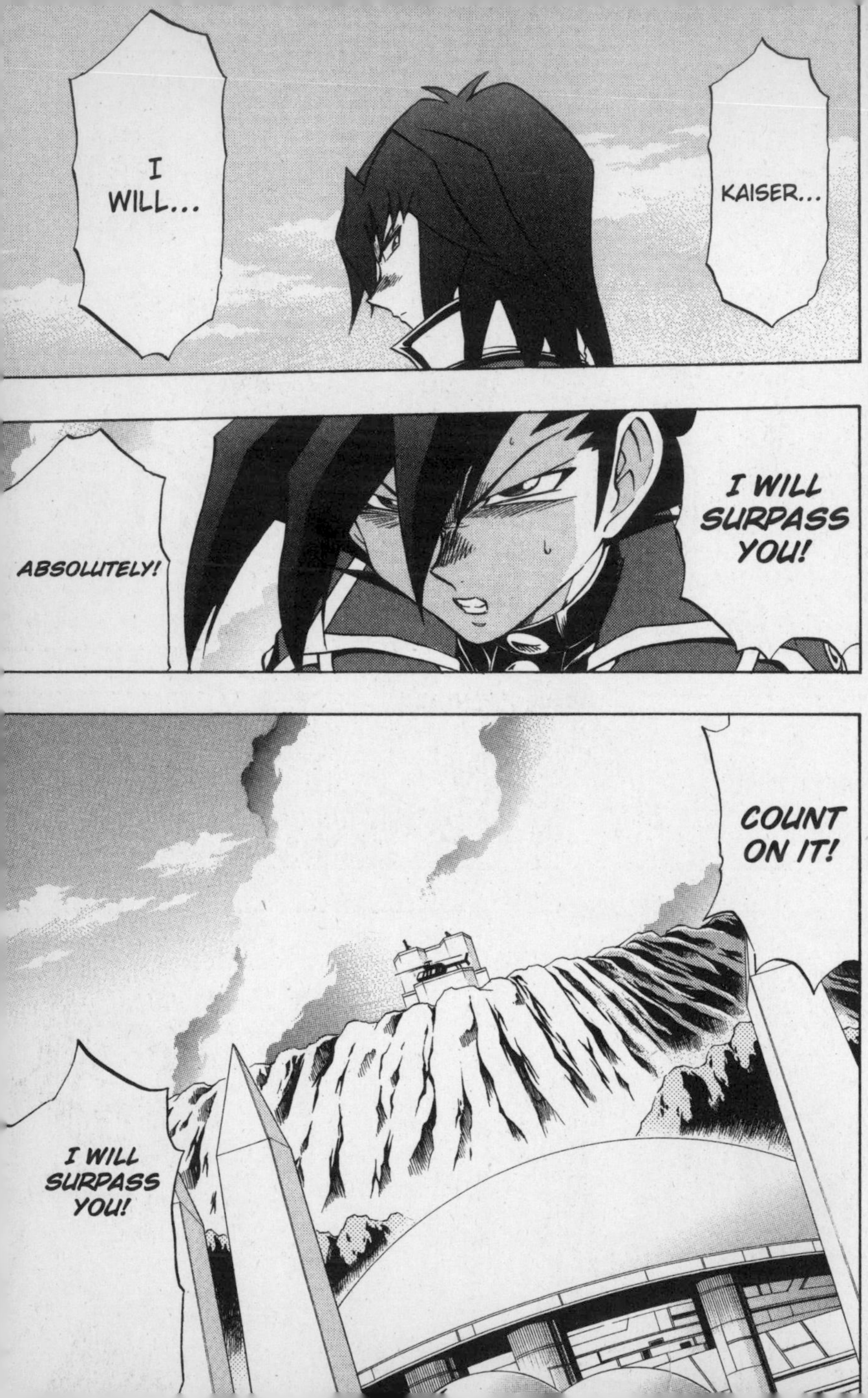
KAISER...
I WILL...
I WILL SURPASS YOU!
ABSOLUTELY!
COUNT ON IT!
I WILL SURPASS YOU!

TELL ME WHY...
WHY ...?!
CRUSHED
WHY SYNCHRO MONSTERS ...?!
THE LIGHT END AND DARK END DRAGONS !!
LIGHT END
I CAN'T MAKE CHAZZ'S DECK!
CAN I HAVE THE LIGHT END AND DARK END DRAGONS SUMMONED JUST AS SACRIFICES?
I MEAN, I DON'T USE SYNCHRO MONSTERS, YOU KNOW...?
WHY DON'T YOU JUST THROW AWAY THAT SILLY PRIDE OF YOURS AND USE SYNCHRO MONSTERS?
ABSOLUTELY NOT.
SATO
WELL, YES, I COULD... BUT I WON'T.

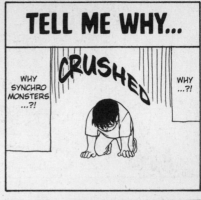

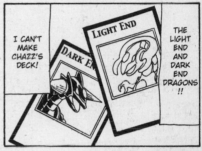

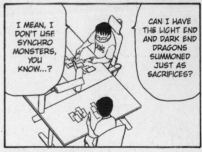

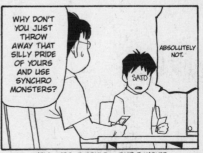

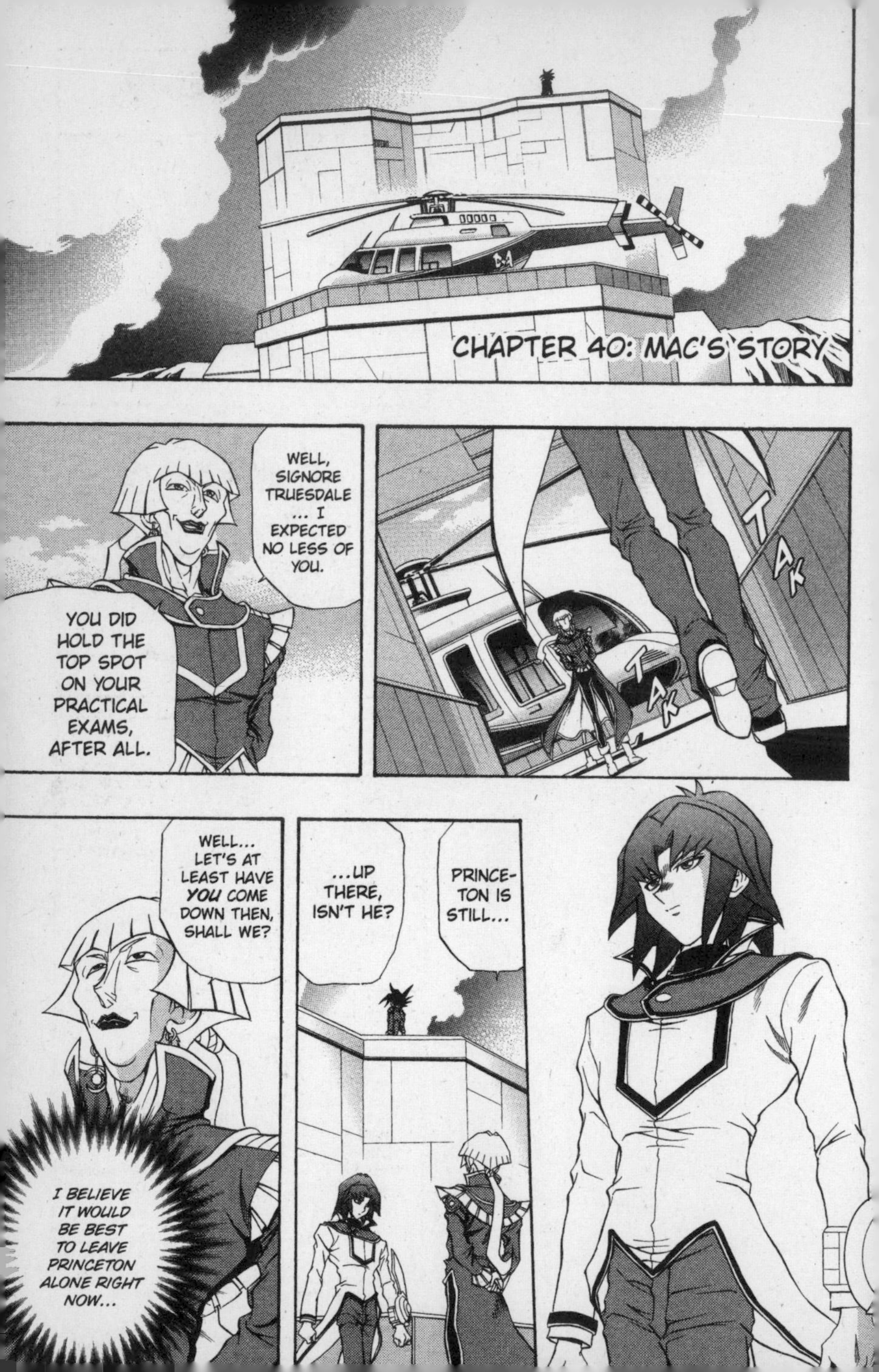
CHAPTER 40: MAC'S STORY
TAK
TAK
WELL, SIGNORE TRUESDALE ... I EXPECTED NO LESS OF YOU.
YOU DID HOLD THE TOP SPOT ON YOUR PRACTICAL EXAMS, AFTER ALL.
PRINCE-TON IS STILL...
...UP THERE, ISN'T HE?
WELL... LET'S AT LEAST HAVE *YOU* COME DOWN THEN, SHALL WE?
*I BELIEVE IT WOULD BE BEST TO LEAVE PRINCETON ALONE RIGHT NOW...*

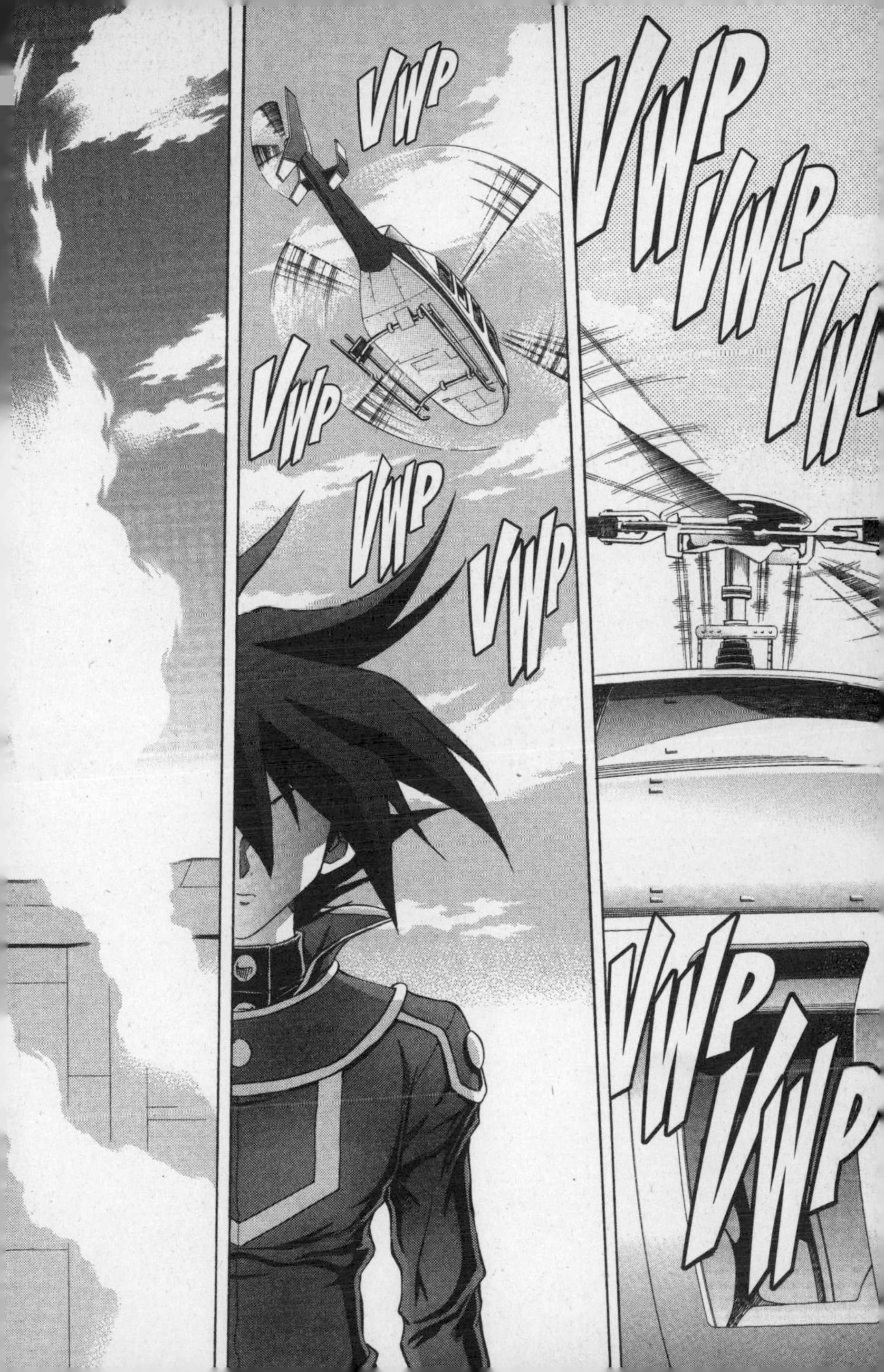
VWP
VWP
VW
VWP
VWP
VWP
VWP
VWP
VWP

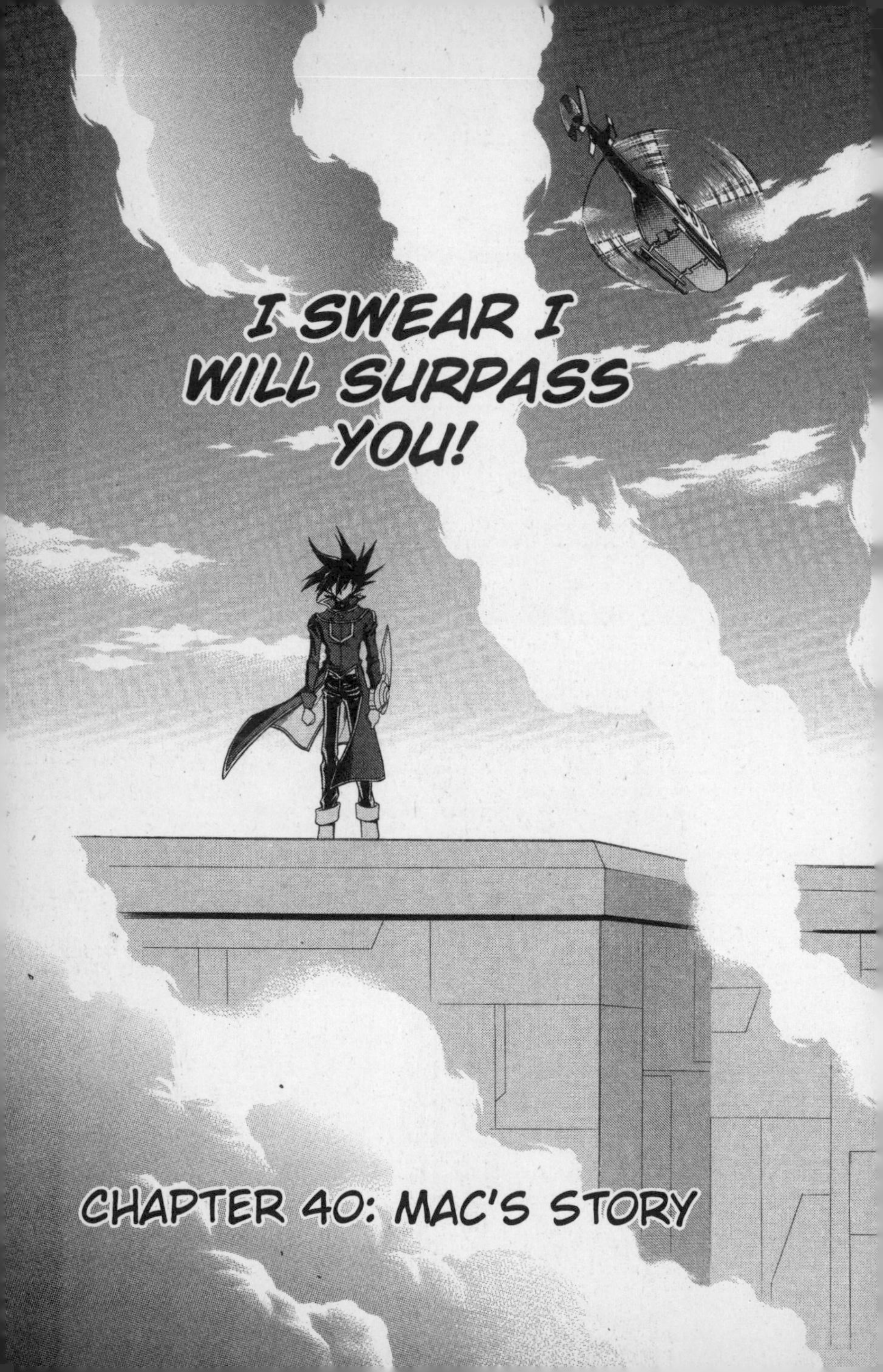
I SWEAR I WILL SURPASS YOU!
CHAPTER 40: MAC'S STORY

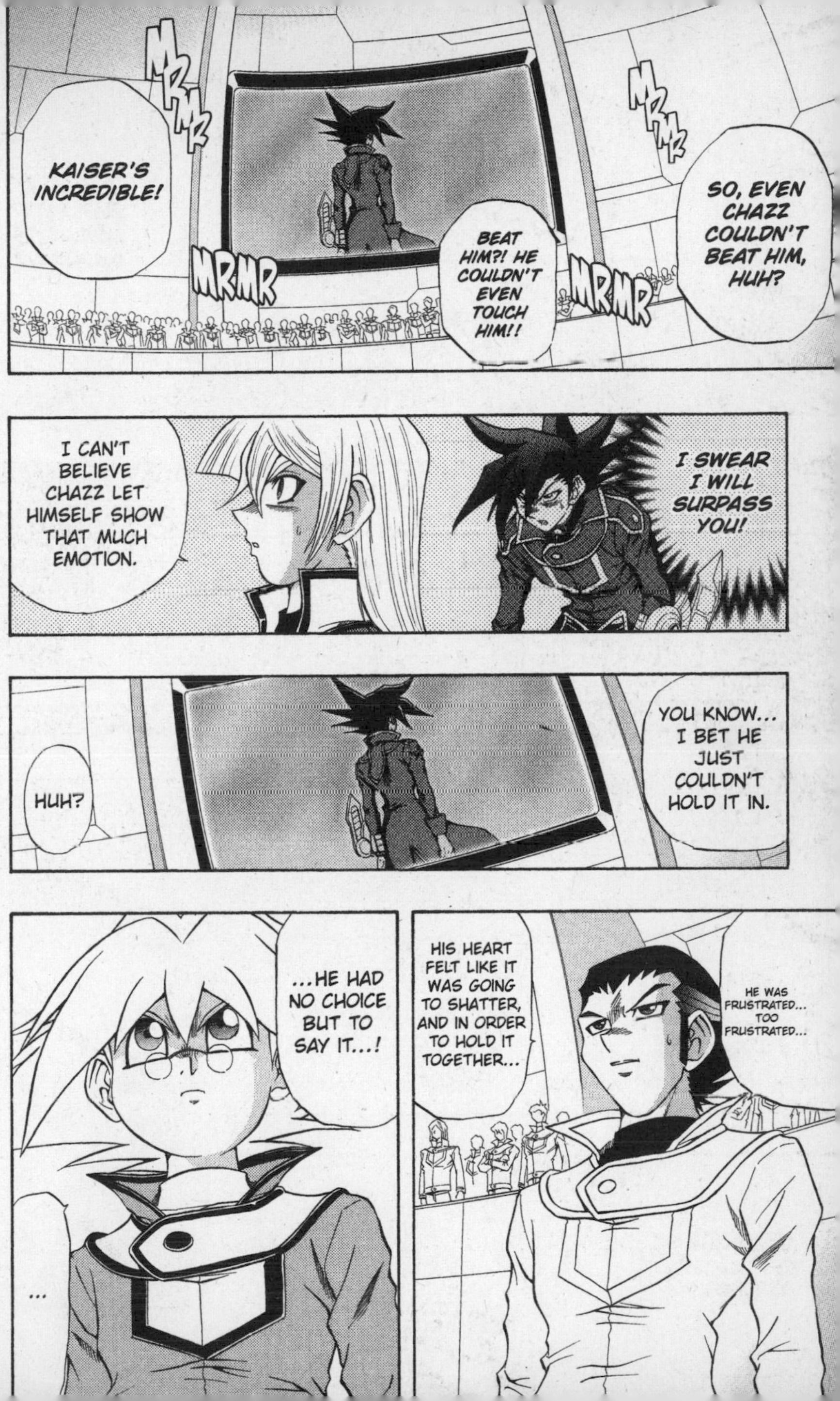
MRMR
SO, EVEN CHAZZ COULDN'T BEAT HIM, HUH?
BEAT HIM?! HE COULDN'T EVEN TOUCH HIM!!
MRMR
KAISER'S INCREDIBLE!
MRMR
MRMR
I SWEAR I WILL SURPASS YOU!
I CAN'T BELIEVE CHAZZ LET HIMSELF SHOW THAT MUCH EMOTION.
YOU KNOW... I BET HE JUST COULDN'T HOLD IT IN.
HUH?
HE WAS FRUSTRATED... TOO FRUSTRATED...
HIS HEART FELT LIKE IT WAS GOING TO SHATTER, AND IN ORDER TO HOLD IT TOGETHER...
...HE HAD NO CHOICE BUT TO SAY IT...!
...

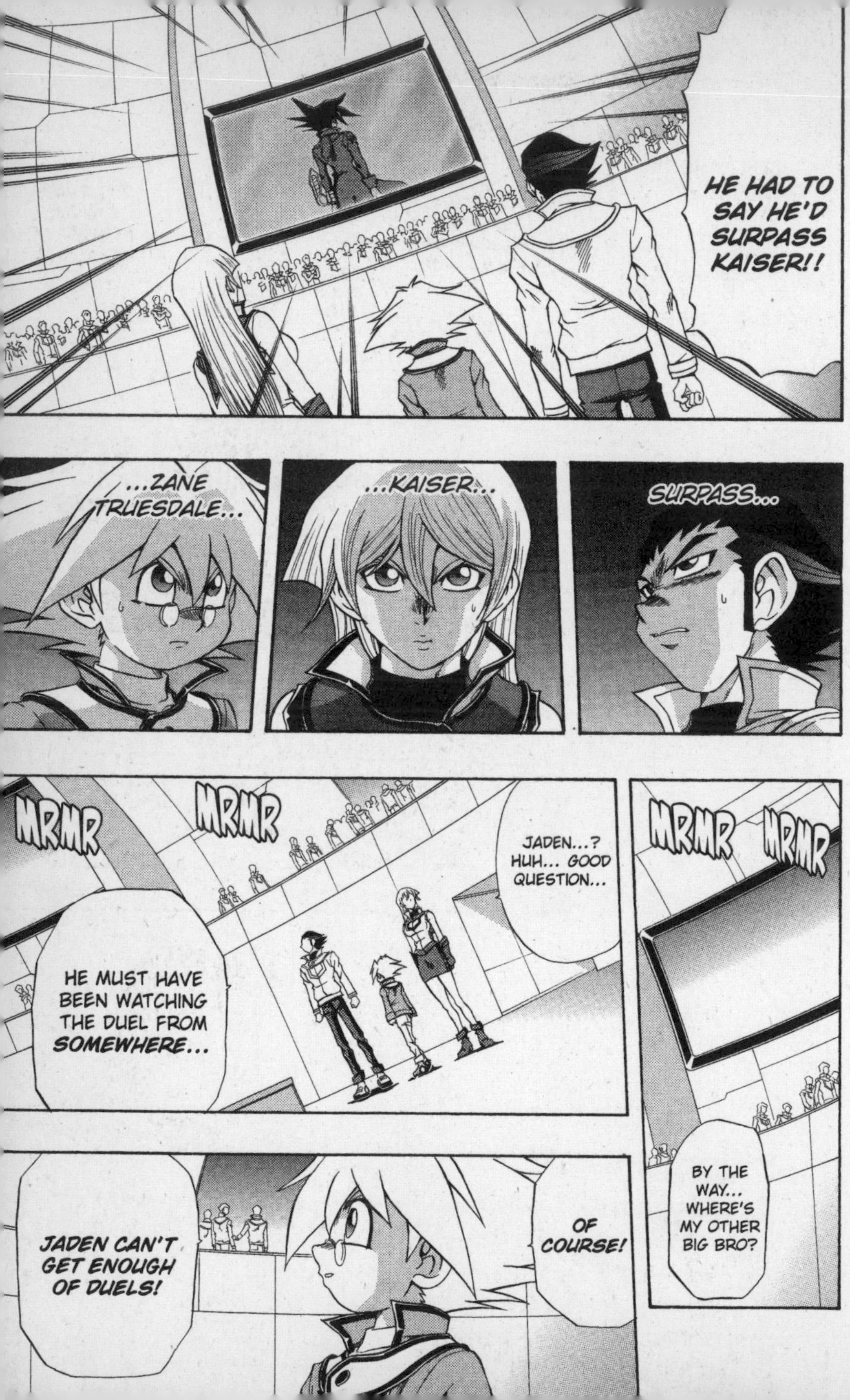
HE HAD TO SAY HE'D SURPASS KAISER!!
SURPASS...
...KAISER...
...ZANE TRUESDALE...
MRMR
MRMR
BY THE WAY... WHERE'S MY OTHER BIG BRO?
MRMR
MRMR
JADEN...? HUH... GOOD QUESTION...
HE MUST HAVE BEEN WATCHING THE DUEL FROM SOMEWHERE...
OF COURSE!
JADEN CAN'T GET ENOUGH OF DUELS!

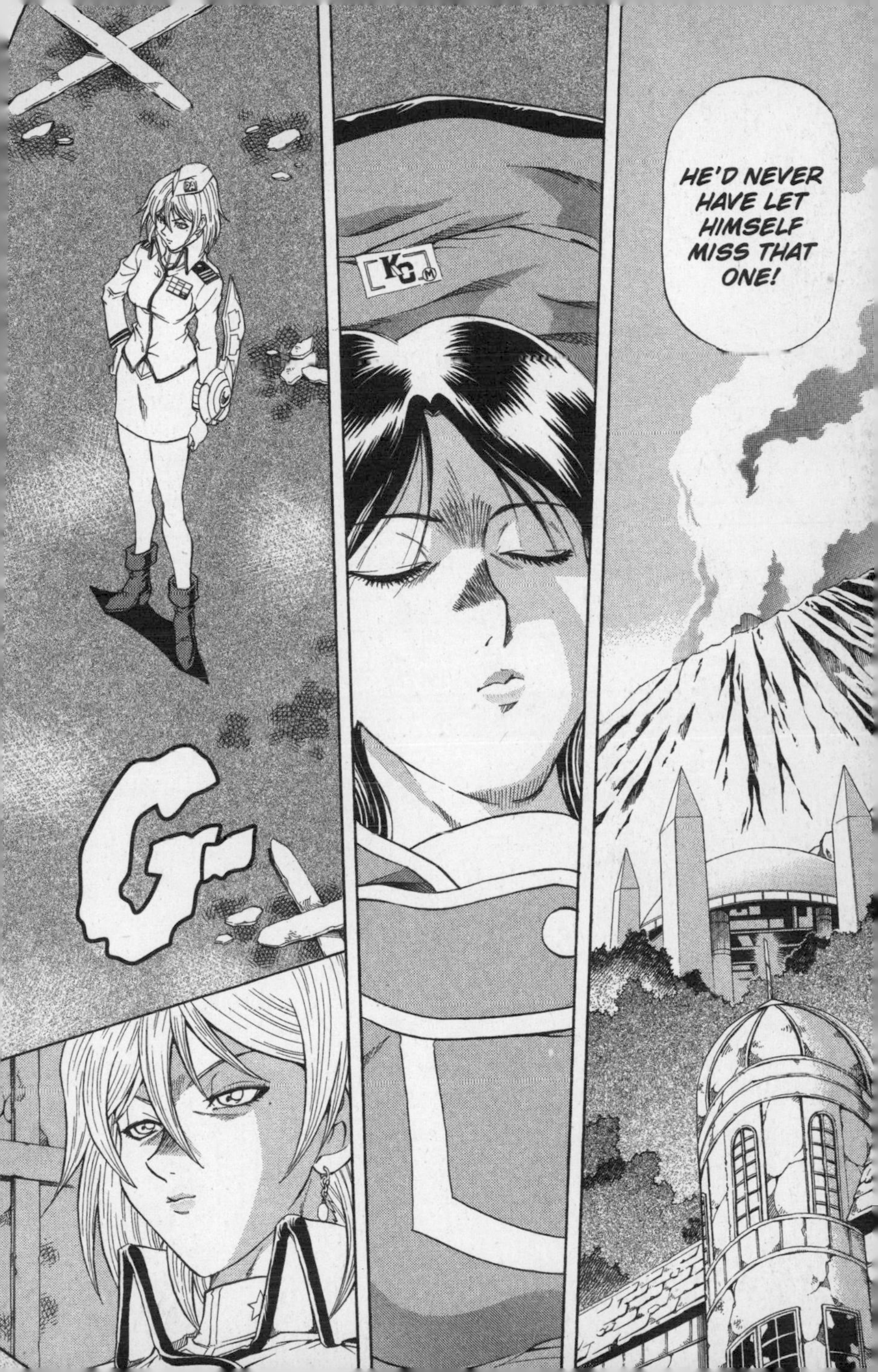
HE'D NEVER HAVE LET HIMSELF MISS THAT ONE!
G

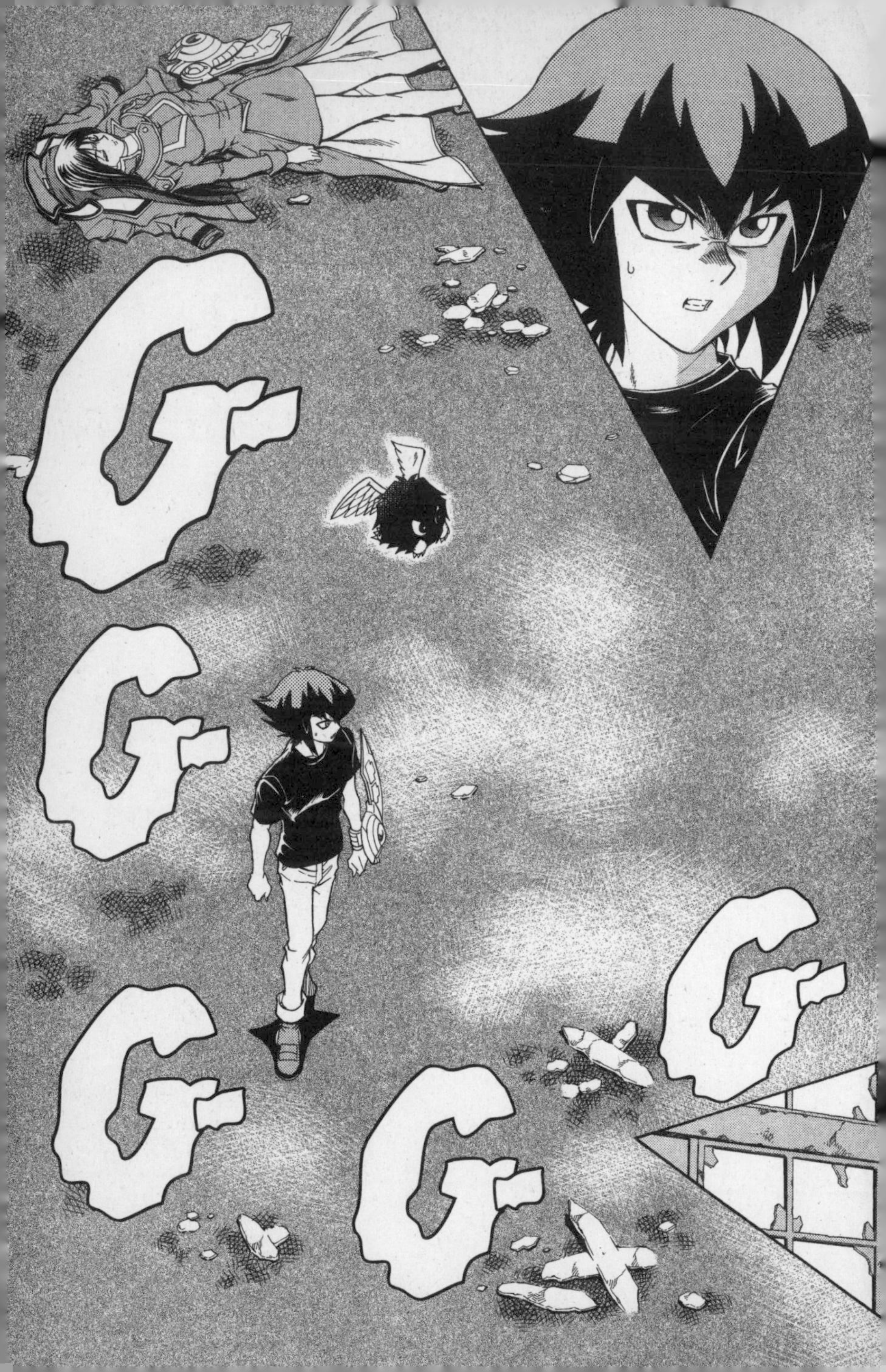
Gr
Gr
Gr
Gr
Gr

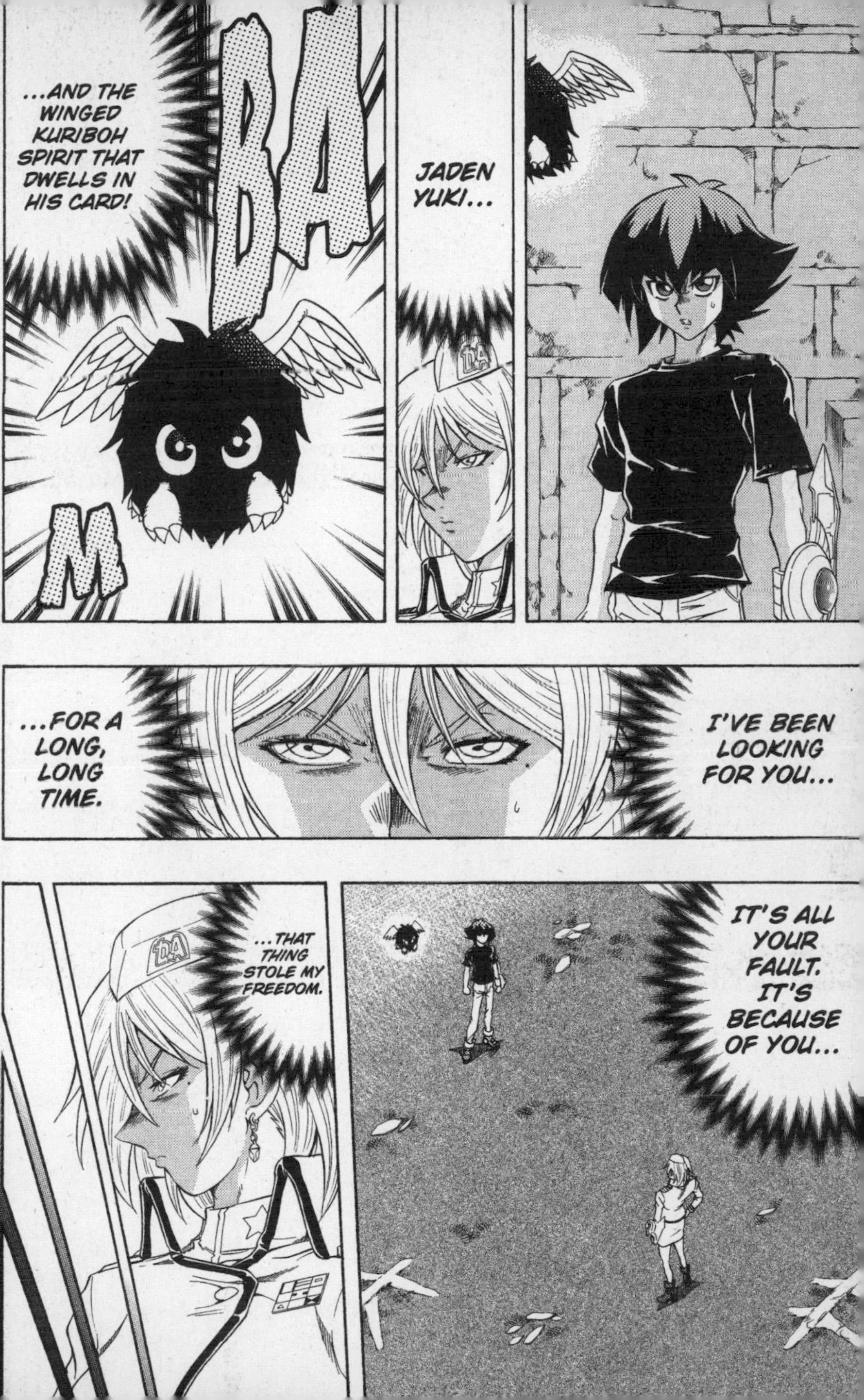
JADEN YUKI...
...AND THE WINGED KURIBOH SPIRIT THAT DWELLS IN HIS CARD!
BA
M
I'VE BEEN LOOKING FOR YOU...
...FOR A LONG, LONG TIME.
IT'S ALL YOUR FAULT. IT'S BECAUSE OF YOU...
...THAT THING STOLE MY FREEDOM.

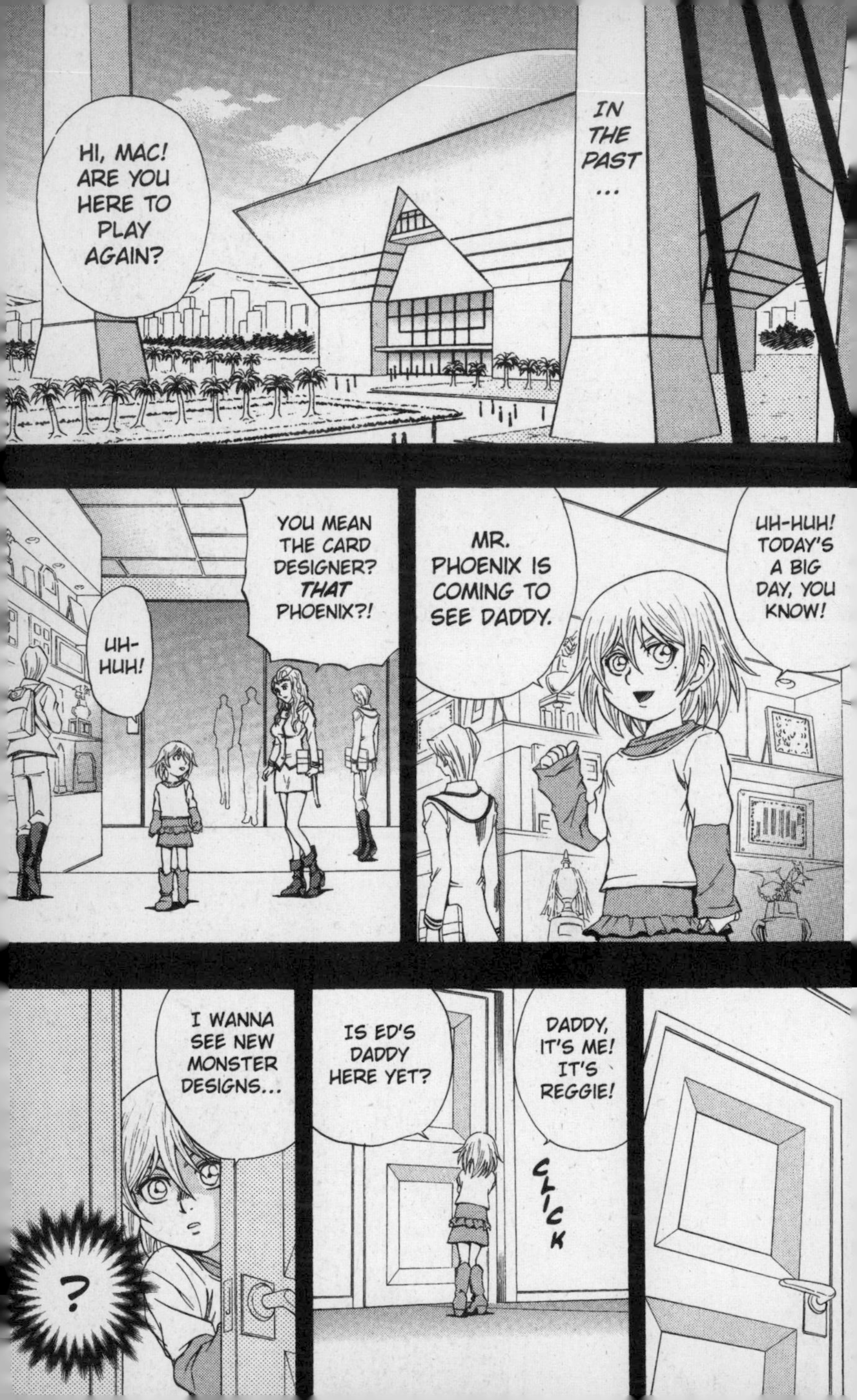
IN THE PAST...
HI, MAC! ARE YOU HERE TO PLAY AGAIN?
UH-HUH! TODAY'S A BIG DAY, YOU KNOW!
MR. PHOENIX IS COMING TO SEE DADDY.
YOU MEAN THE CARD DESIGNER? *THAT* PHOENIX?!
UH-HUH!
DADDY, IT'S ME! IT'S REGGIE!
CLICK
IS ED'S DADDY HERE YET?
I WANNA SEE NEW MONSTER DESIGNS...
?

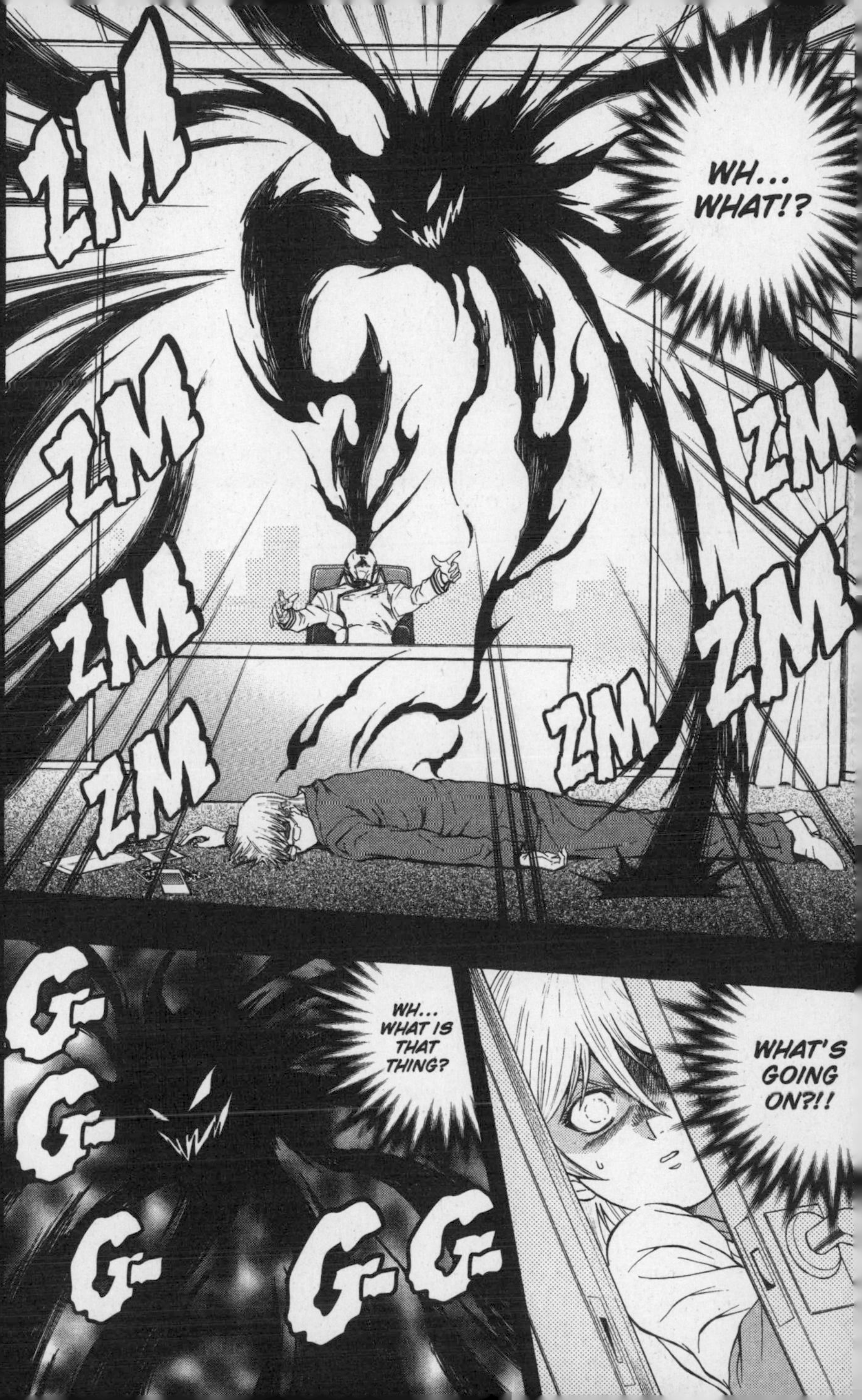
WH... WHAT!?
ZM
ZM
ZM
ZM
ZM
ZM
ZM
WHAT'S GOING ON?!!
WH... WHAT IS THAT THING?
G-G-G-
G-G-

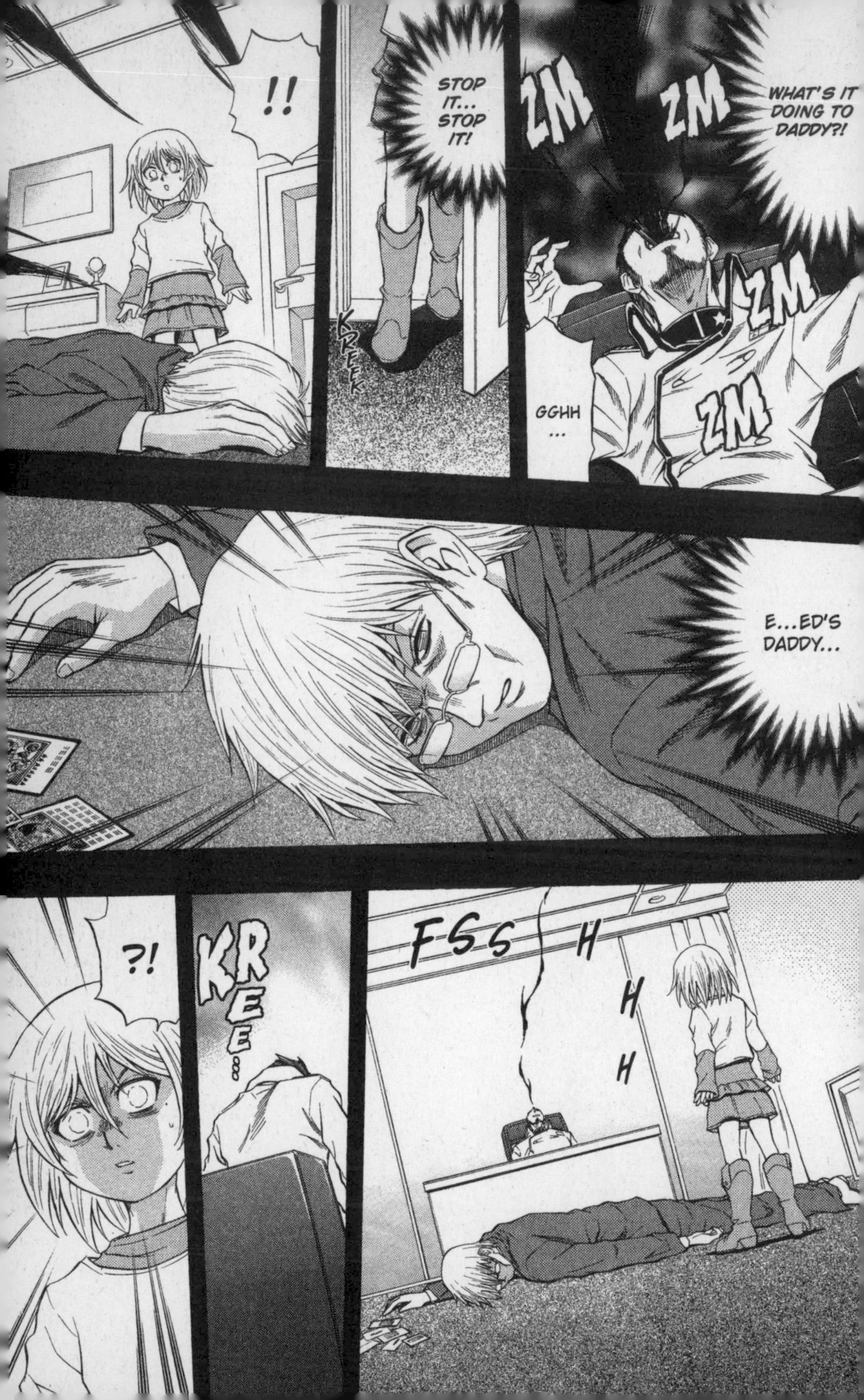
WHAT'S IT DOING TO DADDY?!
ZM
ZM
ZM
ZM
GGHH...
STOP IT... STOP IT!
KREEK
!!
E...ED'S DADDY...
FSSHHHH
KREE..
?!

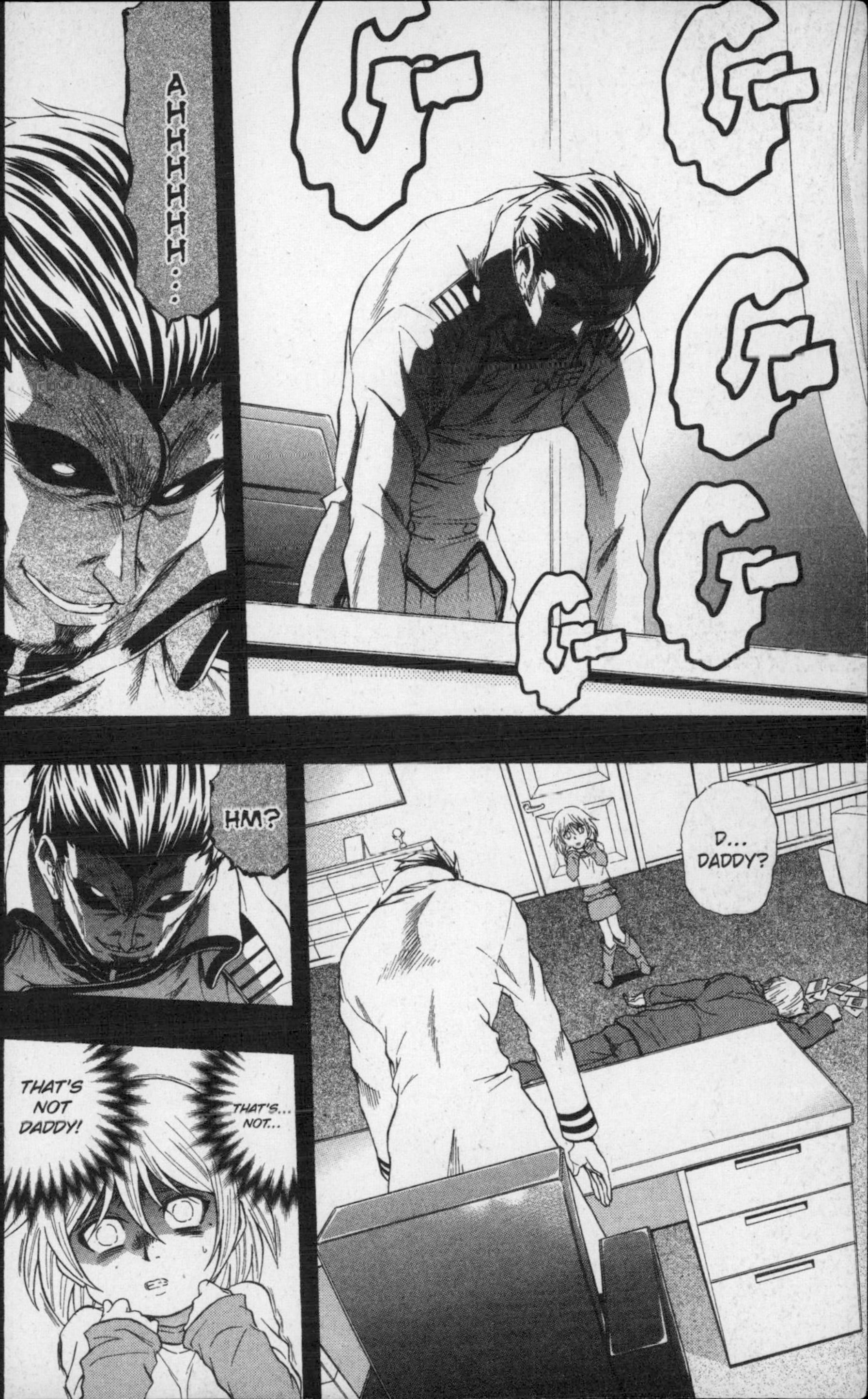
G-G-G-G-G-
AHHHHHHH...
D... DADDY?
HM?
THAT'S... NOT...
THAT'S NOT DADDY!

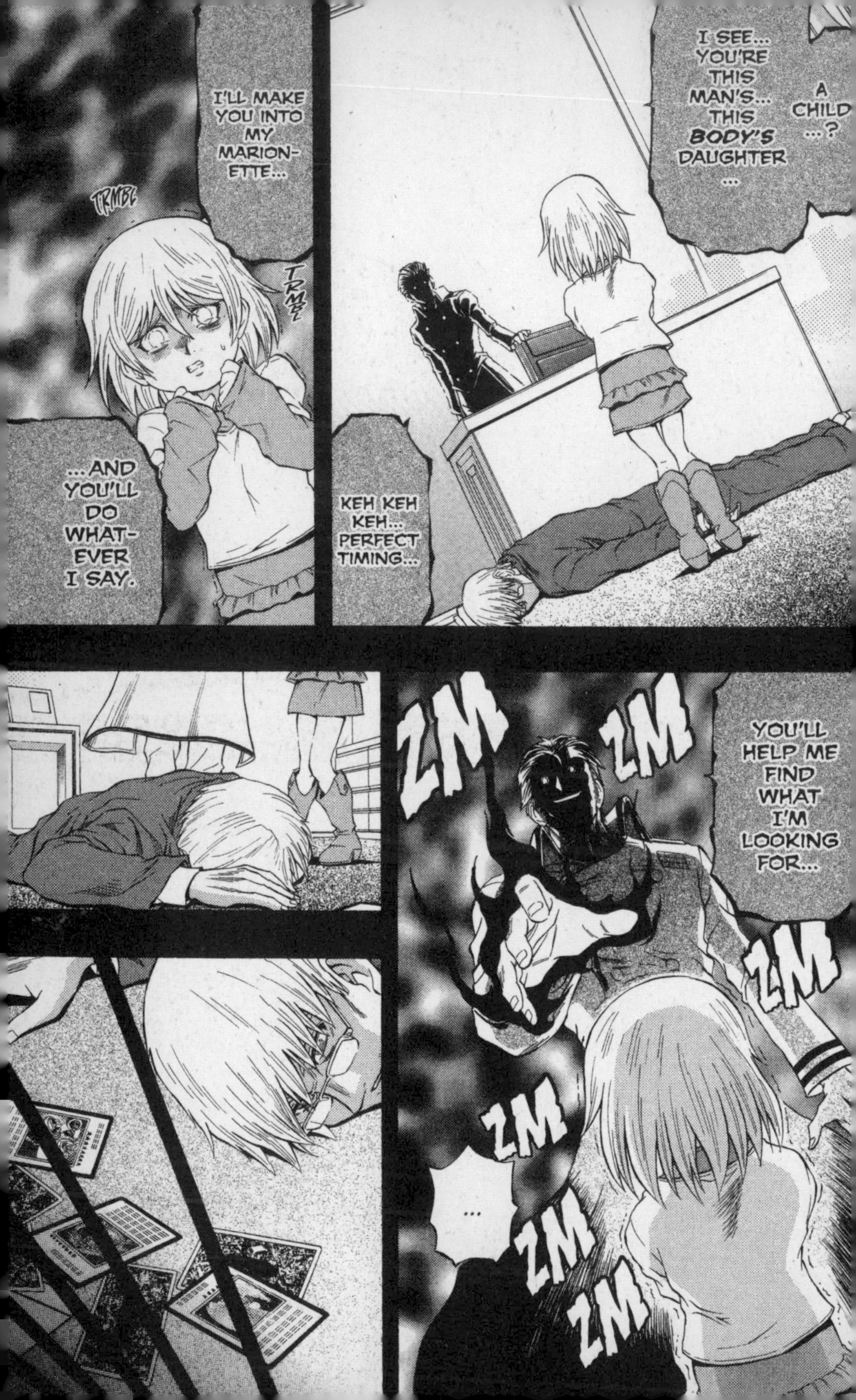
A CHILD ...?
I SEE... YOU'RE THIS MAN'S... THIS BODY'S DAUGHTER ...
KEH KEH KEH... PERFECT TIMING...
I'LL MAKE YOU INTO MY MARION-ETTE...
TRMBL
TRMBL
...AND YOU'LL DO WHAT-EVER I SAY.
YOU'LL HELP ME FIND WHAT I'M LOOKING FOR...
ZM
ZM
ZM
ZM
ZM
ZM
...

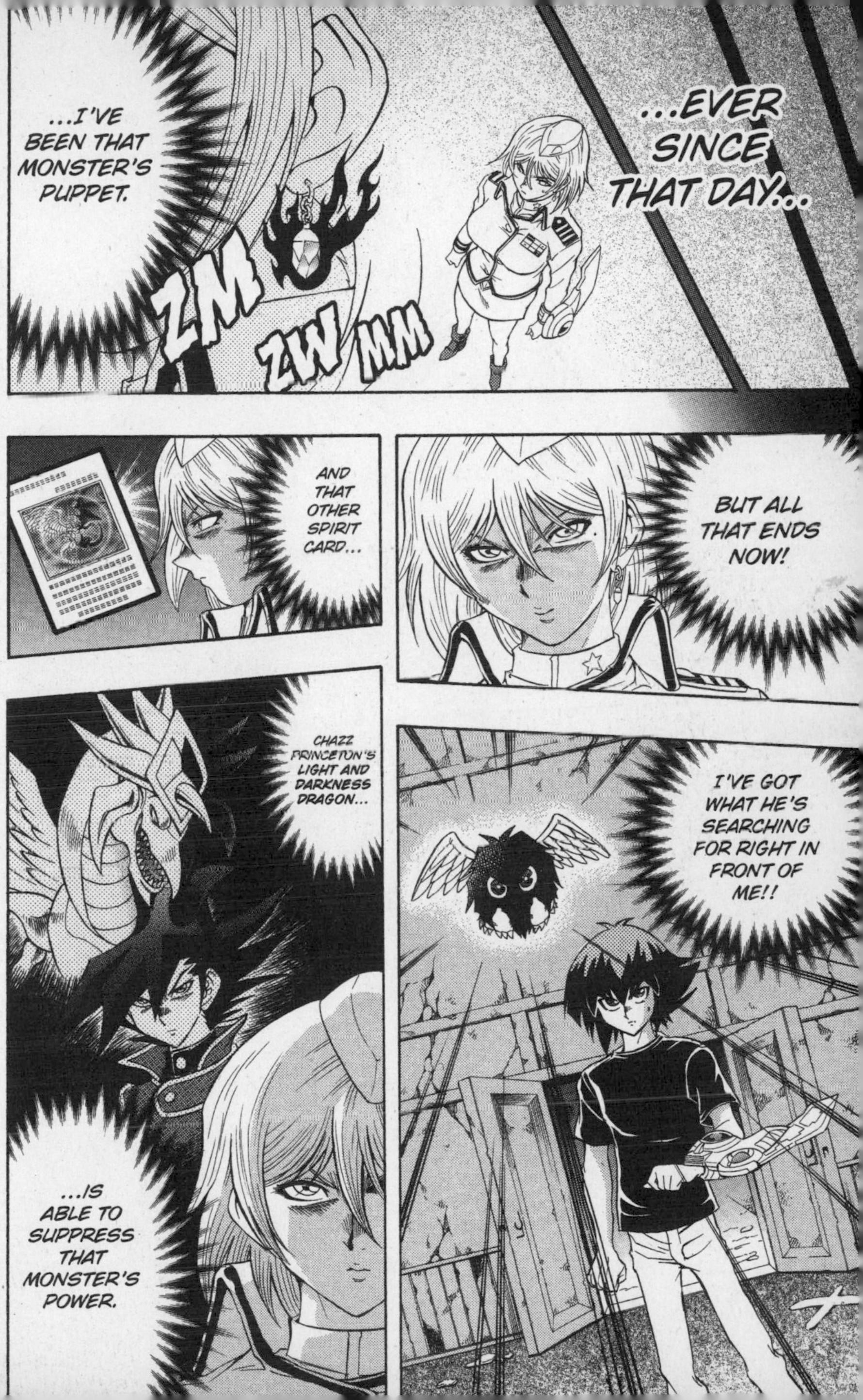
...EVER SINCE THAT DAY...
...I'VE BEEN THAT MONSTER'S PUPPET.
ZM
ZW
MM
BUT ALL THAT ENDS NOW!
AND THAT OTHER SPIRIT CARD...
I'VE GOT WHAT HE'S SEARCHING FOR RIGHT IN FRONT OF ME!!
CHAZZ PRINCETON'S LIGHT AND DARKNESS DRAGON...
...IS ABLE TO SUPPRESS THAT MONSTER'S POWER.

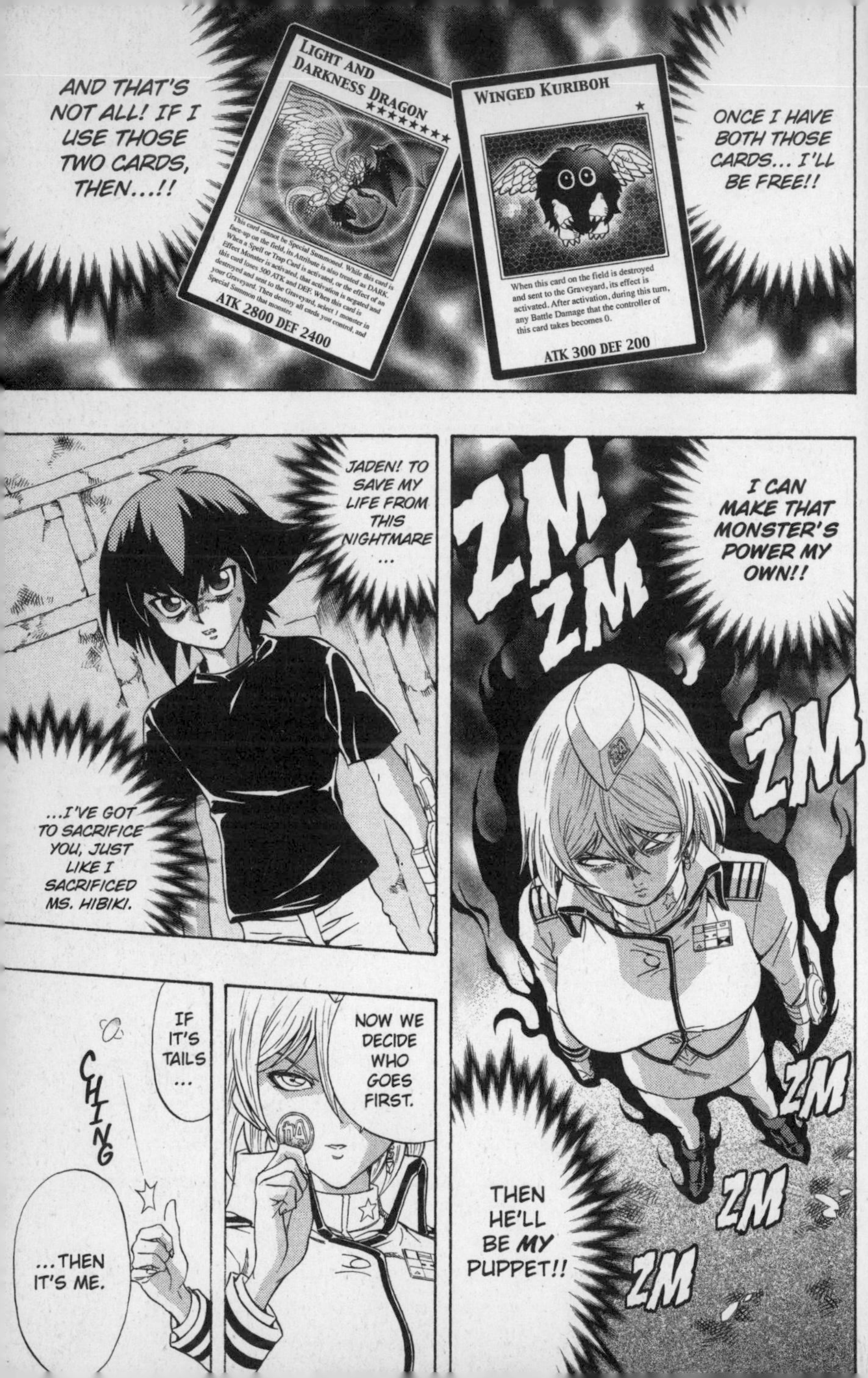
ONCE I HAVE BOTH THOSE CARDS... I'LL BE FREE!!
WINGED KURIBOH
When this card on the field is destroyed and sent to the Graveyard, its effect is activated. After activation, during this turn, any Battle Damage that the controller of this card takes becomes 0.
ATK 300 DEF 200
LIGHT AND DARKNESS DRAGON
This card cannot be Special Summoned. While this card is face-up on the field, its Attribute is also treated as DARK. When a Spell or Trap Card is activated, or the effect of an Effect Monster is activated, that activation is negated and this card loses 500 ATK and DEF. When this card is destroyed and sent to the Graveyard, select 1 monster in your Graveyard. Then destroy all cards you control, and Special Summon that monster.
ATK 2800 DEF 2400
AND THAT'S NOT ALL! IF I USE THOSE TWO CARDS, THEN...!!
I CAN MAKE THAT MONSTER'S POWER MY OWN!!
ZM ZM ZM
ZM
ZM
ZM
ZM
THEN HE'LL BE MY PUPPET!!
JADEN! TO SAVE MY LIFE FROM THIS NIGHTMARE...
...I'VE GOT TO SACRIFICE YOU, JUST LIKE I SACRIFICED MS. HIBIKI.
NOW WE DECIDE WHO GOES FIRST.
IF IT'S TAILS...
CHING
...THEN IT'S ME.

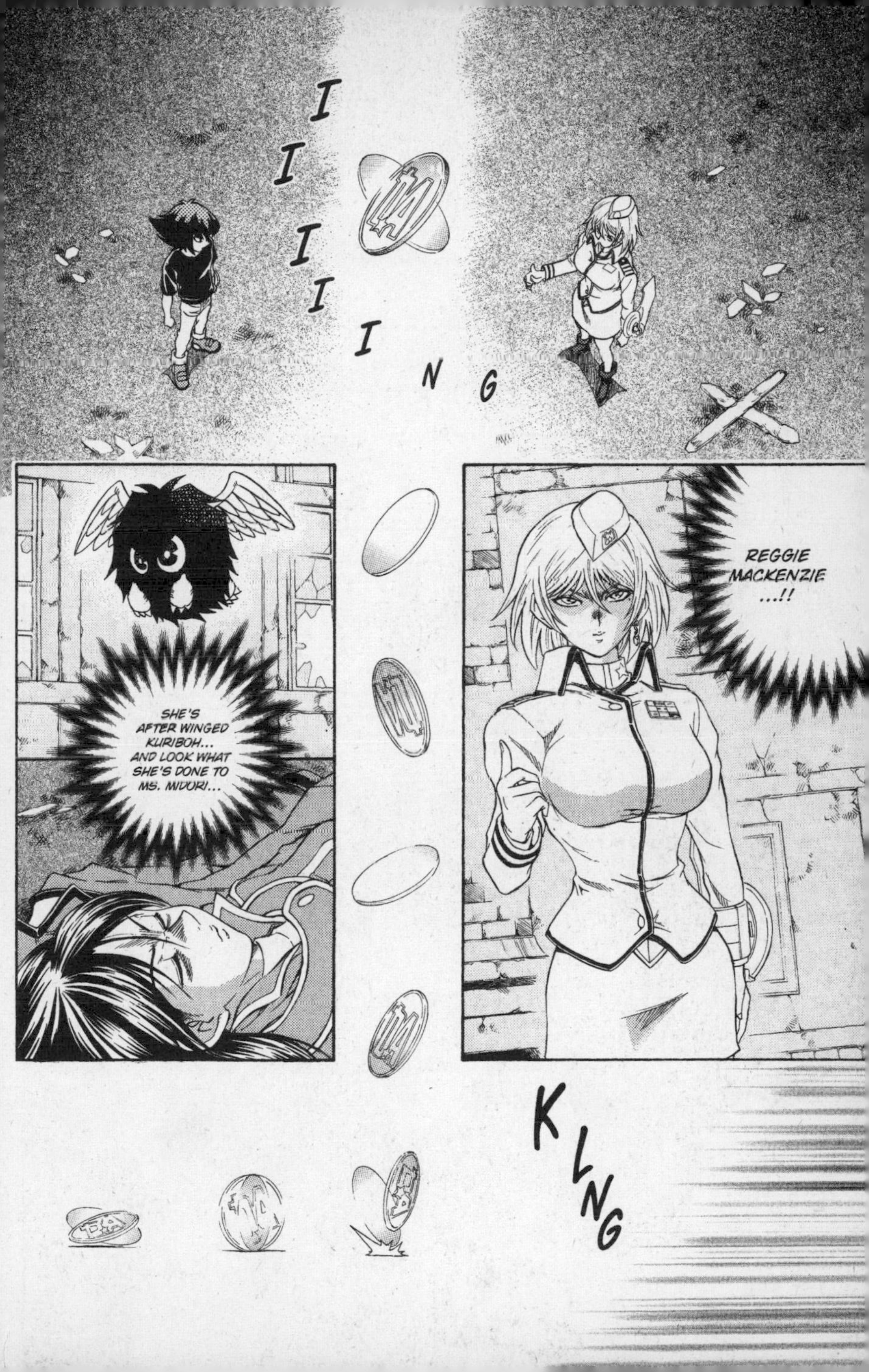
IIIIIING
REGGIE MACKENZIE ...!!
SHE'S AFTER WINGED KURIBOH... AND LOOK WHAT SHE'S DONE TO MS. MIDORI...
KLNG

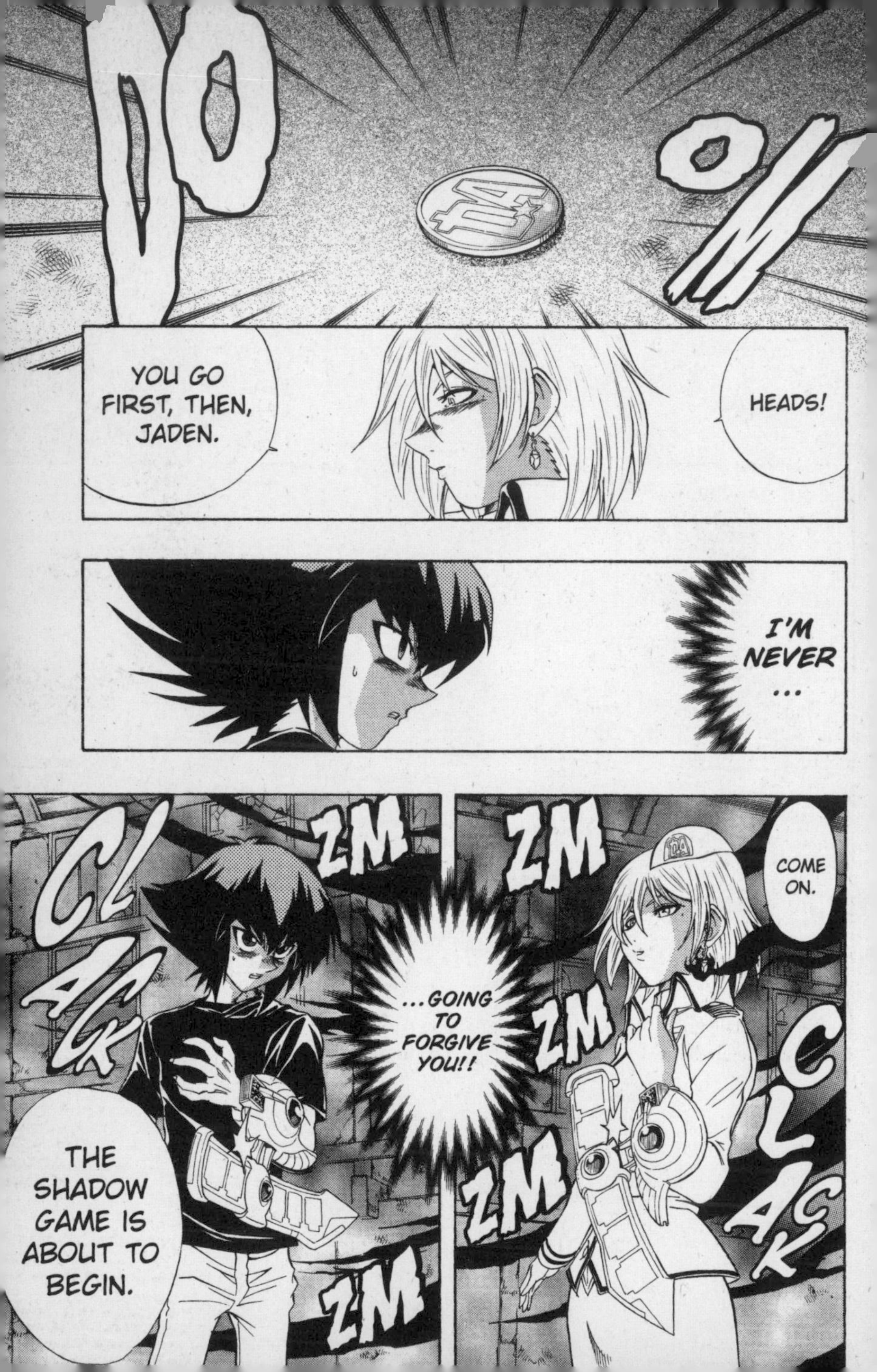
HEADS!
YOU GO FIRST, THEN, JADEN.
I'M NEVER ...
COME ON.
ZM
ZM
CLACK
...GOING TO FORGIVE YOU!!
ZM
ZM
ZM
CLACK
THE SHADOW GAME IS ABOUT TO BEGIN.

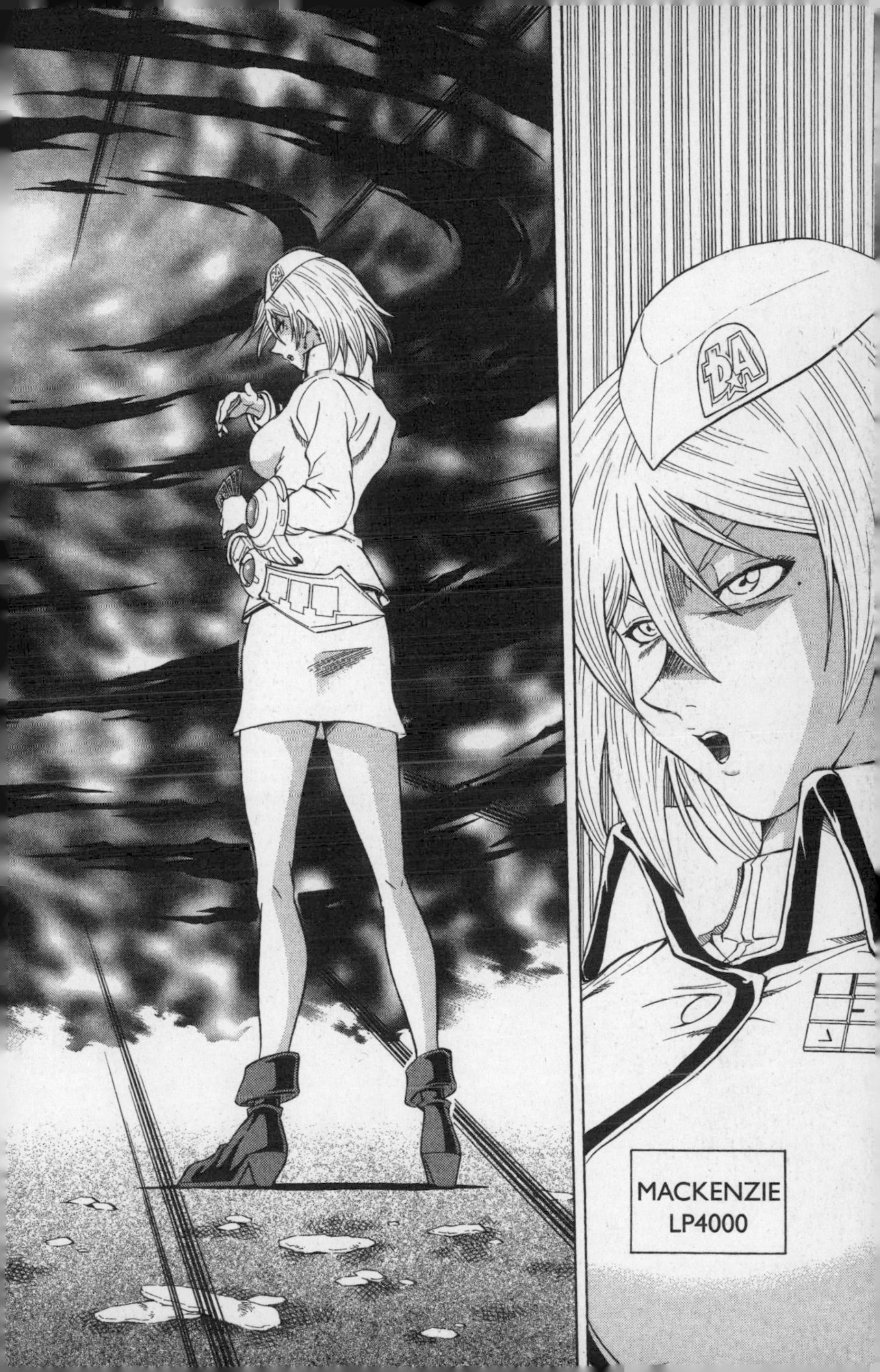
MACKENZIE
LP4000

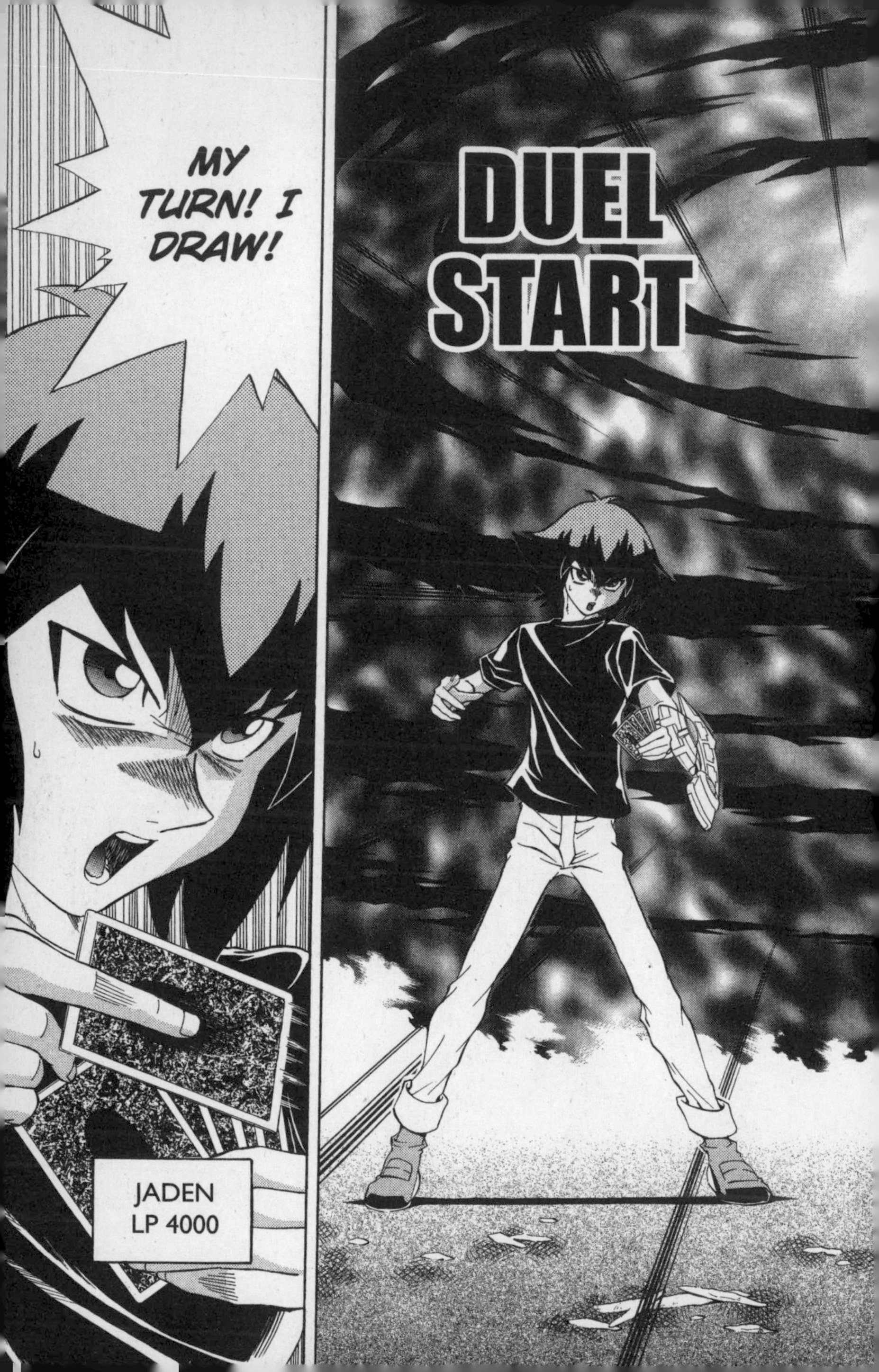
DUEL START
MY TURN! I DRAW!
JADEN
LP 4000

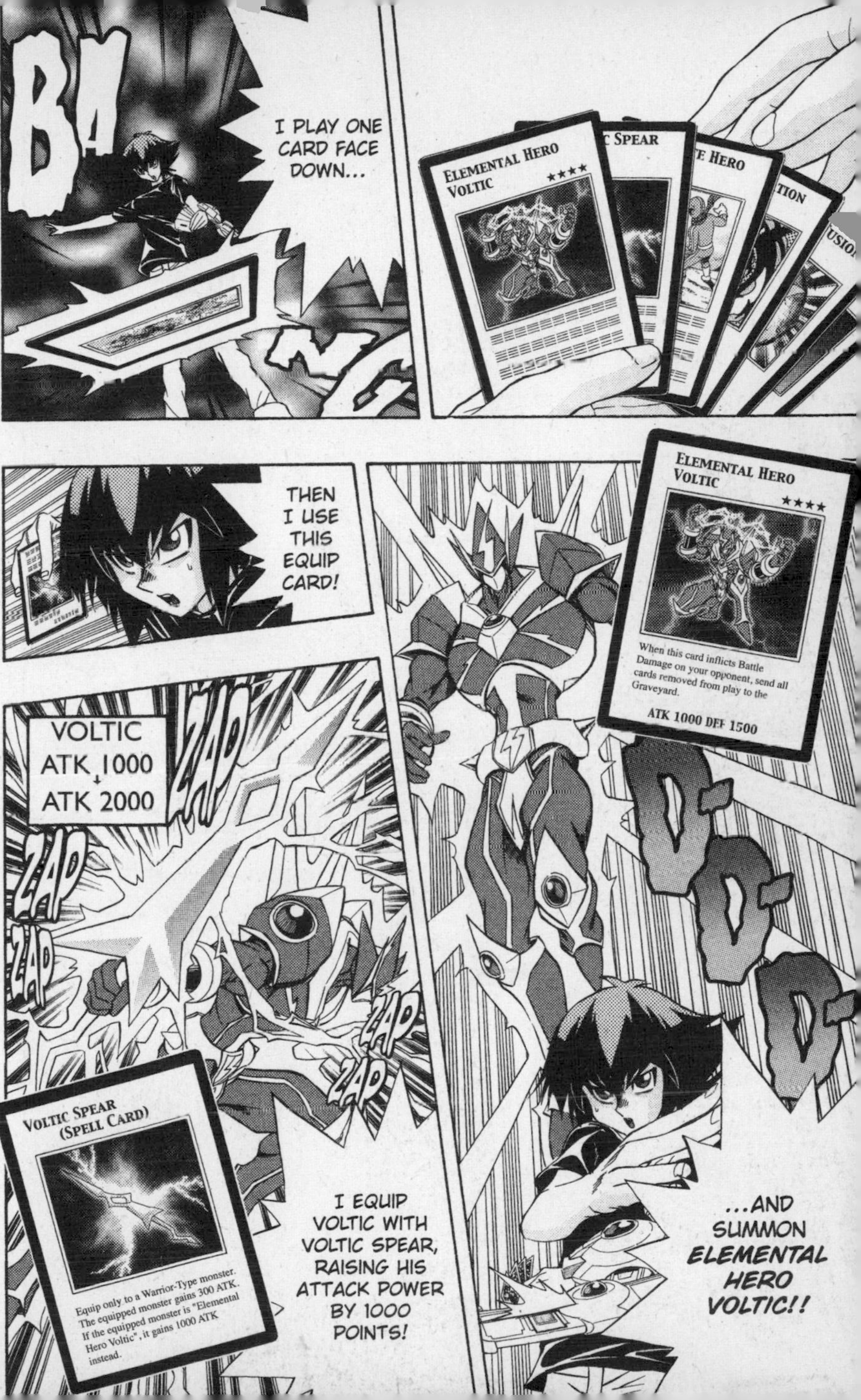
ELEMENTAL HERO VOLTIC
BA
I PLAY ONE CARD FACE DOWN...
ELEMENTAL HERO VOLTIC
When this card inflicts Battle Damage on your opponent, send all cards removed from play to the Graveyard.
ATK 1000 DEF 1500
D-D-D-
...AND SUMMON ELEMENTAL HERO VOLTIC!!
THEN I USE THIS EQUIP CARD!
VOLTIC ATK 1000 ATK 2000
ZAP
ZAP
ZAP
ZAP
ZAP
VOLTIC SPEAR (SPELL CARD)
Equip only to a Warrior-Type monster. The equipped monster gains 300 ATK. If the equipped monster is "Elemental Hero Voltic", it gains 1000 ATK instead.
I EQUIP VOLTIC WITH VOLTIC SPEAR, RAISING HIS ATTACK POWER BY 1000 POINTS!

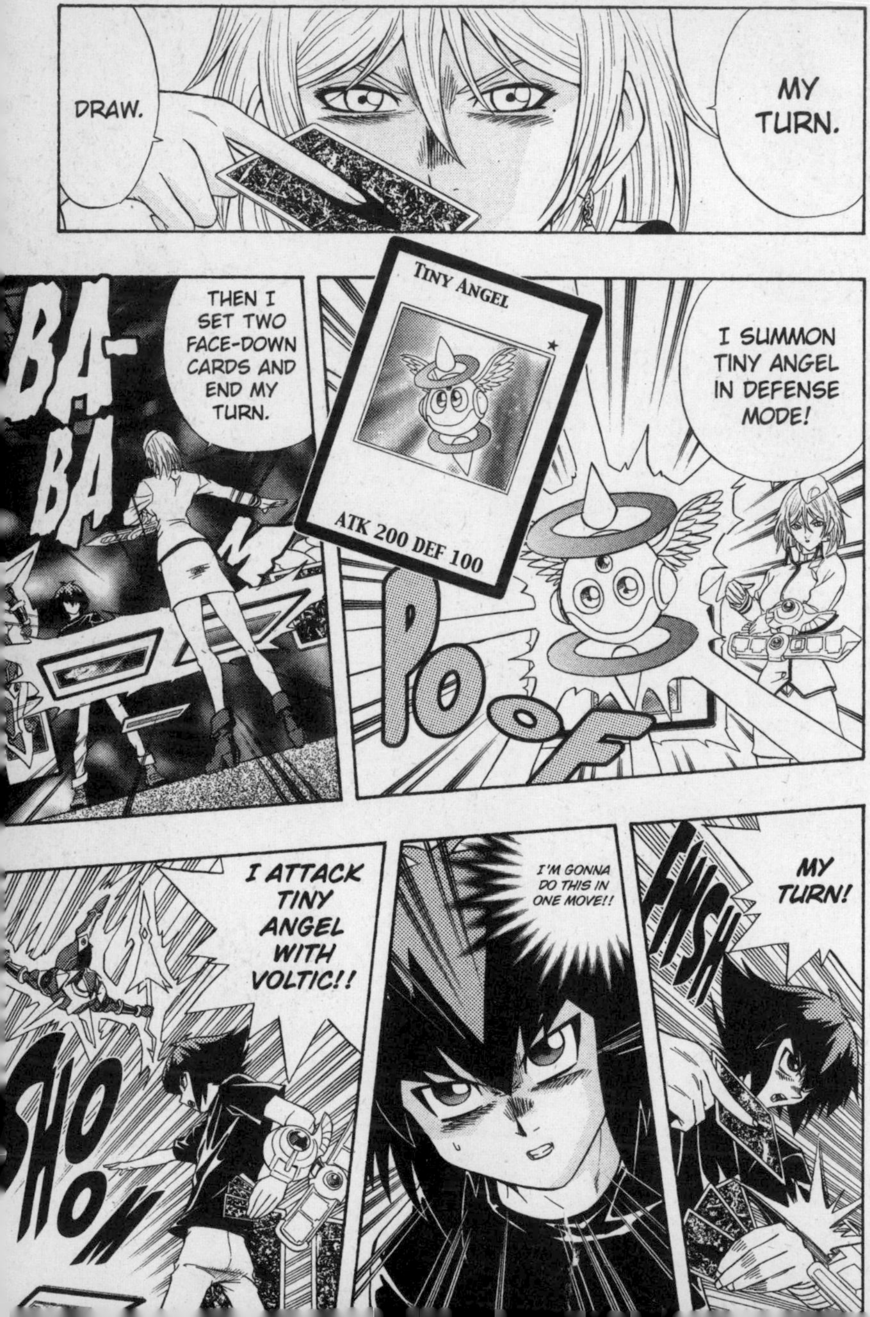
MY TURN.
DRAW.
I SUMMON TINY ANGEL IN DEFENSE MODE!
TINY ANGEL
ATK 200 DEF 100
POOOF
BA-BA-
THEN I SET TWO FACE-DOWN CARDS AND END MY TURN.
MY TURN!
I'M GONNA DO THIS IN ONE MOVE!!
I ATTACK TINY ANGEL WITH VOLTIC!!
SHOOM

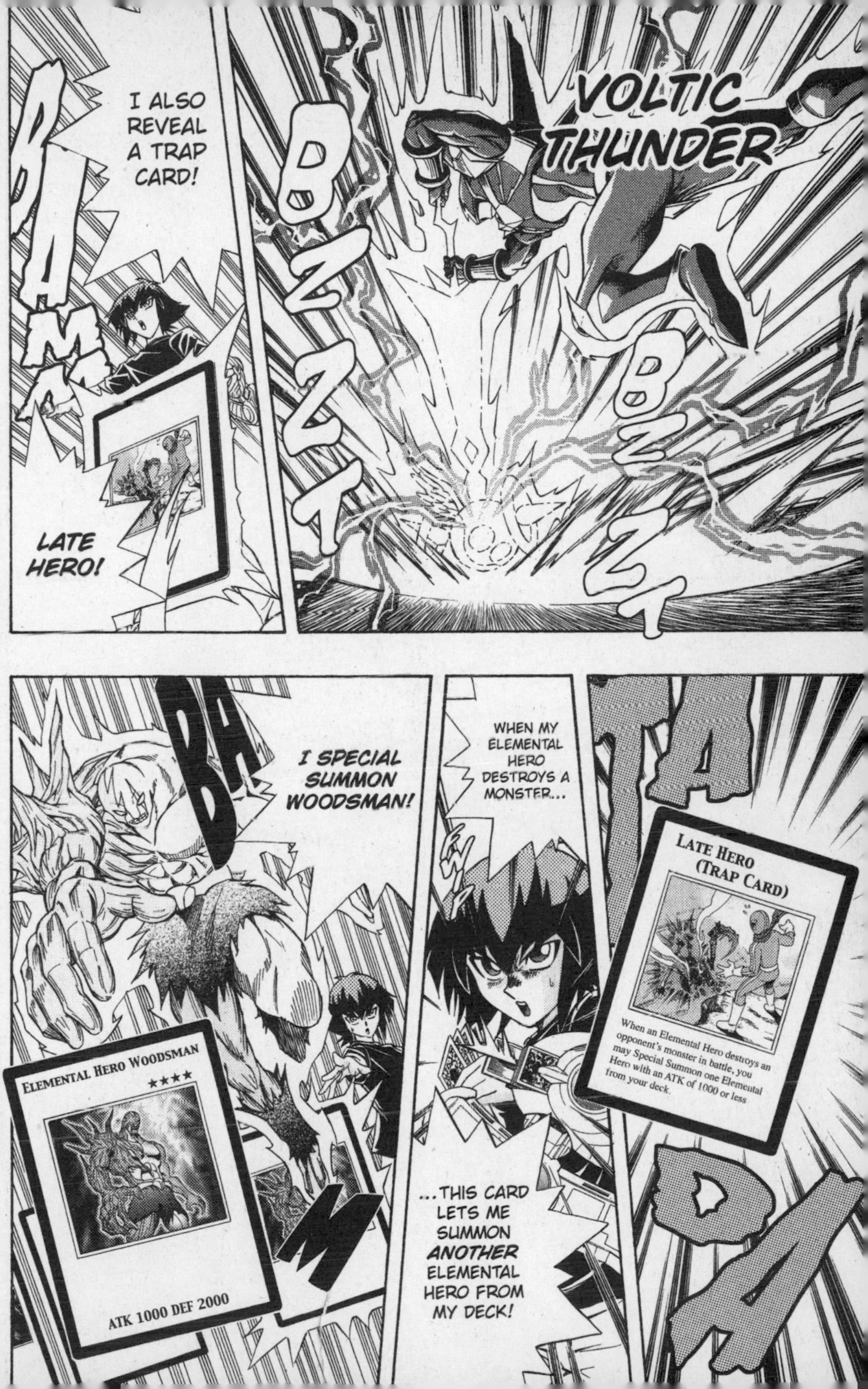
VOLTIC THUNDER
BZZZT
BZZZT
BAM
I ALSO REVEAL A TRAP CARD!
LATE HERO!
TA
LATE HERO (TRAP CARD)
When an Elemental Hero destroys an opponent's monster in battle, you may Special Summon one Elemental Hero with an ATK of 1000 or less from your deck.
DA
WHEN MY ELEMENTAL HERO DESTROYS A MONSTER...
...THIS CARD LETS ME SUMMON ANOTHER ELEMENTAL HERO FROM MY DECK!
BA
I SPECIAL SUMMON WOODSMAN!
ELEMENTAL HERO WOODSMAN
★★★★
ATK 1000 DEF 2000
M

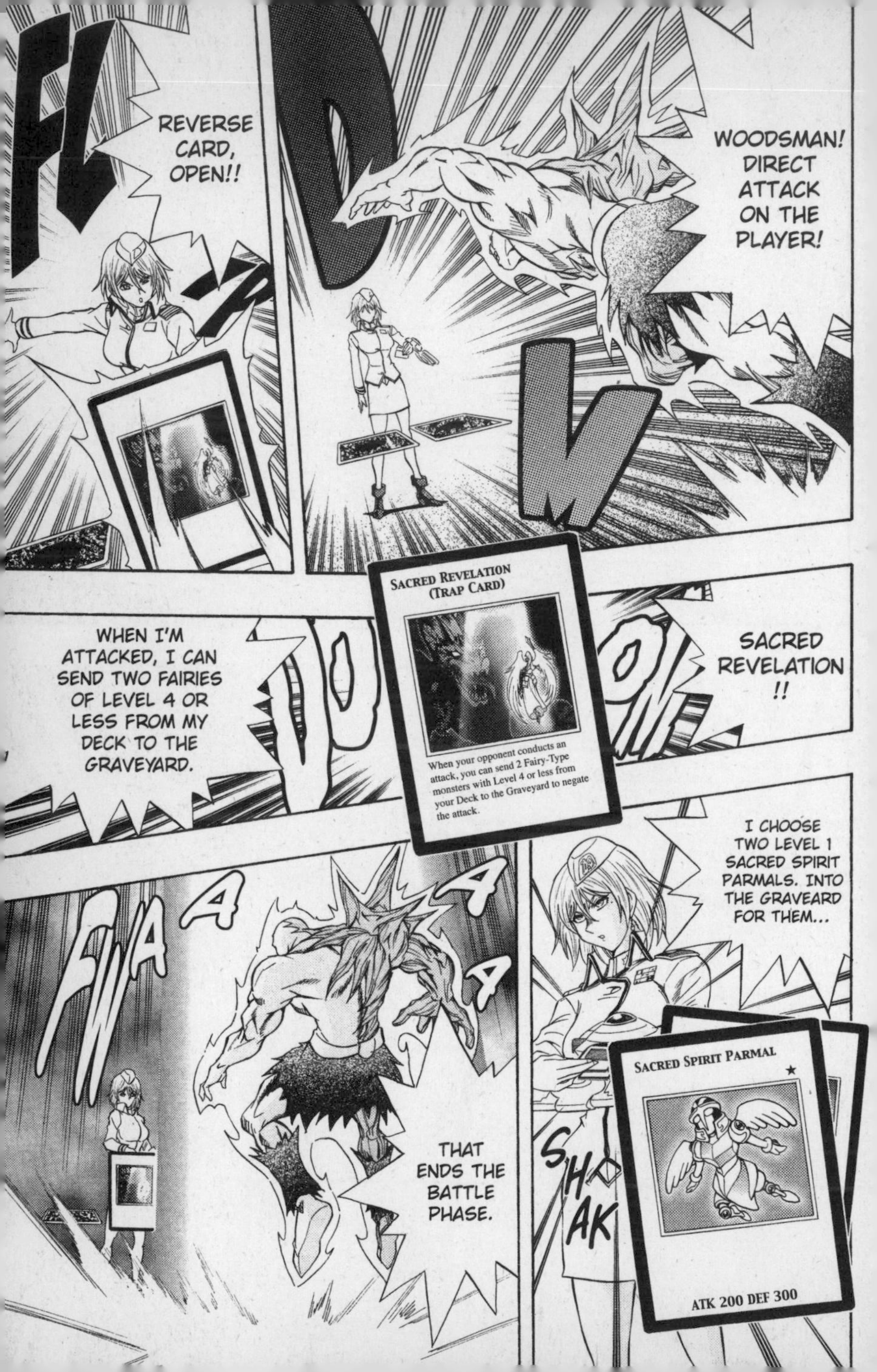
WOODSMAN! DIRECT ATTACK ON THE PLAYER!
REVERSE CARD, OPEN!!
SACRED REVELATION !!
SACRED REVELATION
(TRAP CARD)
When your opponent conducts an attack, you can send 2 Fairy-Type monsters with Level 4 or less from your Deck to the Graveyard to negate the attack.
WHEN I'M ATTACKED, I CAN SEND TWO FAIRIES OF LEVEL 4 OR LESS FROM MY DECK TO THE GRAVEYARD.
I CHOOSE TWO LEVEL 1 SACRED SPIRIT PARMALS. INTO THE GRAVEARD FOR THEM...
SACRED SPIRIT PARMAL
ATK 200 DEF 300
SHAK
THAT ENDS THE BATTLE PHASE.

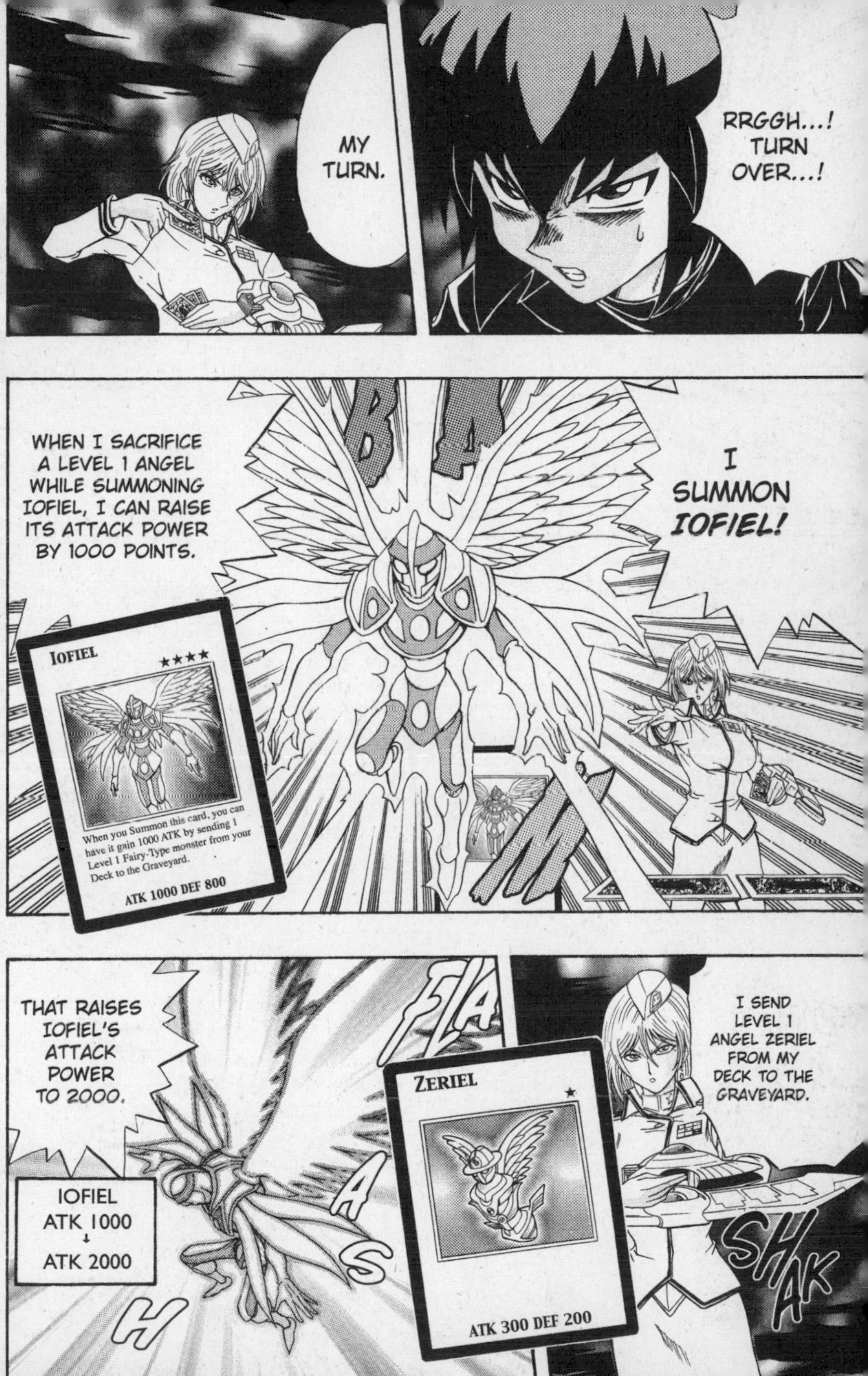

RRGGH...! TURN OVER...!
MY TURN.
I SUMMON IOFIEL!
WHEN I SACRIFICE A LEVEL 1 ANGEL WHILE SUMMONING IOFIEL, I CAN RAISE ITS ATTACK POWER BY 1000 POINTS.
IOFIEL ★★★★
When you Summon this card, you can have it gain 1000 ATK by sending 1 Level 1 Fairy-Type monster from your Deck to the Graveyard.
ATK 1000 DEF 800
I SEND LEVEL 1 ANGEL ZERIEL FROM MY DECK TO THE GRAVEYARD.
SHAK
ZERIEL ★
ATK 300 DEF 200
FLASH
THAT RAISES IOFIEL'S ATTACK POWER TO 2000.
IOFIEL ATK 1000 ↓ ATK 2000

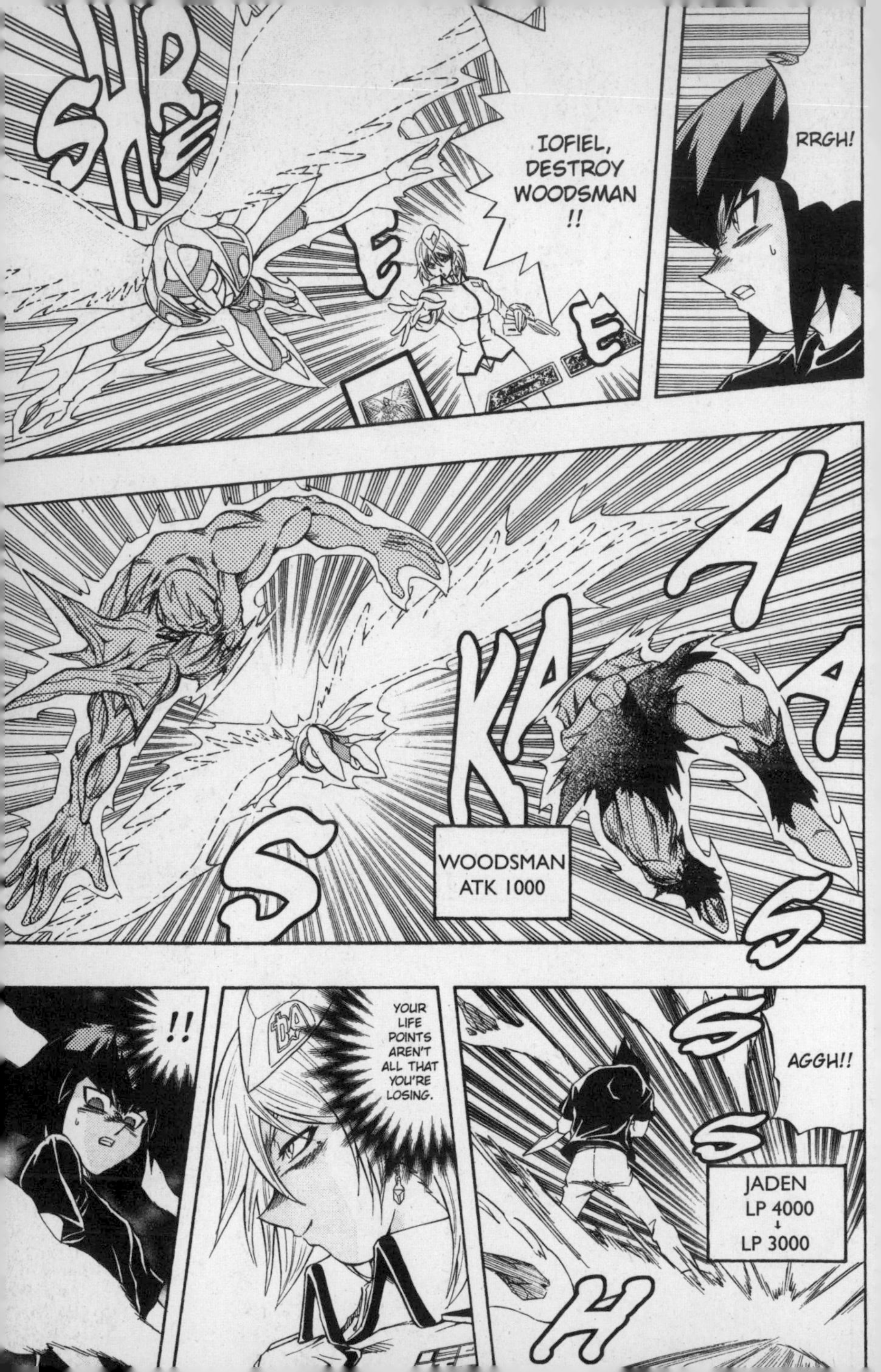
RRGH!
IOFIEL, DESTROY WOODSMAN !!
WOODSMAN ATK 1000
AGGH!!
JADEN LP 4000 ↓ LP 3000
YOUR LIFE POINTS AREN'T ALL THAT YOU'RE LOSING.
!!

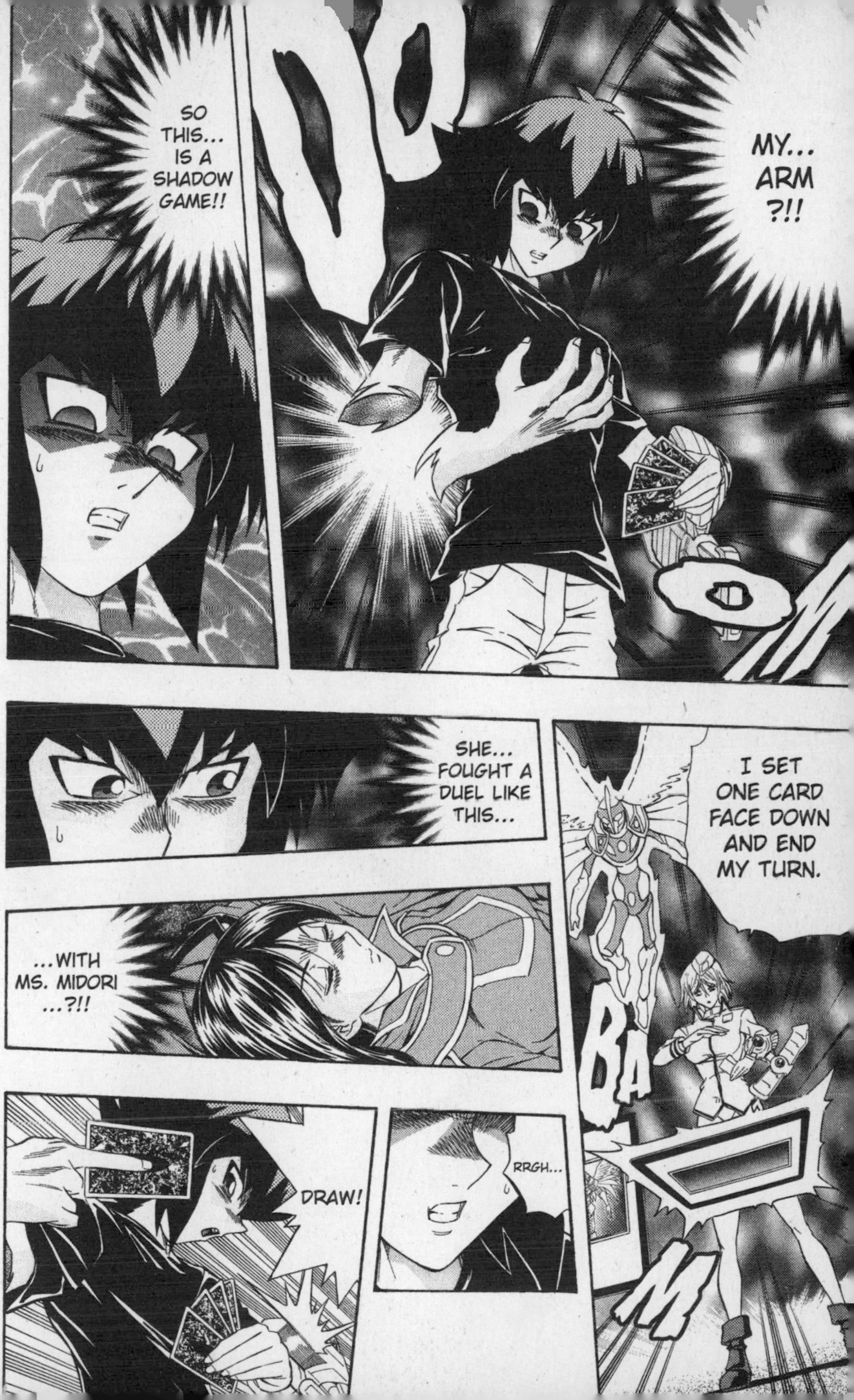
MY... ARM ?!!
SO THIS... IS A SHADOW GAME!!
I SET ONE CARD FACE DOWN AND END MY TURN.
BAM
SHE... FOUGHT A DUEL LIKE THIS...
...WITH MS. MIDORI ...?!!
RRGH...
DRAW!

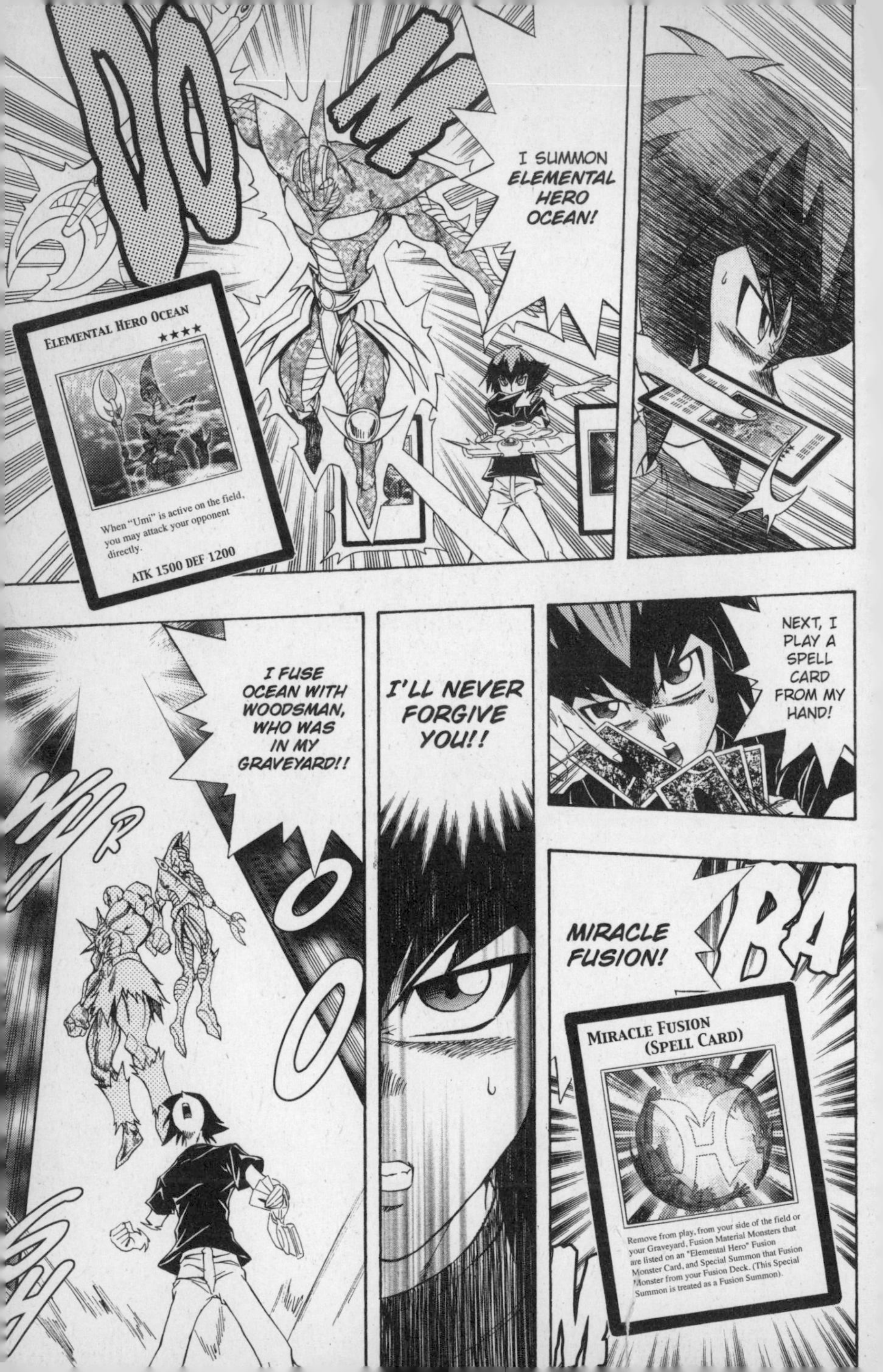
I SUMMON ELEMENTAL HERO OCEAN!
DOM
ELEMENTAL HERO OCEAN ★★★★
When "Umi" is active on the field, you may attack your opponent directly.
ATK 1500 DEF 1200
NEXT, I PLAY A SPELL CARD FROM MY HAND!
MIRACLE FUSION!
MIRACLE FUSION (SPELL CARD)
Remove from play, from your side of the field or your Graveyard, Fusion Material Monsters that are listed on an "Elemental Hero" Fusion Monster Card, and Special Summon that Fusion Monster from your Fusion Deck. (This Special Summon is treated as a Fusion Summon).
I'LL NEVER FORGIVE YOU!!
I FUSE OCEAN WITH WOODSMAN, WHO WAS IN MY GRAVEYARD!!

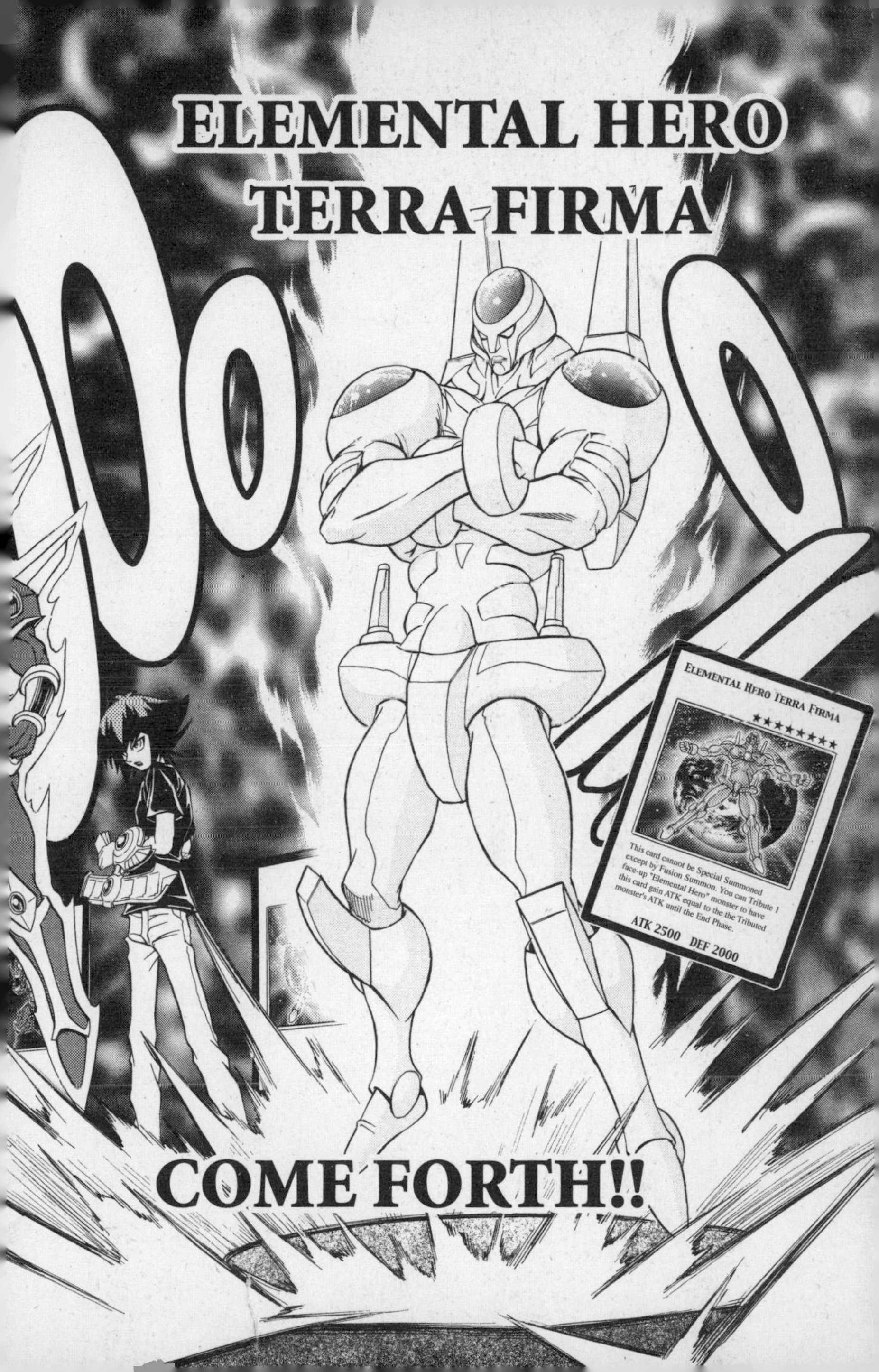
ELEMENTAL HERO TERRA FIRMA
Elemental Hero Terra Firma
This card cannot be Special Summoned except by Fusion Summon. You can Tribute 1 face-up "Elemental Hero" monster to have this card gain ATK equal to the the Tributed monster's ATK until the End Phase.
ATK 2500 DEF 2000
COME FORTH!!

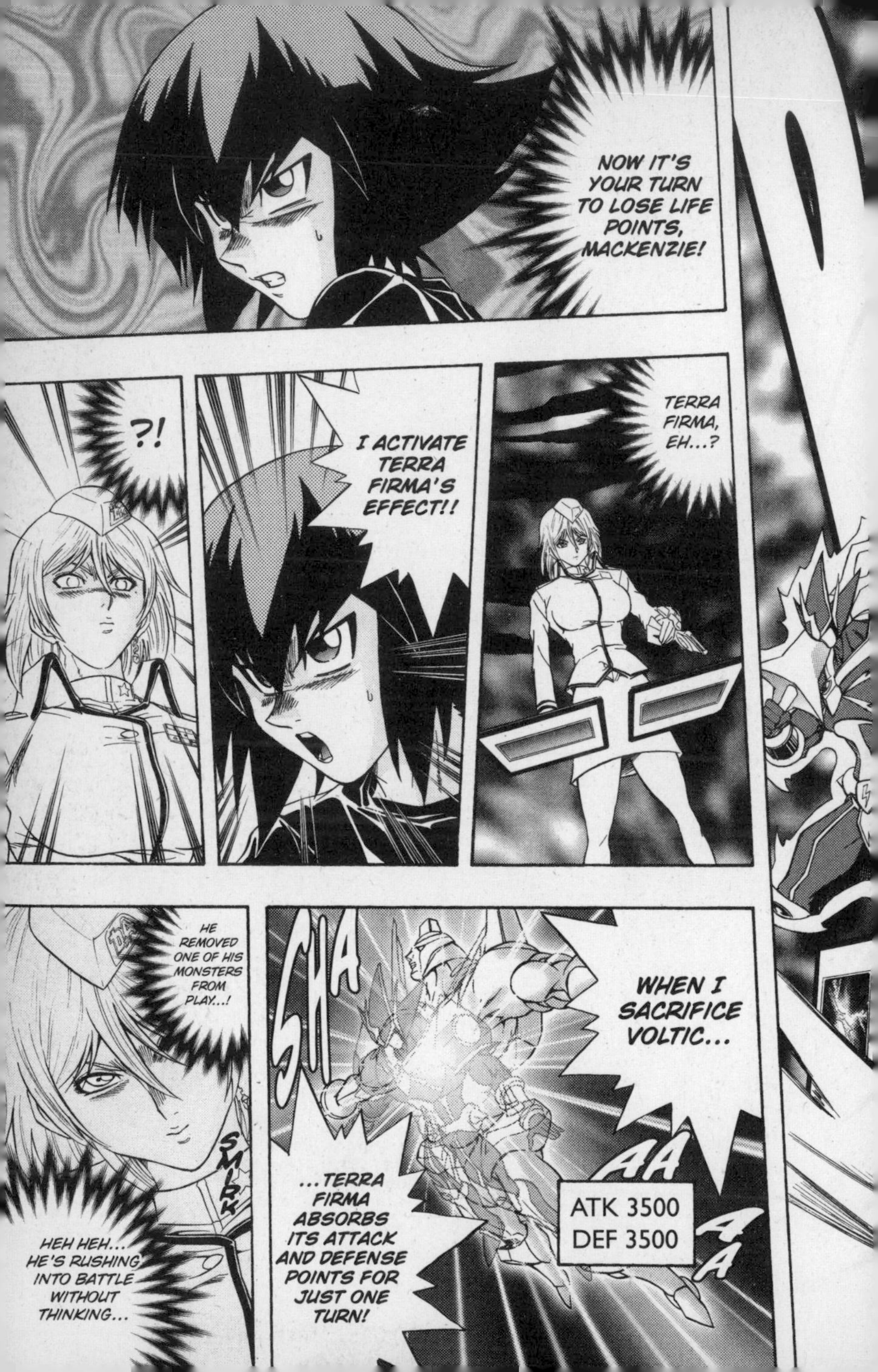
NOW IT'S YOUR TURN TO LOSE LIFE POINTS, MACKENZIE!
TERRA FIRMA, EH...?
I ACTIVATE TERRA FIRMA'S EFFECT!!
?!
WHEN I SACRIFICE VOLTIC...
SHA
AAAA
...TERRA FIRMA ABSORBS ITS ATTACK AND DEFENSE POINTS FOR JUST ONE TURN!
ATK 3500
DEF 3500
HE REMOVED ONE OF HIS MONSTERS FROM PLAY...!
SMIRK
HEH HEH... HE'S RUSHING INTO BATTLE WITHOUT THINKING...

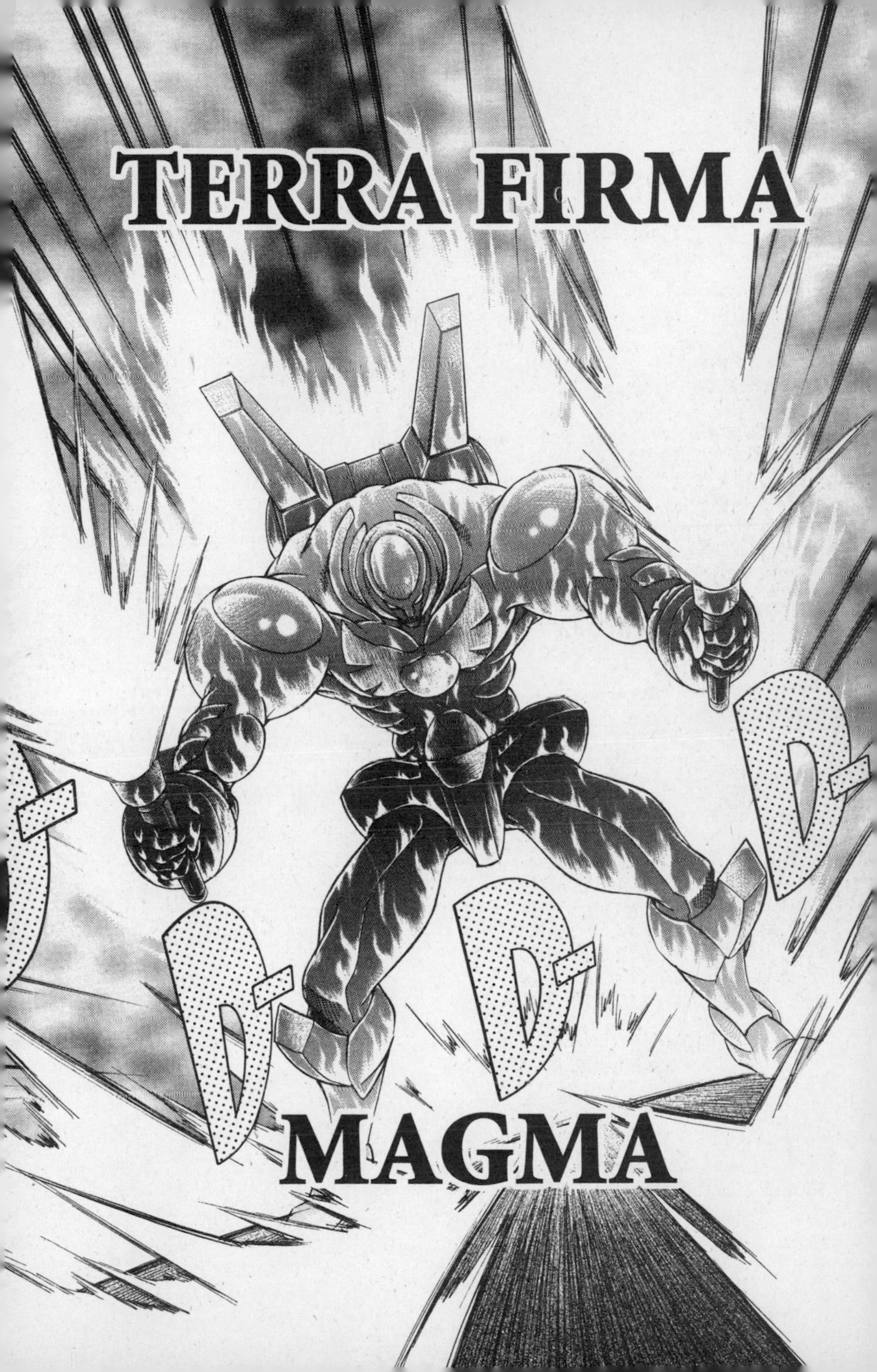
TERRA FIRMA
MAGMA

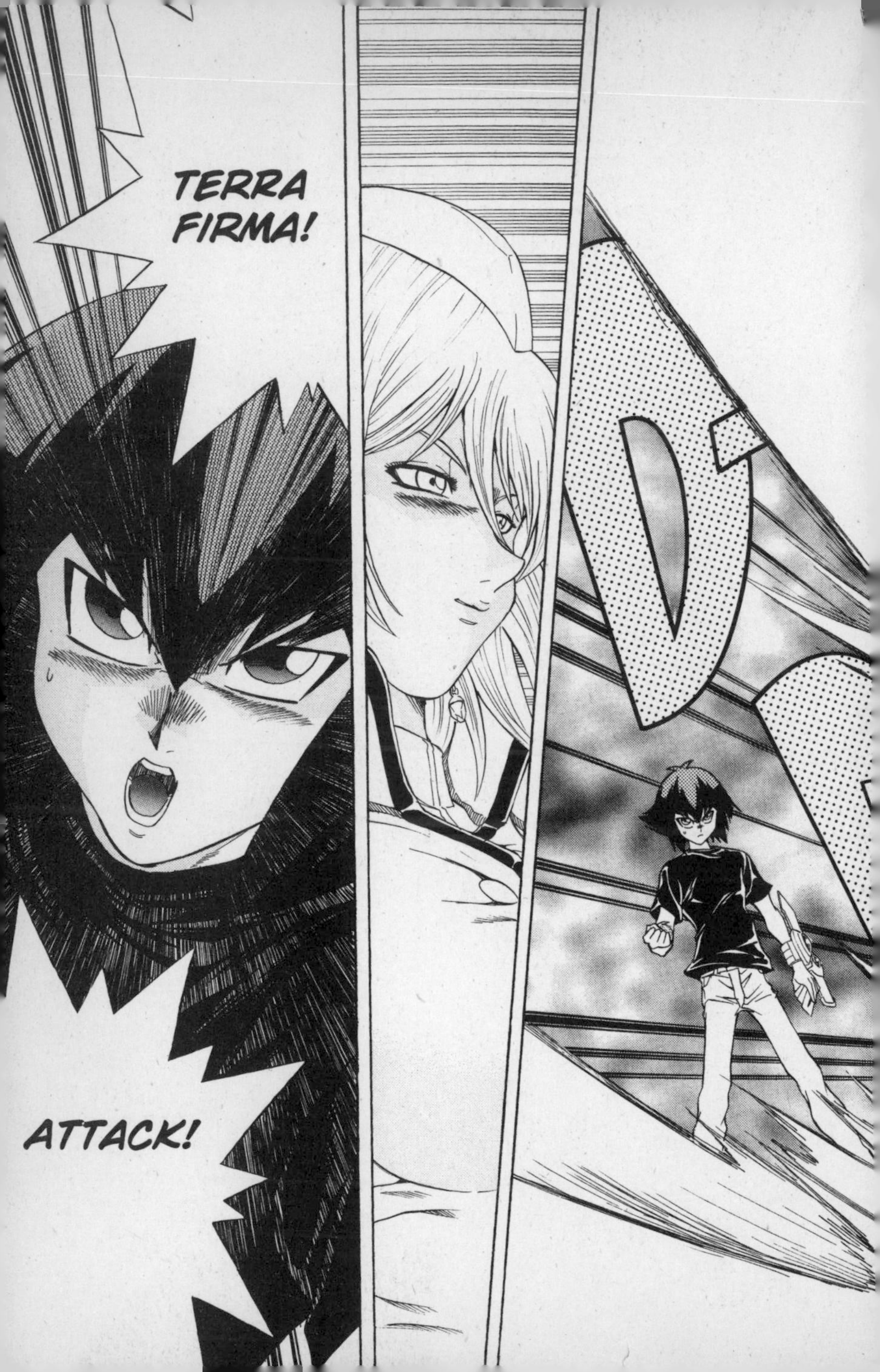
TERRA FIRMA!
ATTACK!

# FAMILY CIRCLE DUEL TOURNAMENT!

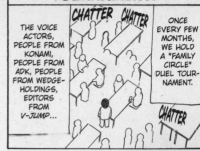

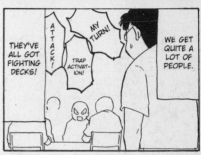

ONCE EVERY FEW MONTHS, WE HOLD A "FAMILY CIRCLE" DUEL TOURNAMENT.
CHATTER
CHATTER
CHATTER
THE VOICE ACTORS, PEOPLE FROM KONAMI, PEOPLE FROM ADK, PEOPLE FROM WEDGE-HOLDINGS, EDITORS FROM V-JUMP...
WE GET QUITE A LOT OF PEOPLE.
MY TURN!
ATTACK!
TRAP ACTIVAT-ION!
THEY'VE ALL GOT FIGHTING DECKS!
I USED MY "FAKE HERO" DECK...
THANK YOU VERY MUCH.
...SHOULD'VE USED MY MAC DECK...
Y... YOU'RE VERY WELCOME.
SATO USED HIS "ANYONE CAN WIN WITH THIS ONE" BLACK FEATHER DECK AND MADE IT INTO THE UPPER RANKS...
I LOST.
I'M TELLING YOU, SYNCHRO'S WHERE IT'S AT!
SATO

MOST OF THE UPPER RANKS WERE MADE UP OF BLACK FEATHER PEOPLE... (BITTER SMILE)

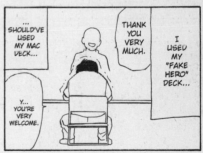

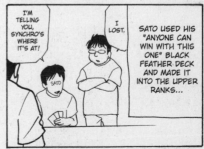

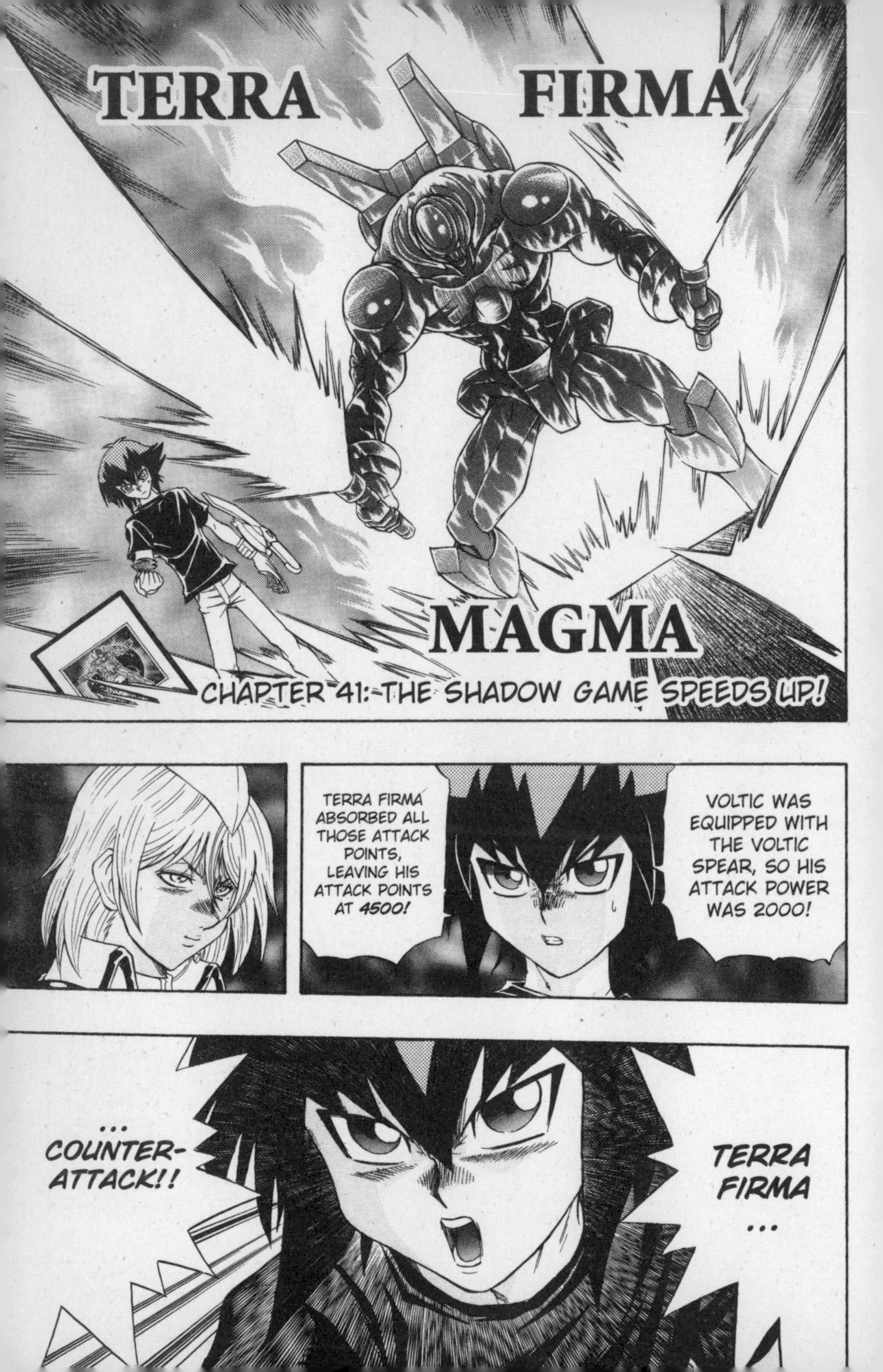
TERRA FIRMA
MAGMA
CHAPTER 41: THE SHADOW GAME SPEEDS UP!
VOLTIC WAS EQUIPPED WITH THE VOLTIC SPEAR, SO HIS ATTACK POWER WAS 2000!
TERRA FIRMA ABSORBED ALL THOSE ATTACK POINTS, LEAVING HIS ATTACK POINTS AT 4500!
TERRA FIRMA ...
... COUNTER-ATTACK!!

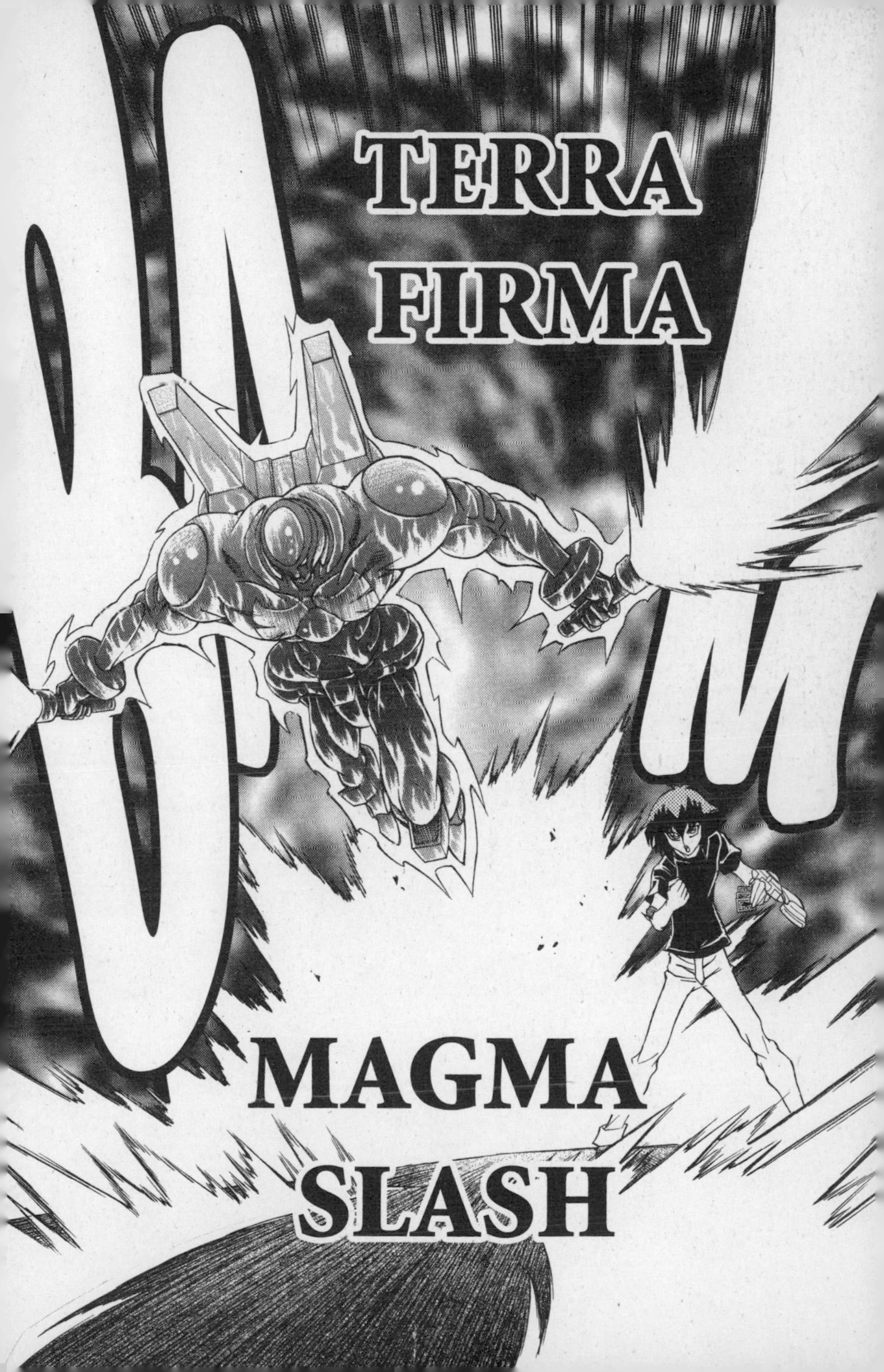
TERRA FIRMA
MAGMA SLASH

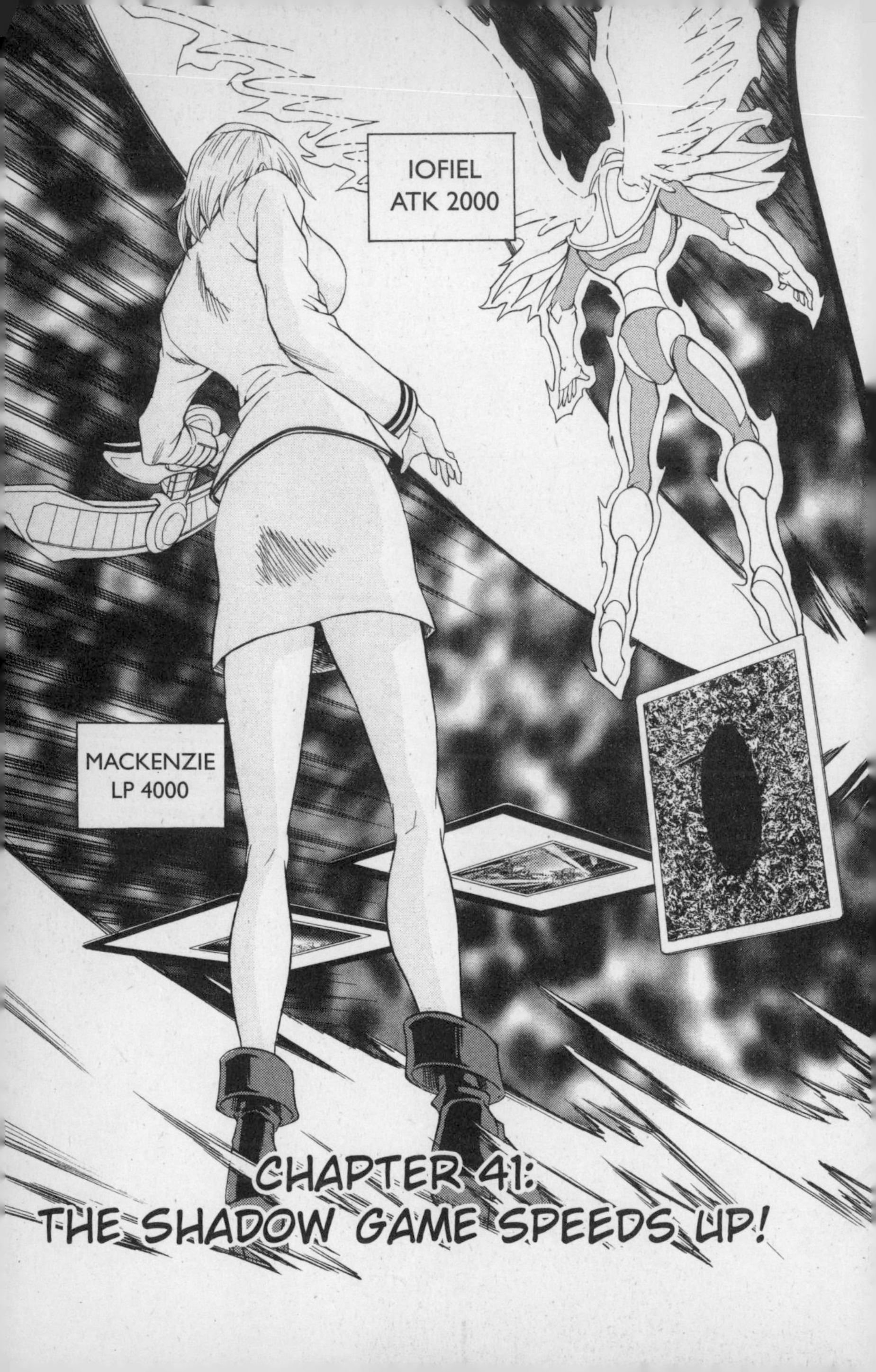
IOFIEL
ATK 2000
MACKENZIE
LP 4000
CHAPTER 41:
THE SHADOW GAME SPEEDS UP!

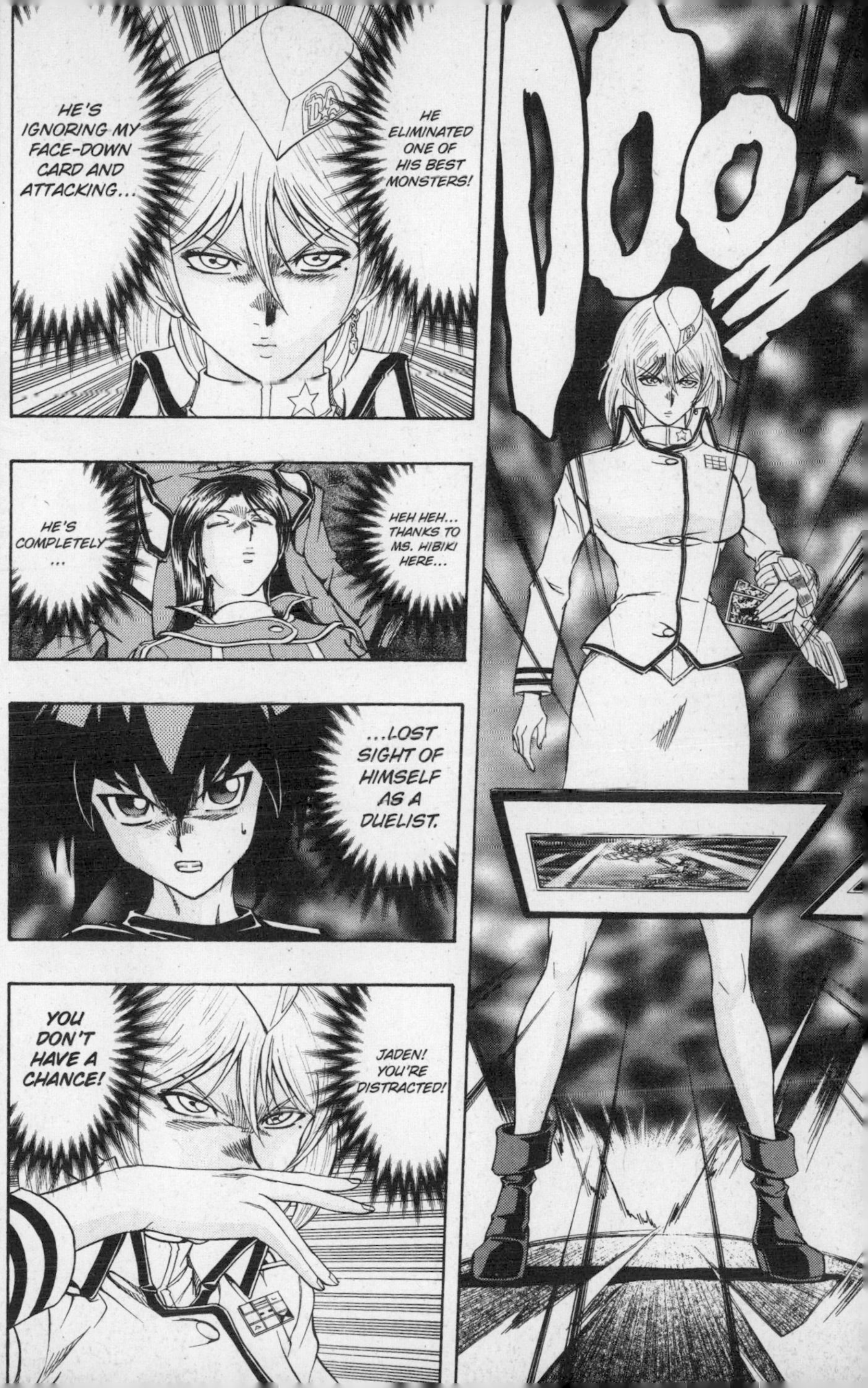
DOOM
HE ELIMINATED ONE OF HIS BEST MONSTERS!
HE'S IGNORING MY FACE-DOWN CARD AND ATTACKING...
HEH HEH... THANKS TO MS. HIBIKI HERE...
HE'S COMPLETELY...
...LOST SIGHT OF HIMSELF AS A DUELIST.
JADEN! YOU'RE DISTRACTED!
YOU DON'T HAVE A CHANCE!

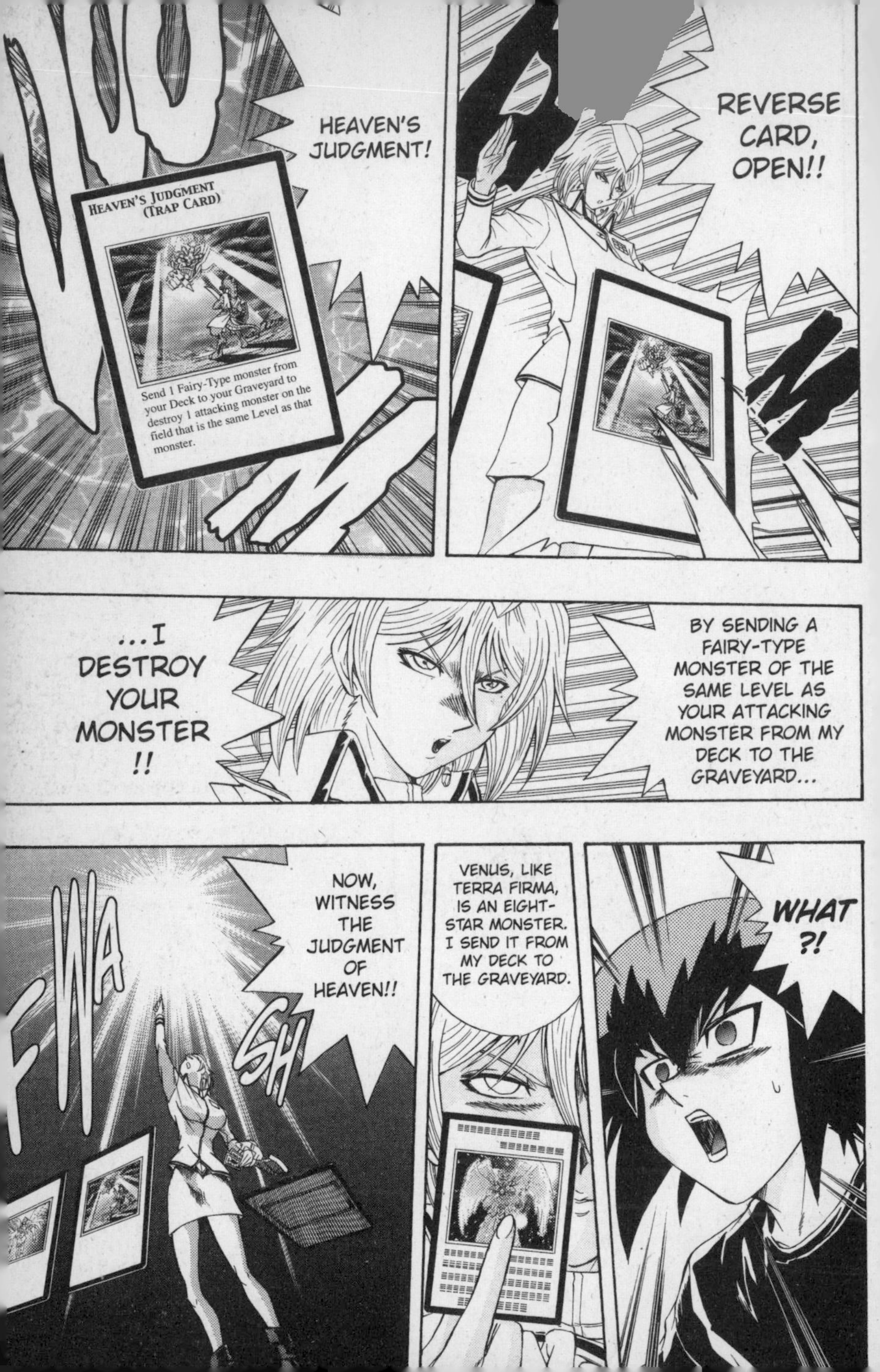
REVERSE CARD, OPEN!!
HEAVEN'S JUDGMENT!
HEAVEN'S JUDGMENT (TRAP CARD)
Send 1 Fairy-Type monster from your Deck to your Graveyard to destroy 1 attacking monster on the field that is the same Level as that monster.
BY SENDING A FAIRY-TYPE MONSTER OF THE SAME LEVEL AS YOUR ATTACKING MONSTER FROM MY DECK TO THE GRAVEYARD...
...I DESTROY YOUR MONSTER!!
WHAT?!
VENUS, LIKE TERRA FIRMA, IS AN EIGHT-STAR MONSTER. I SEND IT FROM MY DECK TO THE GRAVEYARD.
NOW, WITNESS THE JUDGMENT OF HEAVEN!!
FWA
SH

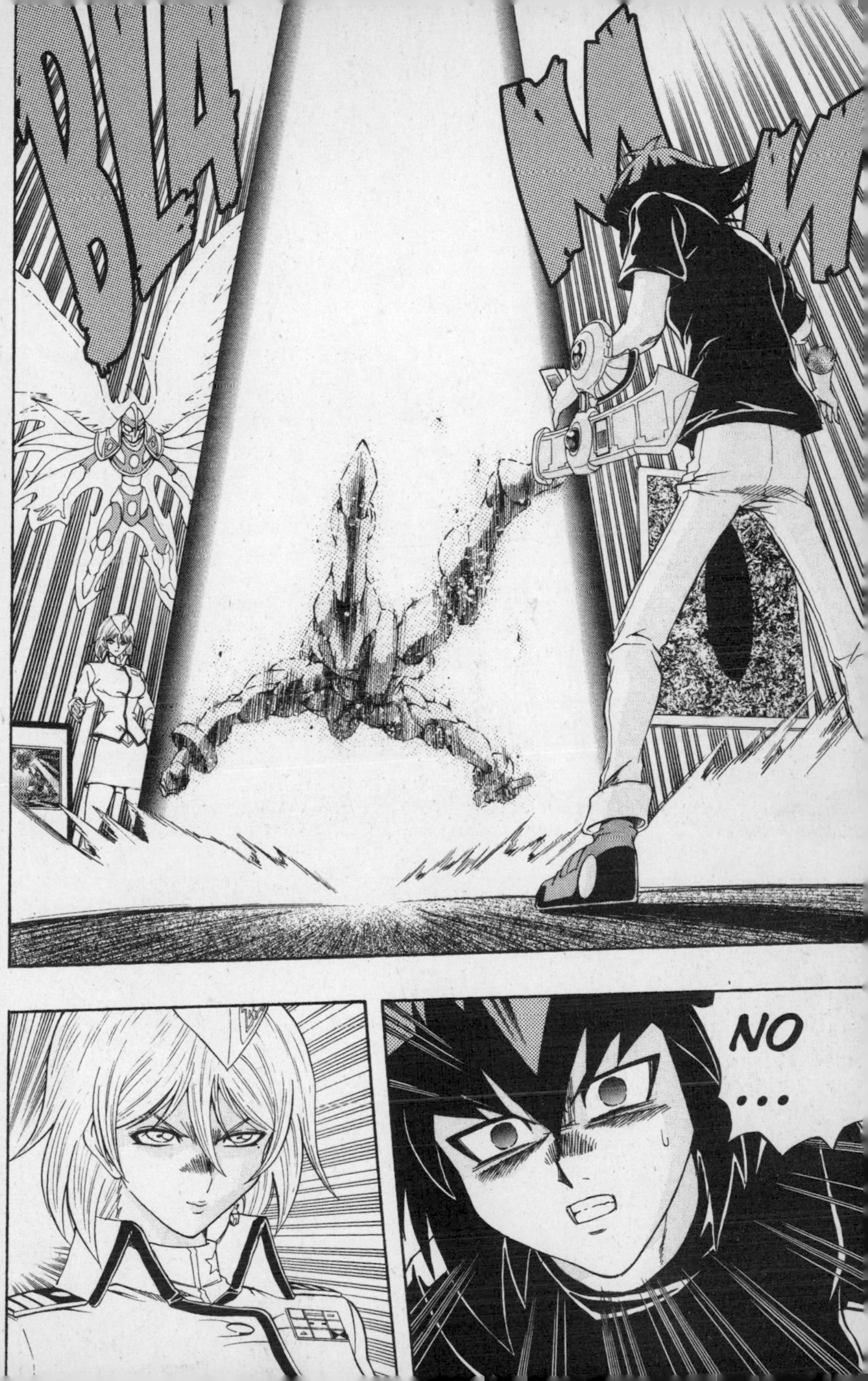
NO
...

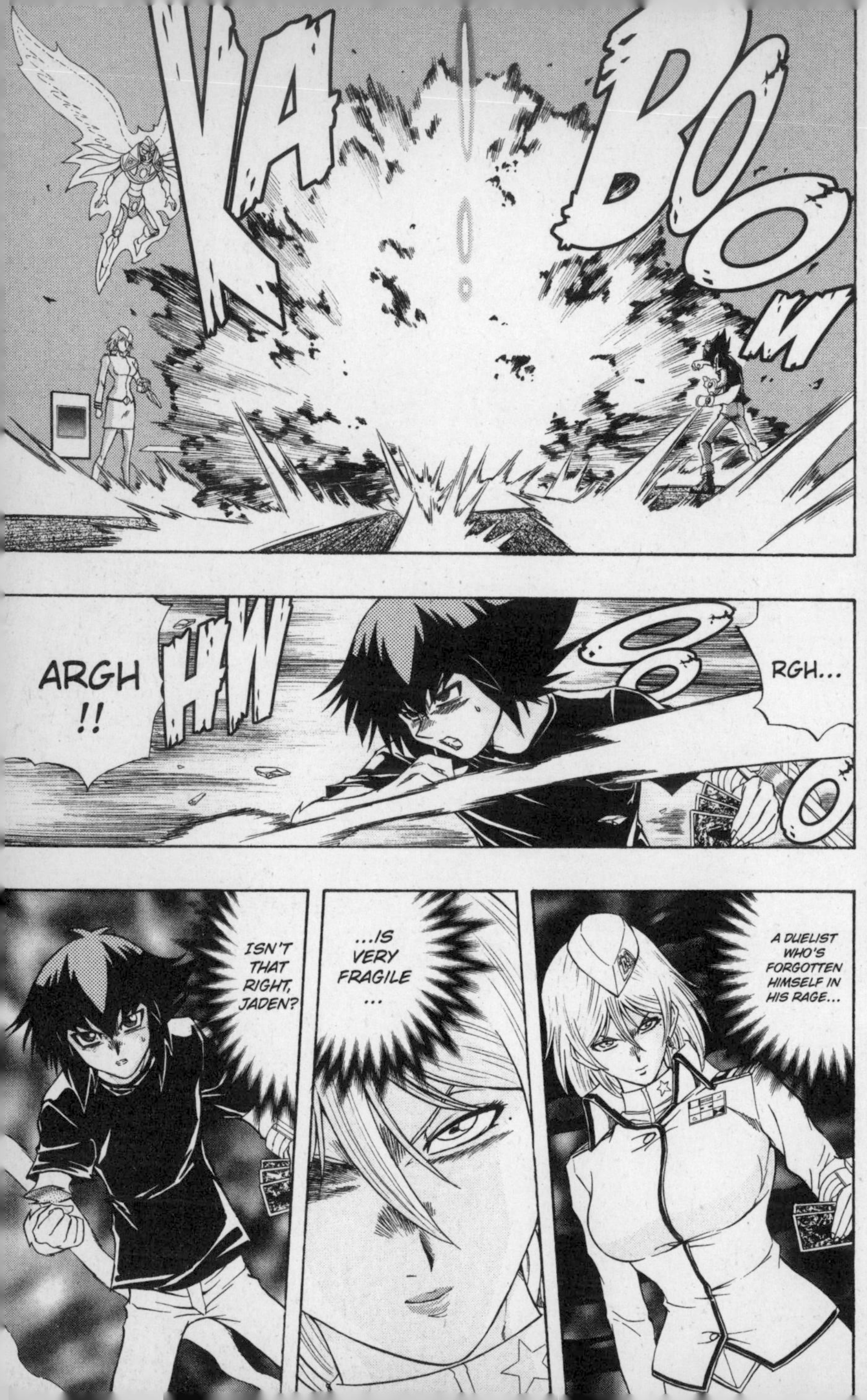
KA
BOOM
RGH...
ARGH !!
A DUELIST WHO'S FORGOTTEN HIMSELF IN HIS RAGE...
...IS VERY FRAGILE ...
ISN'T THAT RIGHT, JADEN?

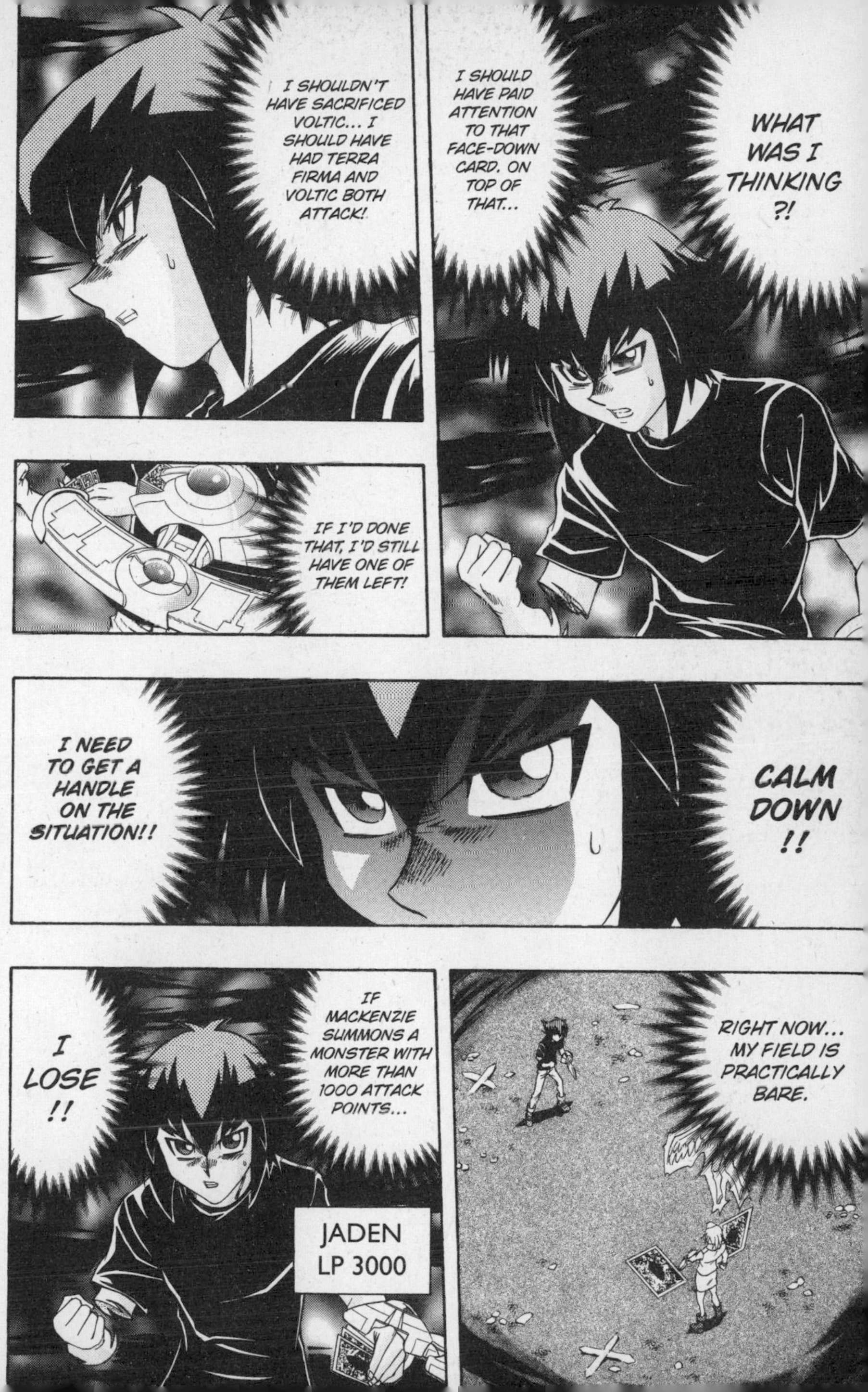
WHAT WAS I THINKING ?!
I SHOULD HAVE PAID ATTENTION TO THAT FACE-DOWN CARD. ON TOP OF THAT...
I SHOULDN'T HAVE SACRIFICED VOLTIC... I SHOULD HAVE HAD TERRA FIRMA AND VOLTIC BOTH ATTACK!
IF I'D DONE THAT, I'D STILL HAVE ONE OF THEM LEFT!
CALM DOWN !!
I NEED TO GET A HANDLE ON THE SITUATION!!
RIGHT NOW... MY FIELD IS PRACTICALLY BARE.
IF MACKENZIE SUMMONS A MONSTER WITH MORE THAN 1000 ATTACK POINTS...
I LOSE !!
JADEN LP 3000

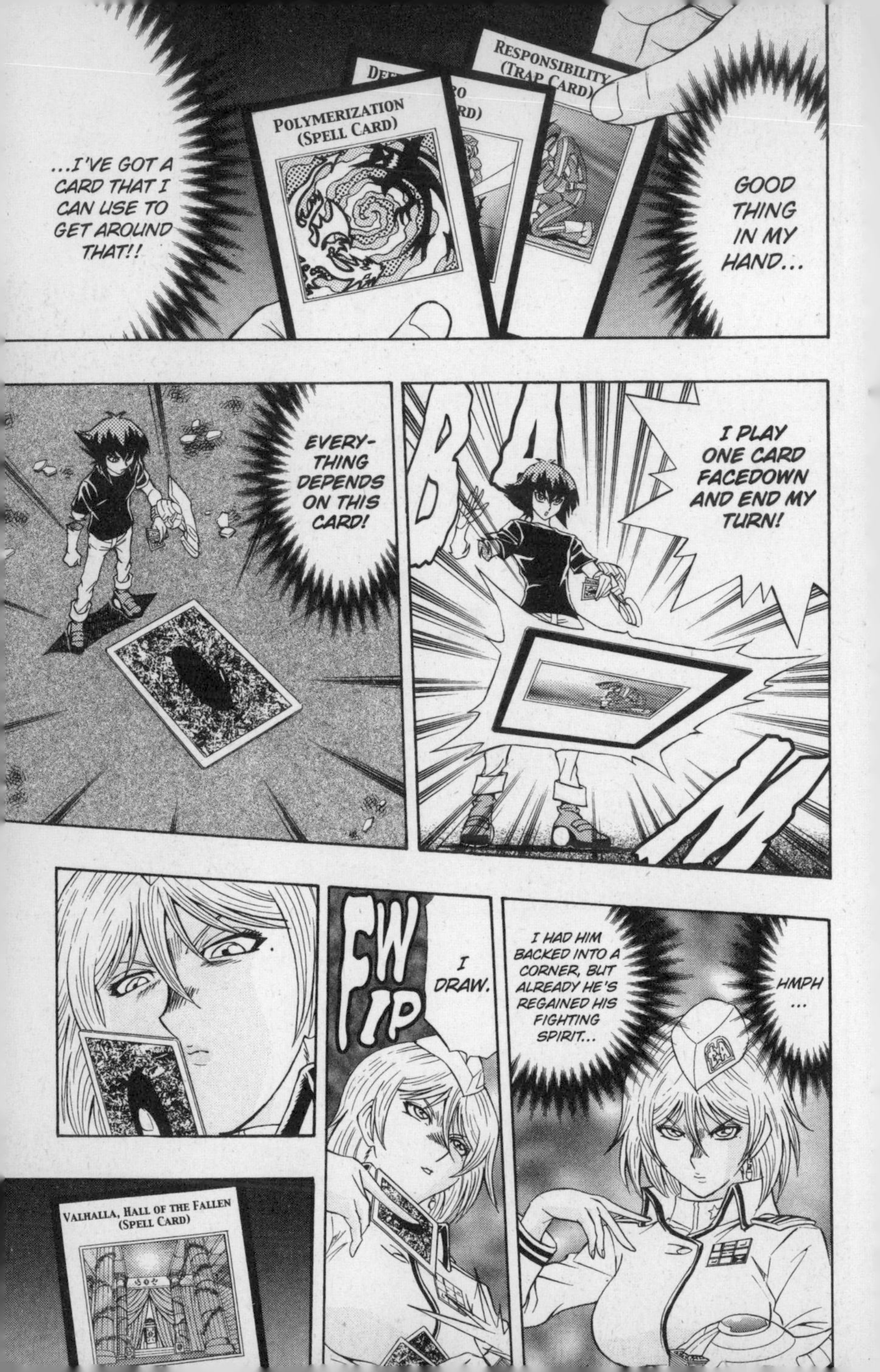

GOOD THING IN MY HAND...
...I'VE GOT A CARD THAT I CAN USE TO GET AROUND THAT!!
RESPONSIBILITY (TRAP CARD)
POLYMERIZATION (SPELL CARD)
BAM
I PLAY ONE CARD FACEDOWN AND END MY TURN!
EVERY-THING DEPENDS ON THIS CARD!
HMPH ...
I HAD HIM BACKED INTO A CORNER, BUT ALREADY HE'S REGAINED HIS FIGHTING SPIRIT...
FWIP
I DRAW.
VALHALLA, HALL OF THE FALLEN (SPELL CARD)

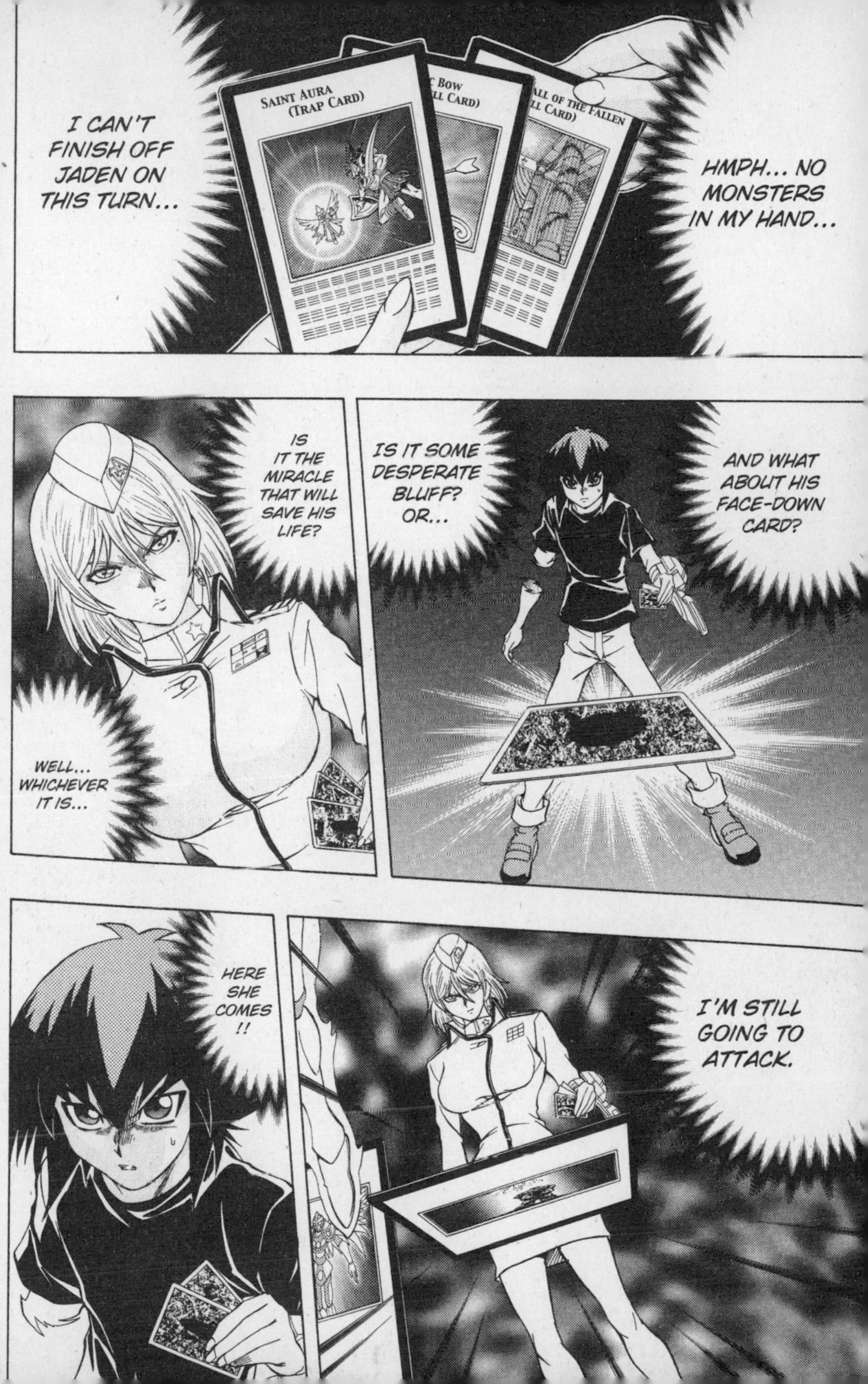
HMPH... NO MONSTERS IN MY HAND...
SAINT AURA (TRAP CARD)
I CAN'T FINISH OFF JADEN ON THIS TURN...
AND WHAT ABOUT HIS FACE-DOWN CARD?
IS IT SOME DESPERATE BLUFF? OR...
IS IT THE MIRACLE THAT WILL SAVE HIS LIFE?
WELL... WHICHEVER IT IS...
I'M STILL GOING TO ATTACK.
HERE SHE COMES!!

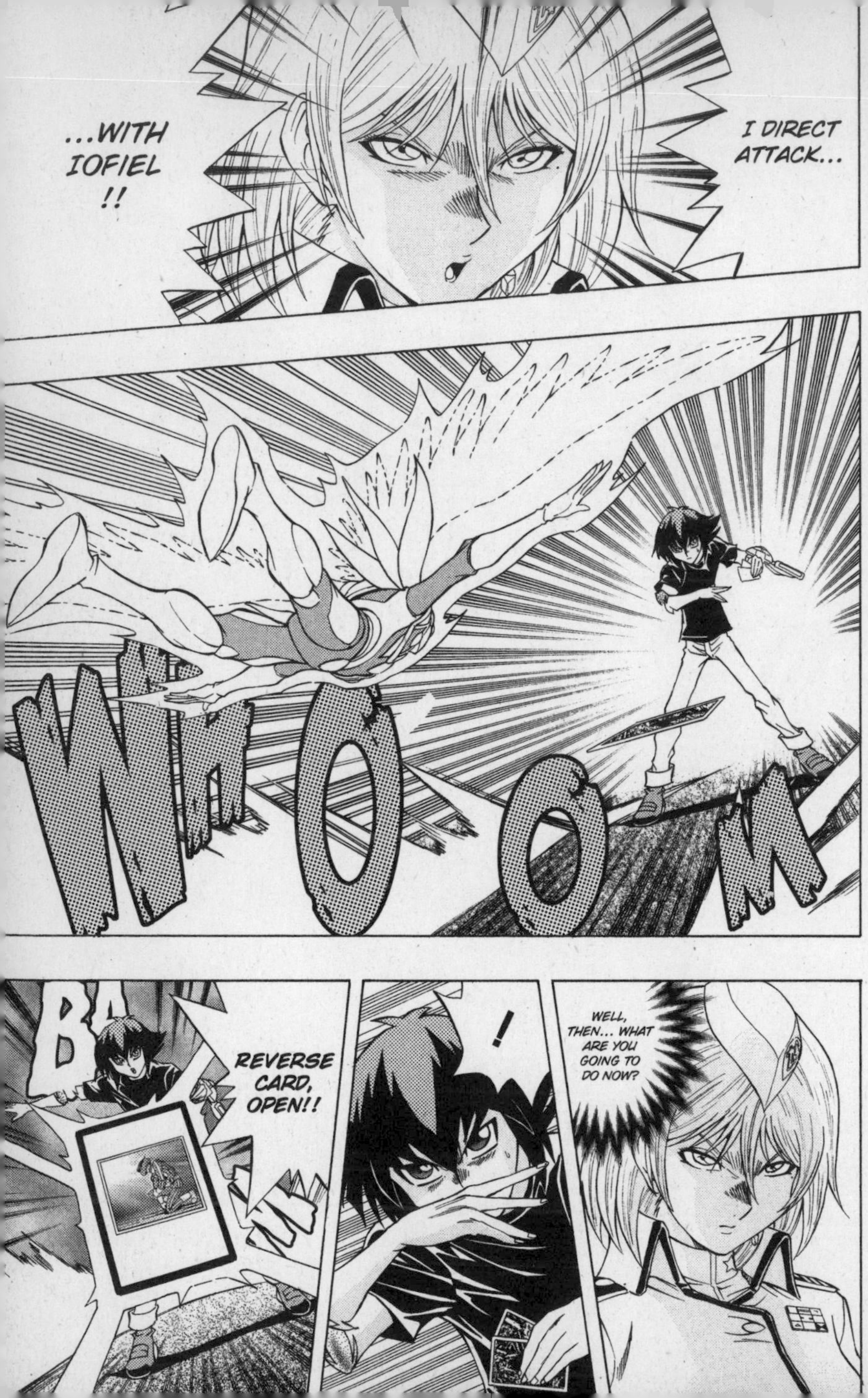
I DIRECT ATTACK...
...WITH IOFIEL !!
WHOOOM
WELL, THEN... WHAT ARE YOU GOING TO DO NOW?
!
REVERSE CARD, OPEN!!
BA

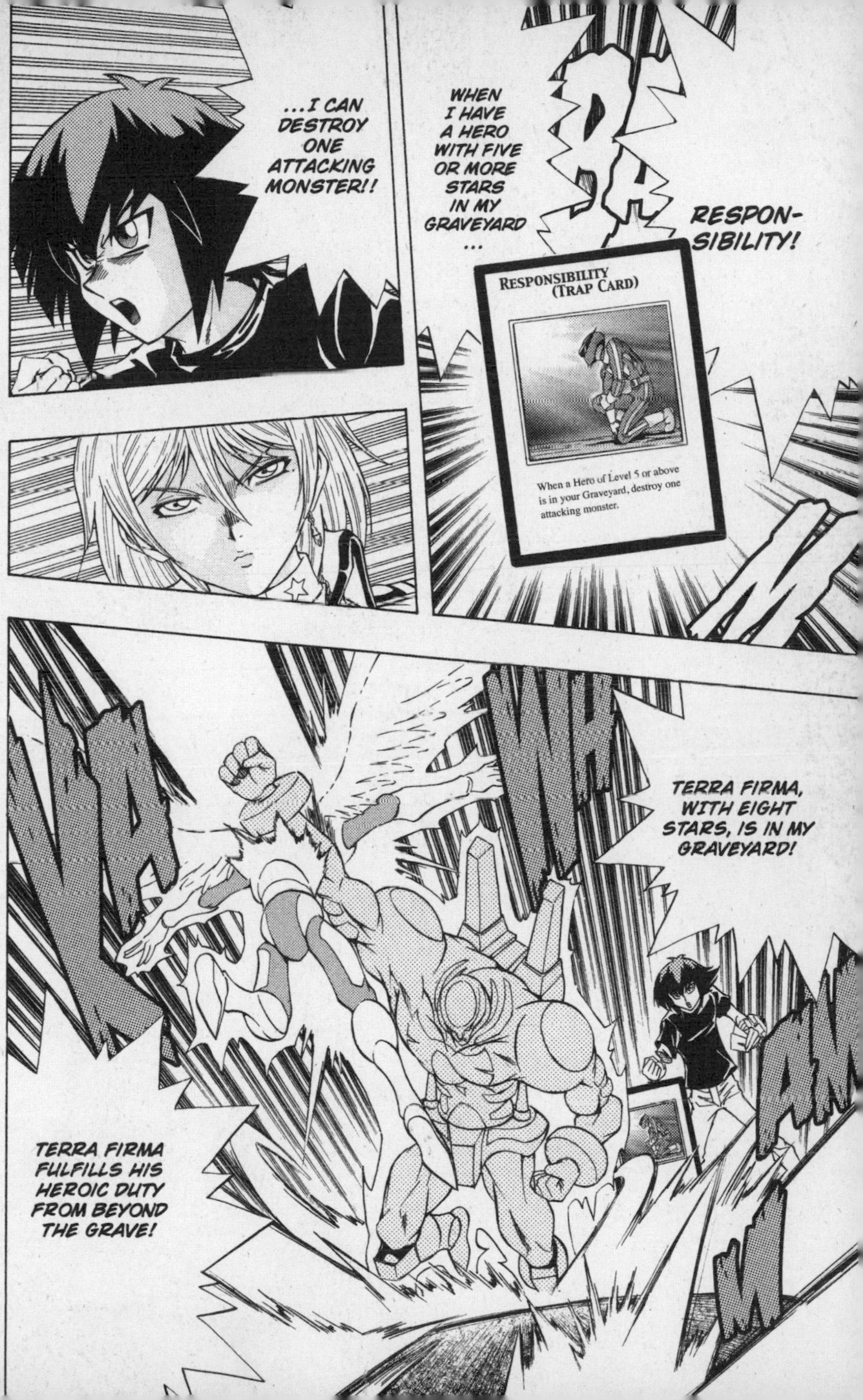
WHEN I HAVE A HERO WITH FIVE OR MORE STARS IN MY GRAVEYARD...
RESPONSIBILITY!
RESPONSIBILITY (TRAP CARD)
When a Hero of Level 5 or above is in your Graveyard, destroy one attacking monster.
...I CAN DESTROY ONE ATTACKING MONSTER!!
TERRA FIRMA, WITH EIGHT STARS, IS IN MY GRAVEYARD!
TERRA FIRMA FULFILLS HIS HEROIC DUTY FROM BEYOND THE GRAVE!

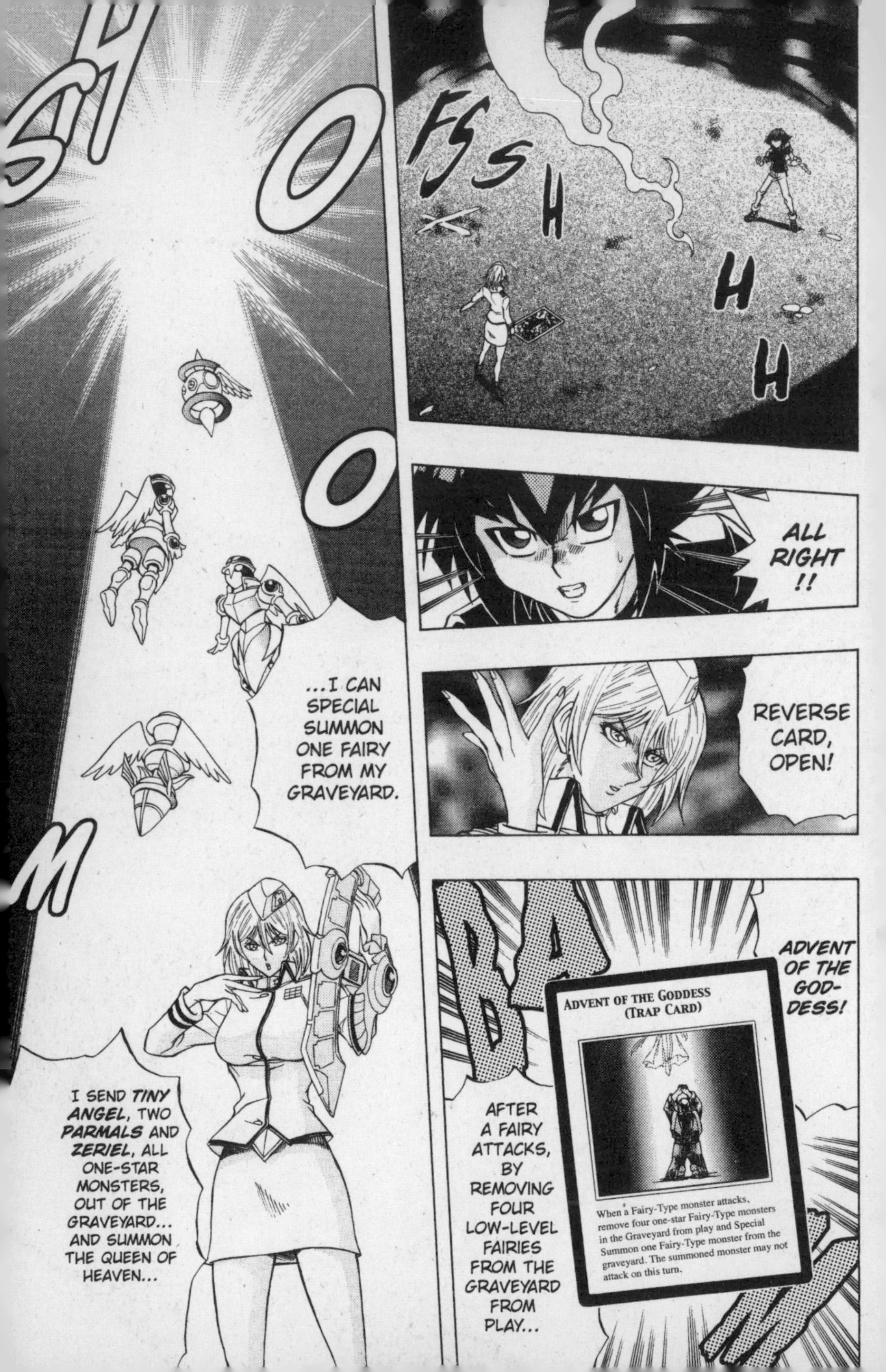
FSSHHHH
ALL RIGHT!!
REVERSE CARD, OPEN!
BA
ADVENT OF THE GOD-DESS!
ADVENT OF THE GODDESS
(TRAP CARD)
When a Fairy-Type monster attacks, remove four one-star Fairy-Type monsters in the Graveyard from play and Special Summon one Fairy-Type monster from the graveyard. The summoned monster may not attack on this turn.
AFTER A FAIRY ATTACKS, BY REMOVING FOUR LOW-LEVEL FAIRIES FROM THE GRAVEYARD FROM PLAY...
WHOOOM
...I CAN SPECIAL SUMMON ONE FAIRY FROM MY GRAVEYARD.
I SEND TINY ANGEL, TWO PARMALS AND ZERIEL, ALL ONE-STAR MONSTERS, OUT OF THE GRAVEYARD... AND SUMMON THE QUEEN OF HEAVEN...

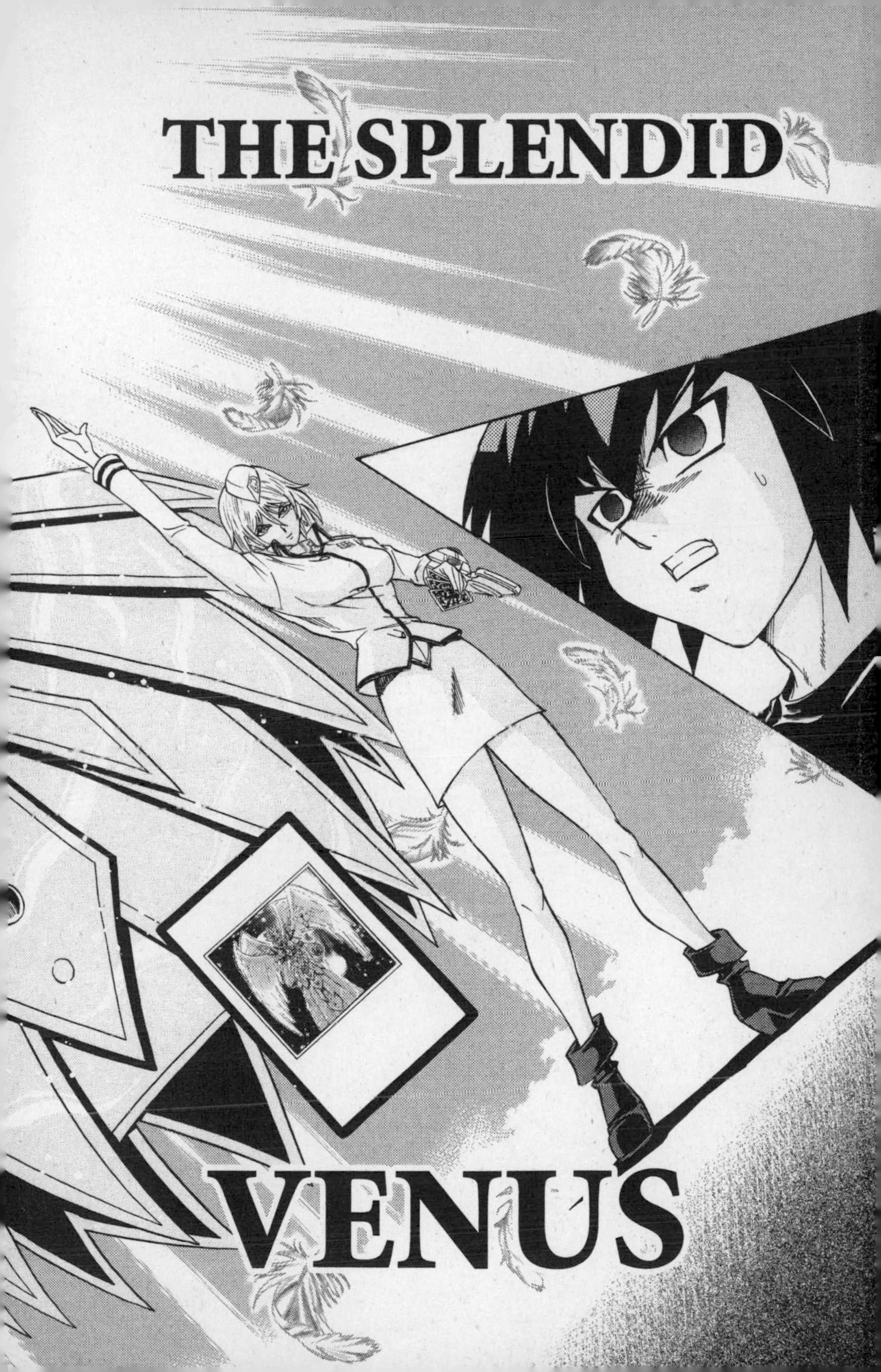
THE SPLENDID
VENUS

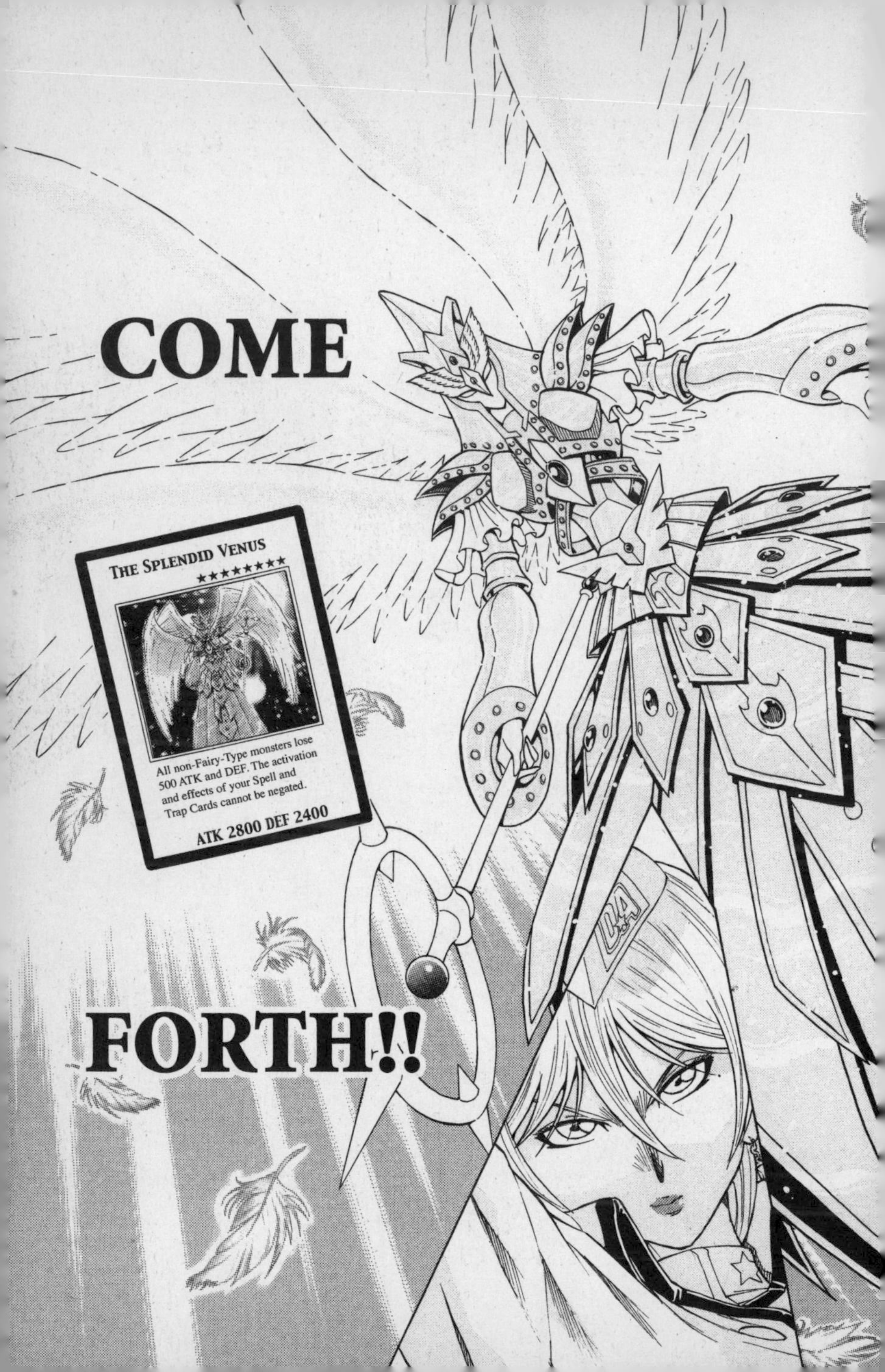
COME
THE SPLENDID VENUS
★★★★★★★★
All non-Fairy-Type monsters lose 500 ATK and DEF. The activation and effects of your Spell and Trap Cards cannot be negated.
ATK 2800 DEF 2400
FORTH!!

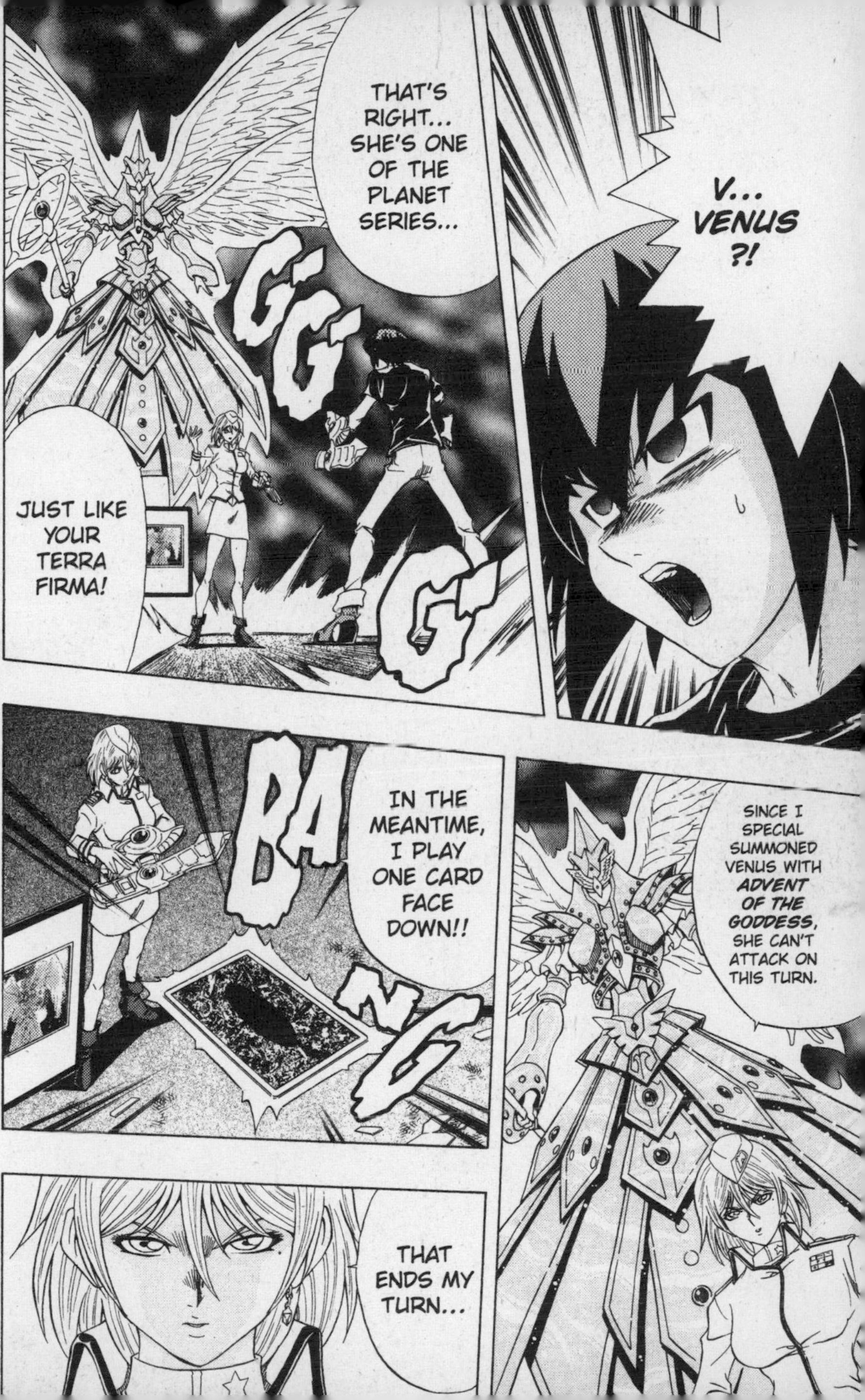
V... VENUS ?!
THAT'S RIGHT... SHE'S ONE OF THE PLANET SERIES...
GG
G
JUST LIKE YOUR TERRA FIRMA!
SINCE I SPECIAL SUMMONED VENUS WITH *ADVENT OF THE GODDESS*, SHE CAN'T ATTACK ON THIS TURN.
BANG
IN THE MEANTIME, I PLAY ONE CARD FACE DOWN!!
THAT ENDS MY TURN...

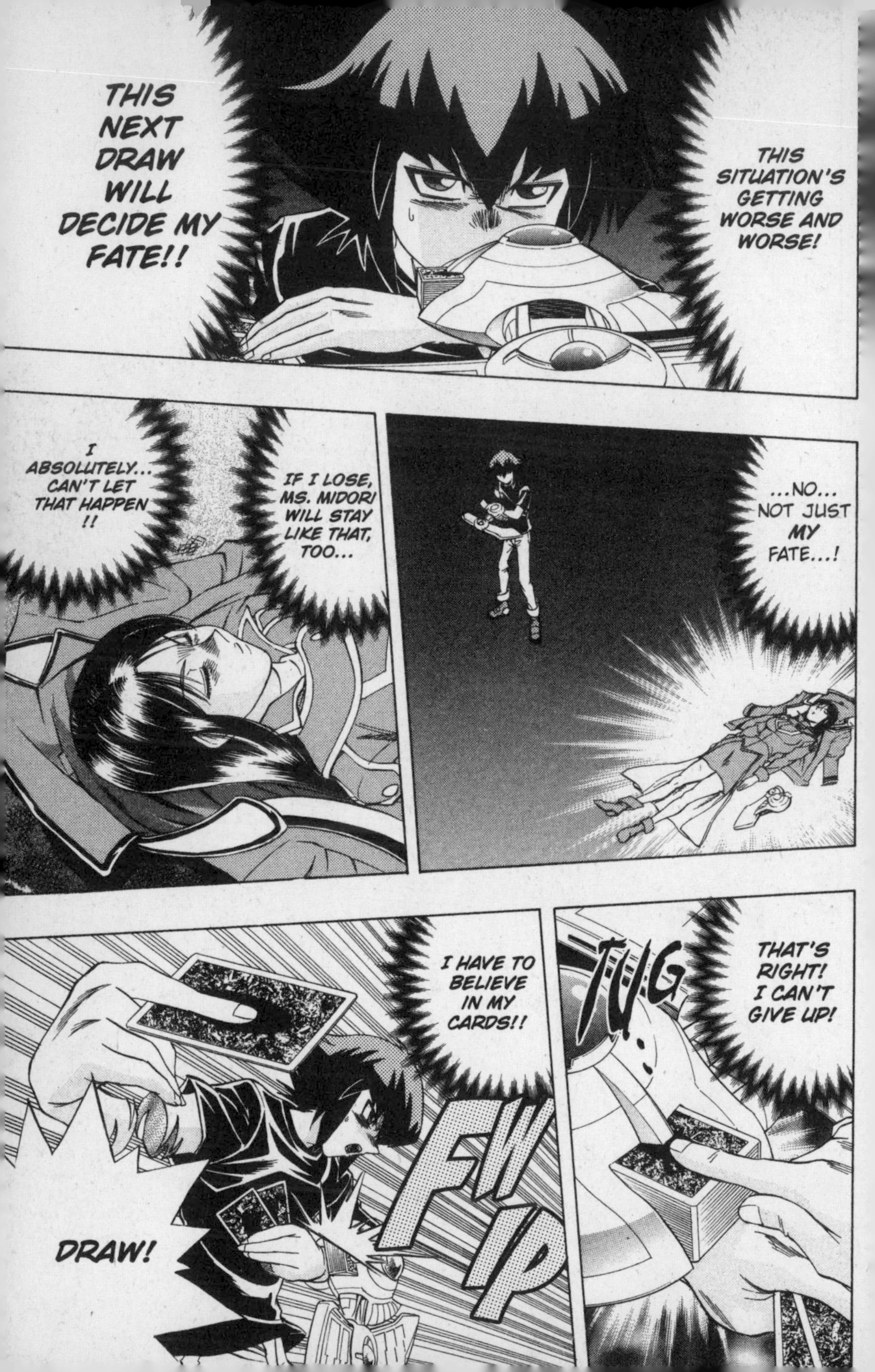
THIS SITUATION'S GETTING WORSE AND WORSE!
THIS NEXT DRAW WILL DECIDE MY FATE!!
...NO... NOT JUST MY FATE...!
IF I LOSE, MS. MIDORI WILL STAY LIKE THAT, TOO...
I ABSOLUTELY... CAN'T LET THAT HAPPEN!!
THAT'S RIGHT! I CAN'T GIVE UP!
TUG
I HAVE TO BELIEVE IN MY CARDS!!
FWIP
DRAW!

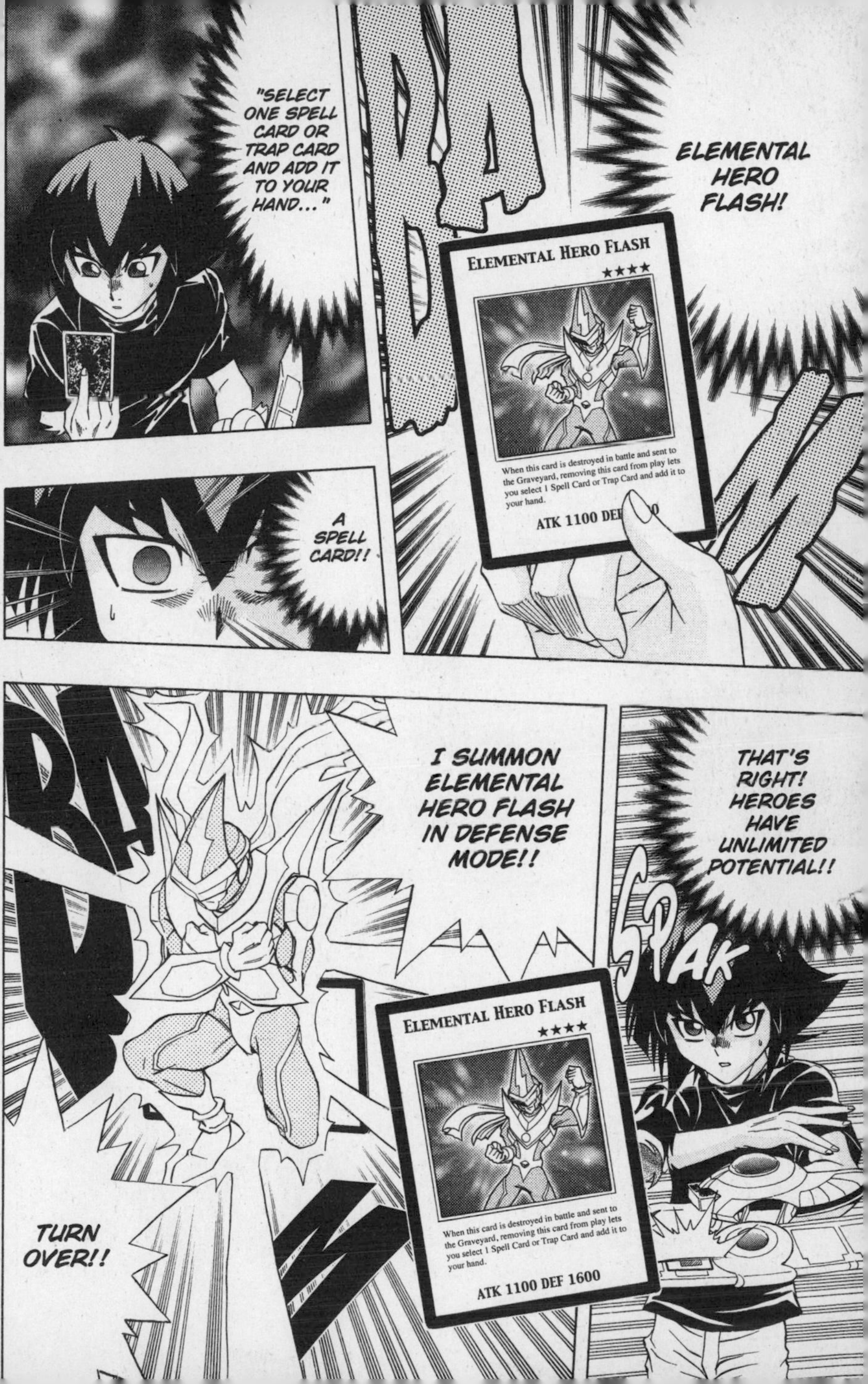
ELEMENTAL HERO FLASH!
ELEMENTAL HERO FLASH
When this card is destroyed in battle and sent to the Graveyard, removing this card from play lets you select 1 Spell Card or Trap Card and add it to your hand.
ATK 1100 DEF
"SELECT ONE SPELL CARD OR TRAP CARD AND ADD IT TO YOUR HAND..."
A SPELL CARD!!
THAT'S RIGHT! HEROES HAVE UNLIMITED POTENTIAL!!
SPAK
ELEMENTAL HERO FLASH
When this card is destroyed in battle and sent to the Graveyard, removing this card from play lets you select 1 Spell Card or Trap Card and add it to your hand.
ATK 1100 DEF 1600
I SUMMON ELEMENTAL HERO FLASH IN DEFENSE MODE!!
TURN OVER!!

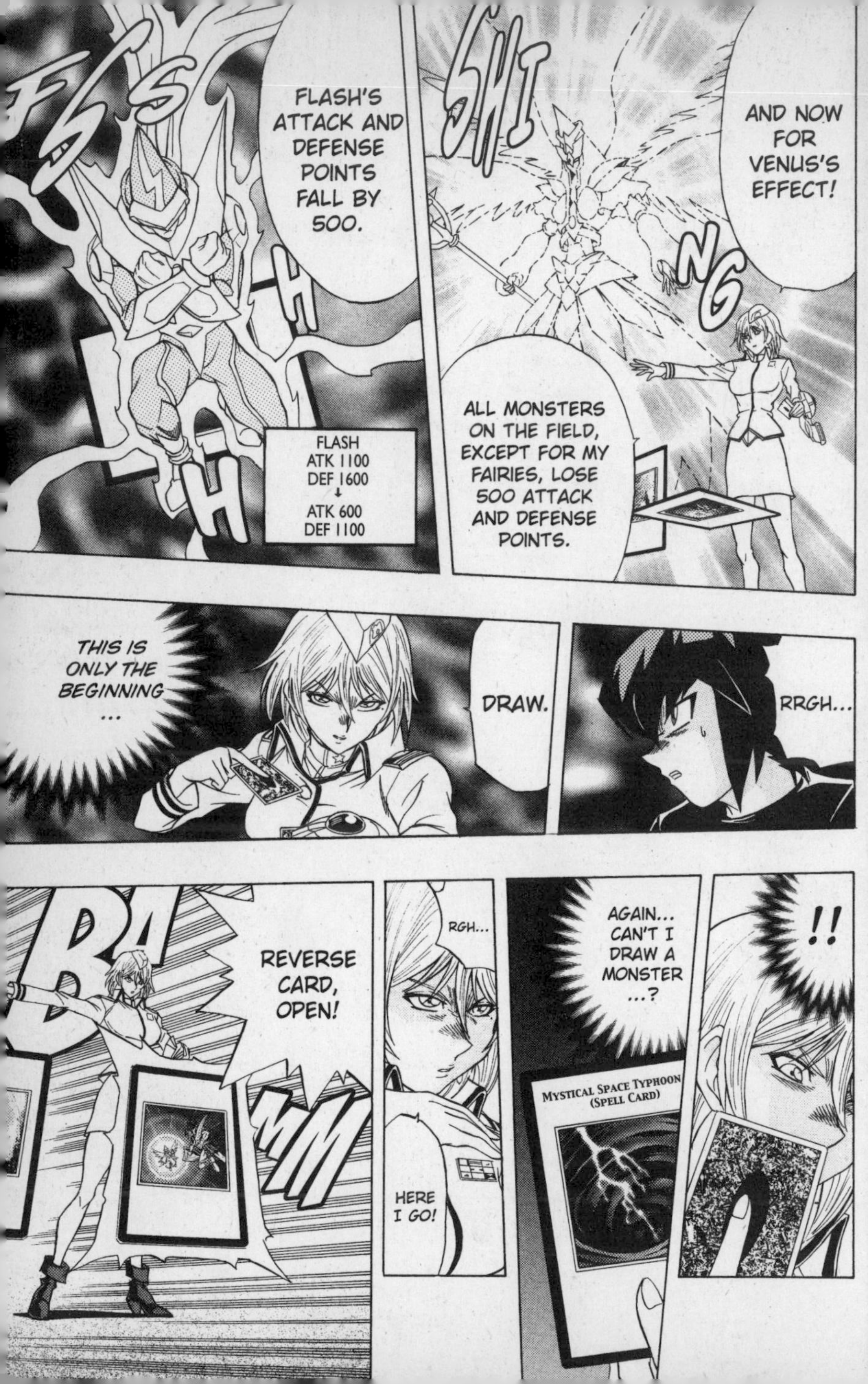
AND NOW FOR VENUS'S EFFECT!
SHING
ALL MONSTERS ON THE FIELD, EXCEPT FOR MY FAIRIES, LOSE 500 ATTACK AND DEFENSE POINTS.
FSS
FLASH'S ATTACK AND DEFENSE POINTS FALL BY 500.
HHH
FLASH
ATK 1100
DEF 1600
↓
ATK 600
DEF 1100
RRGH...
DRAW.
THIS IS ONLY THE BEGINNING...
!!
AGAIN... CAN'T I DRAW A MONSTER...?
MYSTICAL SPACE TYPHOON
(SPELL CARD)
RGH...
HERE I GO!
REVERSE CARD, OPEN!
BA
MM

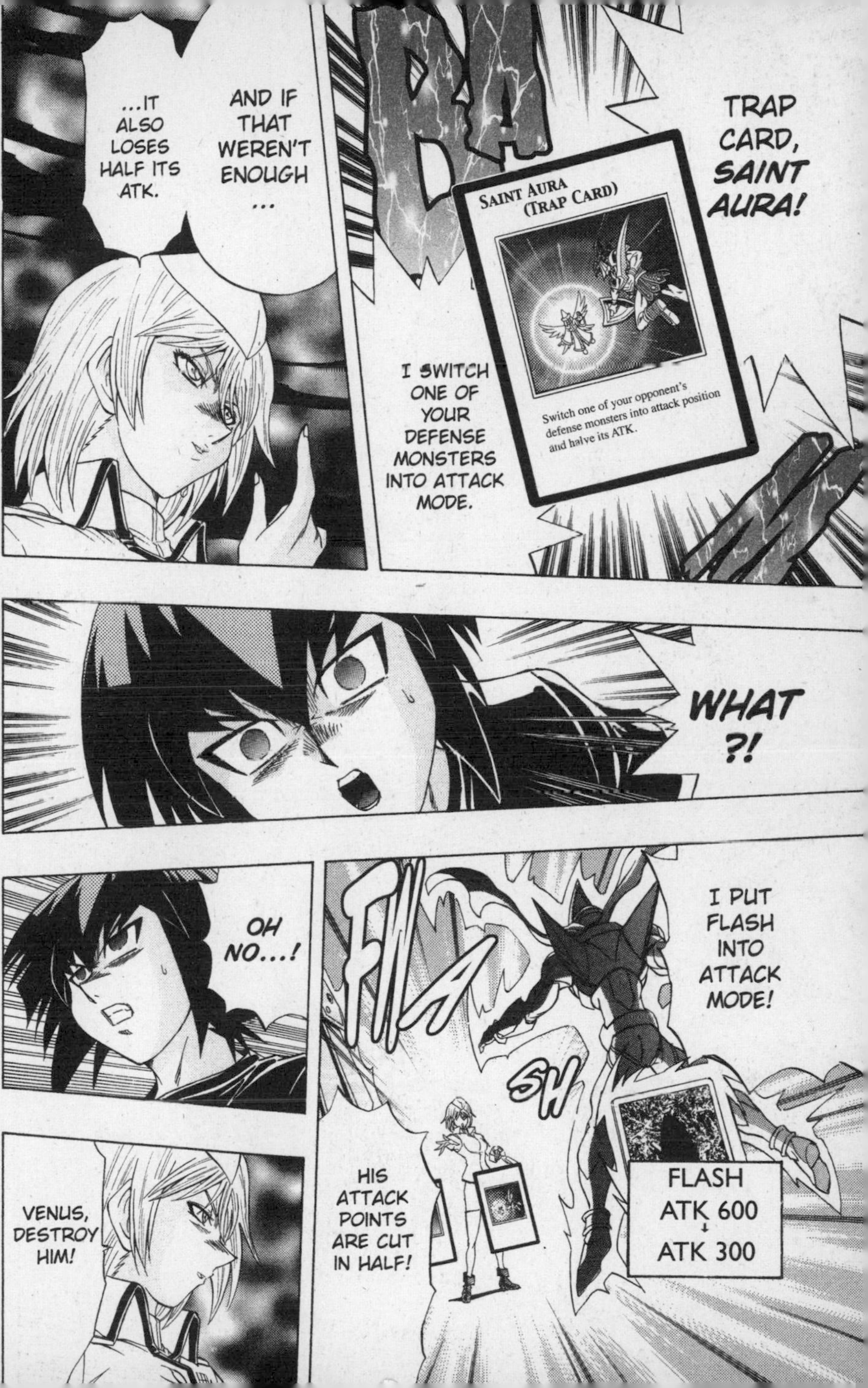
TRAP CARD, SAINT AURA!
SAINT AURA (TRAP CARD)
Switch one of your opponent's defense monsters into attack position and halve its ATK.
I SWITCH ONE OF YOUR DEFENSE MONSTERS INTO ATTACK MODE.
AND IF THAT WEREN'T ENOUGH ...
...IT ALSO LOSES HALF ITS ATK.
WHAT ?!
I PUT FLASH INTO ATTACK MODE!
FWA
SH
HIS ATTACK POINTS ARE CUT IN HALF!
FLASH ATK 600 ATK 300
OH NO...!
VENUS, DESTROY HIM!

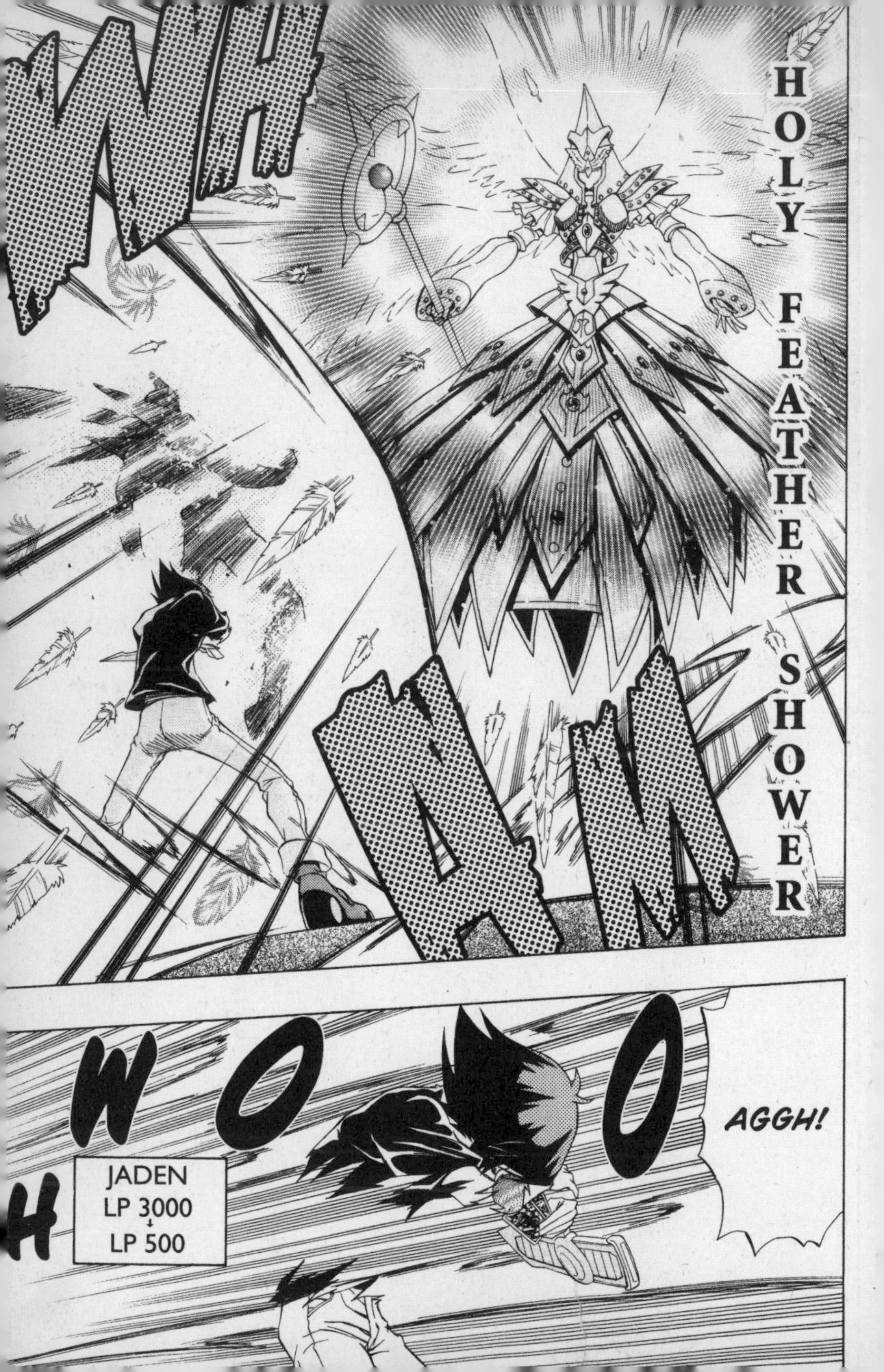
HOLY FEATHER SHOWER
AGGH!
JADEN
LP 3000
LP 500

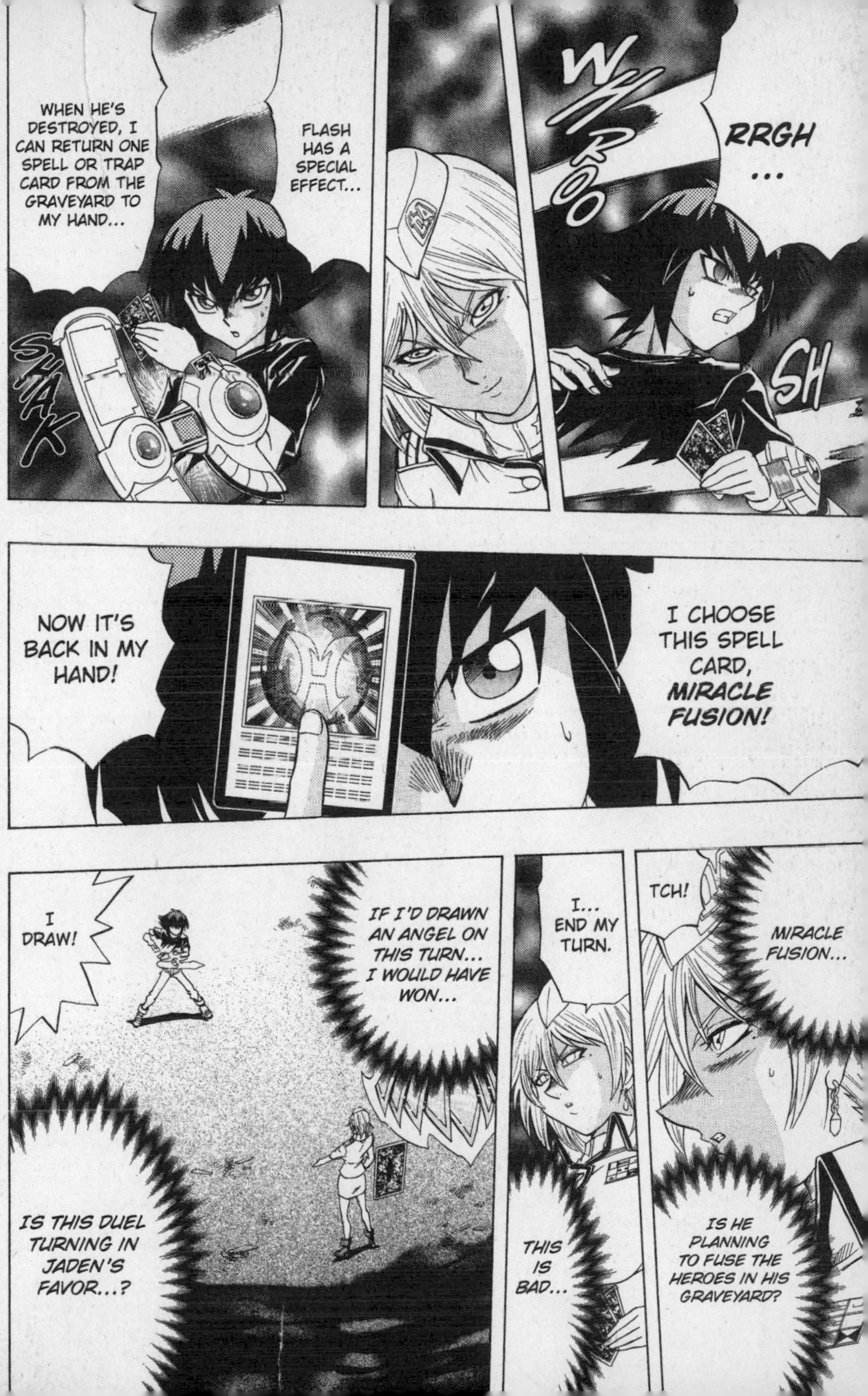
WHROOO
RRGH ...
SH
FLASH HAS A SPECIAL EFFECT...
WHEN HE'S DESTROYED, I CAN RETURN ONE SPELL OR TRAP CARD FROM THE GRAVEYARD TO MY HAND...
SHAAK
I CHOOSE THIS SPELL CARD, *MIRACLE FUSION!*
NOW IT'S BACK IN MY HAND!
TCH!
*MIRACLE FUSION...*
*IS HE PLANNING TO FUSE THE HEROES IN HIS GRAVEYARD?*
I... END MY TURN.
*THIS IS BAD...*
*IF I'D DRAWN AN ANGEL ON THIS TURN... I WOULD HAVE WON...*
I DRAW!
*IS THIS DUEL TURNING IN JADEN'S FAVOR...?*

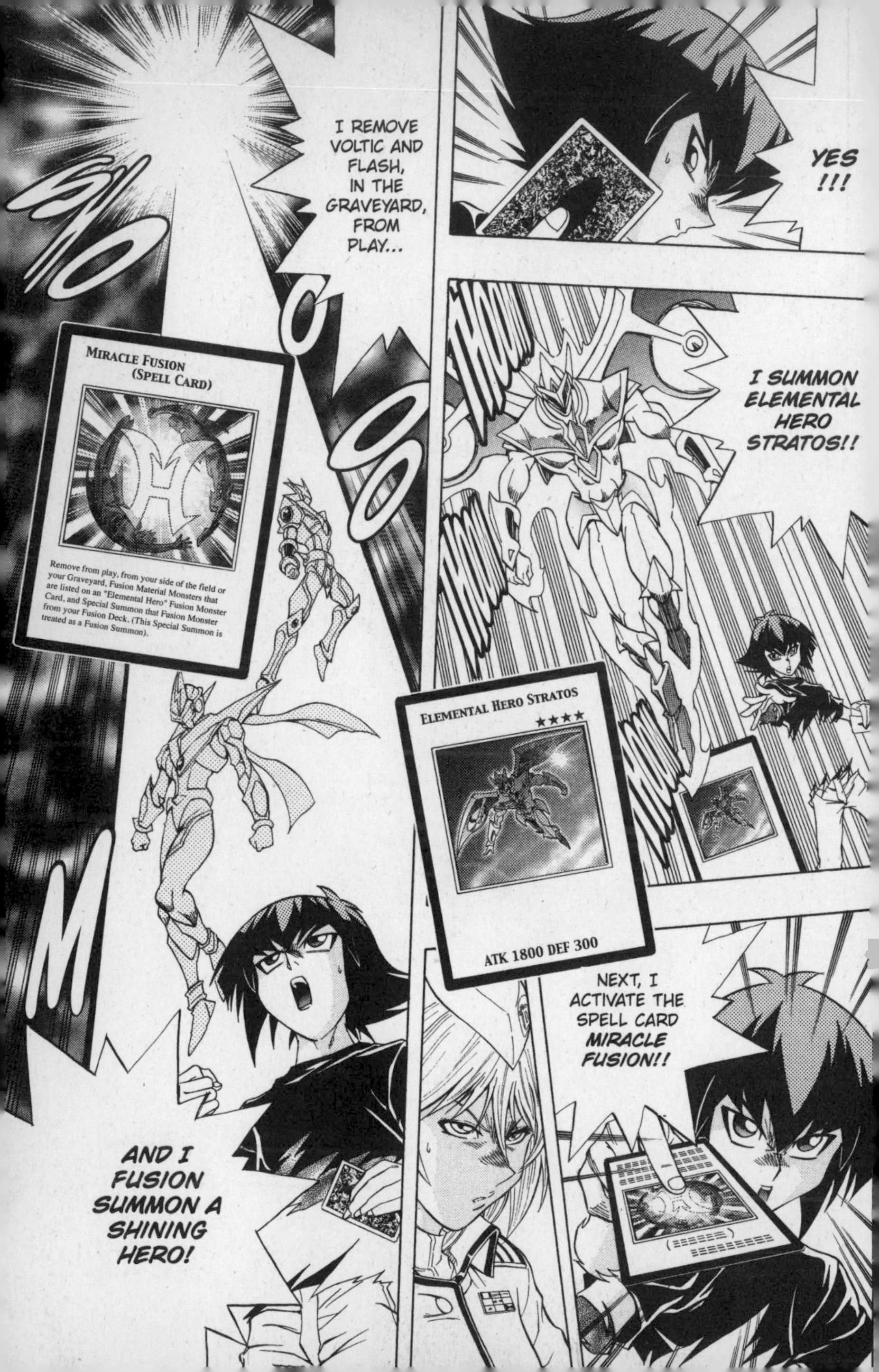
YES!!!
I SUMMON ELEMENTAL HERO STRATOS!!
ELEMENTAL HERO STRATOS
★★★★
ATK 1800 DEF 300
NEXT, I ACTIVATE THE SPELL CARD MIRACLE FUSION!!
I REMOVE VOLTIC AND FLASH, IN THE GRAVEYARD, FROM PLAY...
MIRACLE FUSION
(SPELL CARD)
Remove from play, from your side of the field or your Graveyard, Fusion Material Monsters that are listed on an "Elemental Hero" Fusion Monster Card, and Special Summon that Fusion Monster from your Fusion Deck. (This Special Summon is treated as a Fusion Summon).
AND I FUSION SUMMON A SHINING HERO!

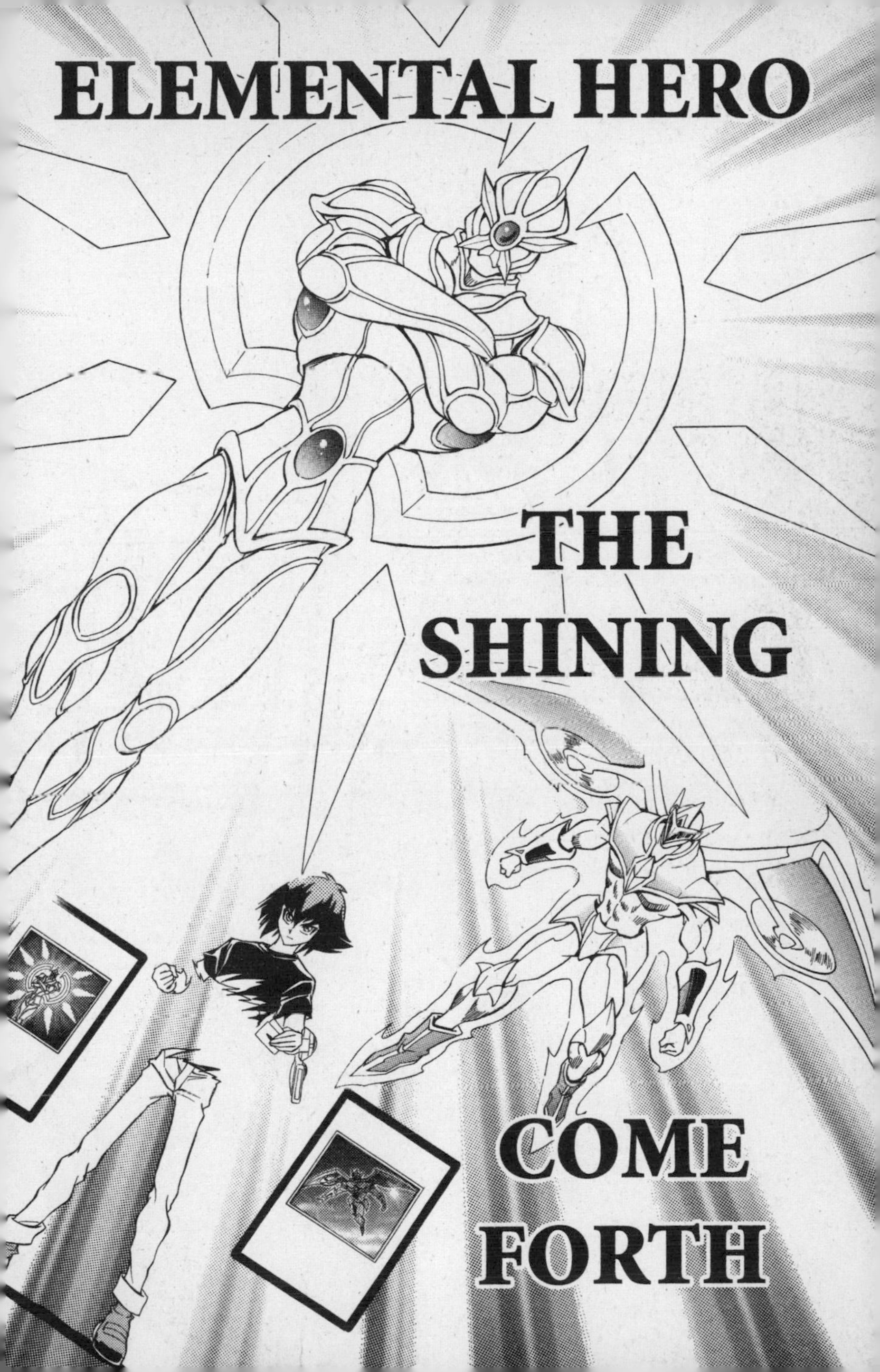
ELEMENTAL HERO
THE SHINING
COME FORTH

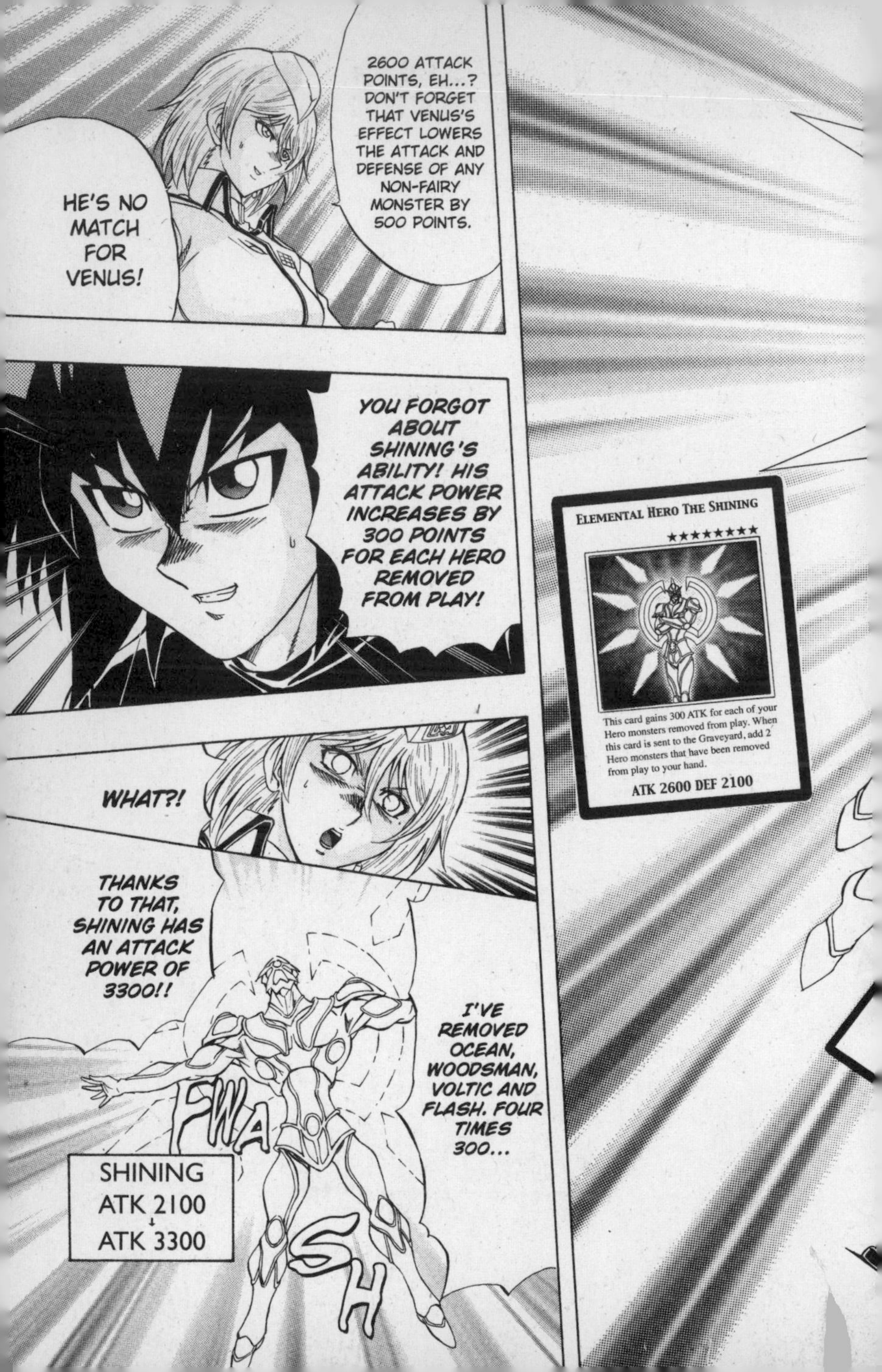
ELEMENTAL HERO THE SHINING
★★★★★★★★
This card gains 300 ATK for each of your Hero monsters removed from play. When this card is sent to the Graveyard, add 2 Hero monsters that have been removed from play to your hand.
ATK 2600 DEF 2100
2600 ATTACK POINTS, EH...? DON'T FORGET THAT VENUS'S EFFECT LOWERS THE ATTACK AND DEFENSE OF ANY NON-FAIRY MONSTER BY 500 POINTS.
HE'S NO MATCH FOR VENUS!
YOU FORGOT ABOUT SHINING'S ABILITY! HIS ATTACK POWER INCREASES BY 300 POINTS FOR EACH HERO REMOVED FROM PLAY!
WHAT?!
I'VE REMOVED OCEAN, WOODSMAN, VOLTIC AND FLASH. FOUR TIMES 300...
THANKS TO THAT, SHINING HAS AN ATTACK POWER OF 3300!!
SHINING ATK 2100 ↓ ATK 3300
FWASH

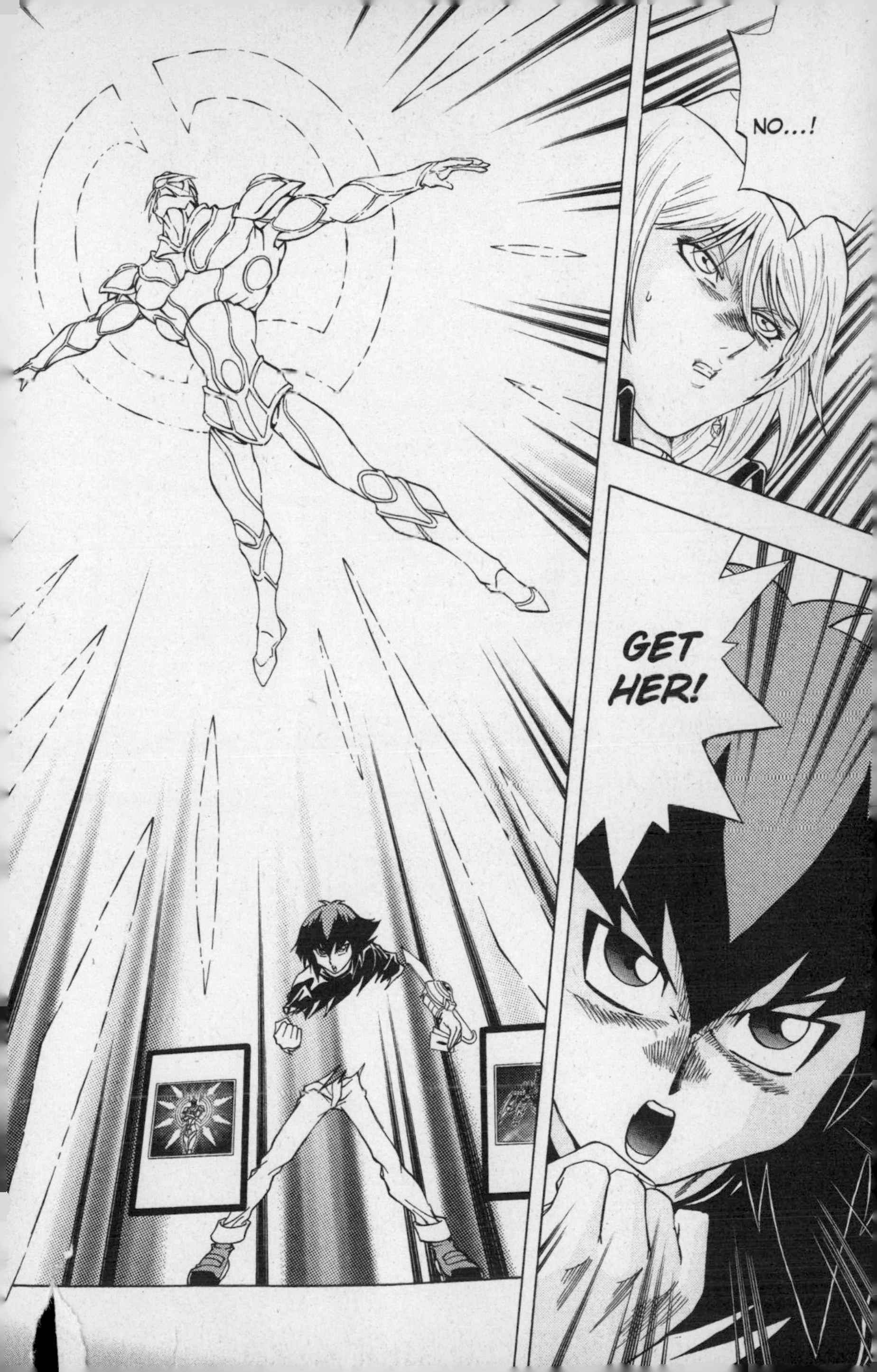
NO...!
GET HER!

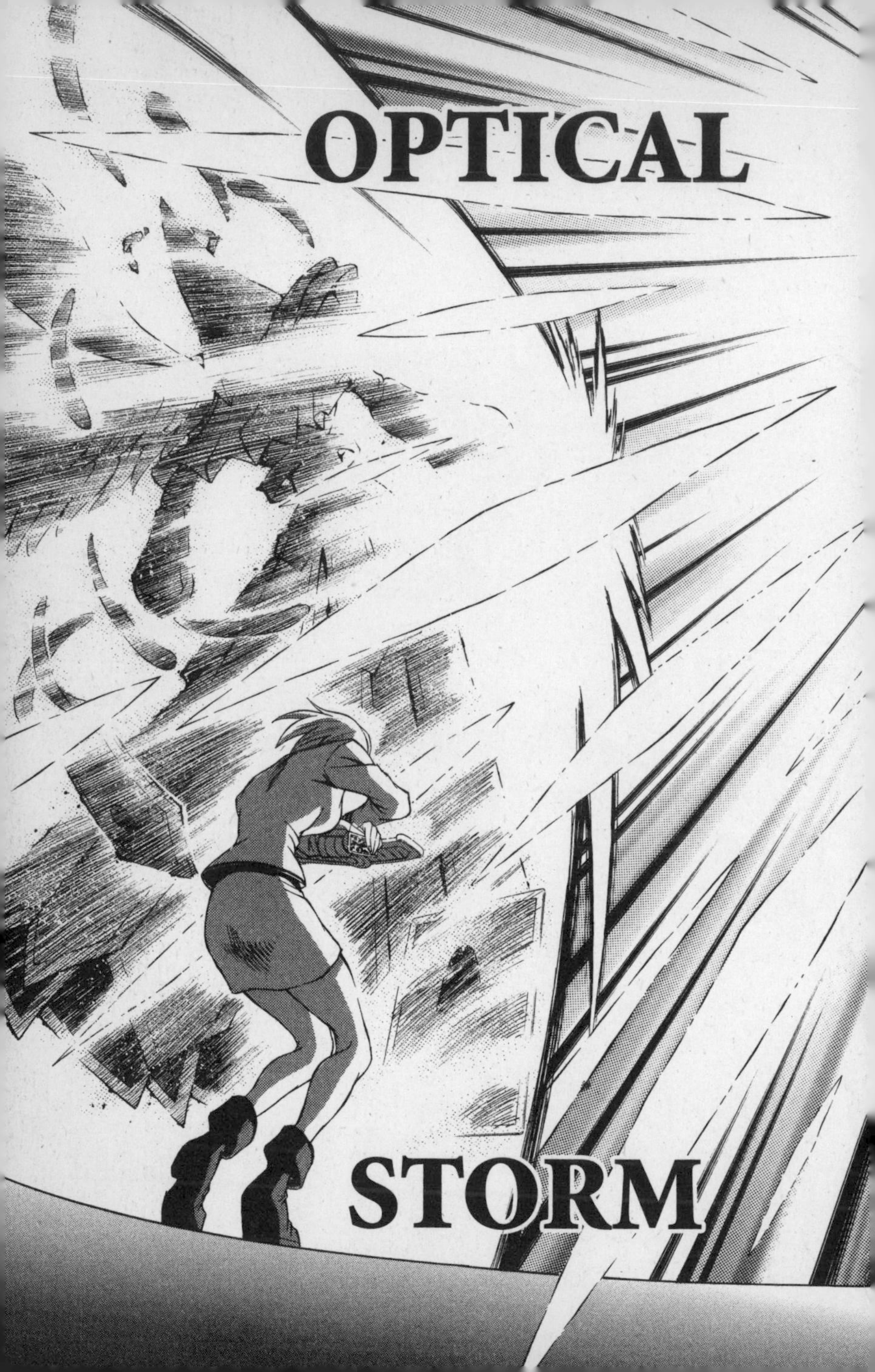
OPTICAL
STORM

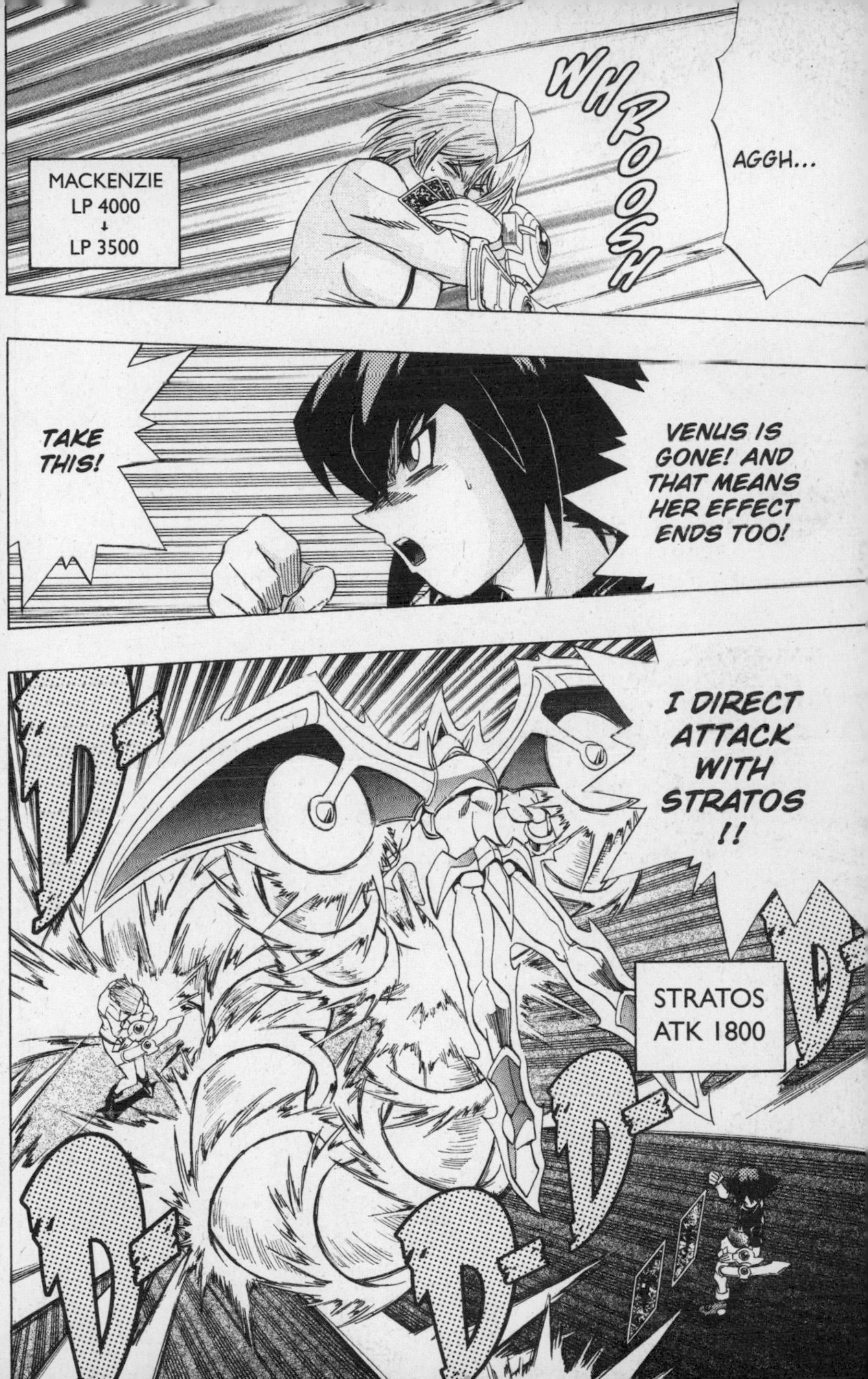
AGGH...
WHROOOSH
MACKENZIE
LP 4000
↓
LP 3500
VENUS IS GONE! AND THAT MEANS HER EFFECT ENDS TOO!
TAKE THIS!
I DIRECT ATTACK WITH STRATOS !!
STRATOS
ATK 1800

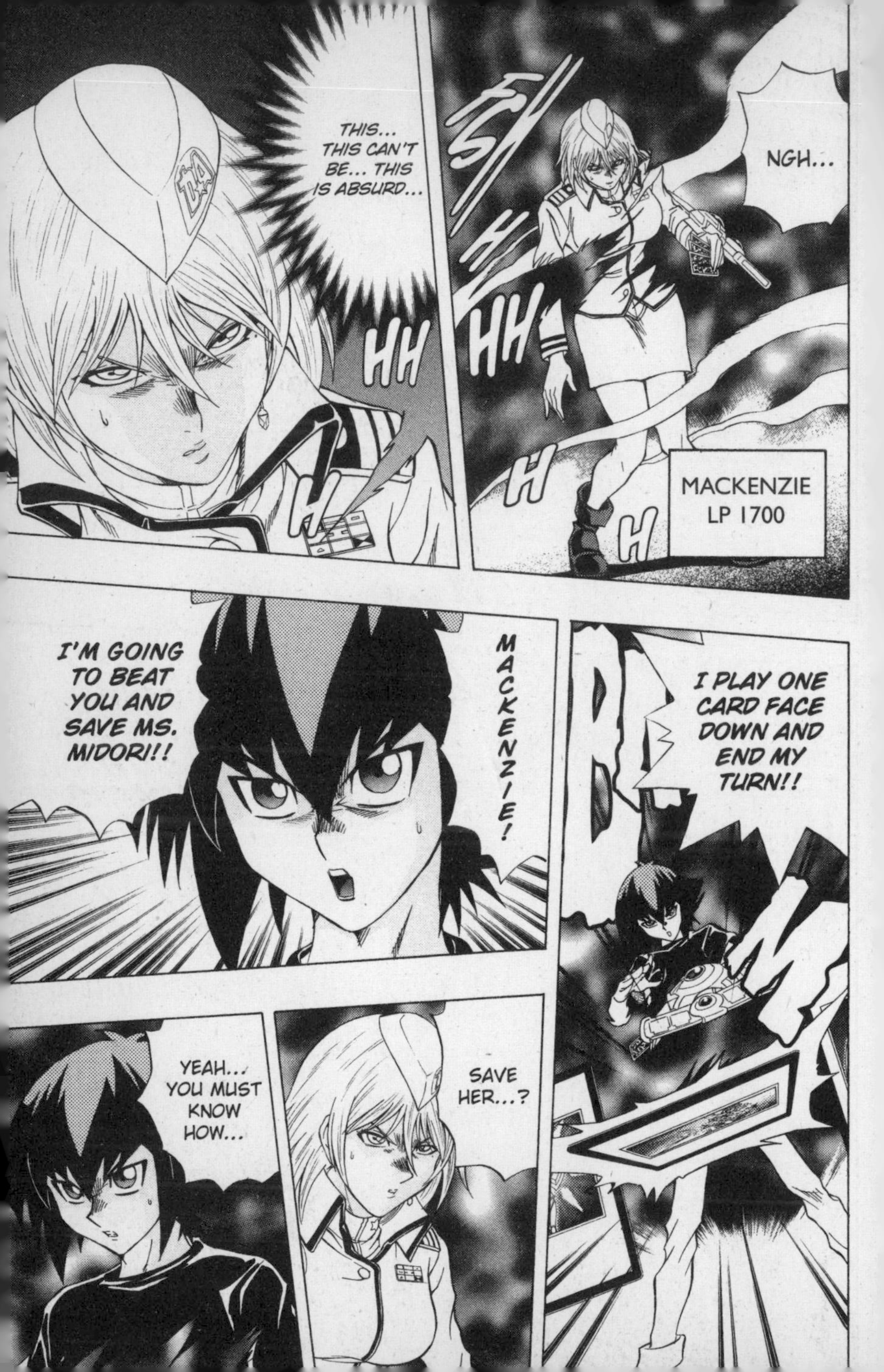
NGH...
MACKENZIE
LP 1700
THIS... THIS CAN'T BE... THIS IS ABSURD...
I PLAY ONE CARD FACE DOWN AND END MY TURN!!
MACKENZIE!
I'M GOING TO BEAT YOU AND SAVE MS. MIDORI!!
SAVE HER...?
YEAH... YOU MUST KNOW HOW...

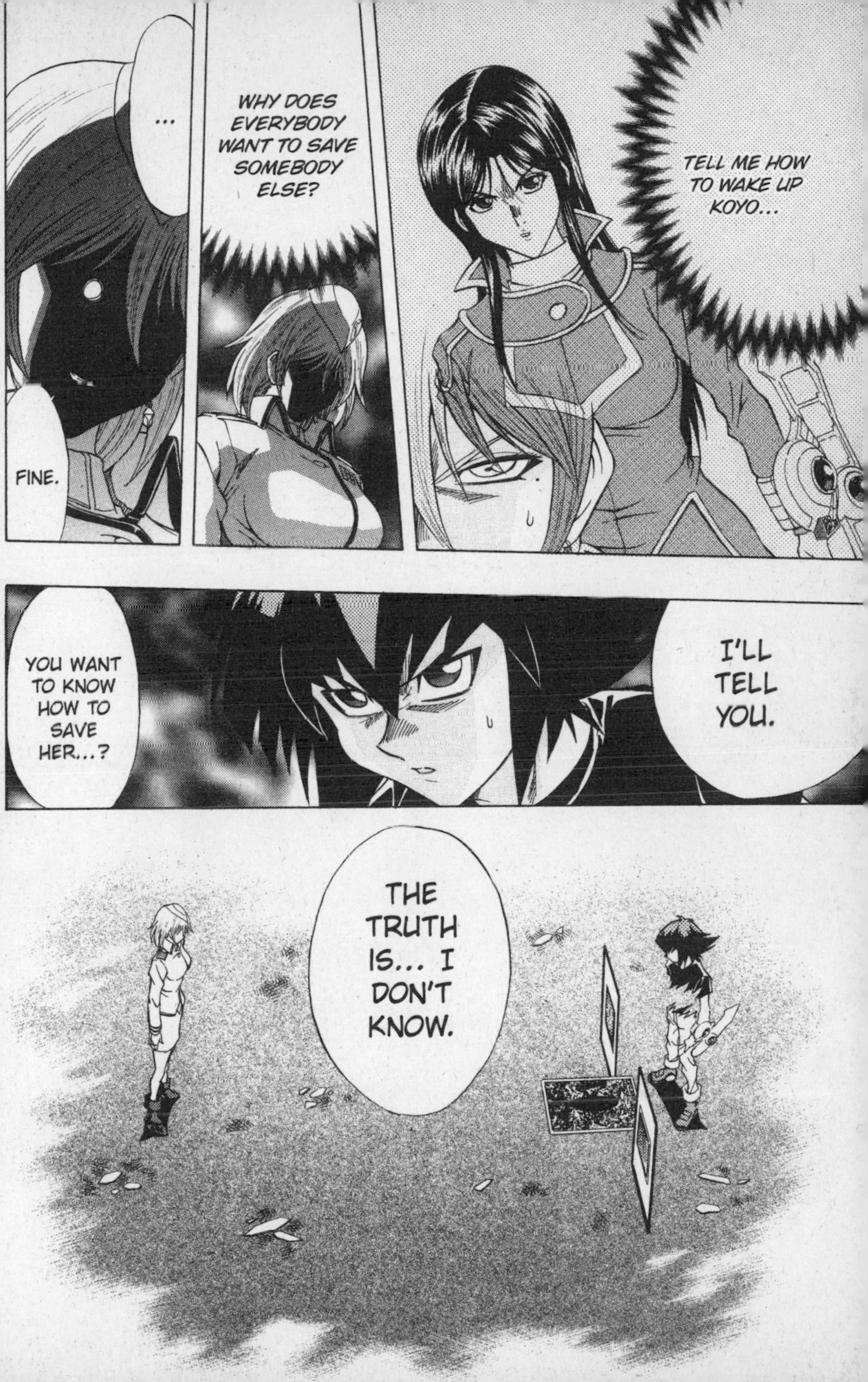
TELL ME HOW TO WAKE UP KOYO...
WHY DOES EVERYBODY WANT TO SAVE SOMEBODY ELSE?
...
FINE.
YOU WANT TO KNOW HOW TO SAVE HER...?
I'LL TELL YOU.
THE TRUTH IS... I DON'T KNOW.

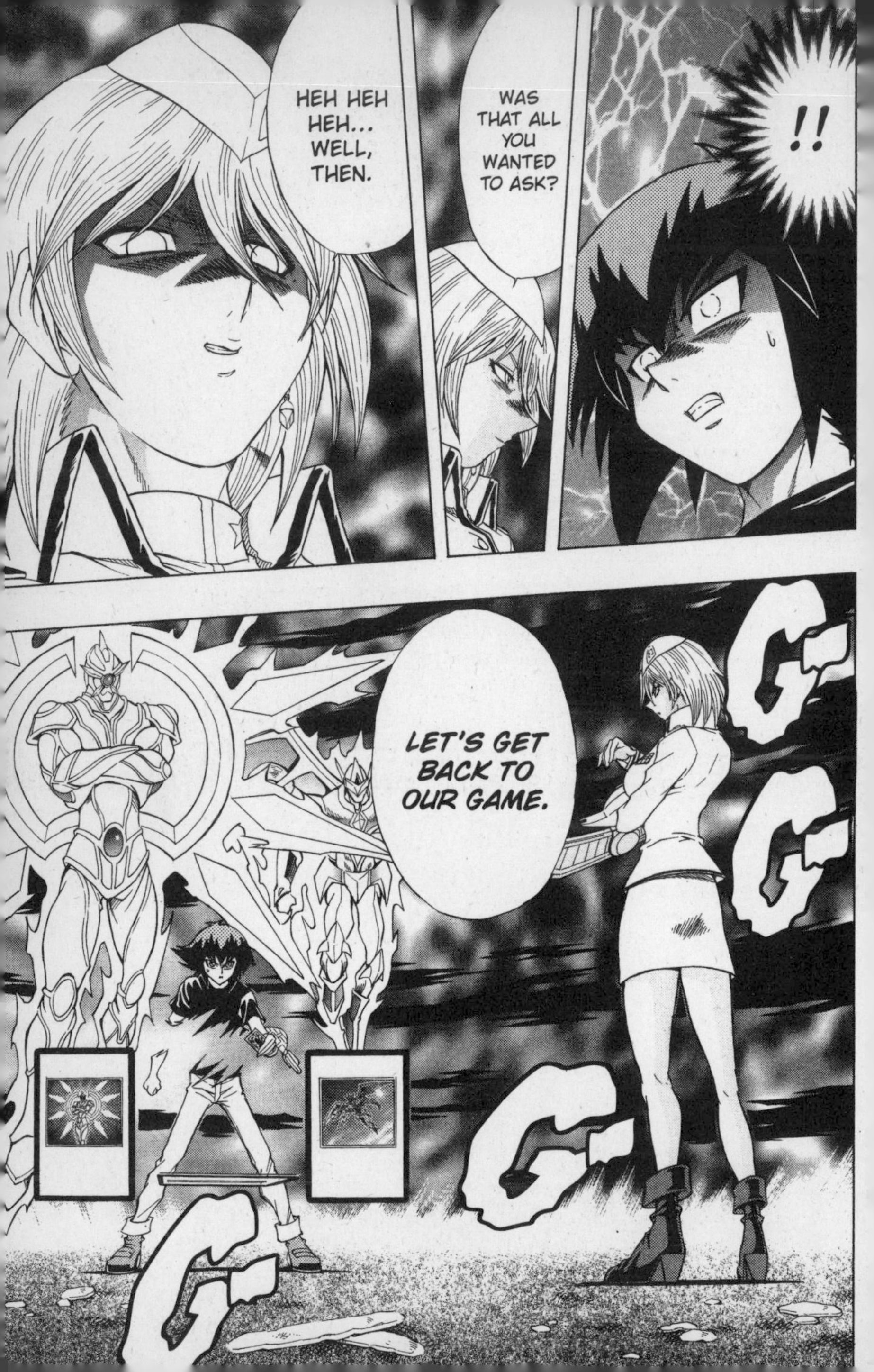
!!
WAS THAT ALL YOU WANTED TO ASK?
HEH HEH HEH... WELL, THEN.
G
G
G
LET'S GET BACK TO OUR GAME.
G
G

A COLLABORATION WITH "INU MAYUGE"?
TOWARDS THE END OF APRIL 2009, I GOT A CALL FROM MR. TERASHI.
MR. KAGEYAMA, I HAVE A FAVOR TO ASK...
LIONS
SURE... WHAT IS IT?
KINDA LOOKS LIKE "INU MAYUGE".
MS. ISHIZUKA SAYS SHE'D LIKE TO SEE WHERE YOU WORK.
I KNOW YOU'RE BUSY, BUT WOULD IT BE ALL RIGHT IF SHE STOPPED BY...?
LIONS
UH. WHAT?
OH...NO... THAT'S FINE, BUT...WHAT DOES SHE WANT HERE...?
...NO IDEA...
TO FIND OUT WHAT HAPPENED NEXT, PLEASE READ THE "LET'S GO WITH 10 PAGES OF INU MAYUGE" INSTALLMENT IN THE JULY 2009 ISSUE OF V-JUMP.
TO THOSE OF YOU WHO DON'T HAVE THAT, CHECK OUT THE "LET'S GO WITH INU MAYUGE" COMIC WHICH WILL HIT THE STORES EVENTUALLY.
(WHEN?!)

THAT WASN'T KIND ENOUGH!
"INU MAYUGE" (DOG EYELASHES) IS ANOTHER MANGA IN *V-JUMP* MAGAZINE IN JAPAN.

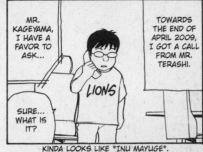

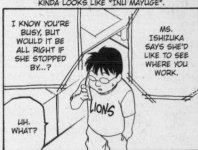

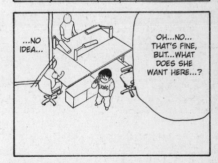

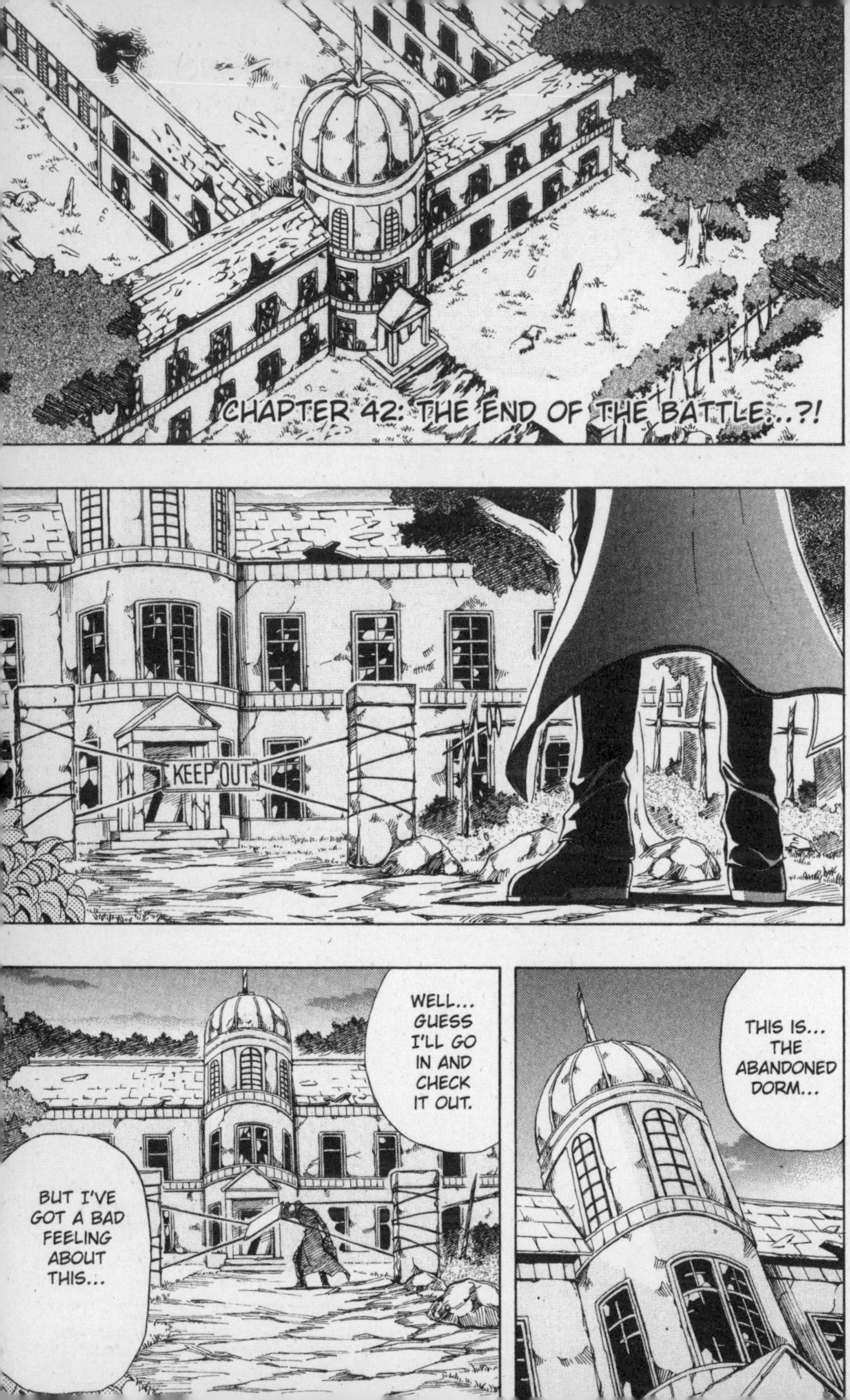
CHAPTER 42: THE END OF THE BATTLE...?!
KEEP OUT
THIS IS... THE ABANDONED DORM...
WELL... GUESS I'LL GO IN AND CHECK IT OUT.
BUT I'VE GOT A BAD FEELING ABOUT THIS...

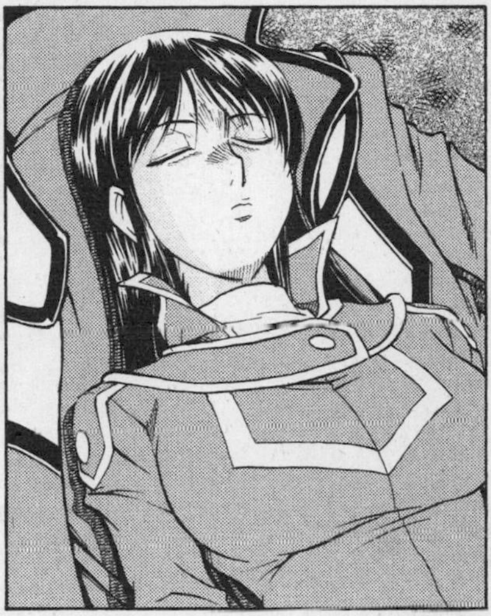

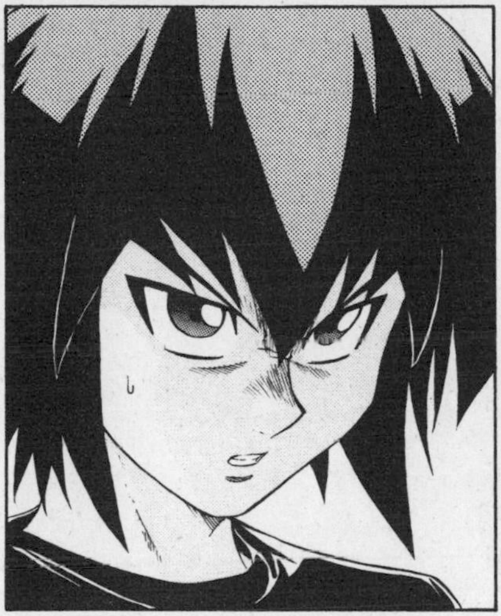

# CHAPTER 42: THE END OF THE BATTLE...?!

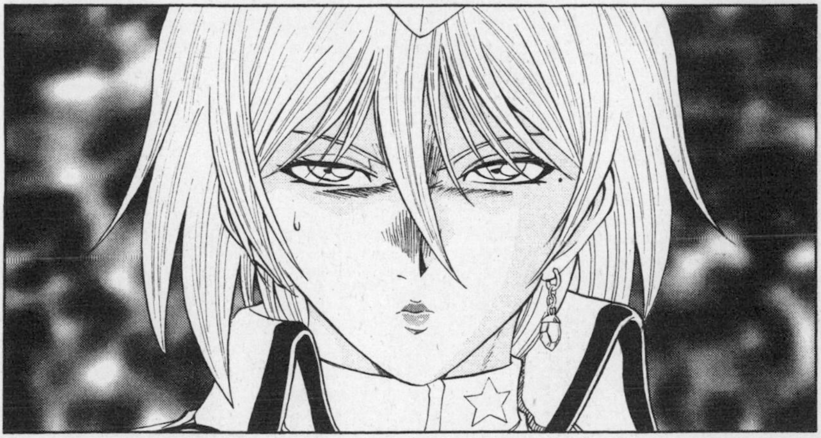

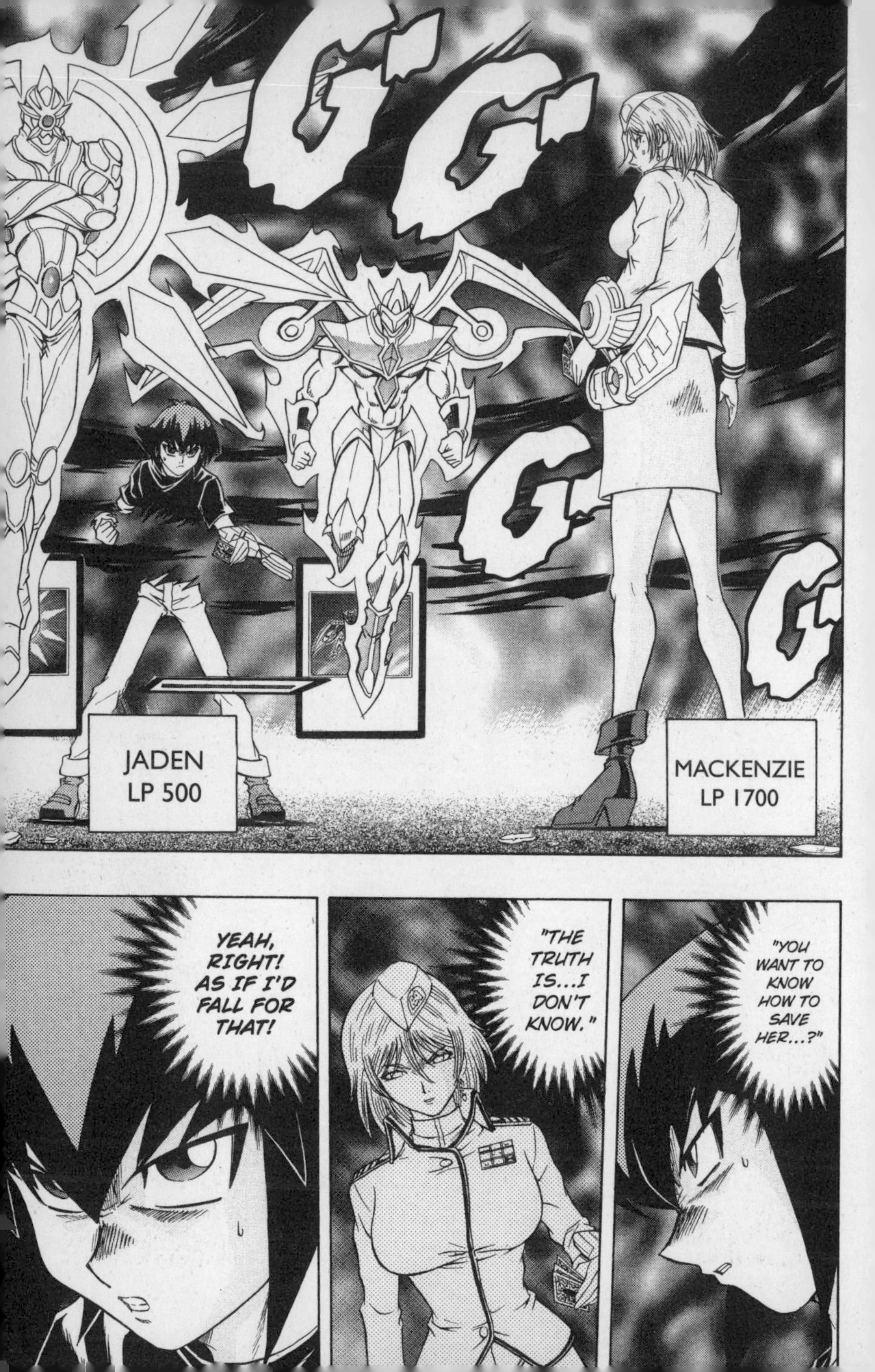
GGGG
MACKENZIE
LP 1700
JADEN
LP 500
"YOU WANT TO KNOW HOW TO SAVE HER...?"
"THE TRUTH IS...I DON'T KNOW."
YEAH, RIGHT! AS IF I'D FALL FOR THAT!

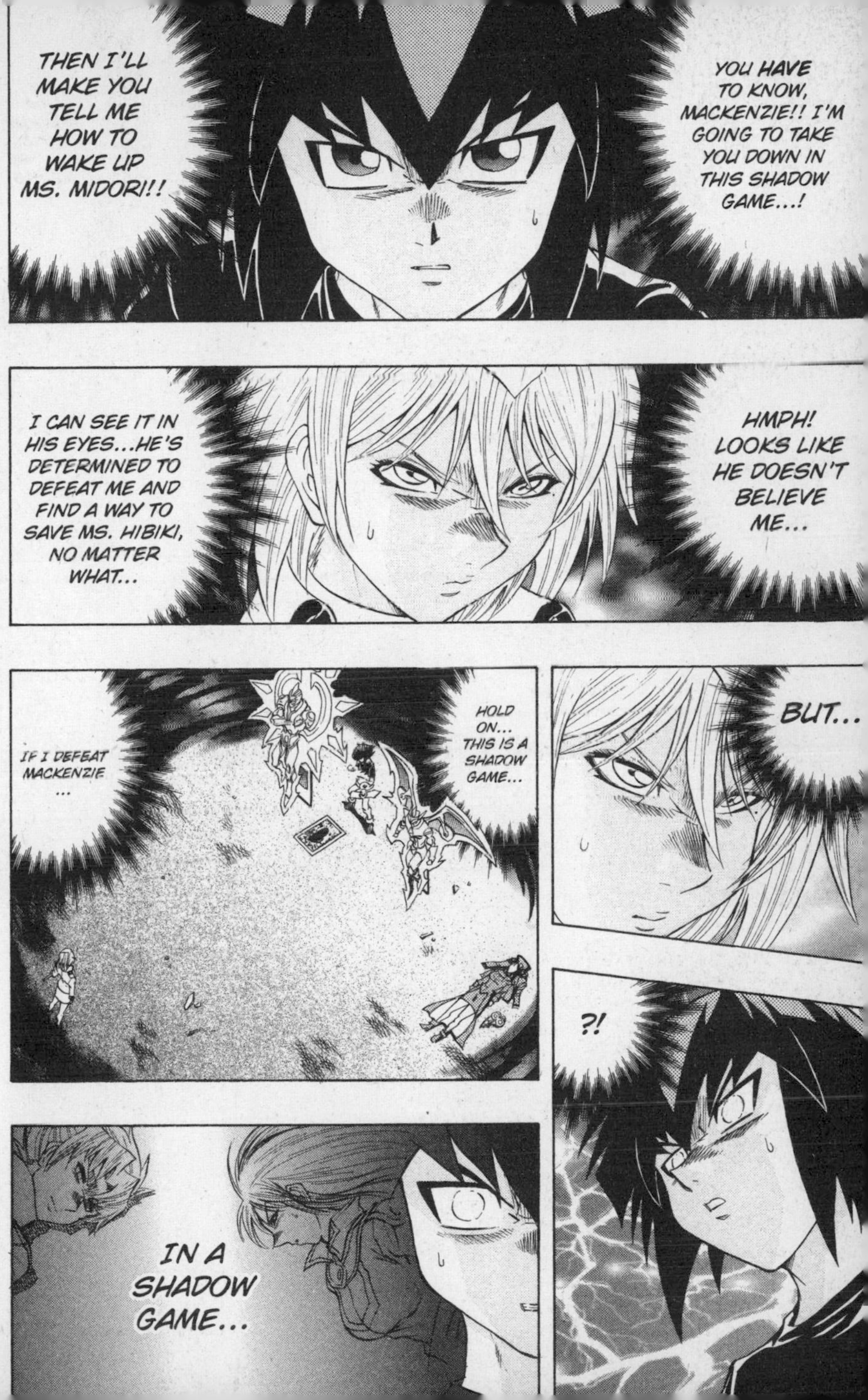
YOU HAVE TO KNOW, MACKENZIE!! I'M GOING TO TAKE YOU DOWN IN THIS SHADOW GAME...!
THEN I'LL MAKE YOU TELL ME HOW TO WAKE UP MS. MIDORI!!
HMPH! LOOKS LIKE HE DOESN'T BELIEVE ME...
I CAN SEE IT IN HIS EYES...HE'S DETERMINED TO DEFEAT ME AND FIND A WAY TO SAVE MS. HIBIKI, NO MATTER WHAT...
BUT...
?!
HOLD ON... THIS IS A SHADOW GAME...
IF I DEFEAT MACKENZIE ...
IN A SHADOW GAME...

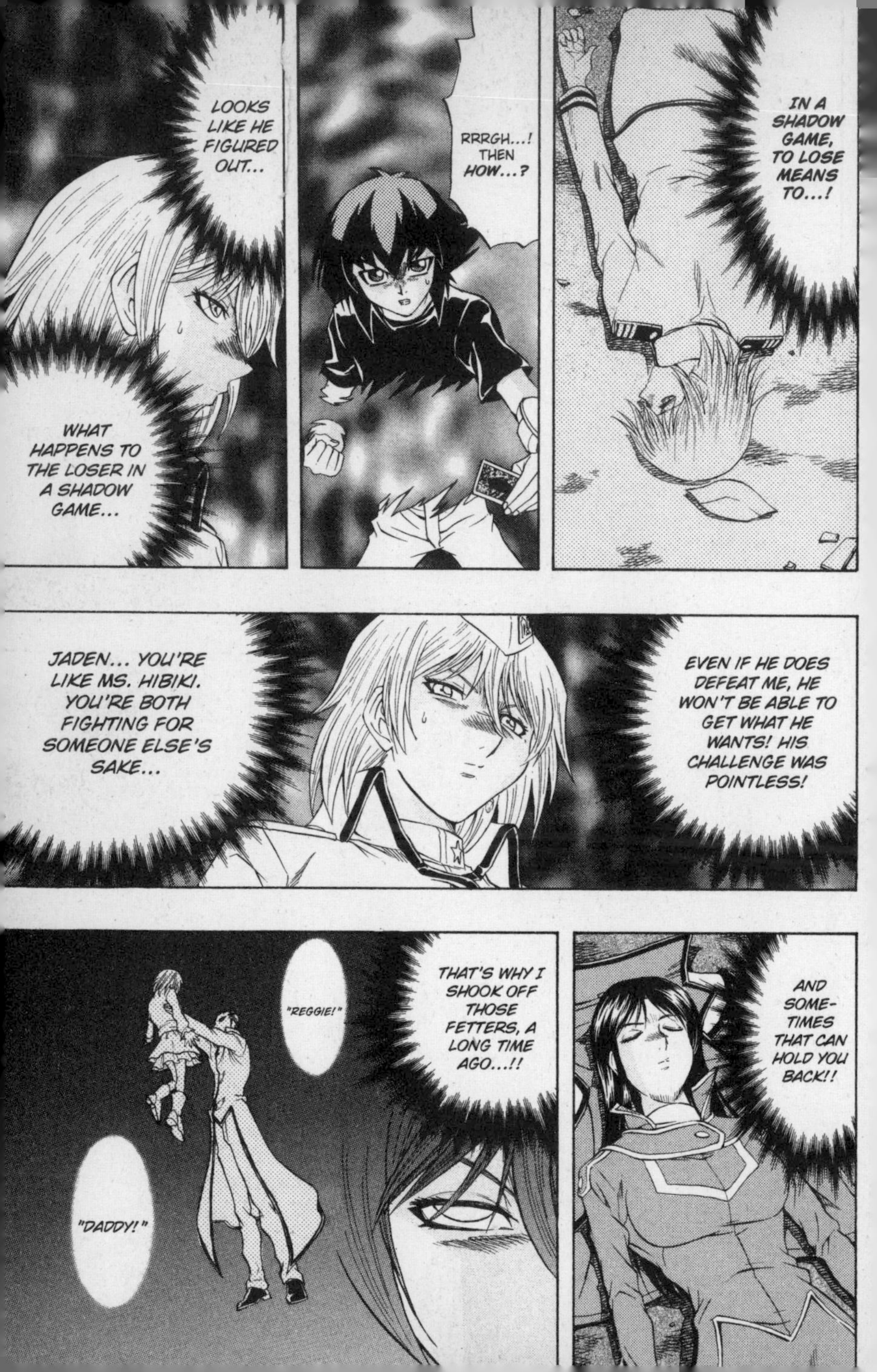
IN A SHADOW GAME, TO LOSE MEANS TO...!
RRRGH...! THEN HOW...?
LOOKS LIKE HE FIGURED OUT...
WHAT HAPPENS TO THE LOSER IN A SHADOW GAME...
EVEN IF HE DOES DEFEAT ME, HE WON'T BE ABLE TO GET WHAT HE WANTS! HIS CHALLENGE WAS POINTLESS!
JADEN... YOU'RE LIKE MS. HIBIKI. YOU'RE BOTH FIGHTING FOR SOMEONE ELSE'S SAKE...
AND SOME-TIMES THAT CAN HOLD YOU BACK!!
THAT'S WHY I SHOOK OFF THOSE FETTERS, A LONG TIME AGO...!!
"REGGIE!"
"DADDY!"

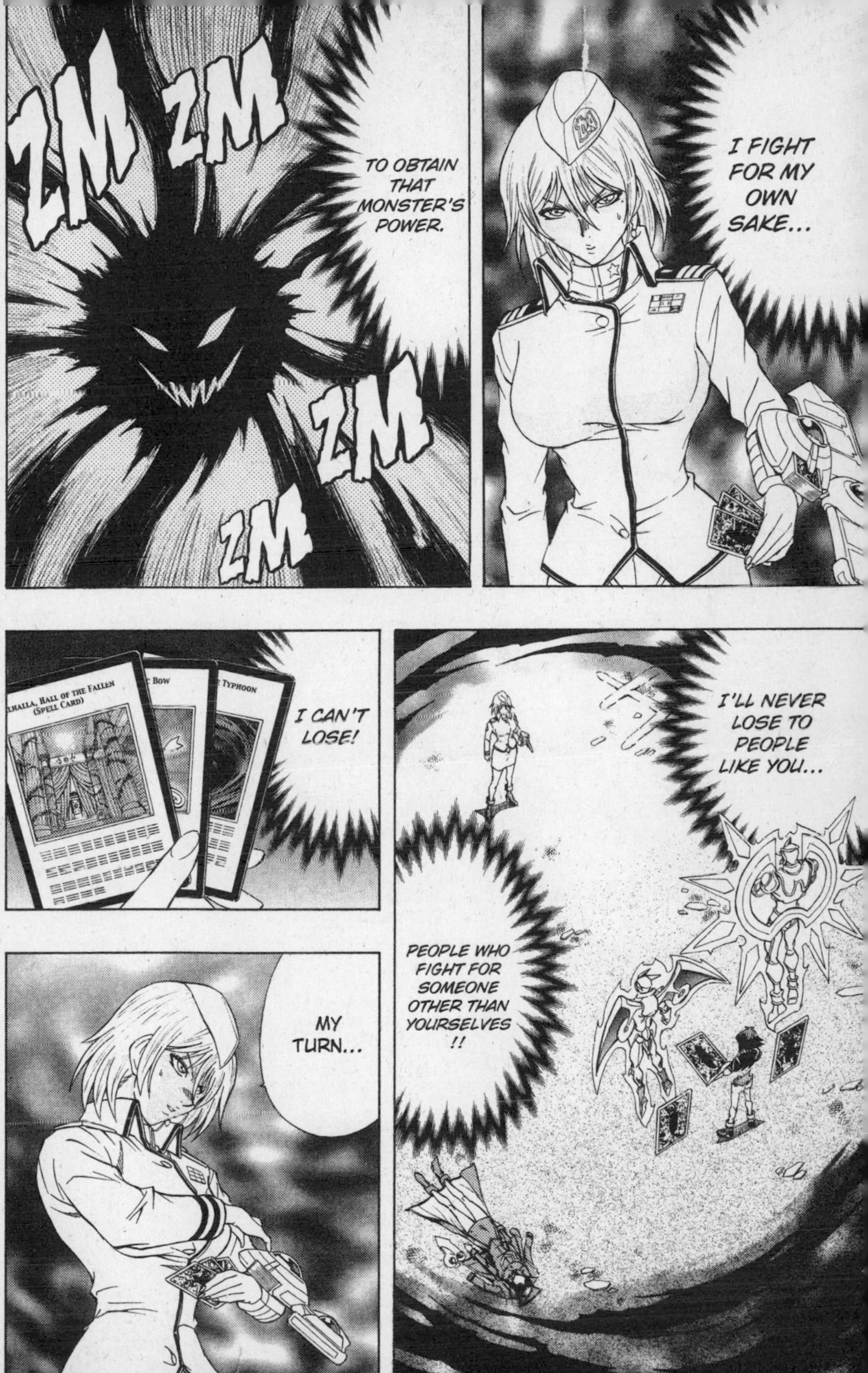
I FIGHT FOR MY OWN SAKE...
TO OBTAIN THAT MONSTER'S POWER.
ZM ZM
ZM
ZM
I'LL NEVER LOSE TO PEOPLE LIKE YOU...
PEOPLE WHO FIGHT FOR SOMEONE OTHER THAN YOURSELVES !!
HALL OF THE FALLEN (SPELL CARD)
BOW
TYPHOON
I CAN'T LOSE!
MY TURN...

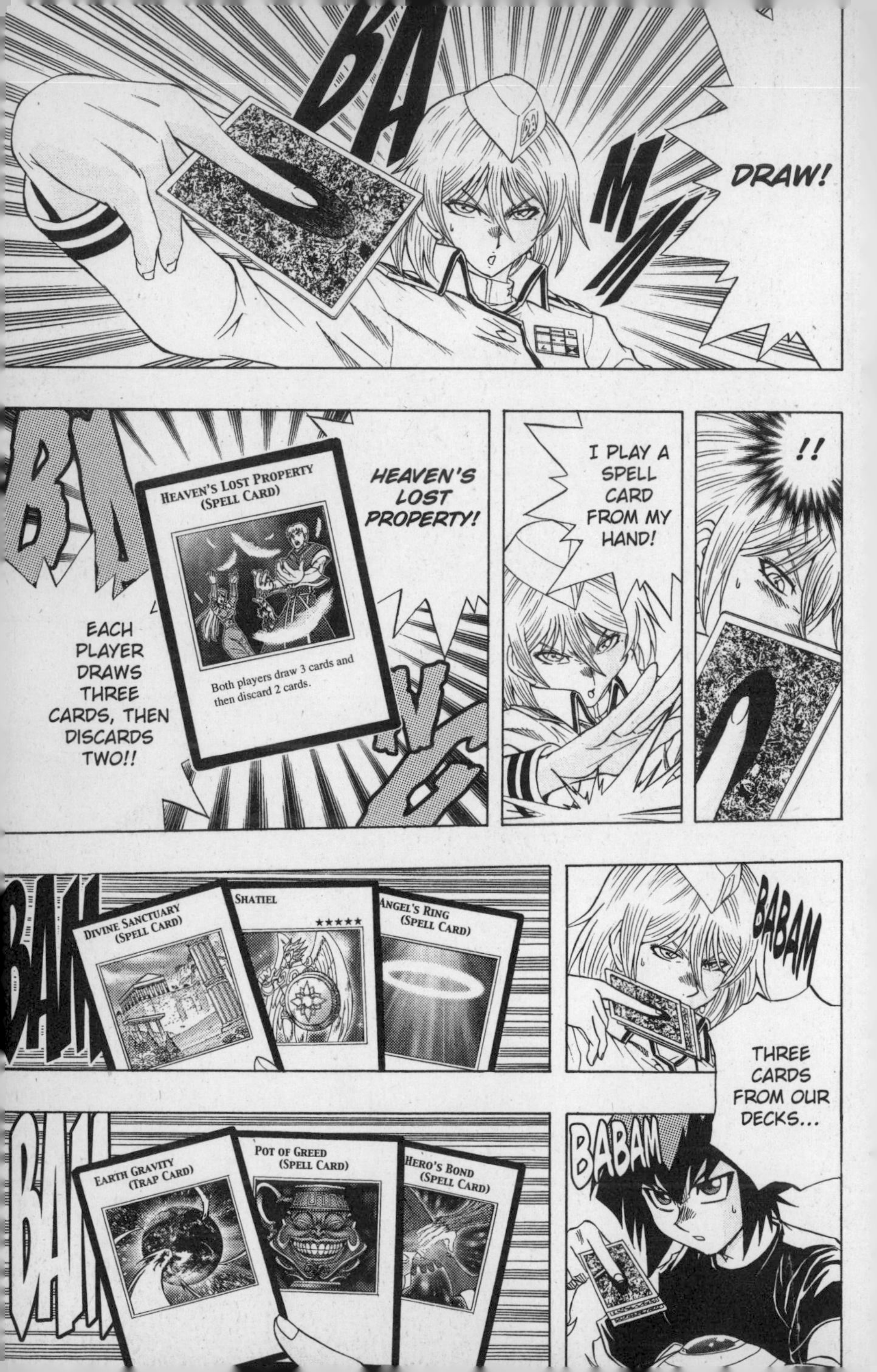
BAMM
DRAW!
!!
I PLAY A SPELL CARD FROM MY HAND!
HEAVEN'S LOST PROPERTY!
HEAVEN'S LOST PROPERTY (SPELL CARD)
Both players draw 3 cards and then discard 2 cards.
EACH PLAYER DRAWS THREE CARDS, THEN DISCARDS TWO!!
BABAM
THREE CARDS FROM OUR DECKS...
DIVINE SANCTUARY (SPELL CARD)
SHATIEL
ANGEL'S RING (SPELL CARD)
BABAM
EARTH GRAVITY (TRAP CARD)
POT OF GREED (SPELL CARD)
HERO'S BOND (SPELL CARD)

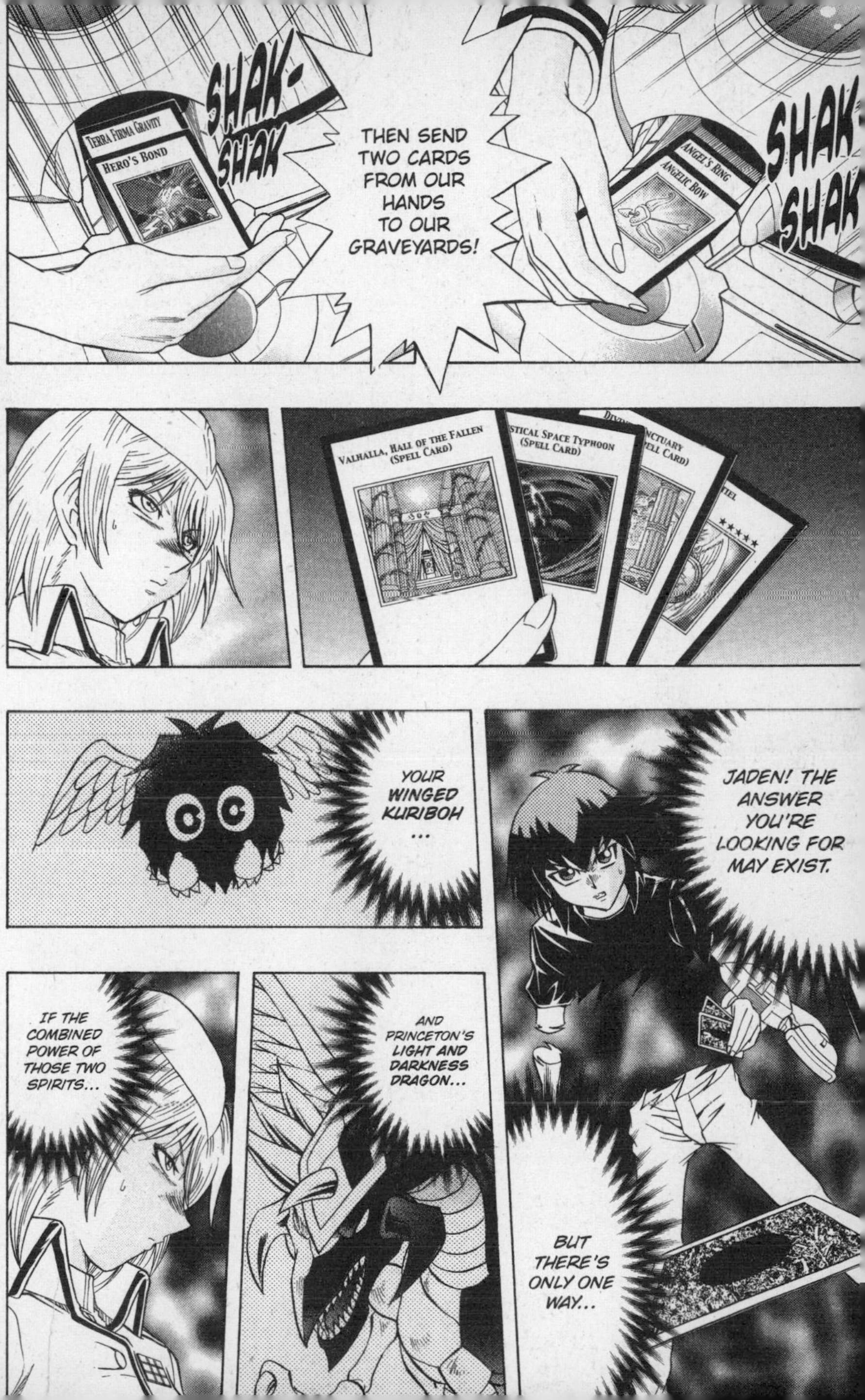
SHAK-SHAK
ANGEL'S RING
ANGELIC BOW
THEN SEND TWO CARDS FROM OUR HANDS TO OUR GRAVEYARDS!
SHAK-SHAK
TERRA FIRMA GRAVITY
HERO'S BOND
VALHALLA, HALL OF THE FALLEN (SPELL CARD)
JADEN! THE ANSWER YOU'RE LOOKING FOR MAY EXIST.
BUT THERE'S ONLY ONE WAY...
YOUR WINGED KURIBOH ...
AND PRINCETON'S LIGHT AND DARKNESS DRAGON...
IF THE COMBINED POWER OF THOSE TWO SPIRITS...

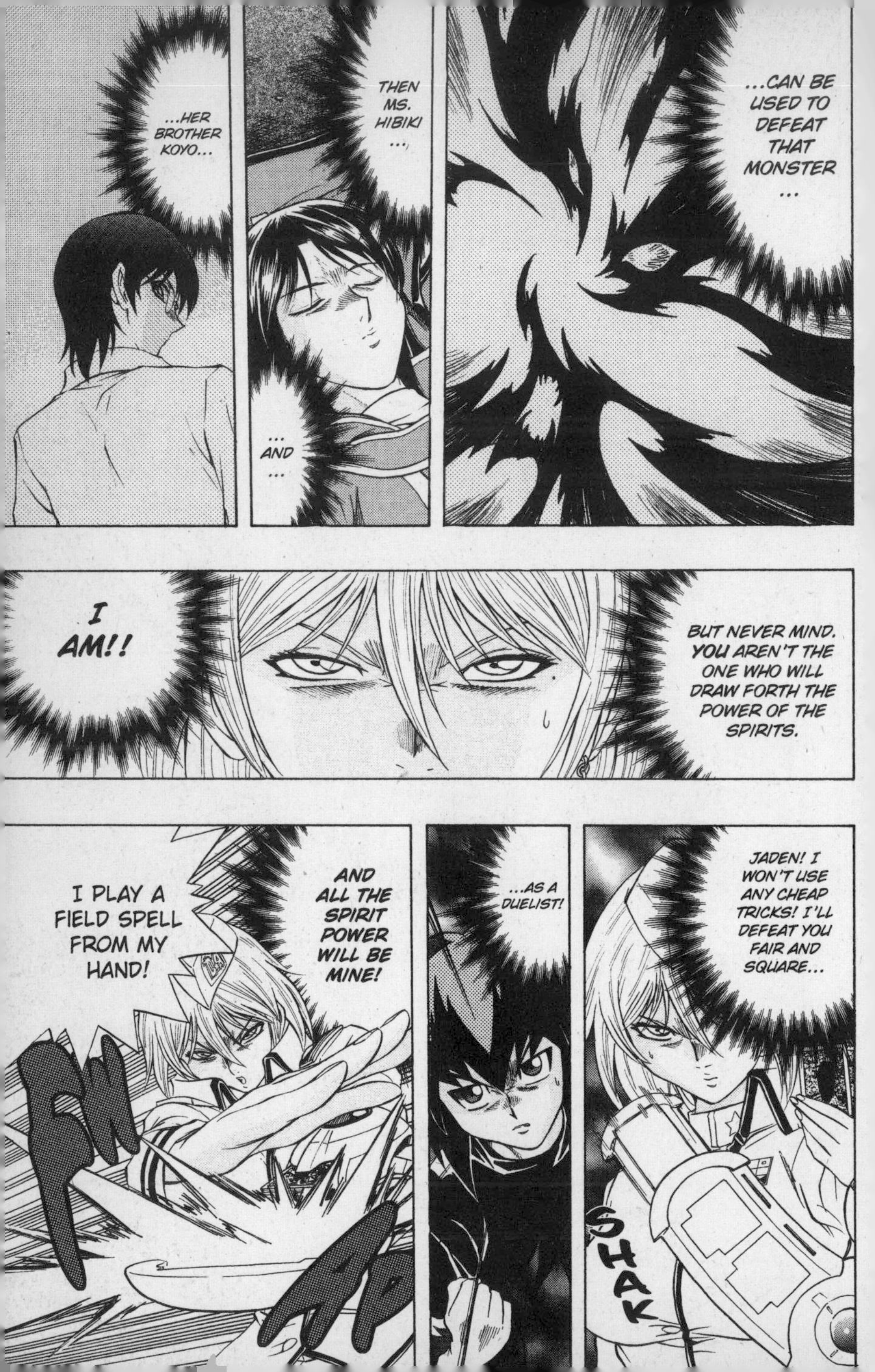
...CAN BE USED TO DEFEAT THAT MONSTER ...
THEN MS. HIBIKI ...,
... AND ...
...HER BROTHER KOYO...
BUT NEVER MIND. YOU AREN'T THE ONE WHO WILL DRAW FORTH THE POWER OF THE SPIRITS.
I AM!!
JADEN! I WON'T USE ANY CHEAP TRICKS! I'LL DEFEAT YOU FAIR AND SQUARE...
SHAK
...AS A DUELIST!
AND ALL THE SPIRIT POWER WILL BE MINE!
I PLAY A FIELD SPELL FROM MY HAND!
FWAP

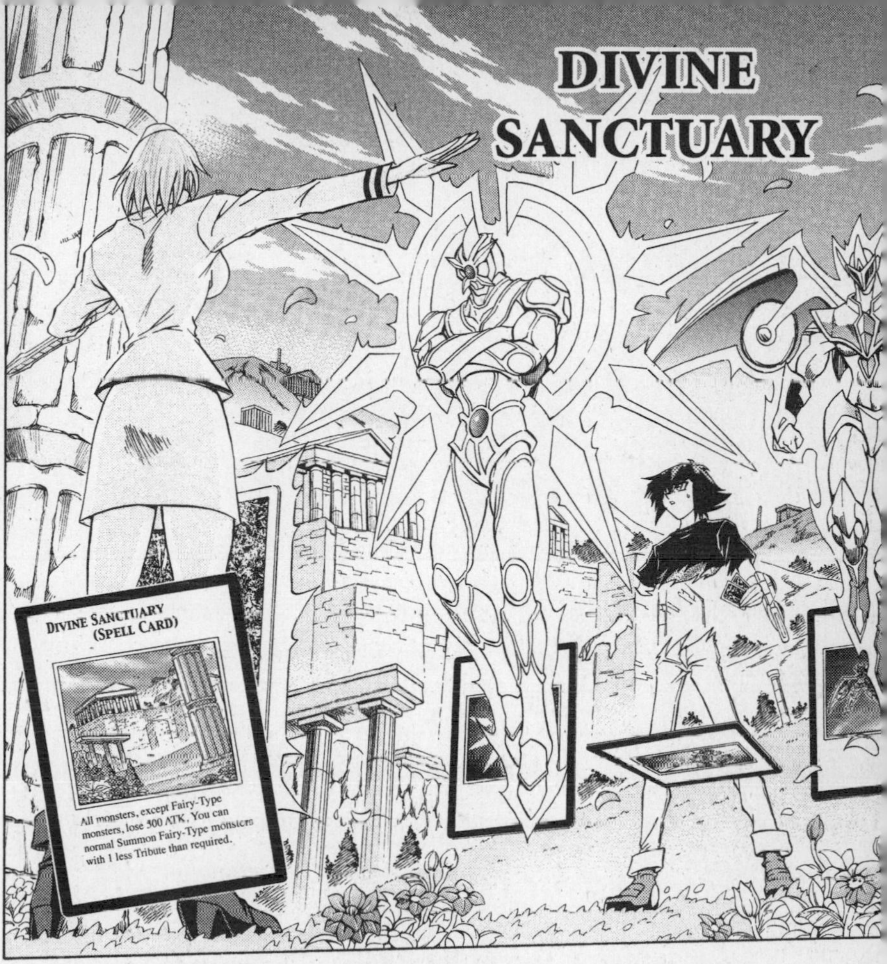
DIVINE SANCTUARY
DIVINE SANCTUARY (SPELL CARD)
All monsters, except Fairy-Type monsters, lose 500 ATK. You can normal Summon Fairy-Type monsters with 1 less Tribute than required.
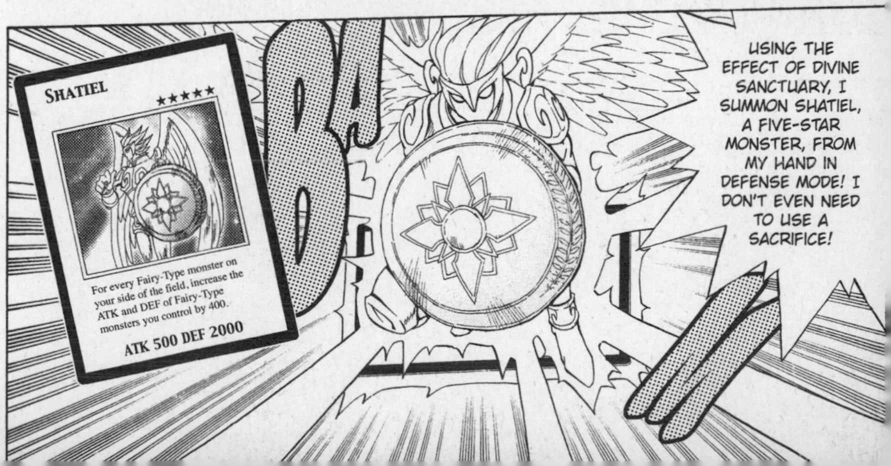
USING THE EFFECT OF DIVINE SANCTUARY, I SUMMON SHATIEL, A FIVE-STAR MONSTER, FROM MY HAND IN DEFENSE MODE! I DON'T EVEN NEED TO USE A SACRIFICE!
SHATIEL ★★★★★
For every Fairy-Type monster on your side of the field, increase the ATK and DEF of Fairy-Type monsters you control by 400.
ATK 500 DEF 2000

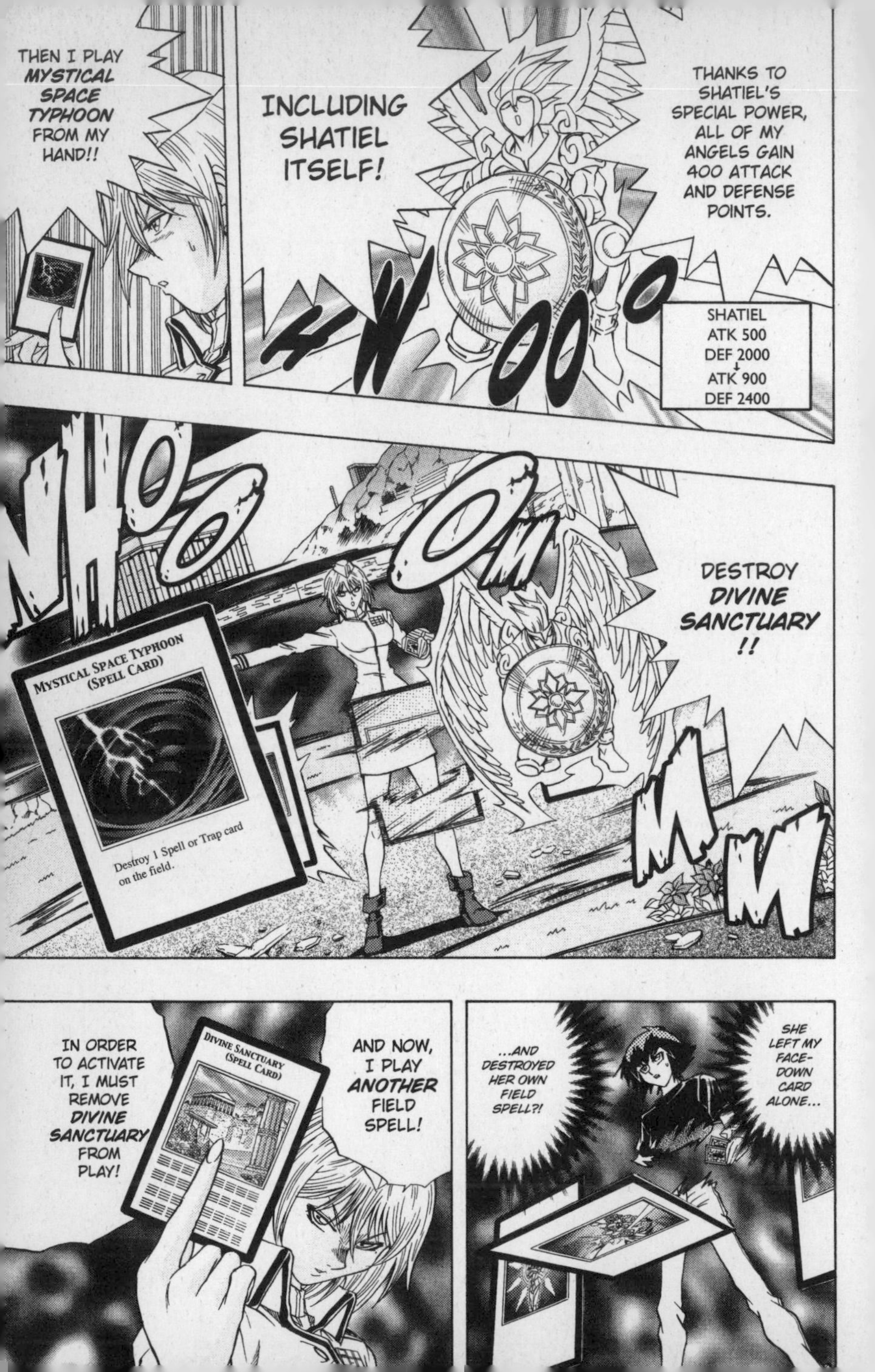
THANKS TO SHATIEL'S SPECIAL POWER, ALL OF MY ANGELS GAIN 400 ATTACK AND DEFENSE POINTS.
INCLUDING SHATIEL ITSELF!
SHATIEL ATK 500 DEF 2000 ↓ ATK 900 DEF 2400
THEN I PLAY MYSTICAL SPACE TYPHOON FROM MY HAND!!
DESTROY DIVINE SANCTUARY!!
MYSTICAL SPACE TYPHOON (SPELL CARD)
Destroy 1 Spell or Trap card on the field.
SHE LEFT MY FACE-DOWN CARD ALONE...
...AND DESTROYED HER OWN FIELD SPELL?!
AND NOW, I PLAY ANOTHER FIELD SPELL!
IN ORDER TO ACTIVATE IT, I MUST REMOVE DIVINE SANCTUARY FROM PLAY!
DIVINE SANCTUARY (SPELL CARD)

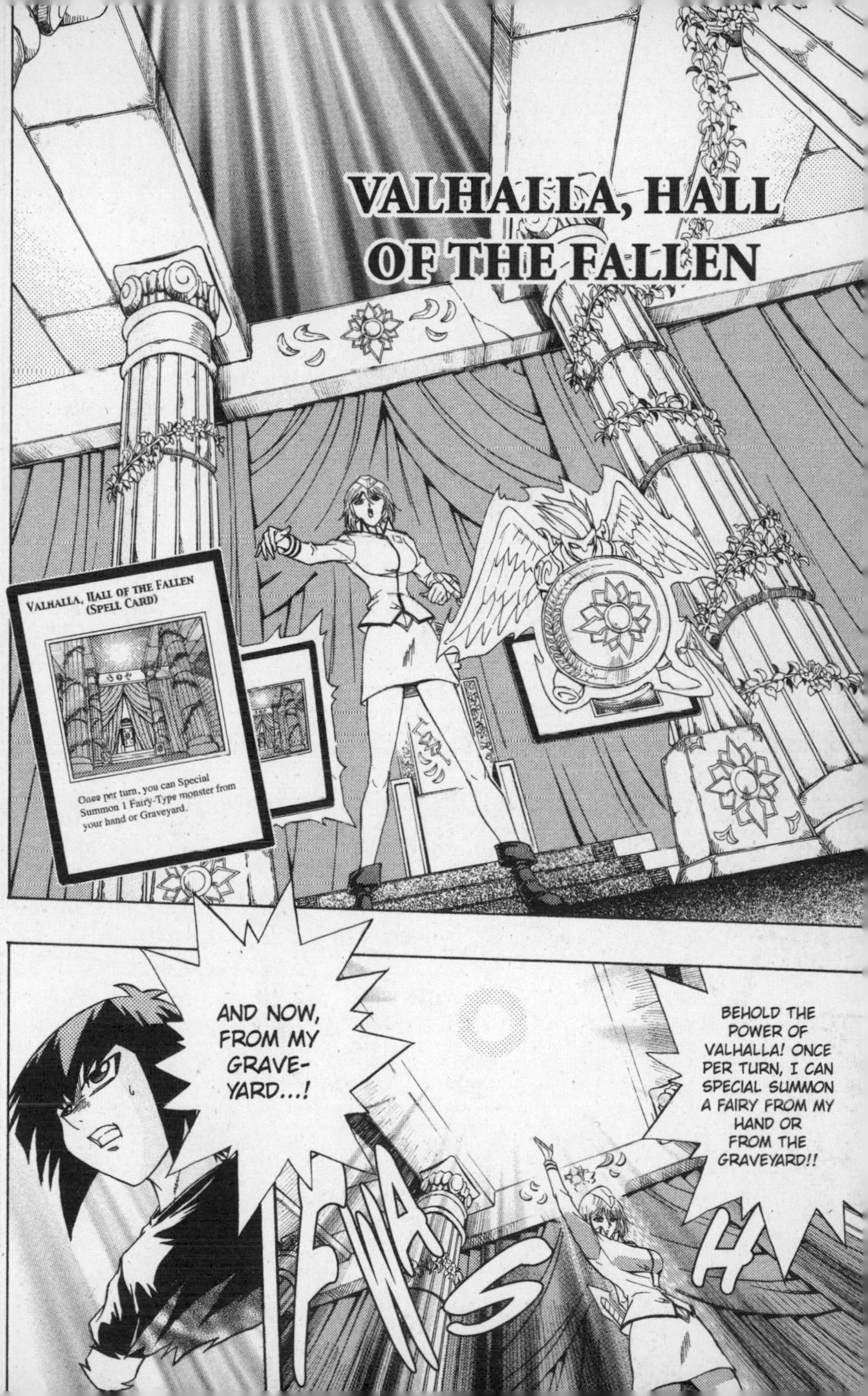
VALHALLA, HALL OF THE FALLEN
VALHALLA, HALL OF THE FALLEN
(SPELL CARD)
Once per turn, you can Special Summon 1 Fairy-Type monster from your hand or Graveyard.
BEHOLD THE POWER OF VALHALLA! ONCE PER TURN, I CAN SPECIAL SUMMON A FAIRY FROM MY HAND OR FROM THE GRAVEYARD!!
AND NOW, FROM MY GRAVE-YARD...!
FWASH

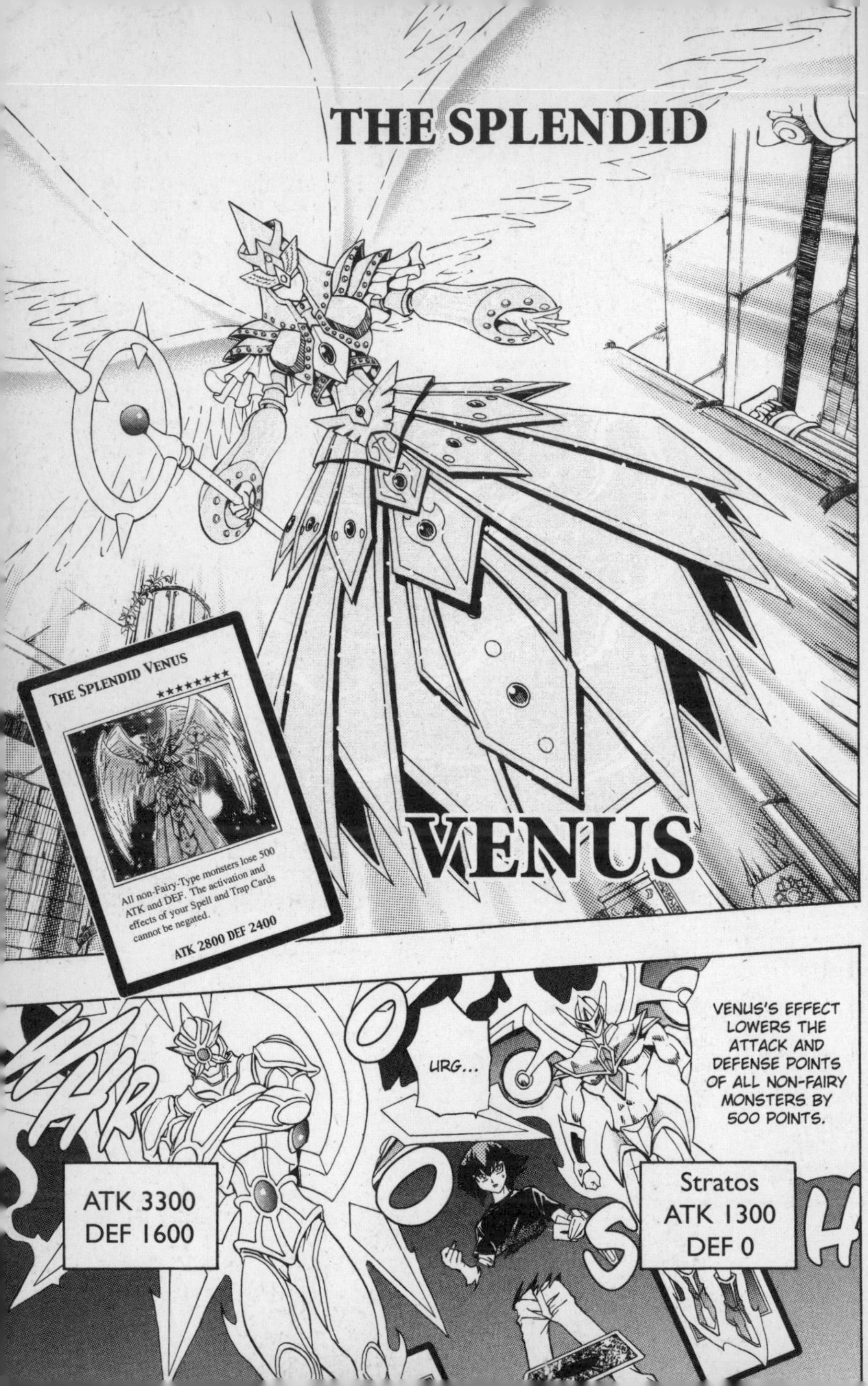
THE SPLENDID
VENUS
The Splendid Venus
All non-Fairy-Type monsters lose 500 ATK and DEF. The activation and effects of your Spell and Trap Cards cannot be negated.
ATK 2800 DEF 2400
VENUS'S EFFECT LOWERS THE ATTACK AND DEFENSE POINTS OF ALL NON-FAIRY MONSTERS BY 500 POINTS.
Stratos
ATK 1300
DEF 0
URG...
ATK 3300
DEF 1600

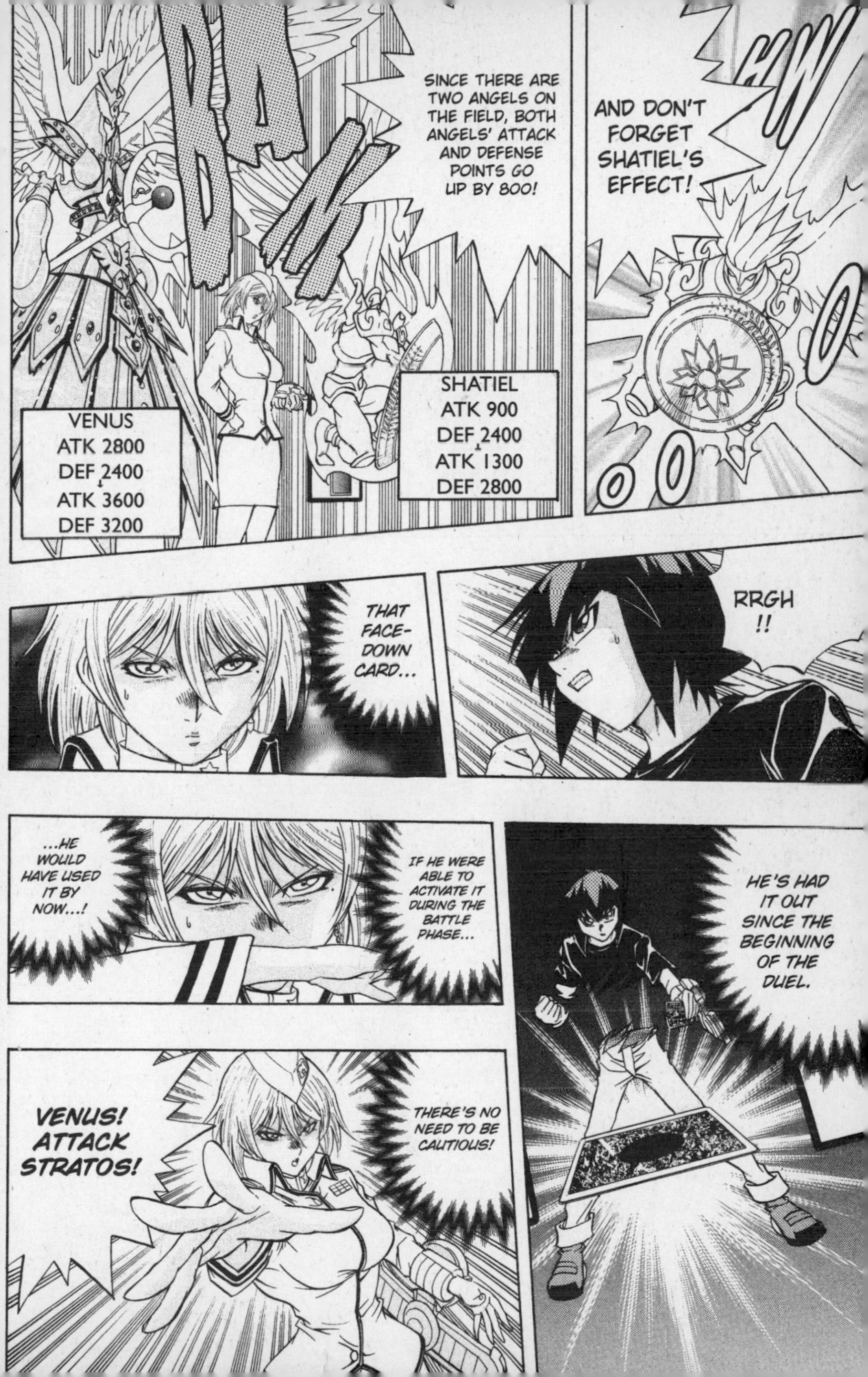
AND DON'T FORGET SHATIEL'S EFFECT!
BAM
SINCE THERE ARE TWO ANGELS ON THE FIELD, BOTH ANGELS' ATTACK AND DEFENSE POINTS GO UP BY 800!
SHATIEL ATK 900 DEF 2400 ATK 1300 DEF 2800
VENUS ATK 2800 DEF 2400 ATK 3600 DEF 3200
RRGH !!
THAT FACE-DOWN CARD...
HE'S HAD IT OUT SINCE THE BEGINNING OF THE DUEL.
IF HE WERE ABLE TO ACTIVATE IT DURING THE BATTLE PHASE...
...HE WOULD HAVE USED IT BY NOW...!
THERE'S NO NEED TO BE CAUTIOUS!
VENUS! ATTACK STRATOS!

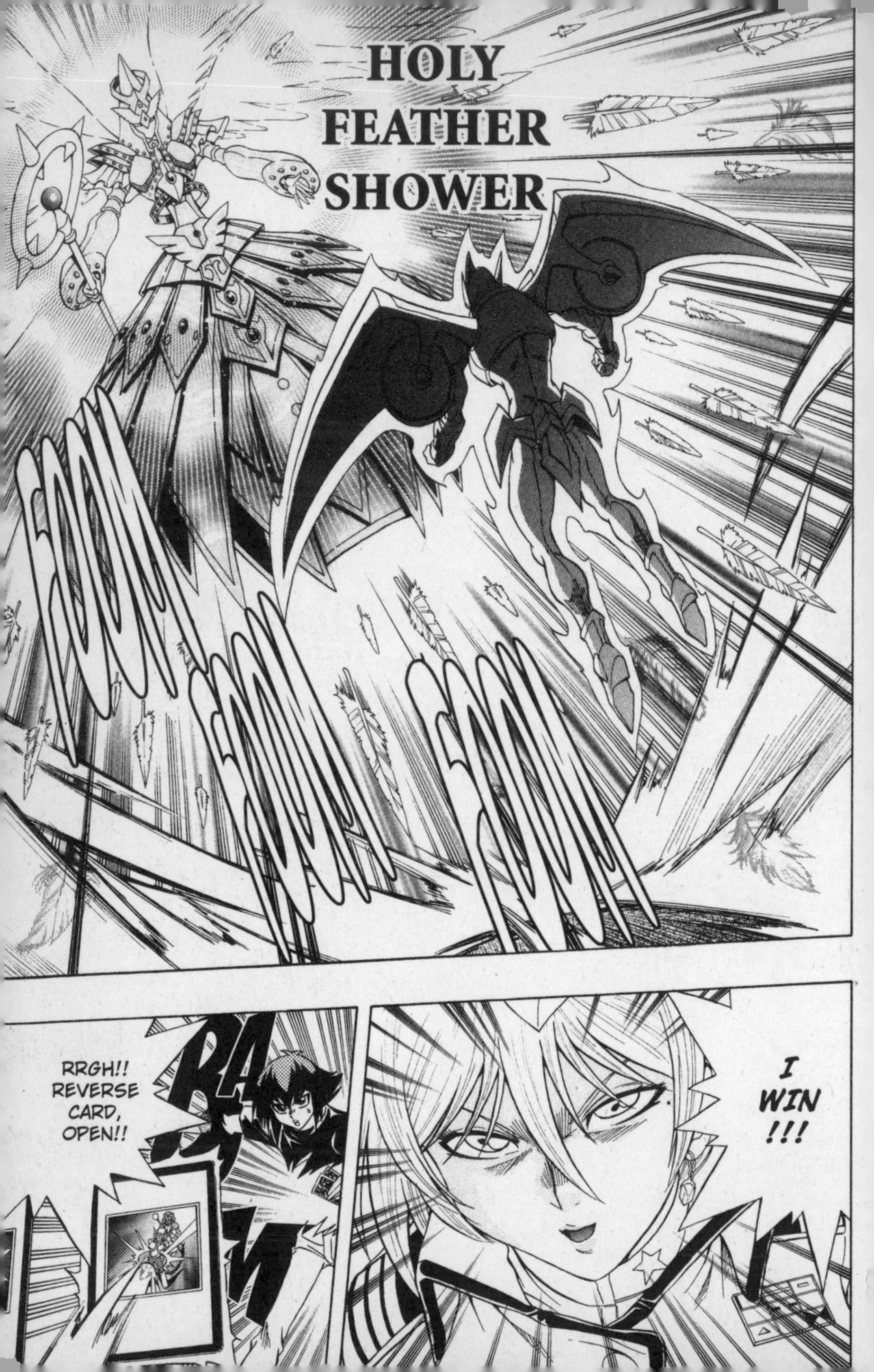
HOLY FEATHER SHOWER
I WIN!!!
RRGH!! REVERSE CARD, OPEN!!

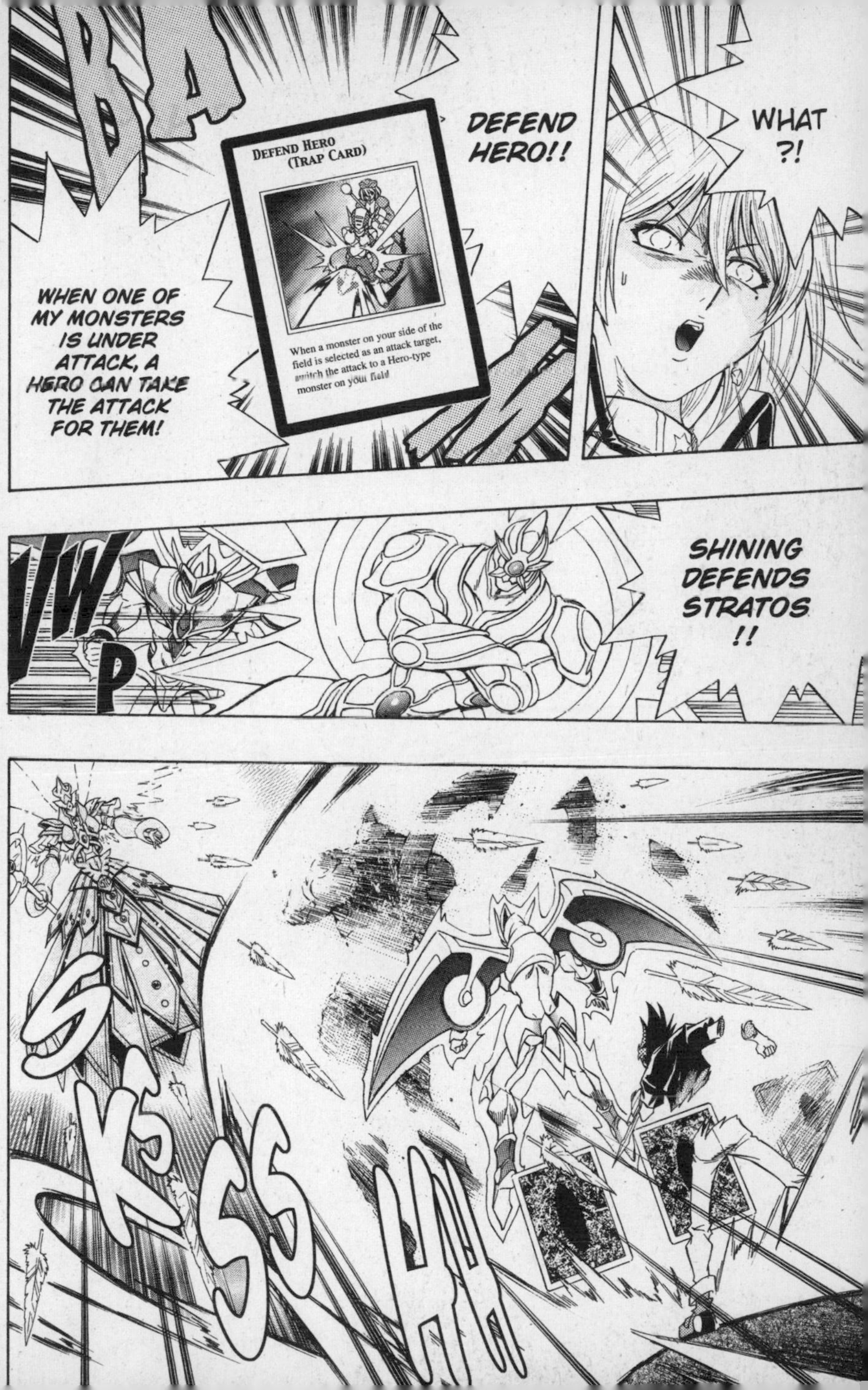
WHAT ?!
BA
DEFEND HERO!!
Defend Hero (Trap Card)
When a monster on your side of the field is selected as an attack target, switch the attack to a Hero-type monster on your field
WHEN ONE OF MY MONSTERS IS UNDER ATTACK, A HERO CAN TAKE THE ATTACK FOR THEM!
SHINING DEFENDS STRATOS !!

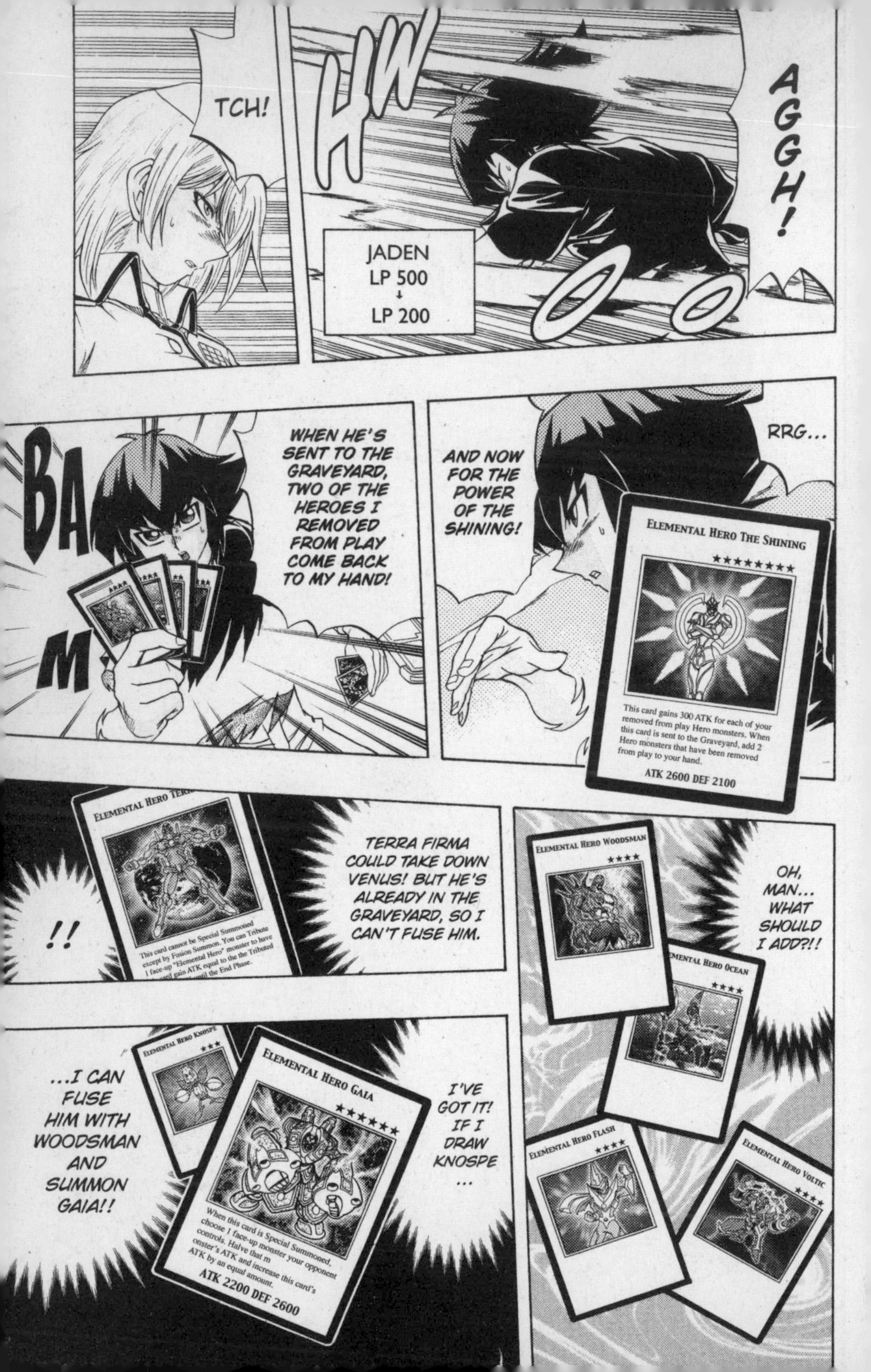
HWW
AGGH!
JADEN
LP 500
↓
LP 200
TCH!
RRG...
AND NOW FOR THE POWER OF THE SHINING!
ELEMENTAL HERO THE SHINING
This card gains 300 ATK for each of your removed from play Hero monsters. When this card is sent to the Graveyard, add 2 Hero monsters that have been removed from play to your hand.
ATK 2600 DEF 2100
WHEN HE'S SENT TO THE GRAVEYARD, TWO OF THE HEROES I REMOVED FROM PLAY COME BACK TO MY HAND!
BAM
ELEMENTAL HERO WOODSMAN
ELEMENTAL HERO OCEAN
ELEMENTAL HERO FLASH
ELEMENTAL HERO VOLTIC
OH, MAN... WHAT SHOULD I ADD?!!
TERRA FIRMA COULD TAKE DOWN VENUS! BUT HE'S ALREADY IN THE GRAVEYARD, SO I CAN'T FUSE HIM.
!!
This card cannot be Special Summoned except by Fusion Summon. You can Tribute 1 face-up "Elemental Hero" monster to have
ELEMENTAL HERO KNOSPE
I'VE GOT IT! IF I DRAW KNOSPE...
ELEMENTAL HERO GAIA
When this card is Special Summoned, choose 1 face-up monster your opponent controls. Halve that monster's ATK and increase this card's ATK by an equal amount.
ATK 2200 DEF 2600
...I CAN FUSE HIM WITH WOODSMAN AND SUMMON GAIA!!

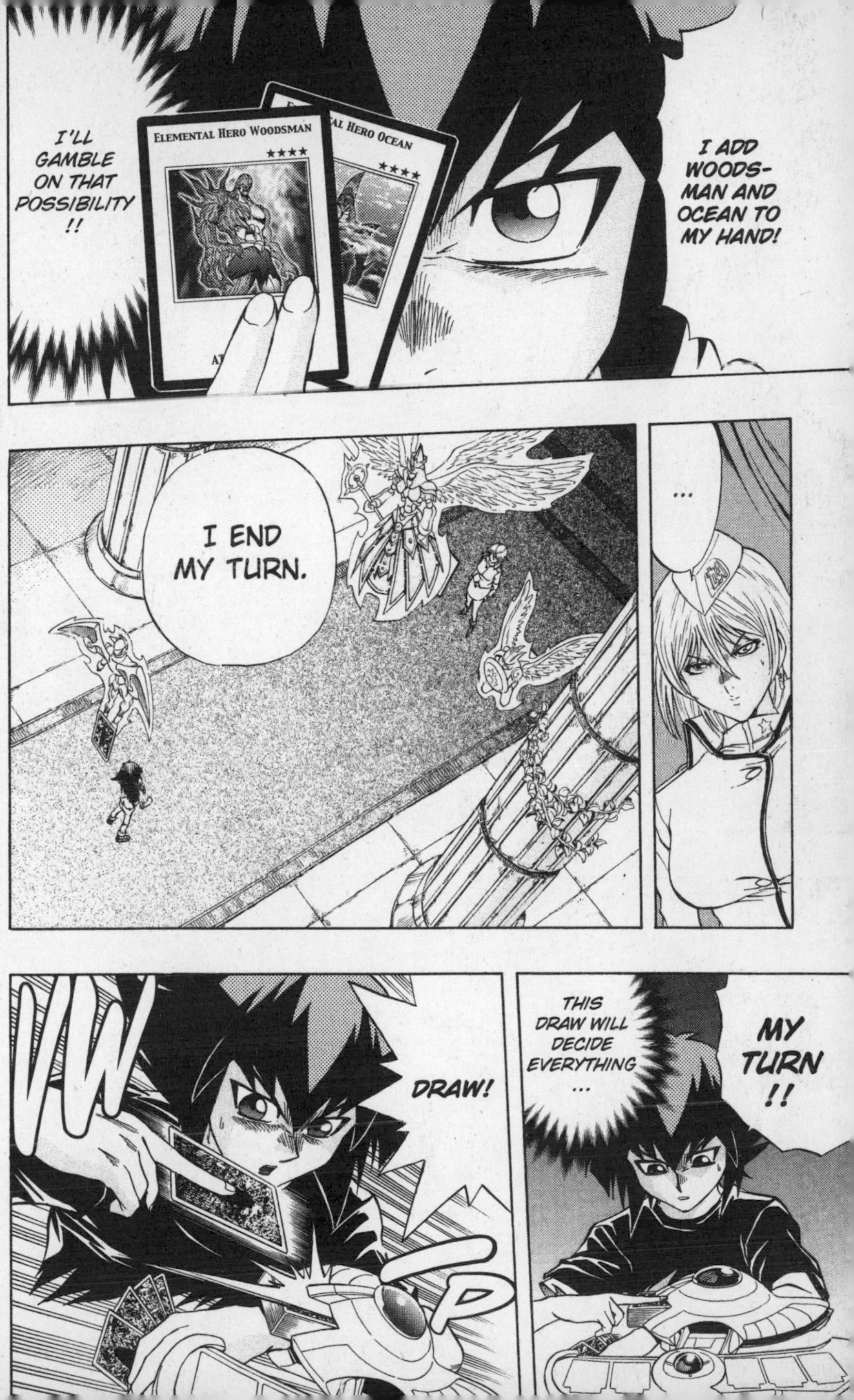
I ADD WOODS-MAN AND OCEAN TO MY HAND!
ELEMENTAL HERO WOODSMAN
I'LL GAMBLE ON THAT POSSIBILITY!!
...
I END MY TURN.
MY TURN!!
THIS DRAW WILL DECIDE EVERYTHING...
DRAW!

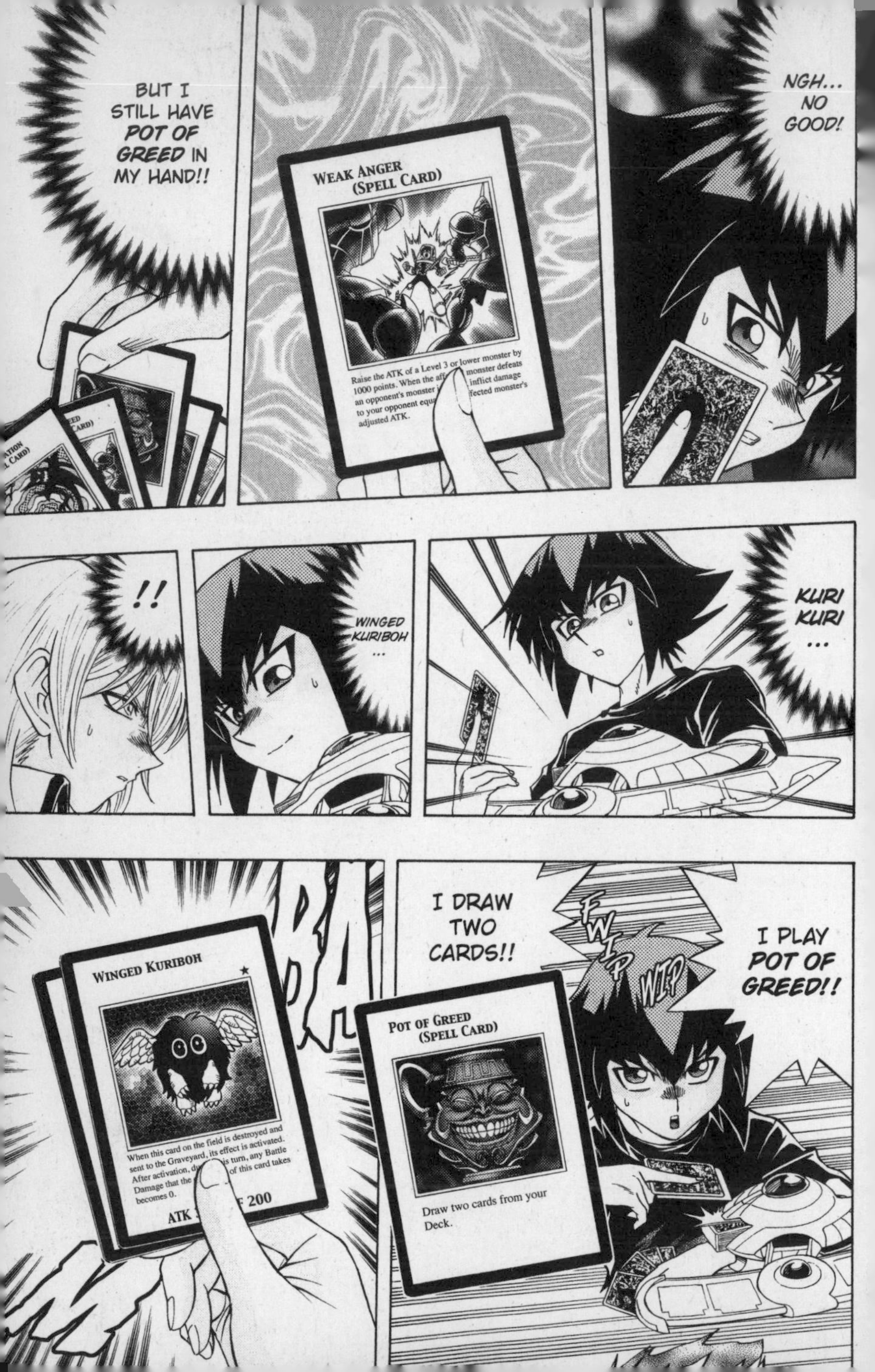
NGH... NO GOOD!
WEAK ANGER (SPELL CARD)
Raise the ATK of a Level 3 or lower monster by
1000 points. When the aff monster defeats
an opponent's monster i inflict damage
to your opponent equ ffected monster's
adjusted ATK.
BUT I STILL HAVE POT OF GREED IN MY HAND!!
KURI KURI ...
WINGED KURIBOH ...
!!
I PLAY POT OF GREED!!
FWIP
WIP
I DRAW TWO CARDS!!
POT OF GREED (SPELL CARD)
Draw two cards from your Deck.
WINGED KURIBOH
When this card on the field is destroyed and
sent to the Graveyard, its effect is activated.
After activation, du is turn, any Battle
Damage that the of this card takes
becomes 0.

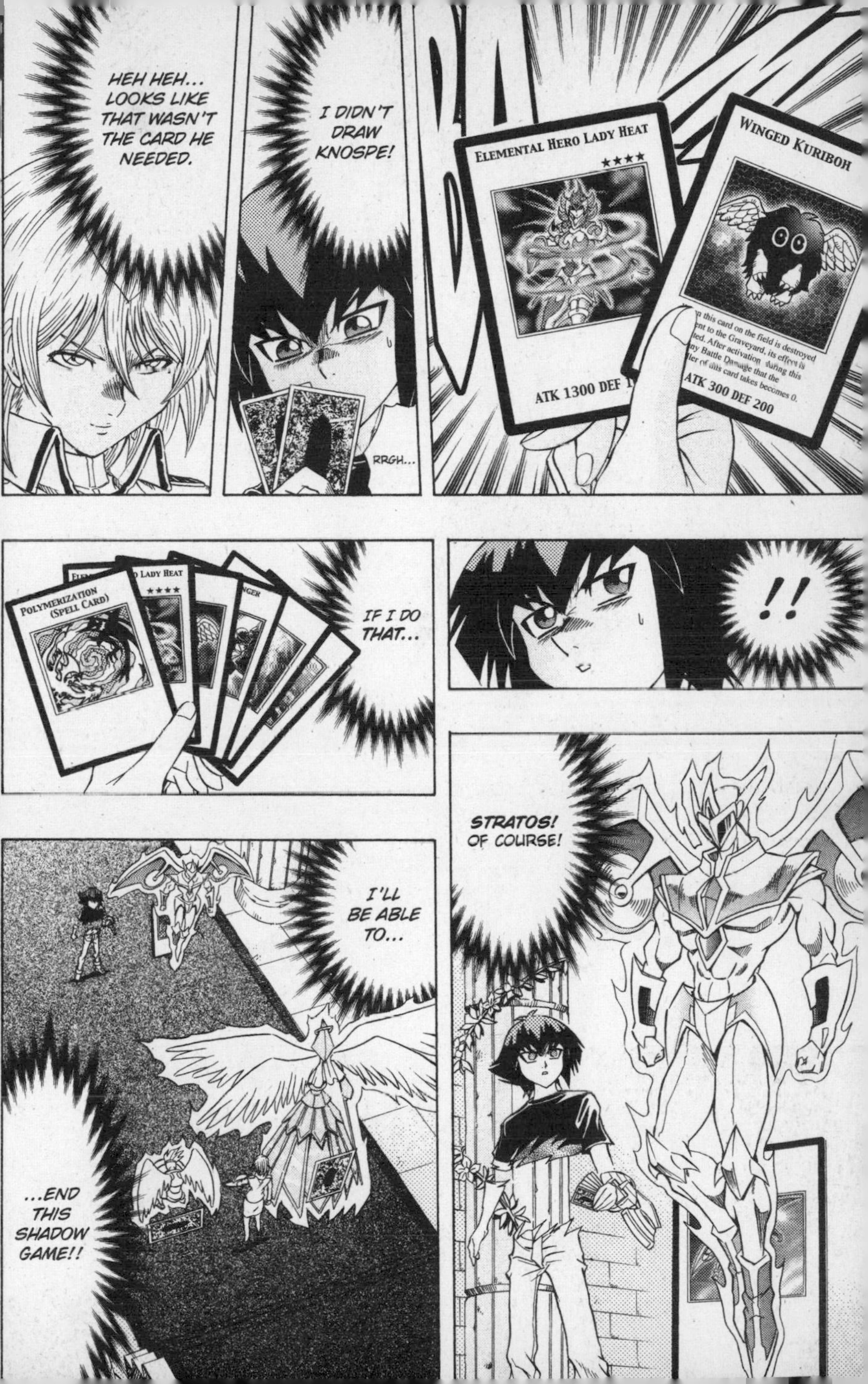

Elemental Hero Lady Heat
ATK 1300 DEF 1
Winged Kuriboh
ATK 300 DEF 200
I DIDN'T DRAW KNOSPE!
RRGH...
HEH HEH... LOOKS LIKE THAT WASN'T THE CARD HE NEEDED.
!!
Polymerization (Spell Card)
IF I DO THAT...
STRATOS! OF COURSE!
I'LL BE ABLE TO...
...END THIS SHADOW GAME!!

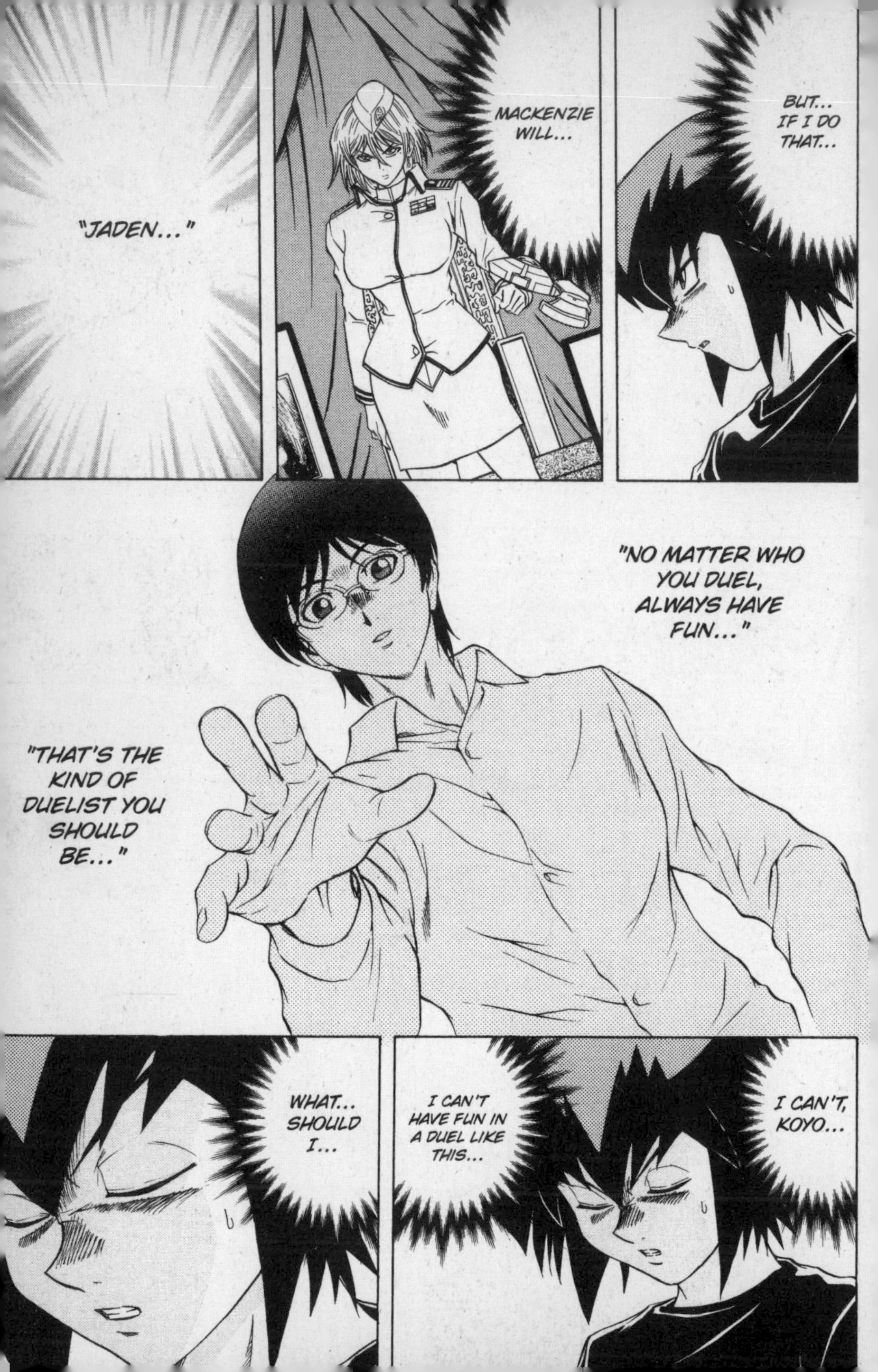
BUT... IF I DO THAT...
MACKENZIE WILL...
"JADEN..."
"NO MATTER WHO YOU DUEL, ALWAYS HAVE FUN..."
"THAT'S THE KIND OF DUELIST YOU SHOULD BE..."
I CAN'T, KOYO...
I CAN'T HAVE FUN IN A DUEL LIKE THIS...
WHAT... SHOULD I...

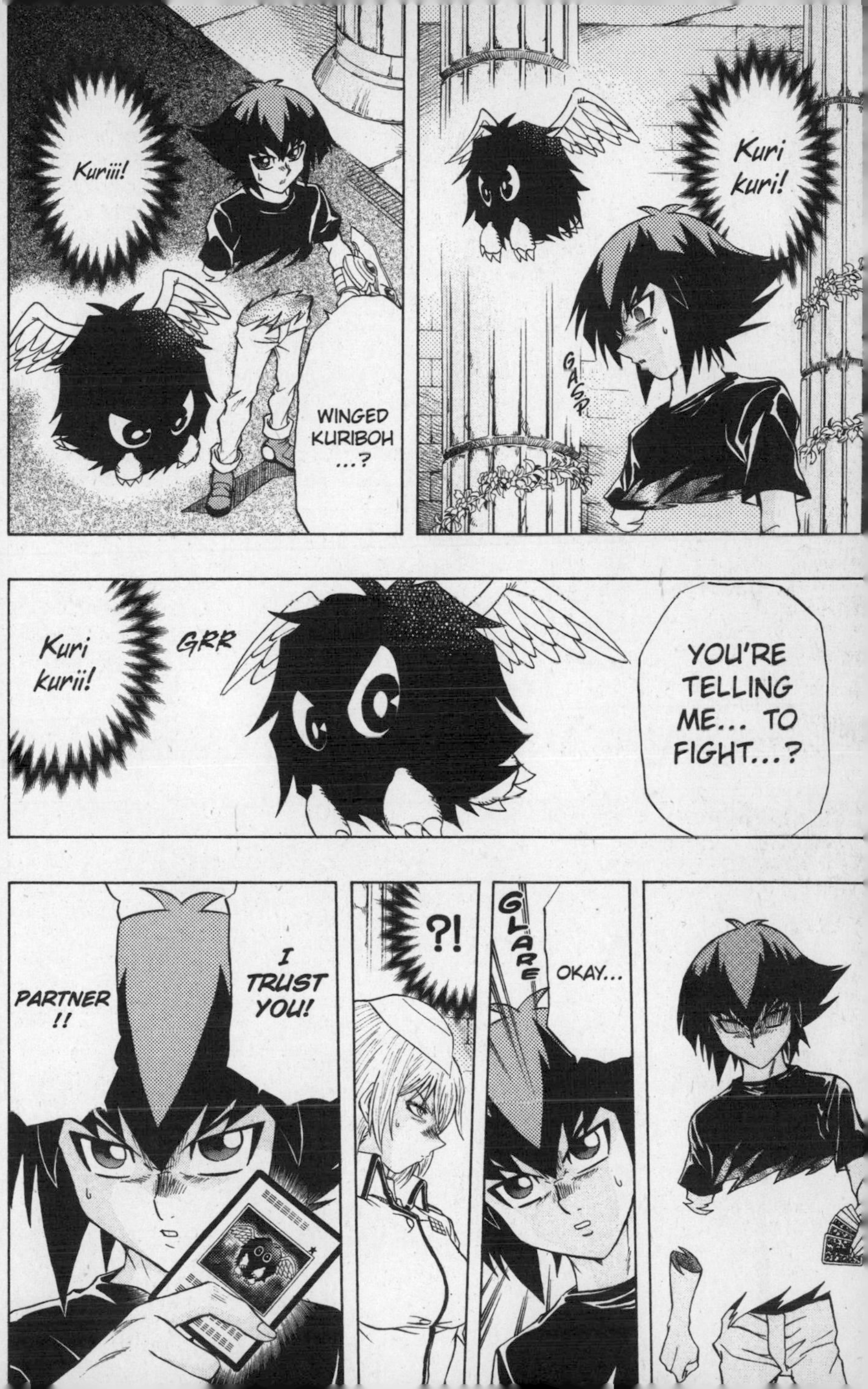
Kuri kuri!
GASP
Kuriii!
WINGED KURIBOH ...?
YOU'RE TELLING ME... TO FIGHT...?
GRR
Kuri kurii!
GLARE
OKAY...
?!
I TRUST YOU!
PARTNER !!

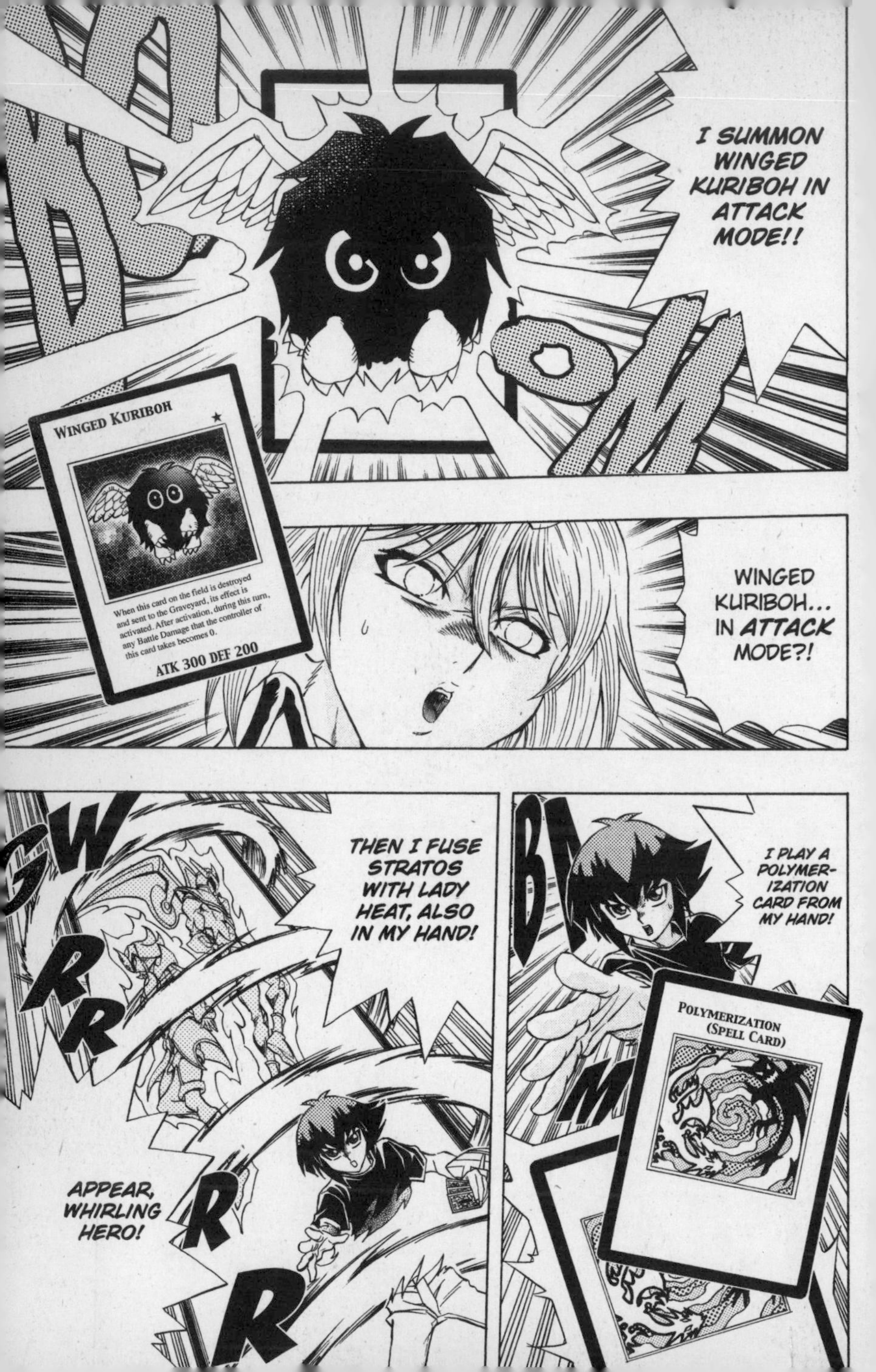
I SUMMON WINGED KURIBOH IN ATTACK MODE!!
WINGED KURIBOH
When this card on the field is destroyed and sent to the Graveyard, its effect is activated. After activation, during this turn, any Battle Damage that the controller of this card takes becomes 0.
ATK 300 DEF 200
WINGED KURIBOH... IN ATTACK MODE?!
I PLAY A POLYMERIZATION CARD FROM MY HAND!
POLYMERIZATION (SPELL CARD)
THEN I FUSE STRATOS WITH LADY HEAT, ALSO IN MY HAND!
APPEAR, WHIRLING HERO!

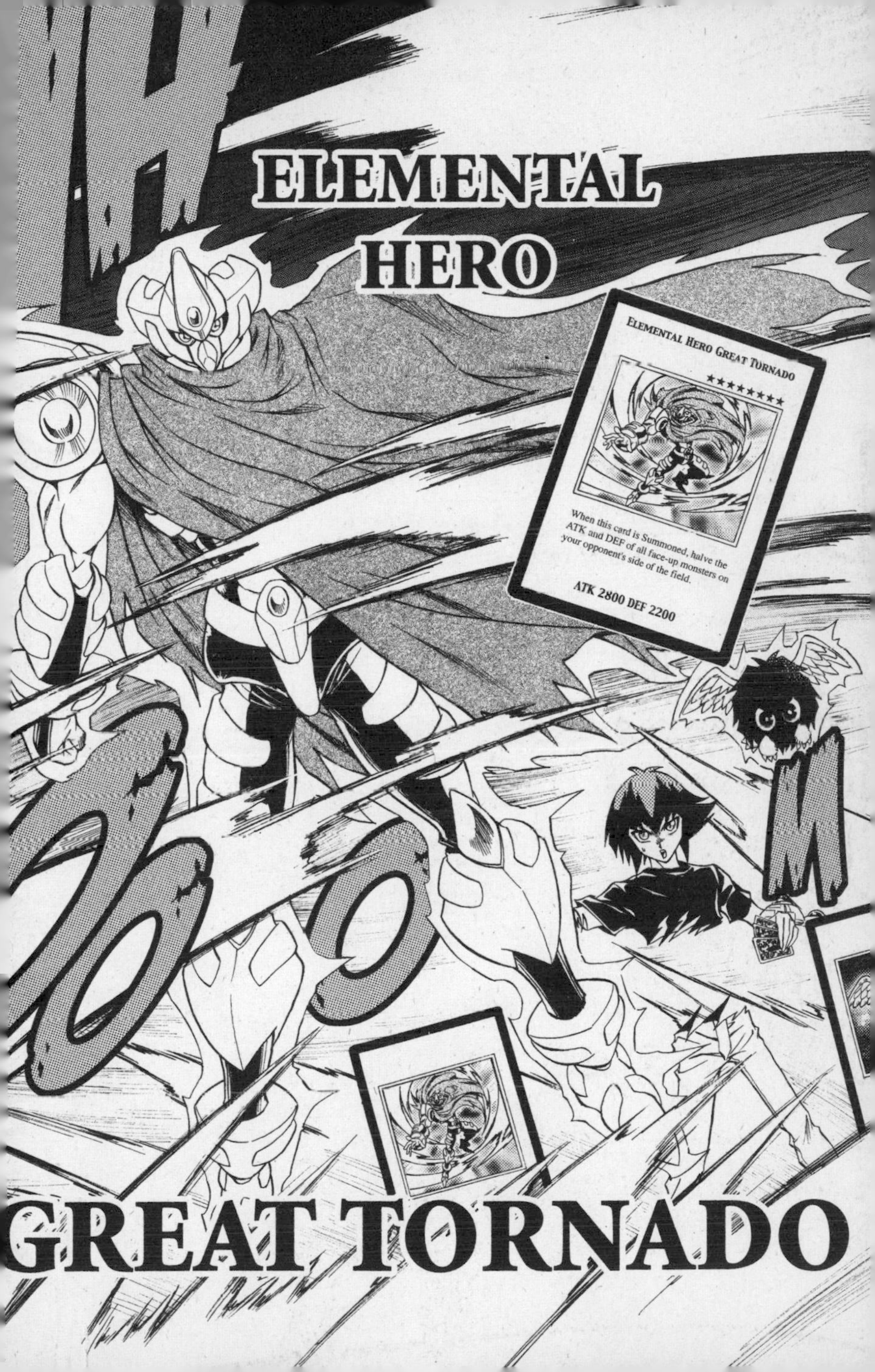
ELEMENTAL HERO
ELEMENTAL HERO GREAT TORNADO
When this card is Summoned, halve the ATK and DEF of all face-up monsters on your opponent's side of the field.
ATK 2800 DEF 2200
GREAT TORNADO

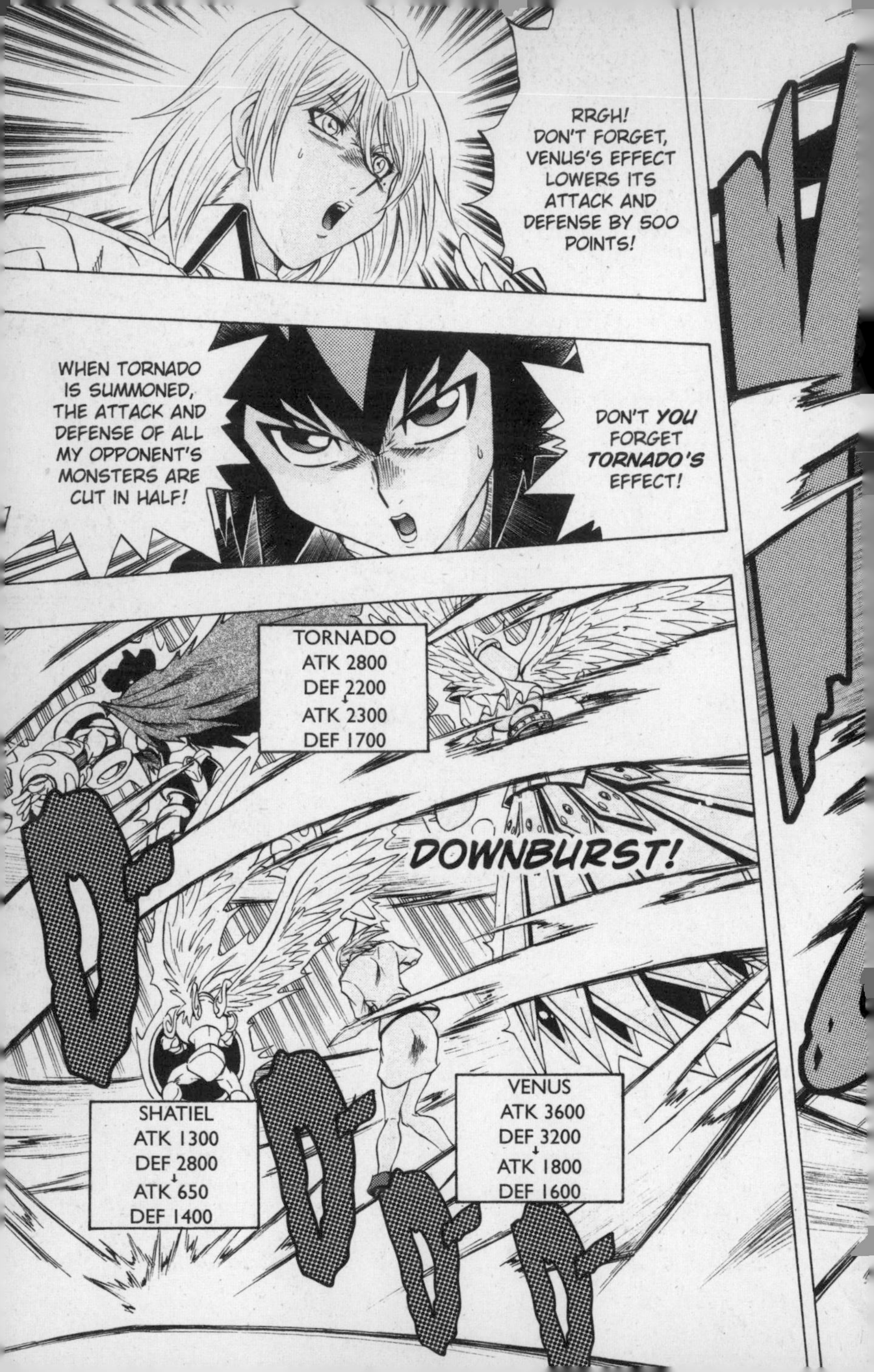
RRGH! DON'T FORGET, VENUS'S EFFECT LOWERS ITS ATTACK AND DEFENSE BY 500 POINTS!
DON'T YOU FORGET TORNADO'S EFFECT!
WHEN TORNADO IS SUMMONED, THE ATTACK AND DEFENSE OF ALL MY OPPONENT'S MONSTERS ARE CUT IN HALF!
TORNADO ATK 2800 DEF 2200 ↓ ATK 2300 DEF 1700
DOWNBURST!
VENUS ATK 3600 DEF 3200 ↓ ATK 1800 DEF 1600
SHATIEL ATK 1300 DEF 2800 ↓ ATK 650 DEF 1400

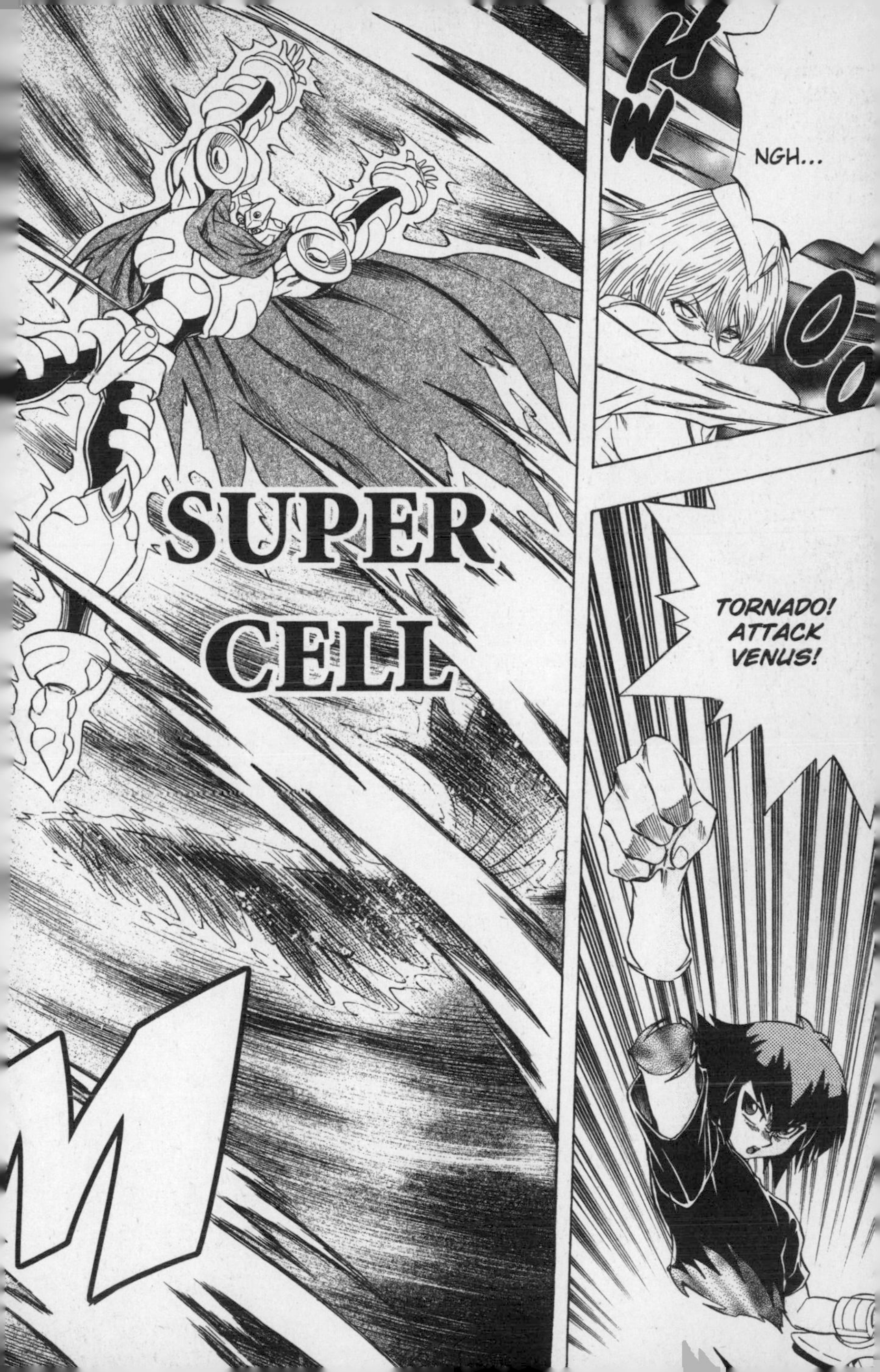
NGH...
TORNADO! ATTACK VENUS!
SUPER CELL

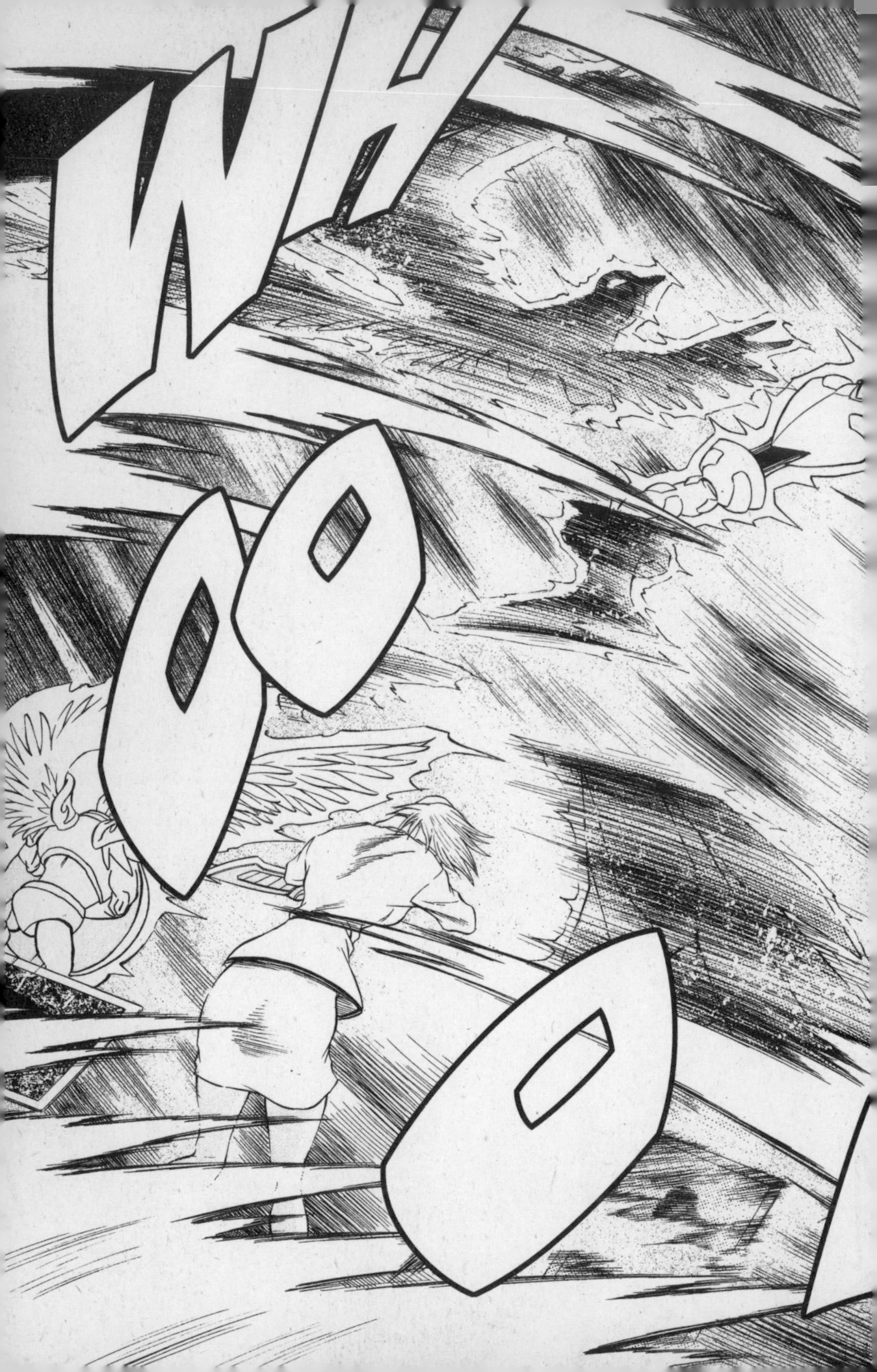
WHOOO

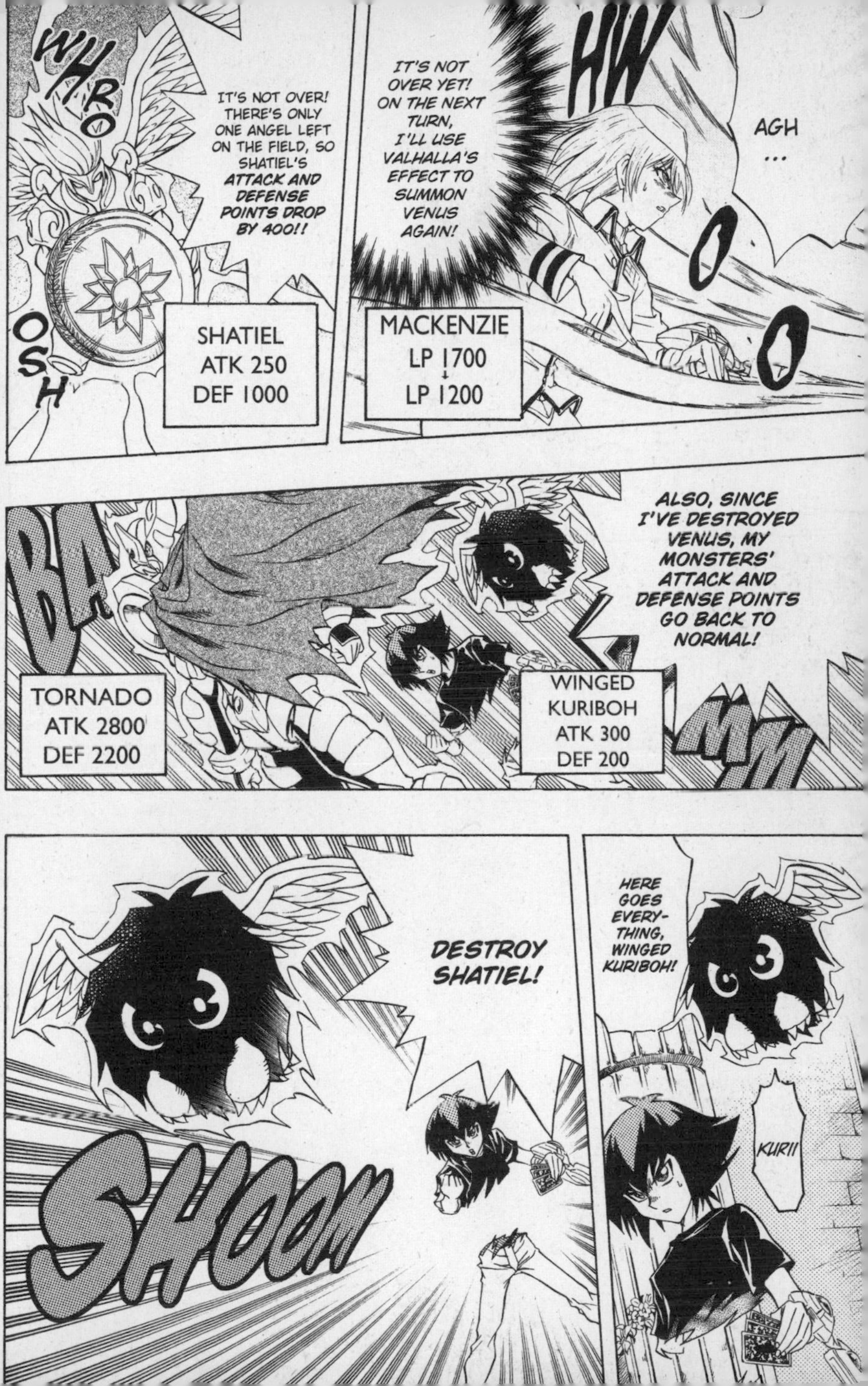
HWOOO
AGH...
IT'S NOT OVER YET! ON THE NEXT TURN, I'LL USE VALHALLA'S EFFECT TO SUMMON VENUS AGAIN!
MACKENZIE
LP 1700
LP 1200
WHROOSH
IT'S NOT OVER! THERE'S ONLY ONE ANGEL LEFT ON THE FIELD, SO SHATIEL'S ATTACK AND DEFENSE POINTS DROP BY 400!!
SHATIEL
ATK 250
DEF 1000
ALSO, SINCE I'VE DESTROYED VENUS, MY MONSTERS' ATTACK AND DEFENSE POINTS GO BACK TO NORMAL!
MM
WINGED KURIBOH
ATK 300
DEF 200
BA
TORNADO
ATK 2800
DEF 2200
HERE GOES EVERY-THING, WINGED KURIBOH!
KURII
DESTROY SHATIEL!
SHOOM

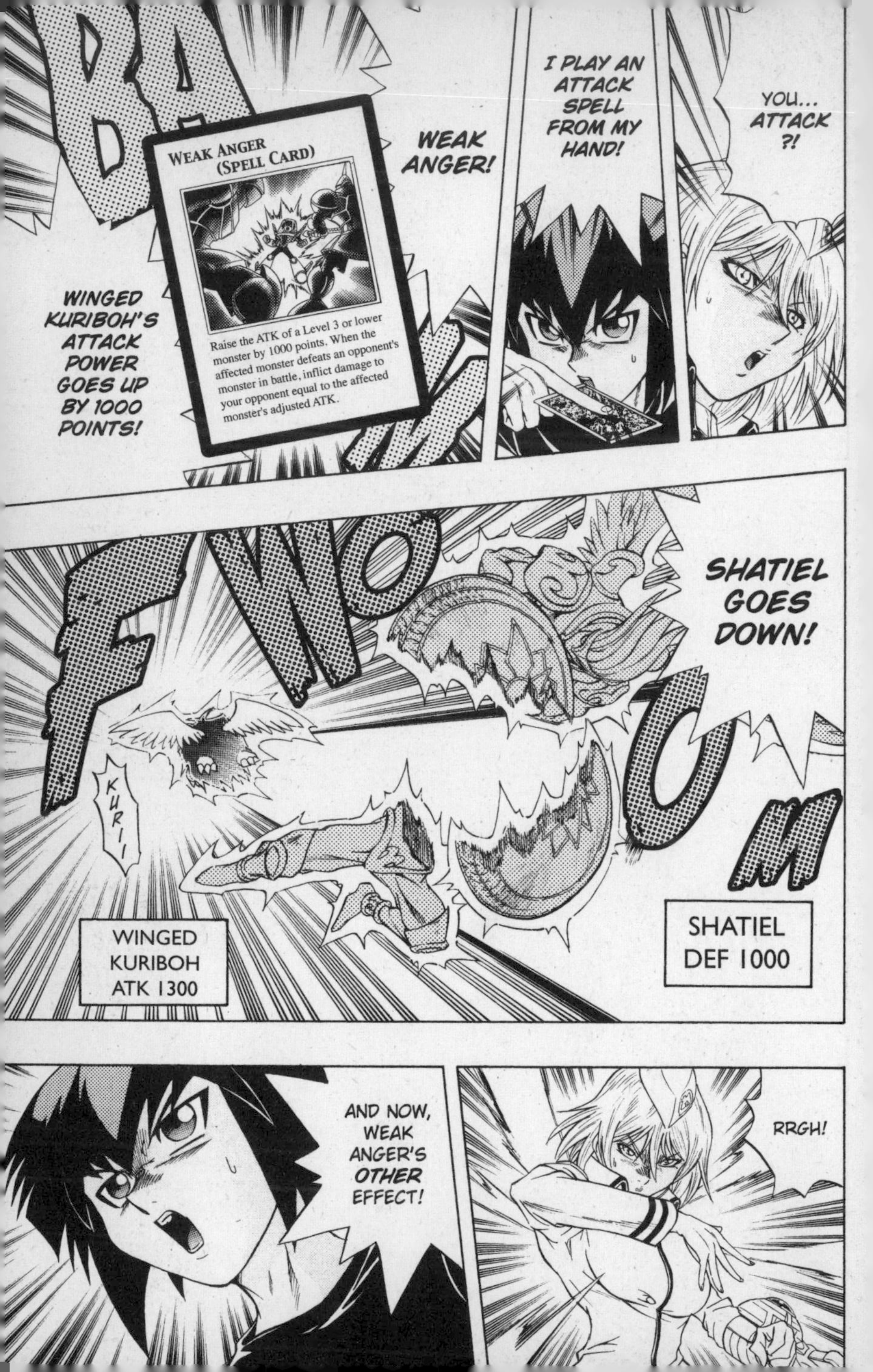
YOU... ATTACK ?!
I PLAY AN ATTACK SPELL FROM MY HAND!
WEAK ANGER!
WEAK ANGER (SPELL CARD)
Raise the ATK of a Level 3 or lower monster by 1000 points. When the affected monster defeats an opponent's monster in battle, inflict damage to your opponent equal to the affected monster's adjusted ATK.
WINGED KURIBOH'S ATTACK POWER GOES UP BY 1000 POINTS!
SHATIEL GOES DOWN!
FWOOM
SHATIEL DEF 1000
KURIII
WINGED KURIBOH ATK 1300
RRGH!
AND NOW, WEAK ANGER'S OTHER EFFECT!

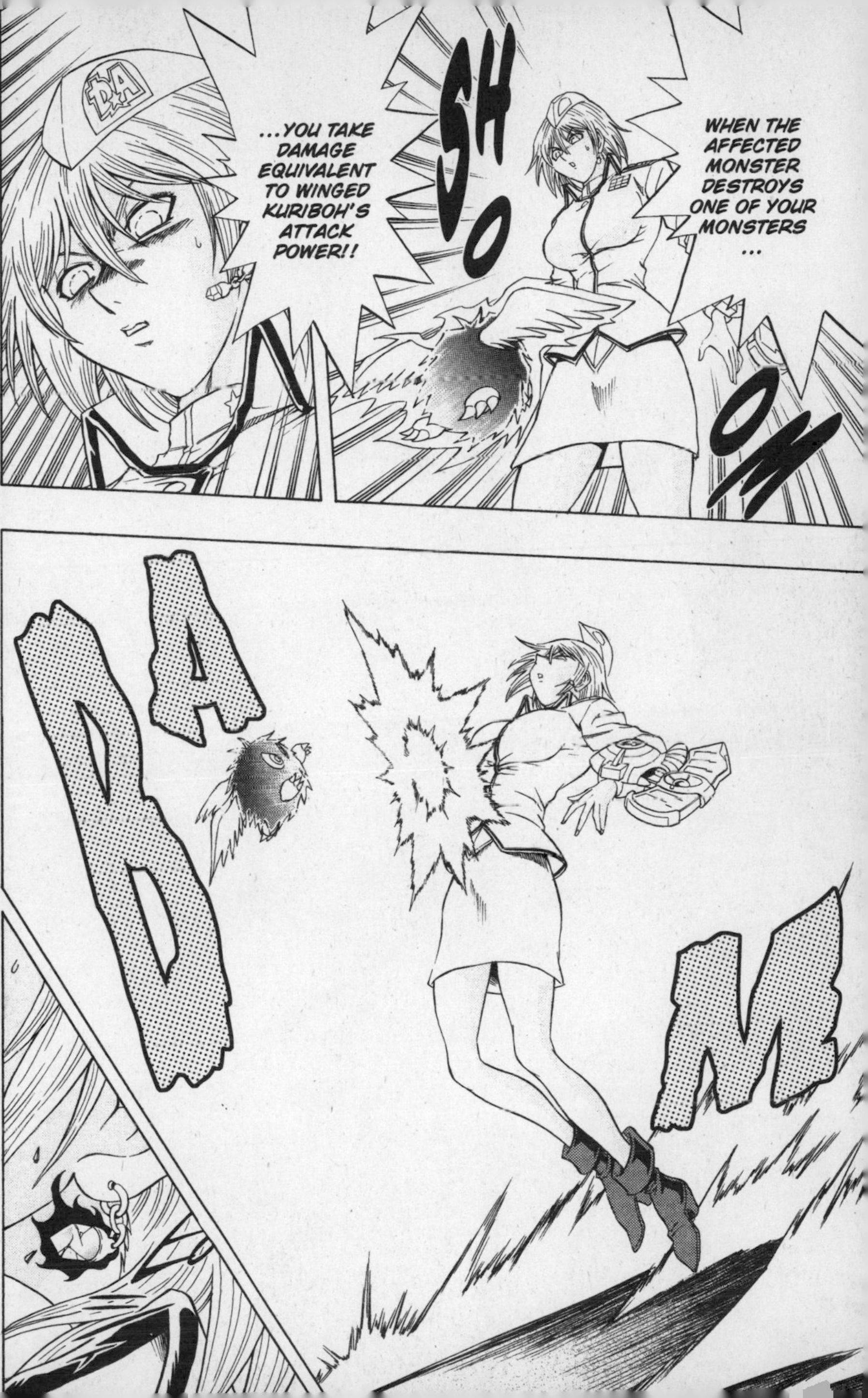
WHEN THE AFFECTED MONSTER DESTROYS ONE OF YOUR MONSTERS ...
SHOOM
...YOU TAKE DAMAGE EQUIVALENT TO WINGED KURIBOH'S ATTACK POWER!!
BAM

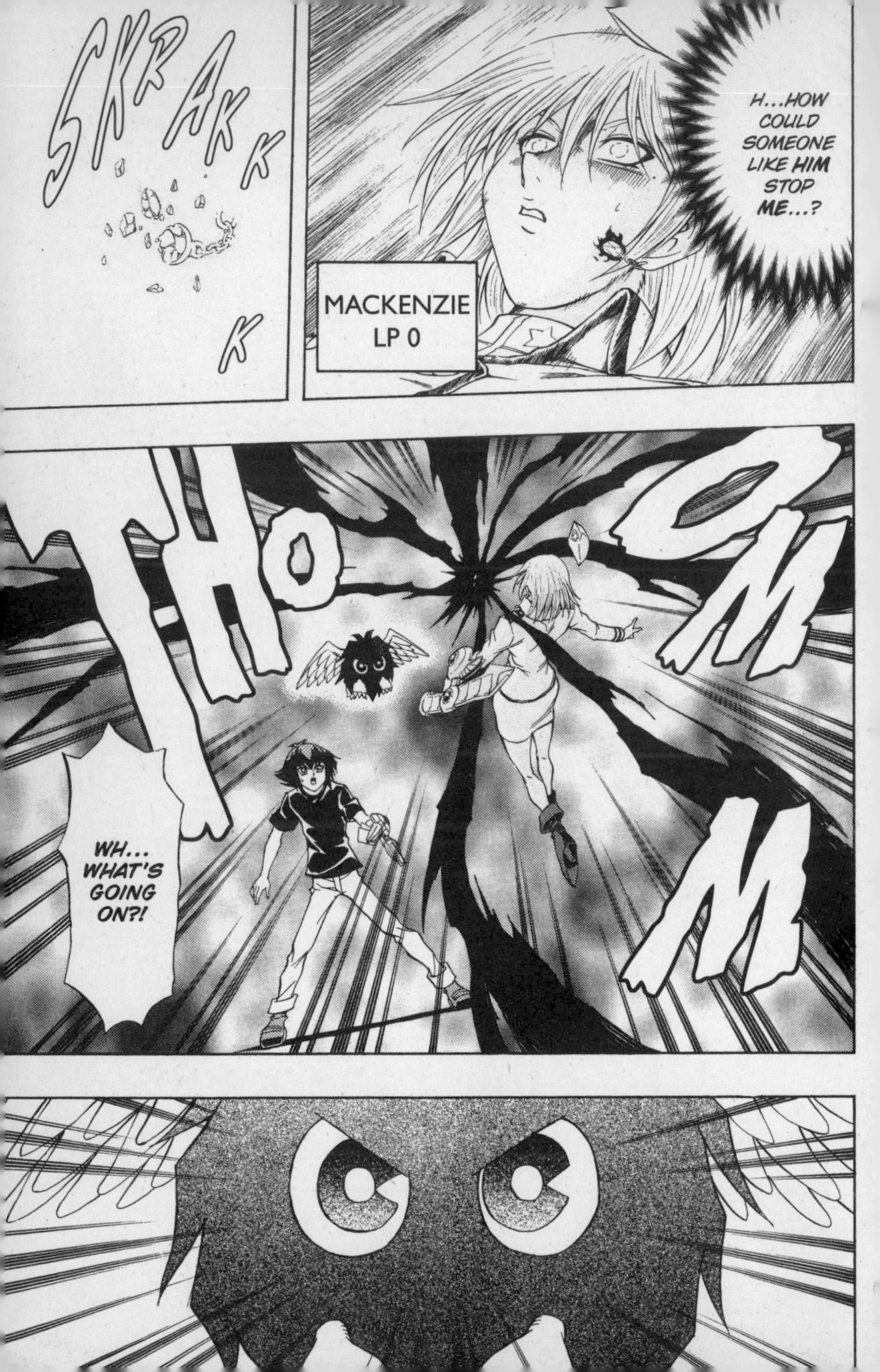
H...HOW COULD SOMEONE LIKE HIM STOP ME...?
MACKENZIE
LP 0
SKRAKKK
WH... WHAT'S GOING ON?!

V JUMP CARD FEST '09
AUGUST 29, 2009 MAKUHARI MESSE
MURMUR MURMUR MURMUR
WOW...
I GOT THERE BEFORE THE HALL OPENED... BUT THE LINE WAS ALREADY ENORMOUS.
I'M AMAZED EVERY YEAR!
ONCE THE DOORS OPENED, YOU COULD DUEL THE "CHARISMATIC" DUELISTS AT THE FREE DUEL BOOTH, AND THERE WAS A HUGE CROWD AROUND THEM, TOO...
CHAT-T-ER CHATT-ER
THAT'S KAISER KAIBA FOR YOU. A NATIONAL FOLLOWING...
THE "CHARISMATICS" DUELED FROM MORNING UNTIL AFTER LUNCH! YEEK!
I MEANDERED AROUND THE HALL, AND THEN IN A WAITING ROOM...
...DREW JADEN'S SIGNATURES TO DECORATE THE V-JUMP BOOTH.
WITH NO ROUGH SKETCHES! AND YEAH, THE BALANCE WAS A LITTLE...
OH, MR. KAGEYAMA, MS. ISHIZUKA WILL BE BY LATER!
HUH? SHE WILL!? I'LL HAVE TO GO SAY HI.
← Mr. Saito
SHE CAME!

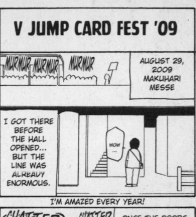

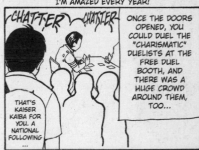

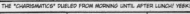

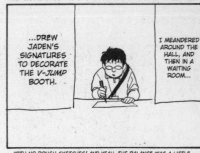

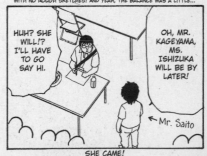

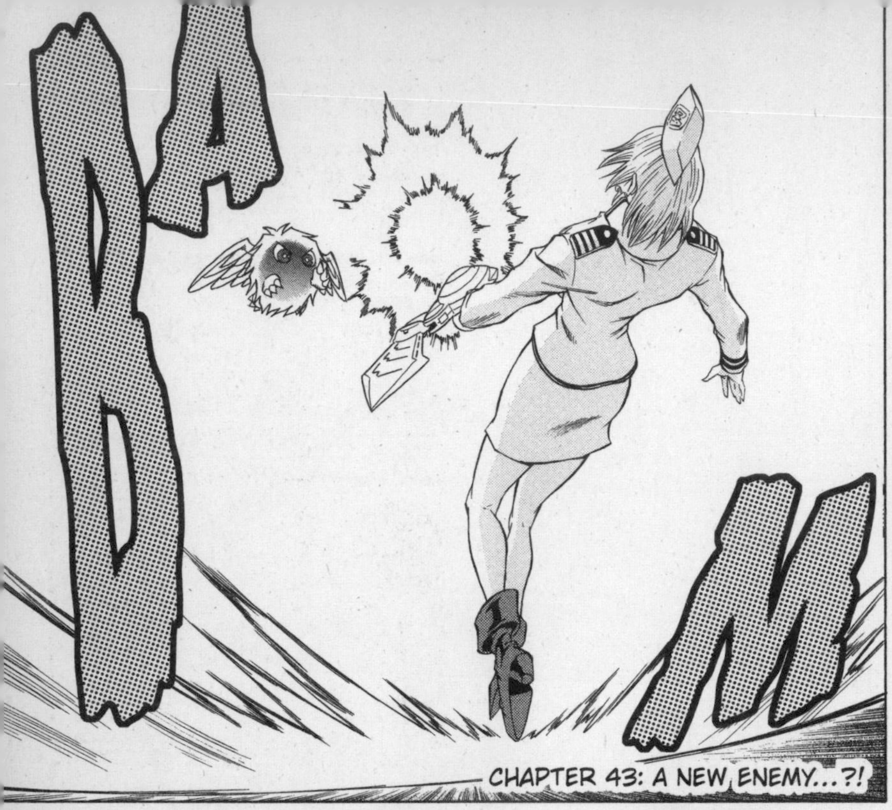
BAM
CHAPTER 43: A NEW ENEMY...?!

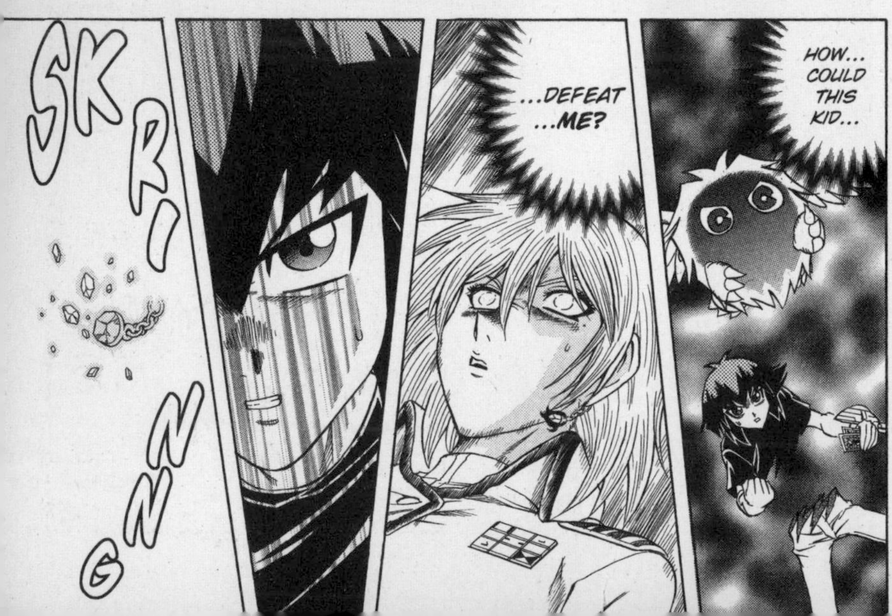
HOW... COULD THIS KID...
...DEFEAT ...ME?
SKRINNG

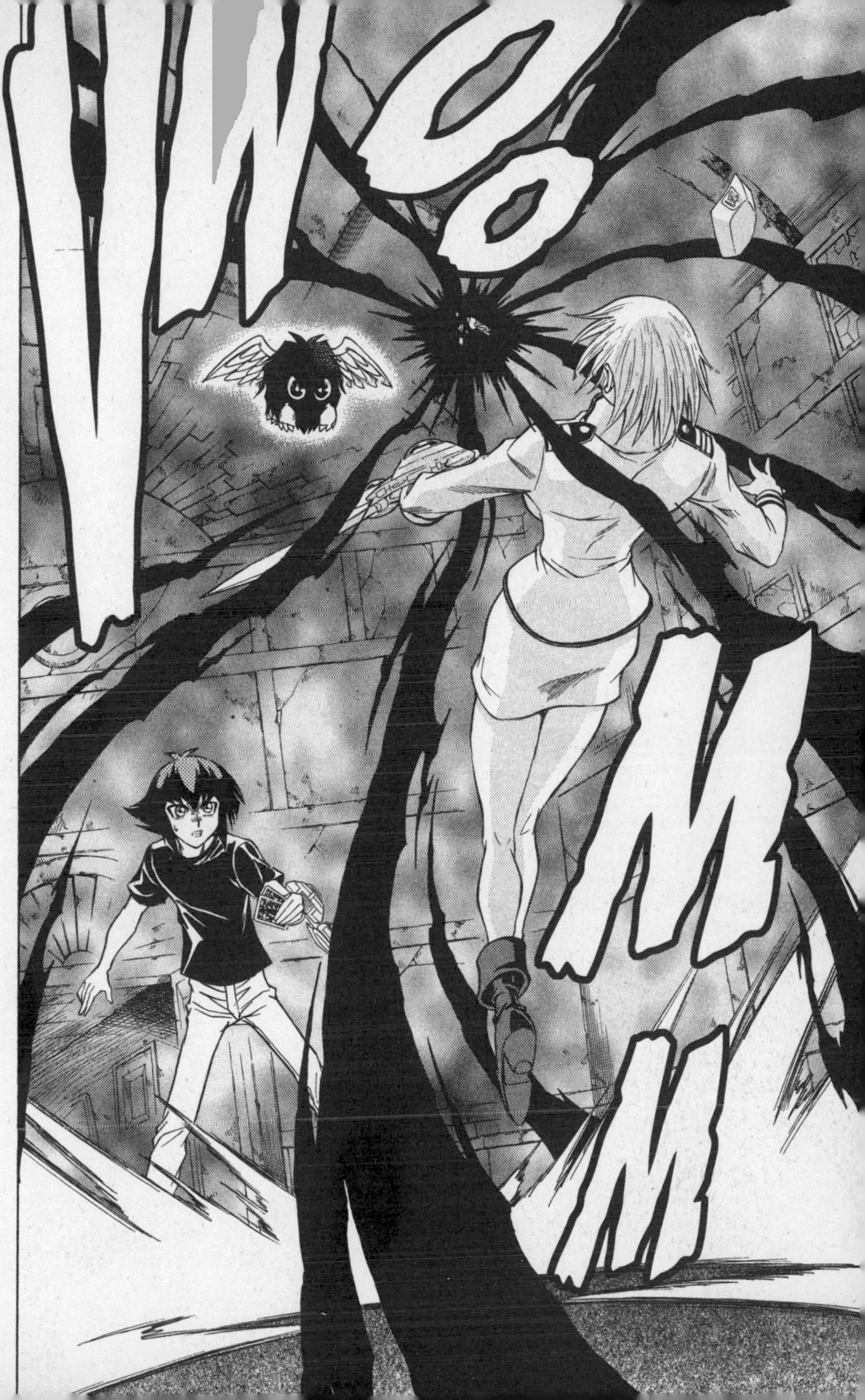

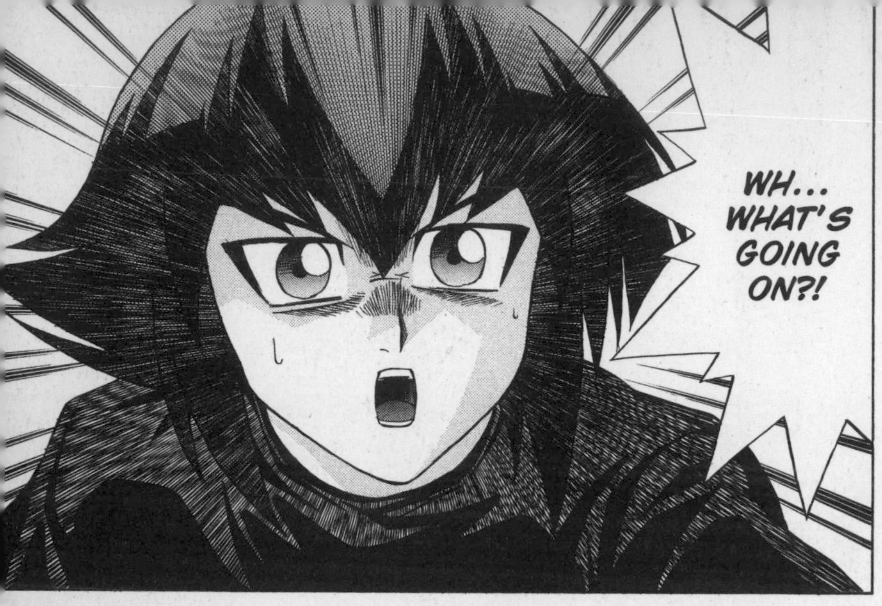
WH... WHAT'S GOING ON?!

# CHAPTER 43: A NEW ENEMY...?!

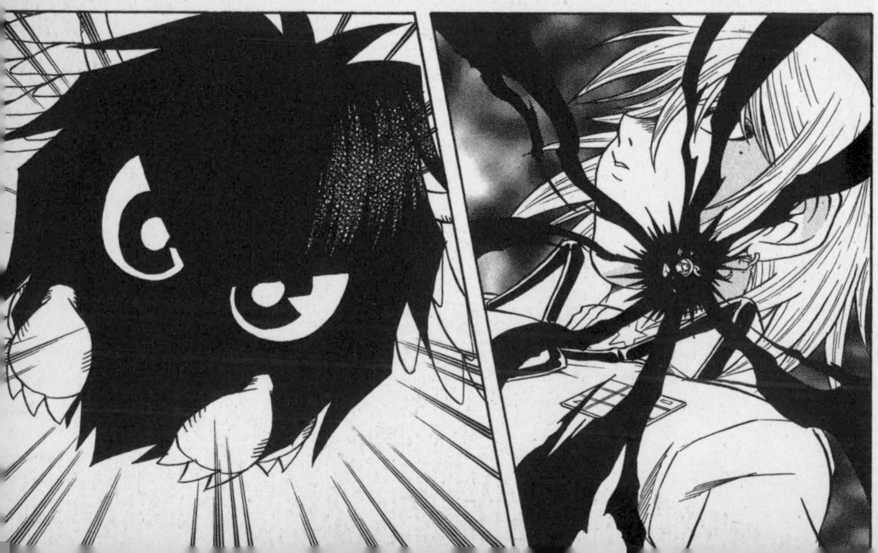

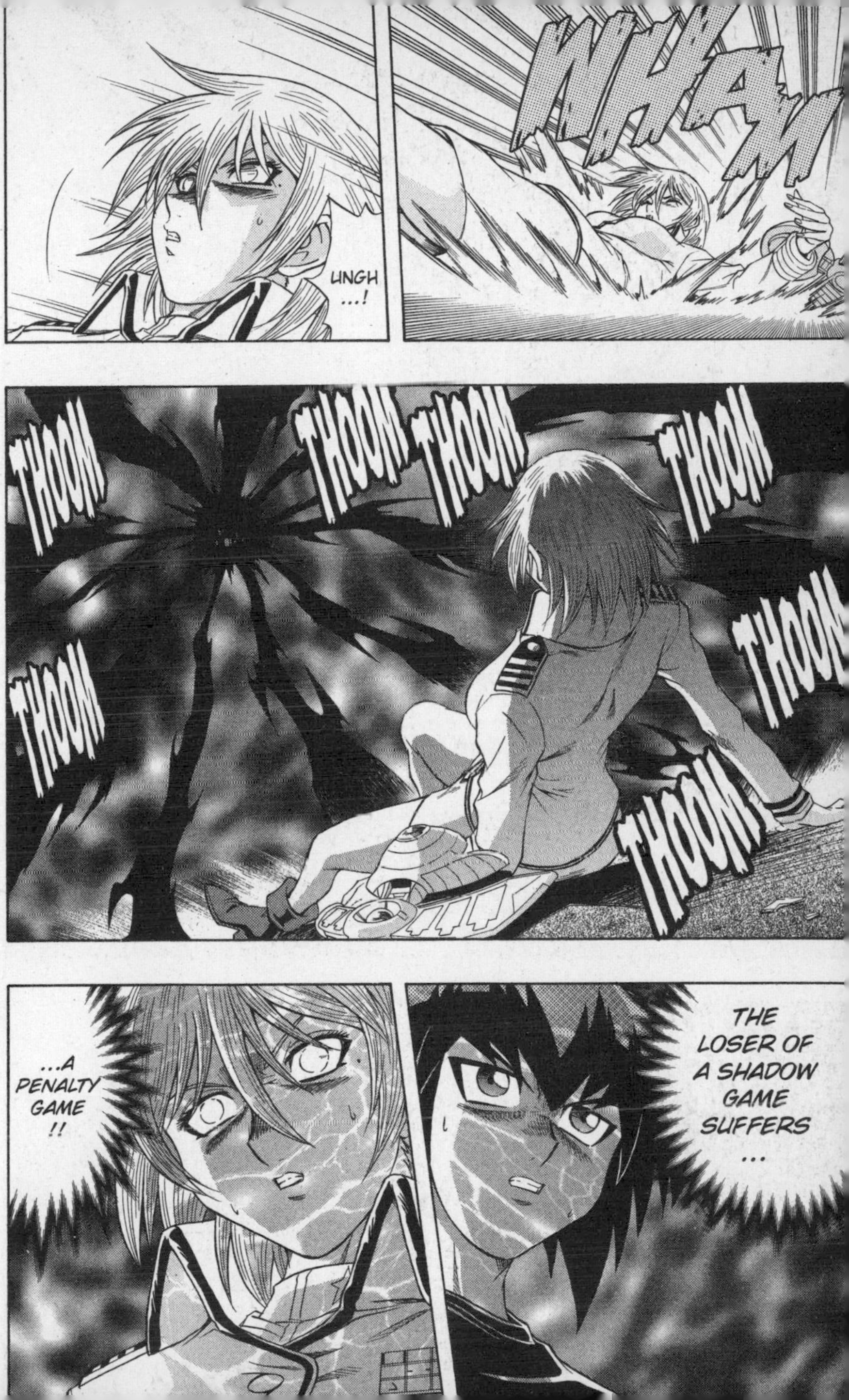
WHAM
UNGH ...!
THOOM
THOOM
THOOM
THOOM
THOOM
THOOM
THOOM
THOOM
THE LOSER OF A SHADOW GAME SUFFERS ...
...A PENALTY GAME !!

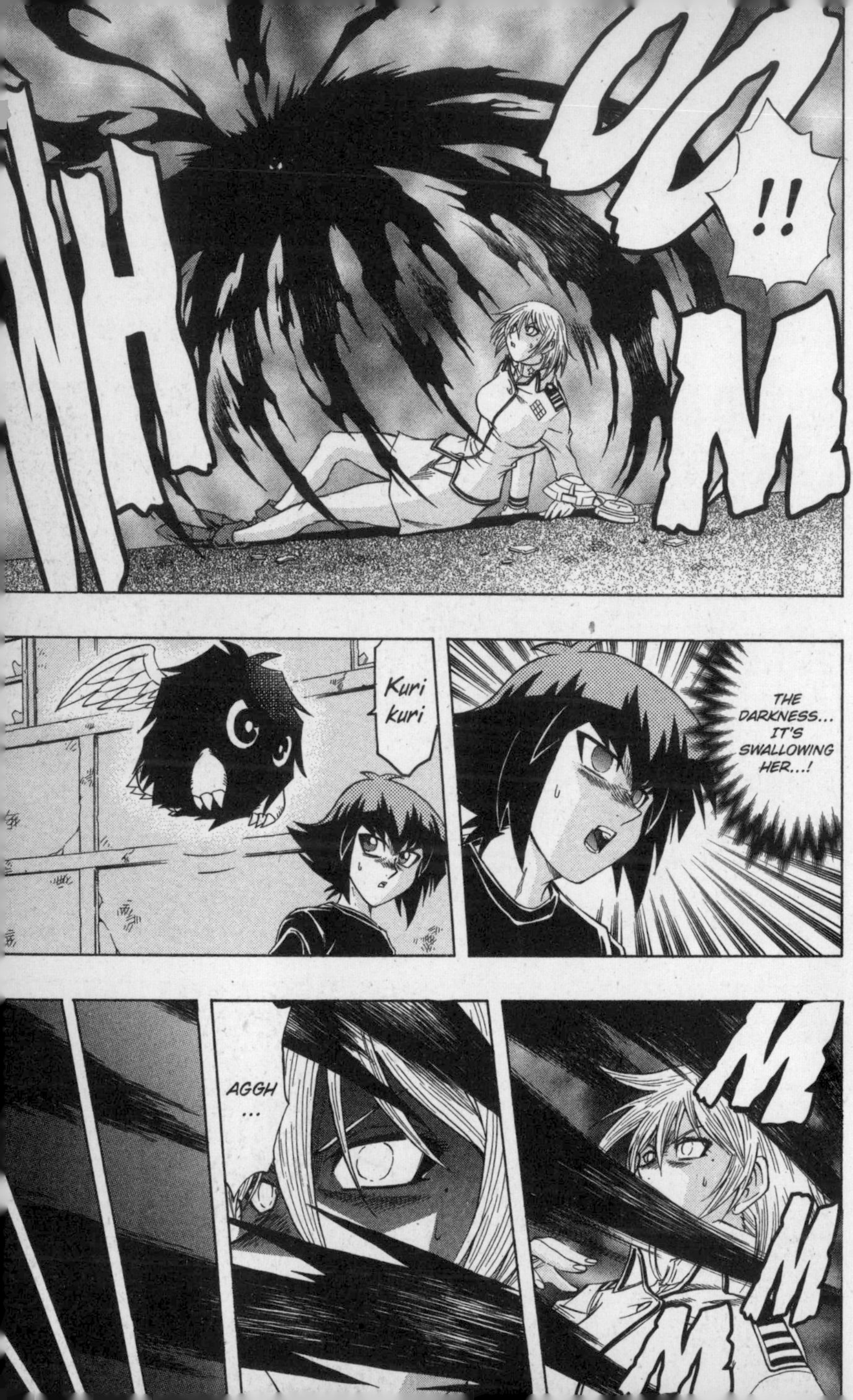
!!
THE DARKNESS... IT'S SWALLOWING HER...!
Kuri kuri
AGGH
...

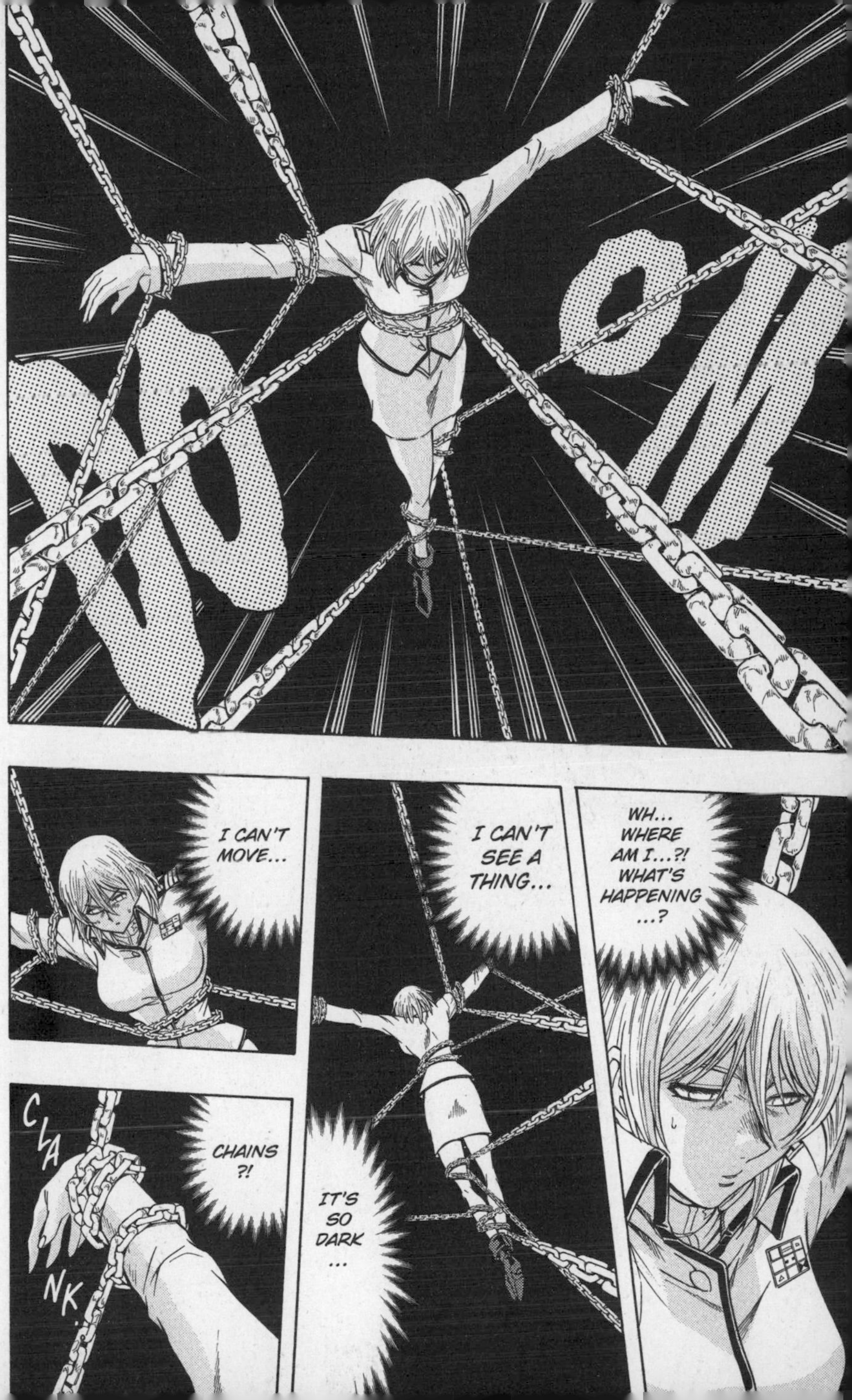
DOOM
WH... WHERE AM I...?! WHAT'S HAPPENING ...?
I CAN'T SEE A THING...
IT'S SO DARK ...
I CAN'T MOVE...
CHAINS ?!
CLANK.

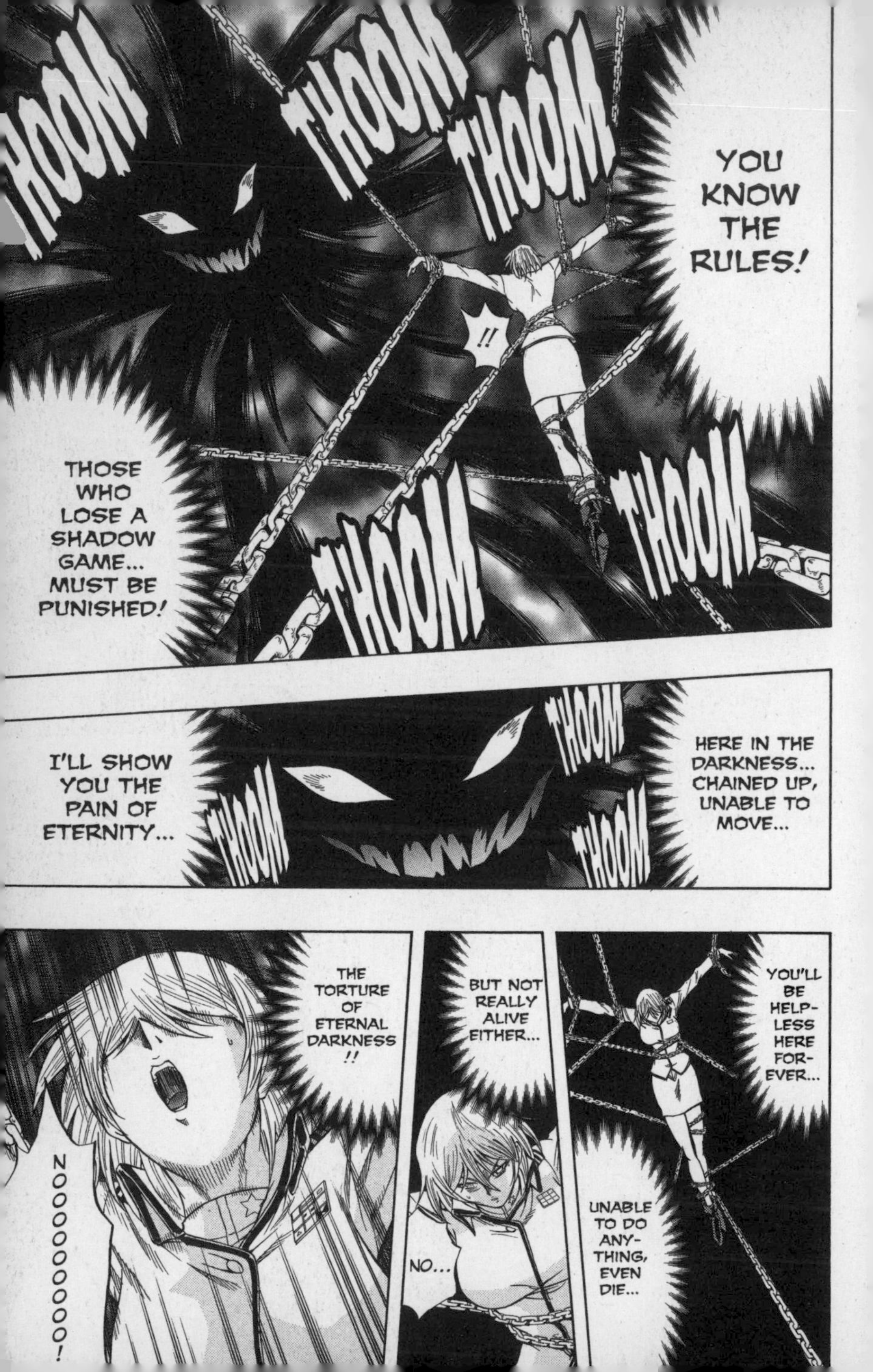
THOOM
THOOM
THOOM
YOU KNOW THE RULES!
!!
THOOM
THOOM
THOSE WHO LOSE A SHADOW GAME... MUST BE PUNISHED!
HERE IN THE DARKNESS... CHAINED UP, UNABLE TO MOVE...
THOOM
THOOM
THOOM
I'LL SHOW YOU THE PAIN OF ETERNITY...
YOU'LL BE HELP-LESS HERE FOR-EVER...
UNABLE TO DO ANY-THING, EVEN DIE...
BUT NOT REALLY ALIVE EITHER...
NO...
THE TORTURE OF ETERNAL DARKNESS !!
NOOOOOOOOOO!

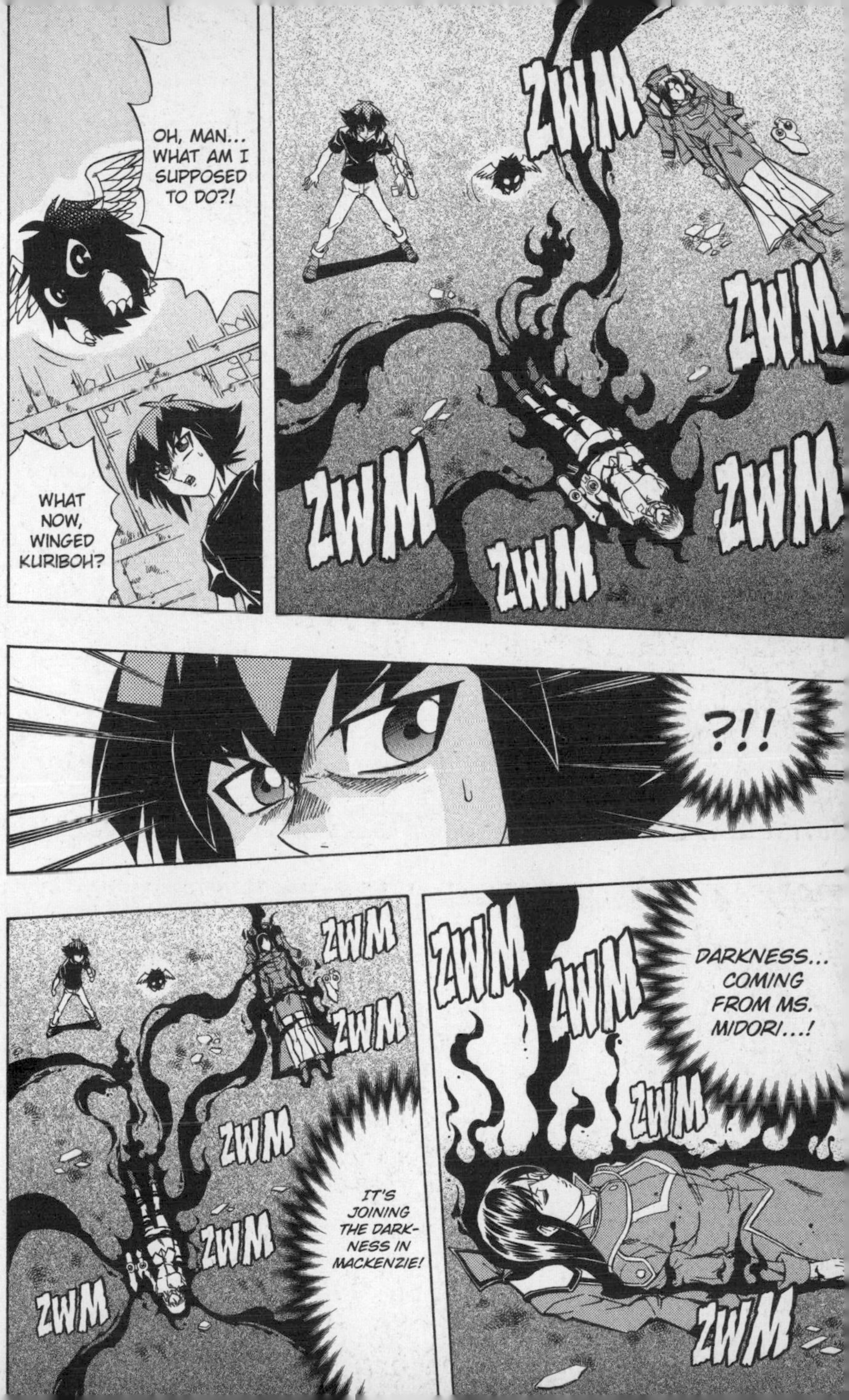
ZWM
ZWM
ZWM
ZWM
ZWM
OH, MAN... WHAT AM I SUPPOSED TO DO?!
WHAT NOW, WINGED KURIBOH?
?!!
DARKNESS... COMING FROM MS. MIDORI...!
ZWM
ZWM
ZWM
ZWM
ZWM
ZWM
ZWM
IT'S JOINING THE DARK-NESS IN MACKENZIE!
ZWM
ZWM

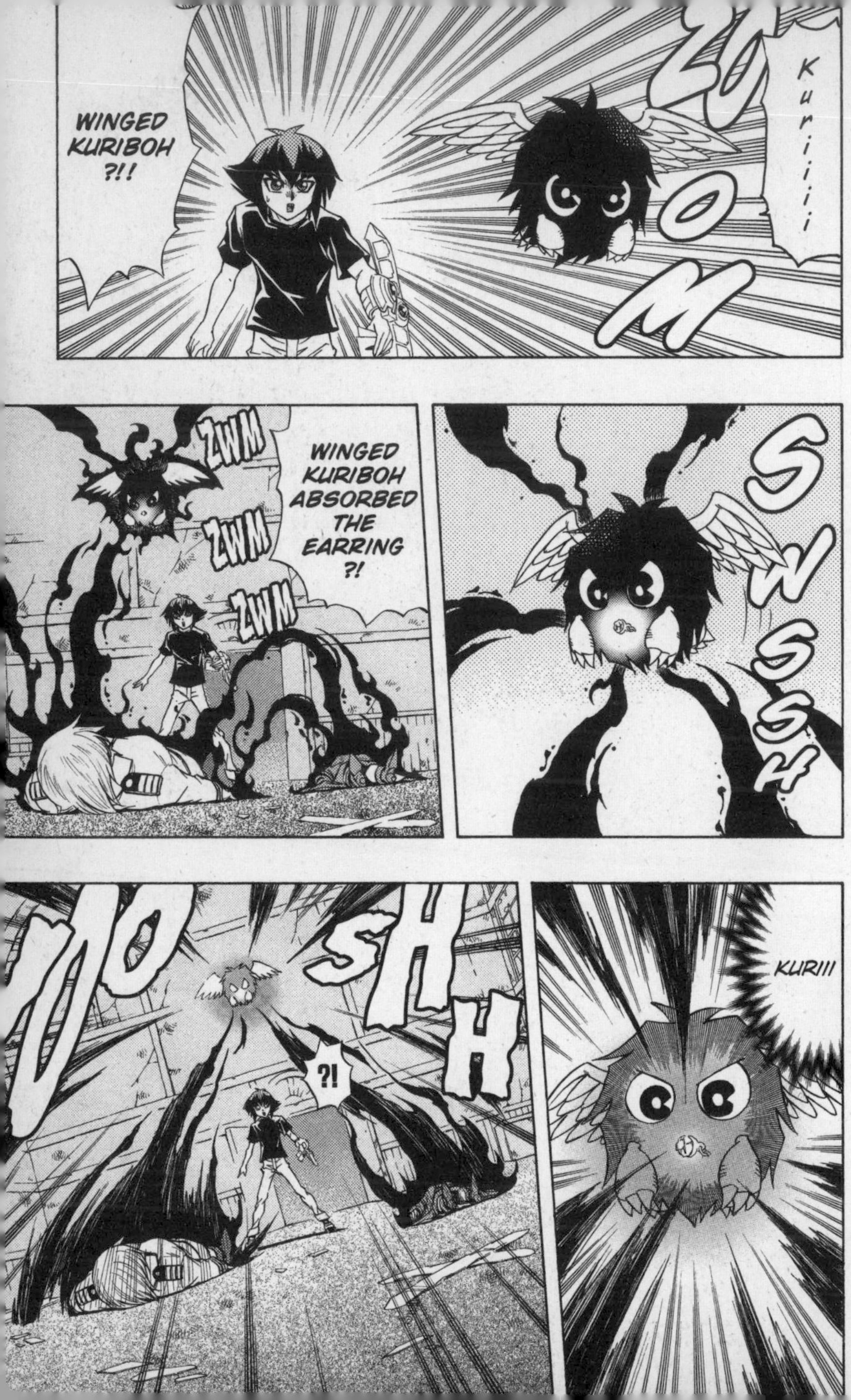

Kuriiiii
ZOOM
WINGED KURIBOH ?!!
SWSSH
WINGED KURIBOH ABSORBED THE EARRING ?!
ZWM
ZWM
ZWM
KURIII
?!

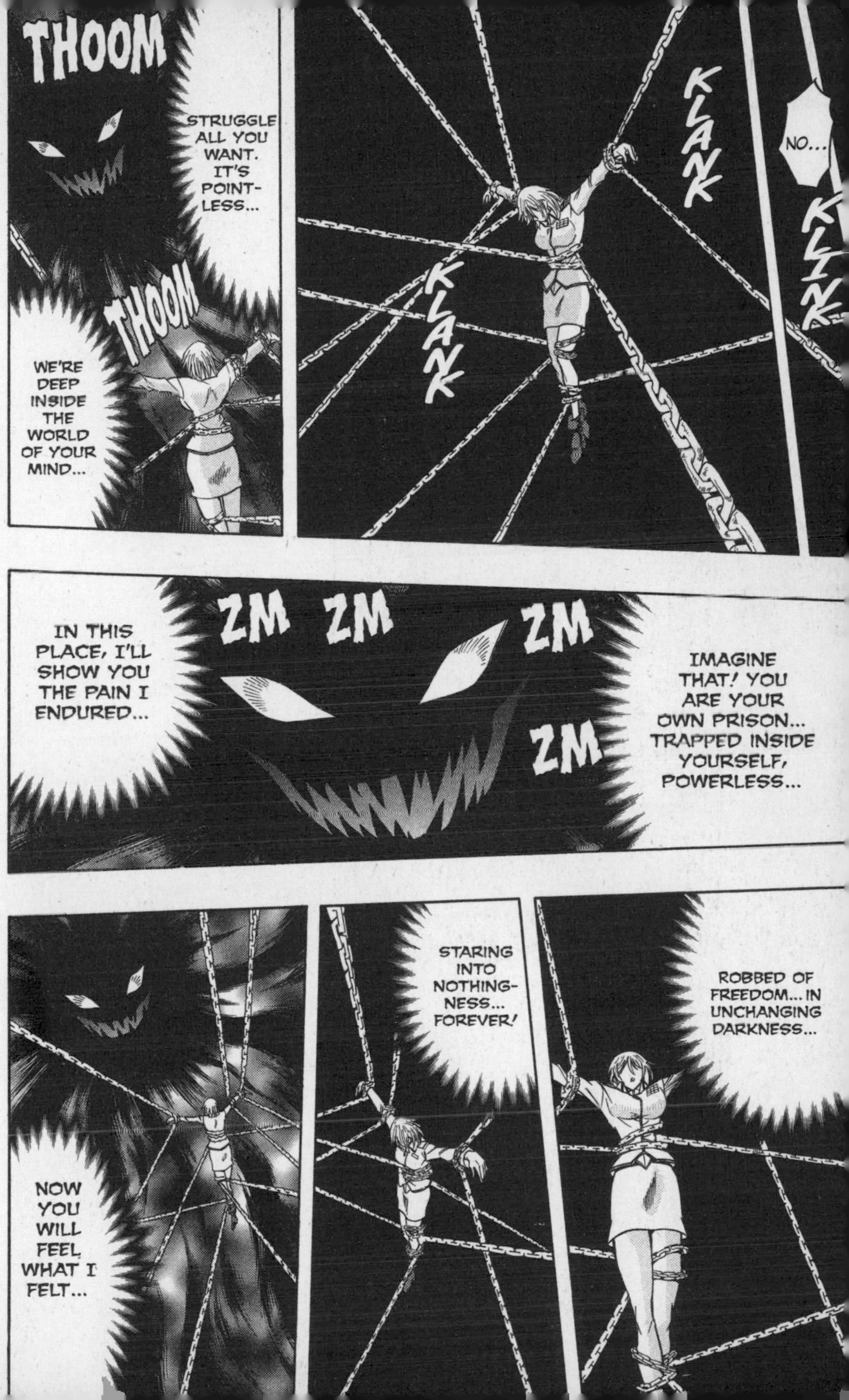
NO...
KLINK
KLANK
KLANK
THOOM
STRUGGLE ALL YOU WANT. IT'S POINTLESS...
THOOM
WE'RE DEEP INSIDE THE WORLD OF YOUR MIND...
IMAGINE THAT! YOU ARE YOUR OWN PRISON... TRAPPED INSIDE YOURSELF, POWERLESS...
ZM ZM ZM ZM
IN THIS PLACE, I'LL SHOW YOU THE PAIN I ENDURED...
ROBBED OF FREEDOM... IN UNCHANGING DARKNESS...
STARING INTO NOTHINGNESS... FOREVER!
NOW YOU WILL FEEL WHAT I FELT...

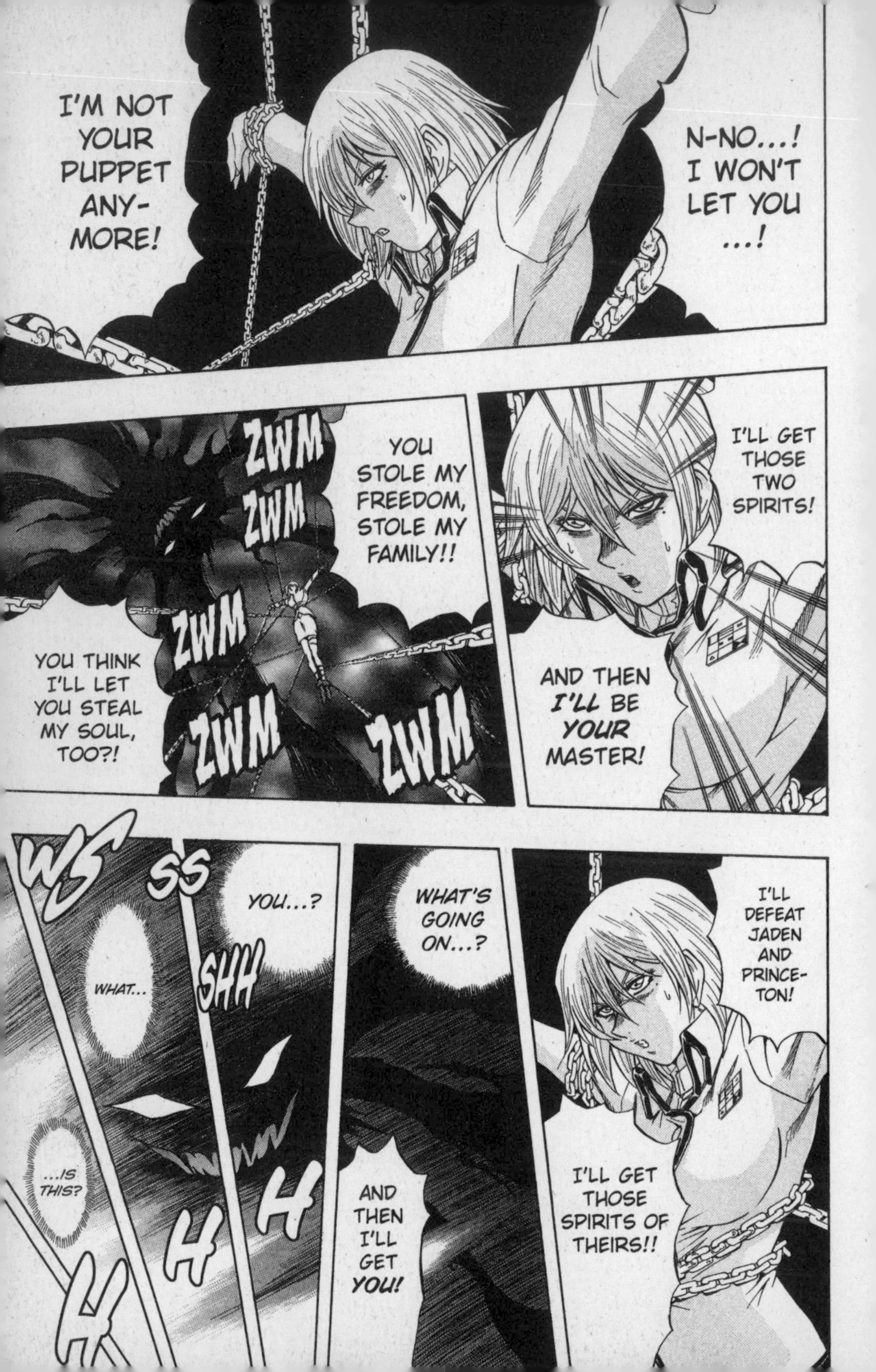
N-NO...! I WON'T LET YOU ...!
I'M NOT YOUR PUPPET ANY-MORE!
I'LL GET THOSE TWO SPIRITS!
AND THEN *I'LL* BE *YOUR* MASTER!
YOU STOLE MY FREEDOM, STOLE MY FAMILY!!
ZWM
ZWM
ZWM
ZWM
ZWM
YOU THINK I'LL LET YOU STEAL MY SOUL, TOO?!
I'LL DEFEAT JADEN AND PRINCE-TON!
I'LL GET THOSE SPIRITS OF THEIRS!!
*WHAT'S GOING ON...?*
AND THEN I'LL GET *YOU!*
*YOU...?*
SHH
H
H
WSS
*WHAT...*
*...IS THIS?*
H

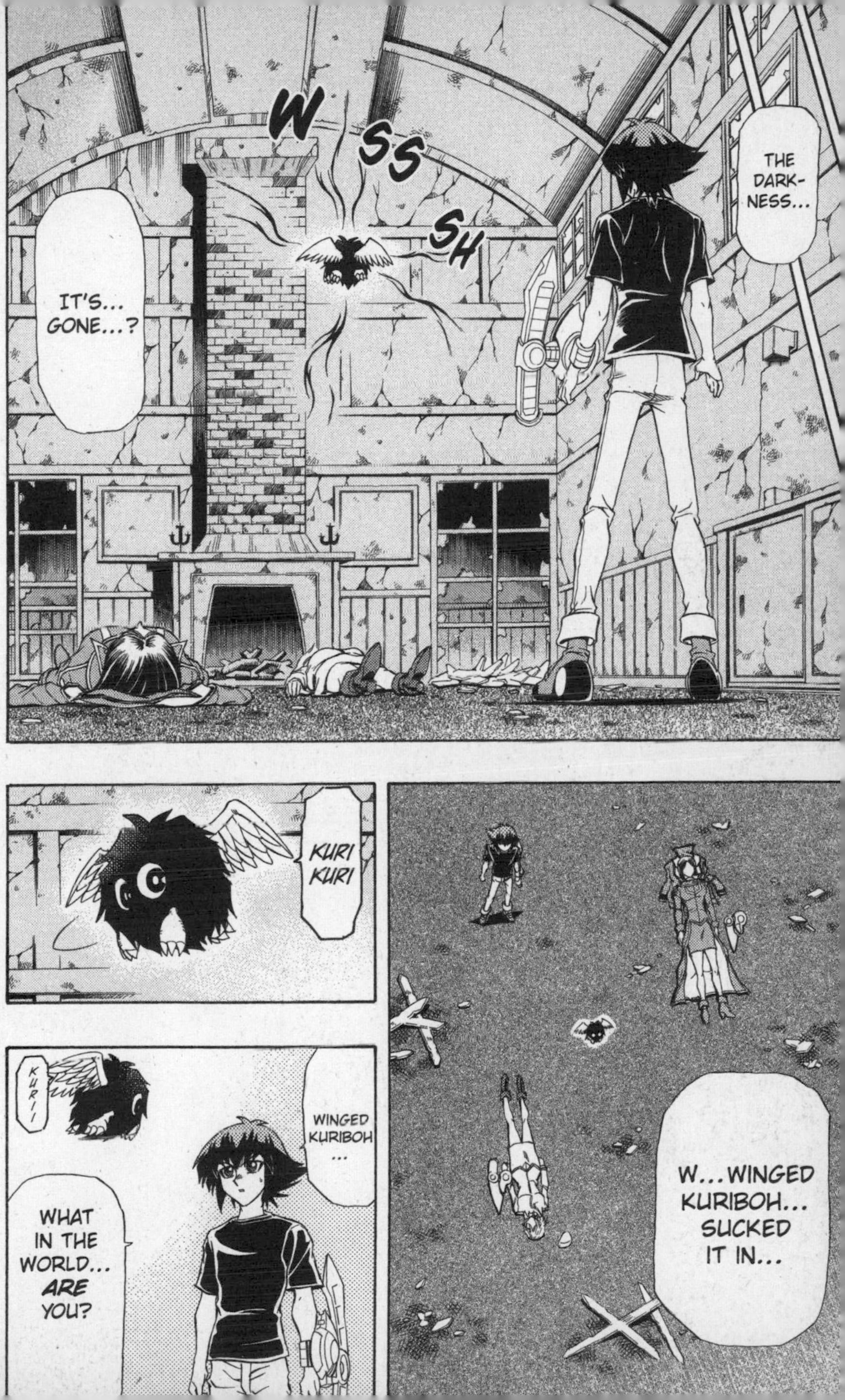
THE DARKNESS...
WSSSH
IT'S... GONE...?
W...WINGED KURIBOH... SUCKED IT IN...
KURI KURI
KURI!
WINGED KURIBOH...
WHAT IN THE WORLD... ARE YOU?

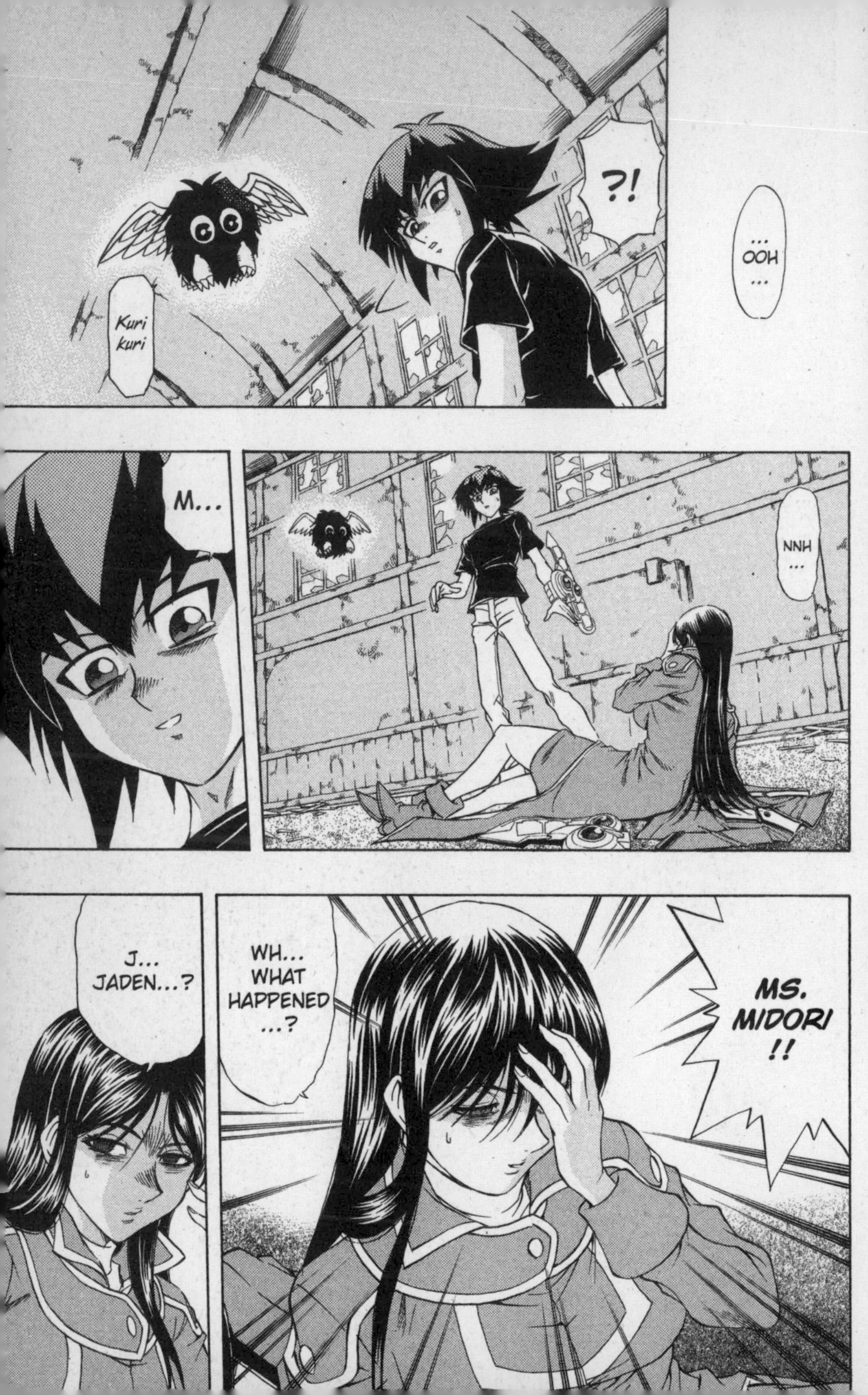
...OOH...
?!
Kuri kuri
NNH...
M...
MS. MIDORI!!
WH... WHAT HAPPENED...?
J... JADEN...?

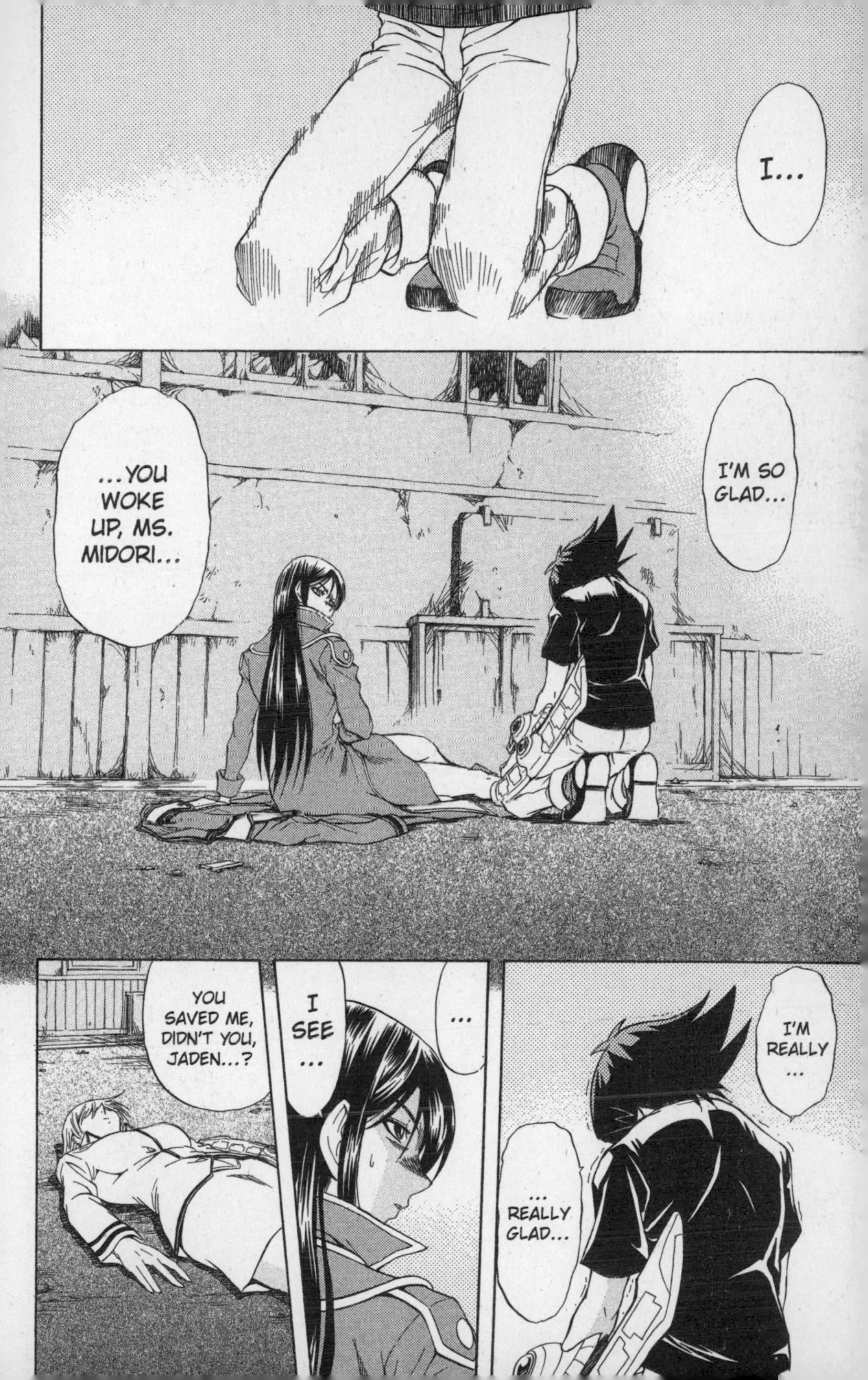
I...
I'M SO GLAD...
...YOU WOKE UP, MS. MIDORI...
I'M REALLY ...
... REALLY GLAD...
...
I SEE ...
YOU SAVED ME, DIDN'T YOU, JADEN...?

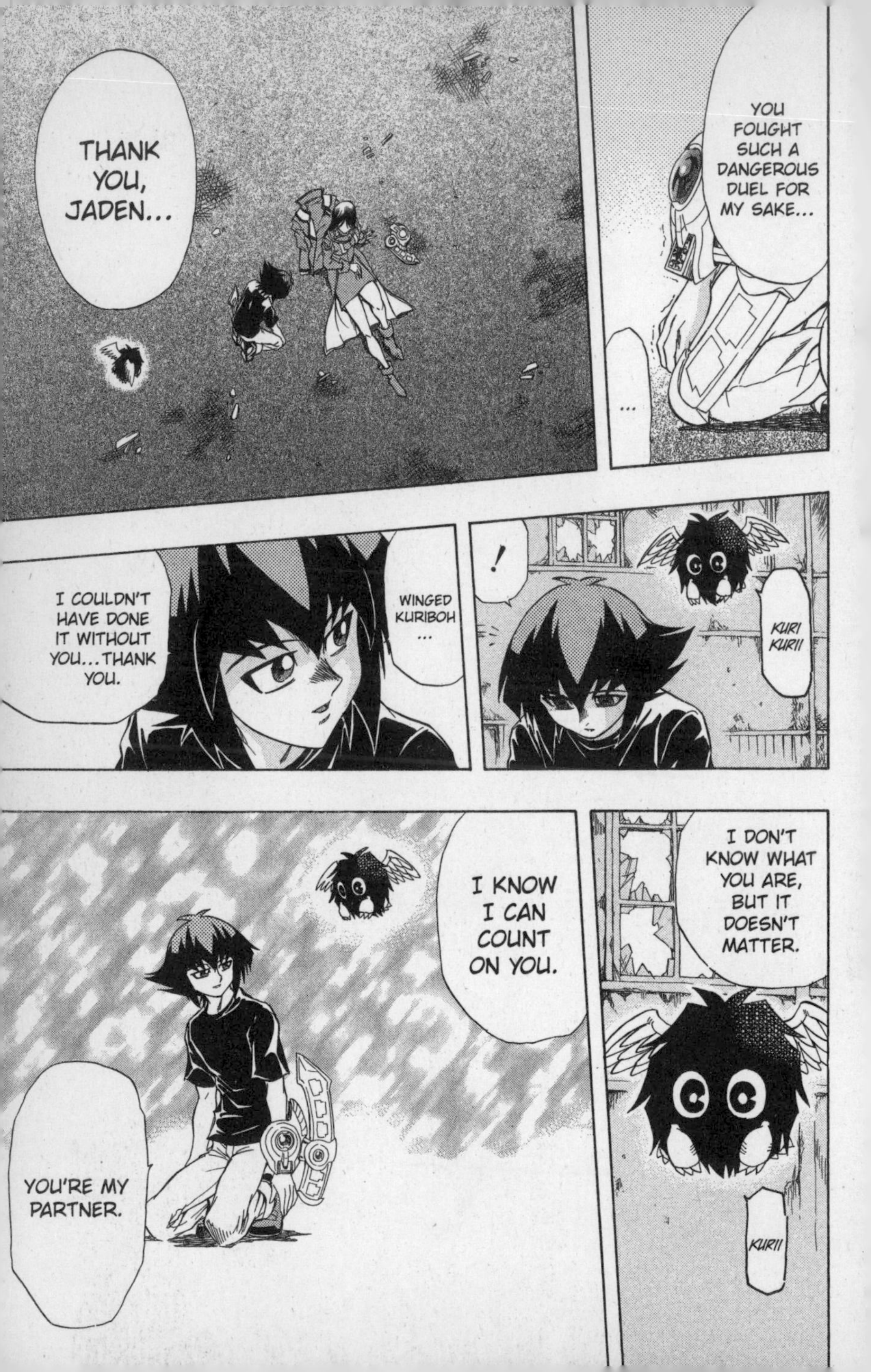
YOU FOUGHT SUCH A DANGEROUS DUEL FOR MY SAKE...
...
THANK YOU, JADEN...
!
KURI KURII
WINGED KURIBOH ...
I COULDN'T HAVE DONE IT WITHOUT YOU...THANK YOU.
I DON'T KNOW WHAT YOU ARE, BUT IT DOESN'T MATTER.
KURII
I KNOW I CAN COUNT ON YOU.
YOU'RE MY PARTNER.

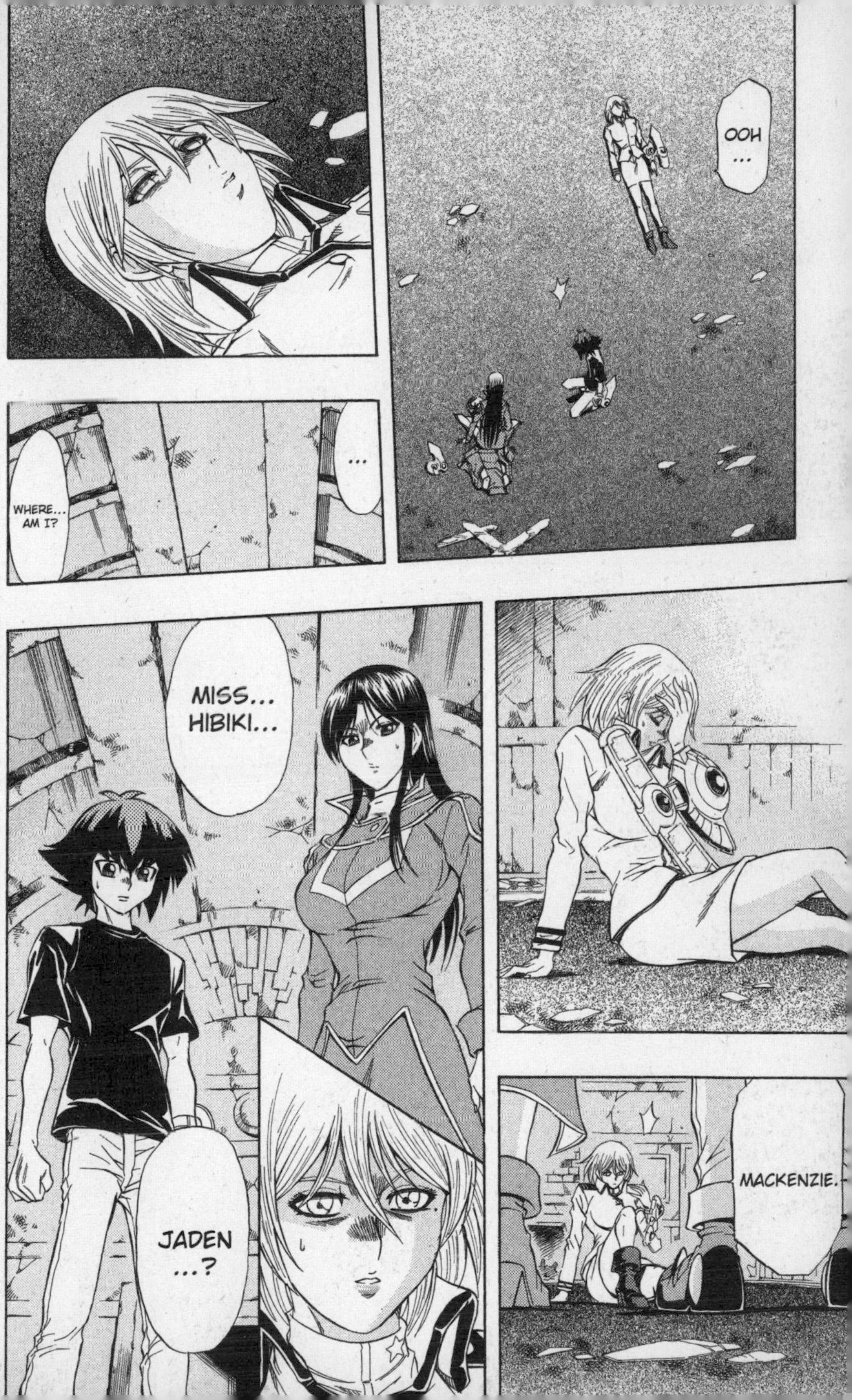
OOH ...
...
WHERE... AM I?
MACKENZIE.
MISS... HIBIKI...
JADEN ...?

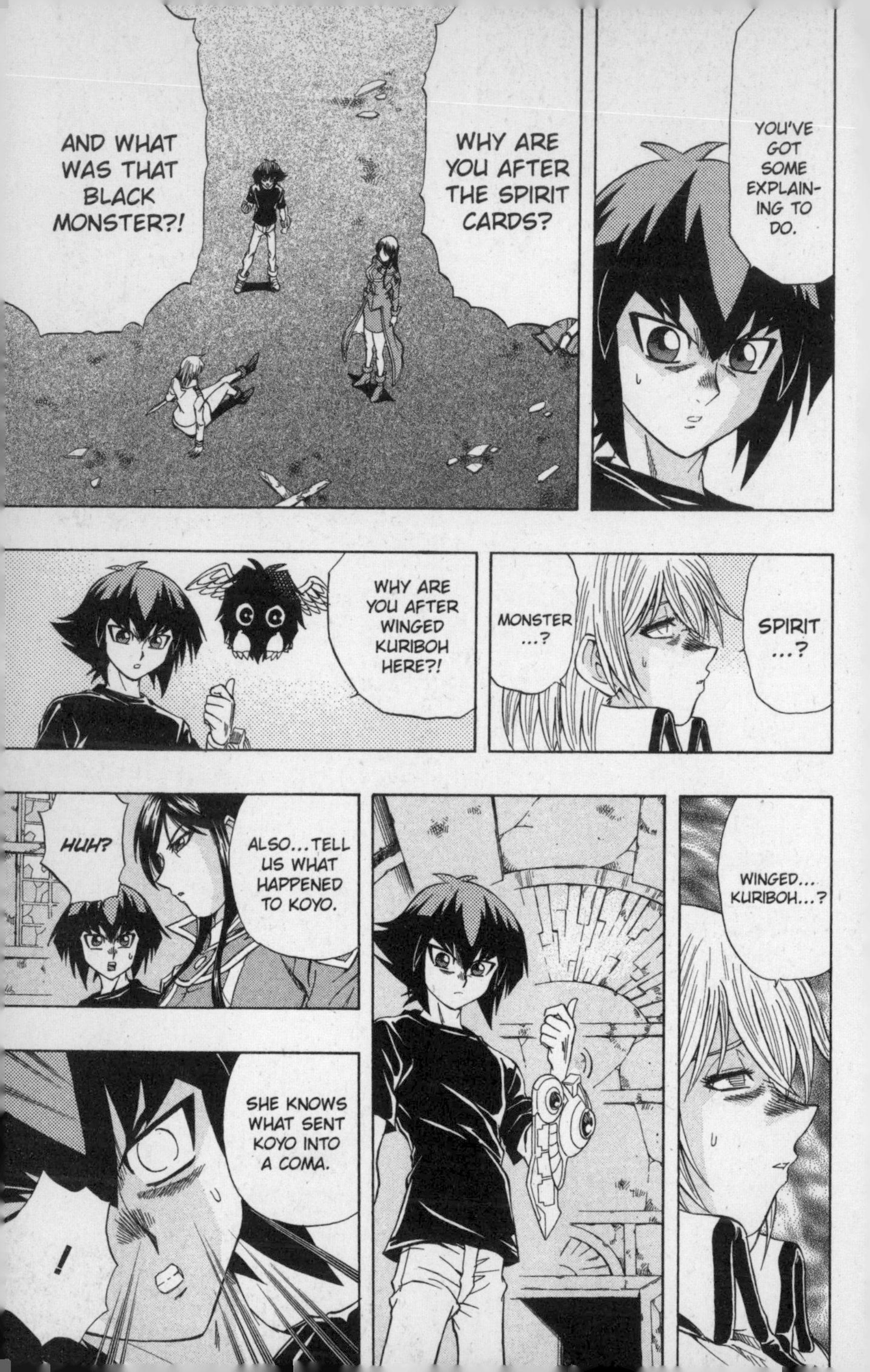
YOU'VE GOT SOME EXPLAINING TO DO.
WHY ARE YOU AFTER THE SPIRIT CARDS?
AND WHAT WAS THAT BLACK MONSTER?!
SPIRIT ...?
MONSTER ...?
WHY ARE YOU AFTER WINGED KURIBOH HERE?!
WINGED... KURIBOH...?
ALSO...TELL US WHAT HAPPENED TO KOYO.
HUH?
SHE KNOWS WHAT SENT KOYO INTO A COMA.
!

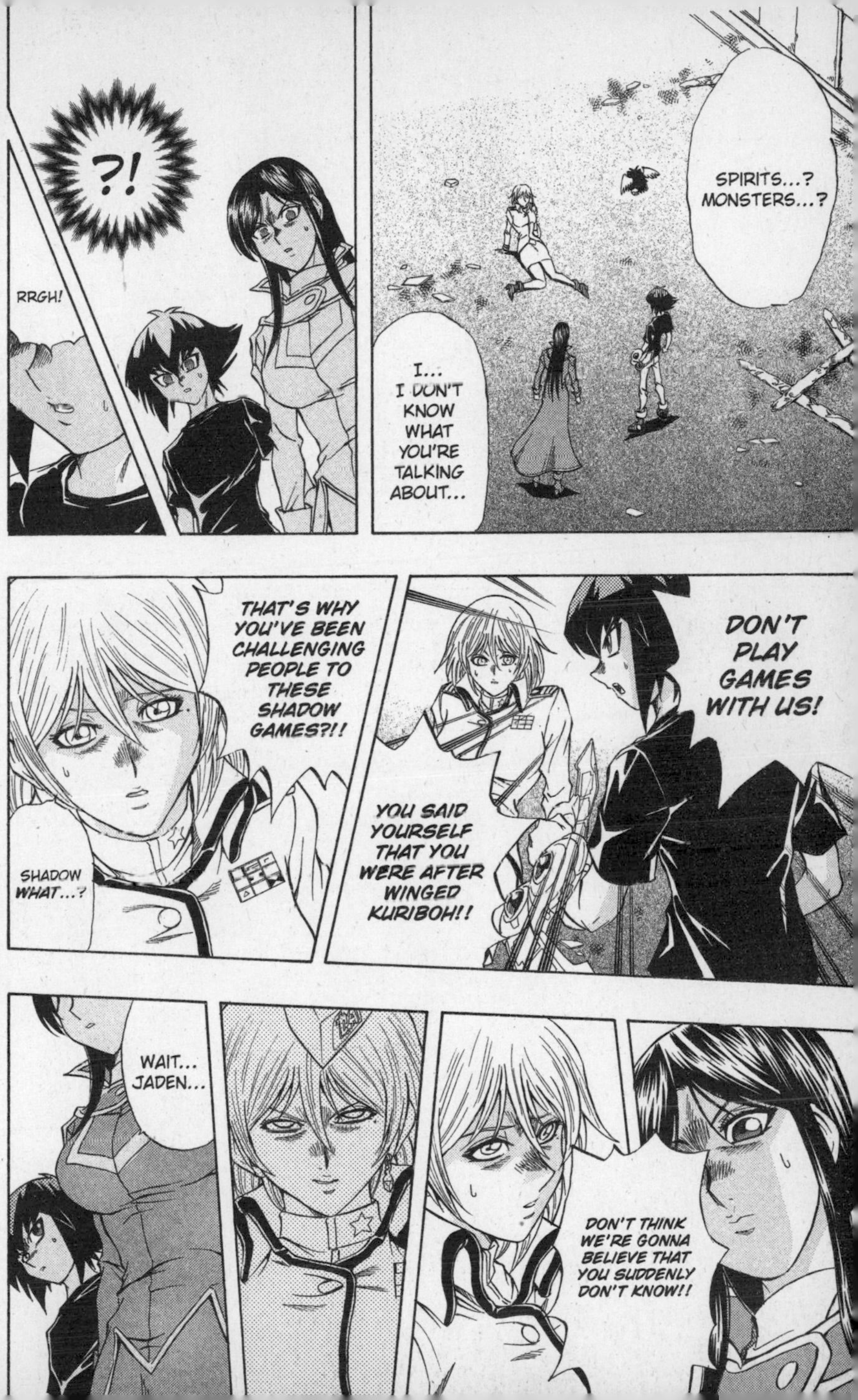
SPIRITS...? MONSTERS...?
I... I DON'T KNOW WHAT YOU'RE TALKING ABOUT...
?!
RRGH!
DON'T PLAY GAMES WITH US!
YOU SAID YOURSELF THAT YOU WERE AFTER WINGED KURIBOH!!
THAT'S WHY YOU'VE BEEN CHALLENGING PEOPLE TO THESE SHADOW GAMES?!!
SHADOW WHAT...?
DON'T THINK WE'RE GONNA BELIEVE THAT YOU SUDDENLY DON'T KNOW!!
WAIT... JADEN...

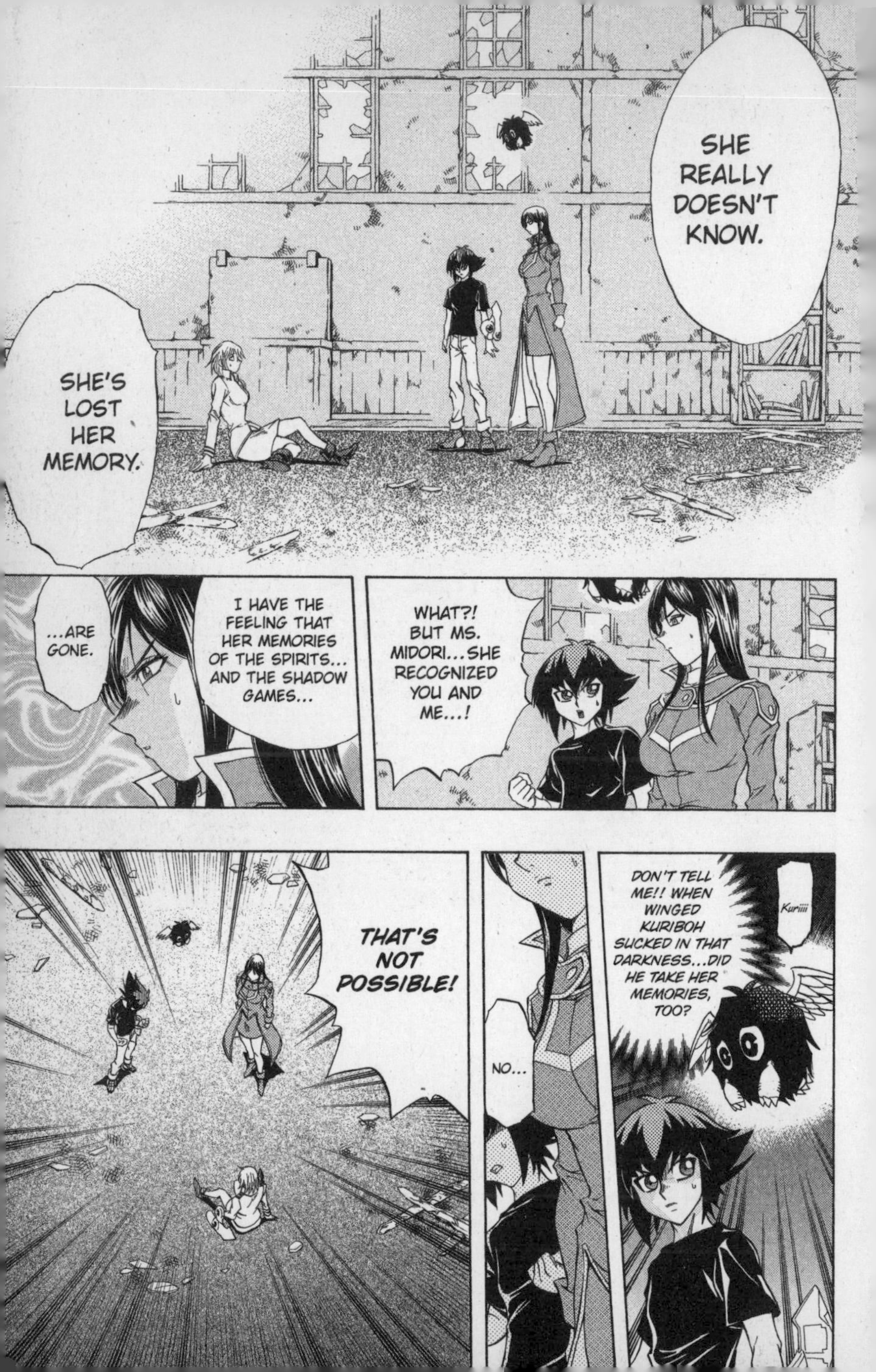
SHE REALLY DOESN'T KNOW.
SHE'S LOST HER MEMORY.
WHAT?! BUT MS. MIDORI...SHE RECOGNIZED YOU AND ME...!
I HAVE THE FEELING THAT HER MEMORIES OF THE SPIRITS... AND THE SHADOW GAMES...
...ARE GONE.
Kuriiii
DON'T TELL ME!! WHEN WINGED KURIBOH SUCKED IN THAT DARKNESS...DID HE TAKE HER MEMORIES, TOO?
NO...
THAT'S NOT POSSIBLE!

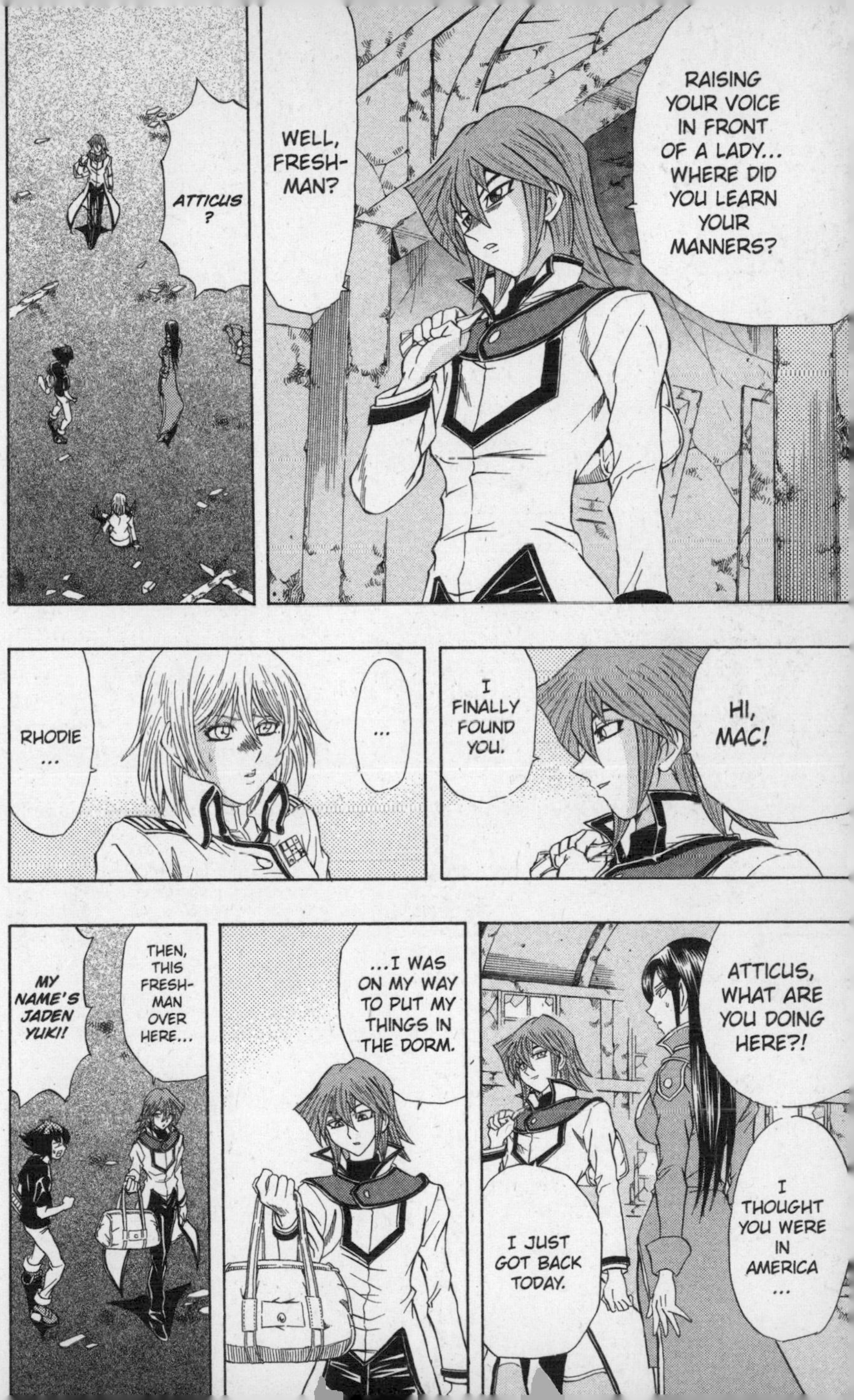
RAISING YOUR VOICE IN FRONT OF A LADY... WHERE DID YOU LEARN YOUR MANNERS?
WELL, FRESH-MAN?
ATTICUS?
HI, MAC!
I FINALLY FOUND YOU.
...
RHODIE...
ATTICUS, WHAT ARE YOU DOING HERE?!
I THOUGHT YOU WERE IN AMERICA...
I JUST GOT BACK TODAY.
...I WAS ON MY WAY TO PUT MY THINGS IN THE DORM.
THEN, THIS FRESH-MAN OVER HERE...
MY NAME'S JADEN YUKI!

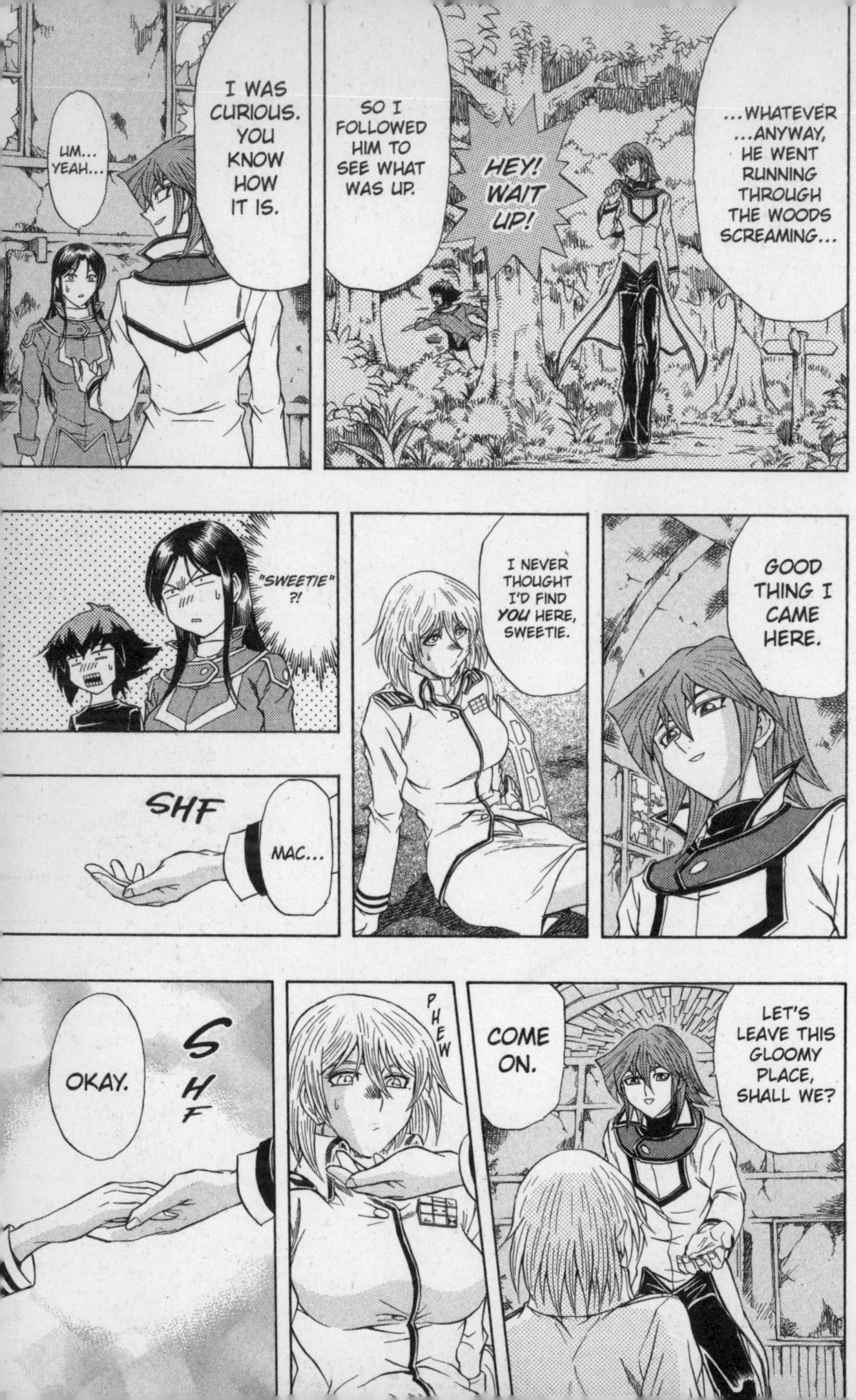
...WHATEVER ...ANYWAY, HE WENT RUNNING THROUGH THE WOODS SCREAMING...
HEY! WAIT UP!
SO I FOLLOWED HIM TO SEE WHAT WAS UP.
I WAS CURIOUS. YOU KNOW HOW IT IS.
UM... YEAH...
GOOD THING I CAME HERE.
I NEVER THOUGHT I'D FIND *YOU* HERE, SWEETIE.
"SWEETIE"?!
SHF
MAC...
LET'S LEAVE THIS GLOOMY PLACE, SHALL WE?
COME ON.
PHEW
SHF
OKAY.

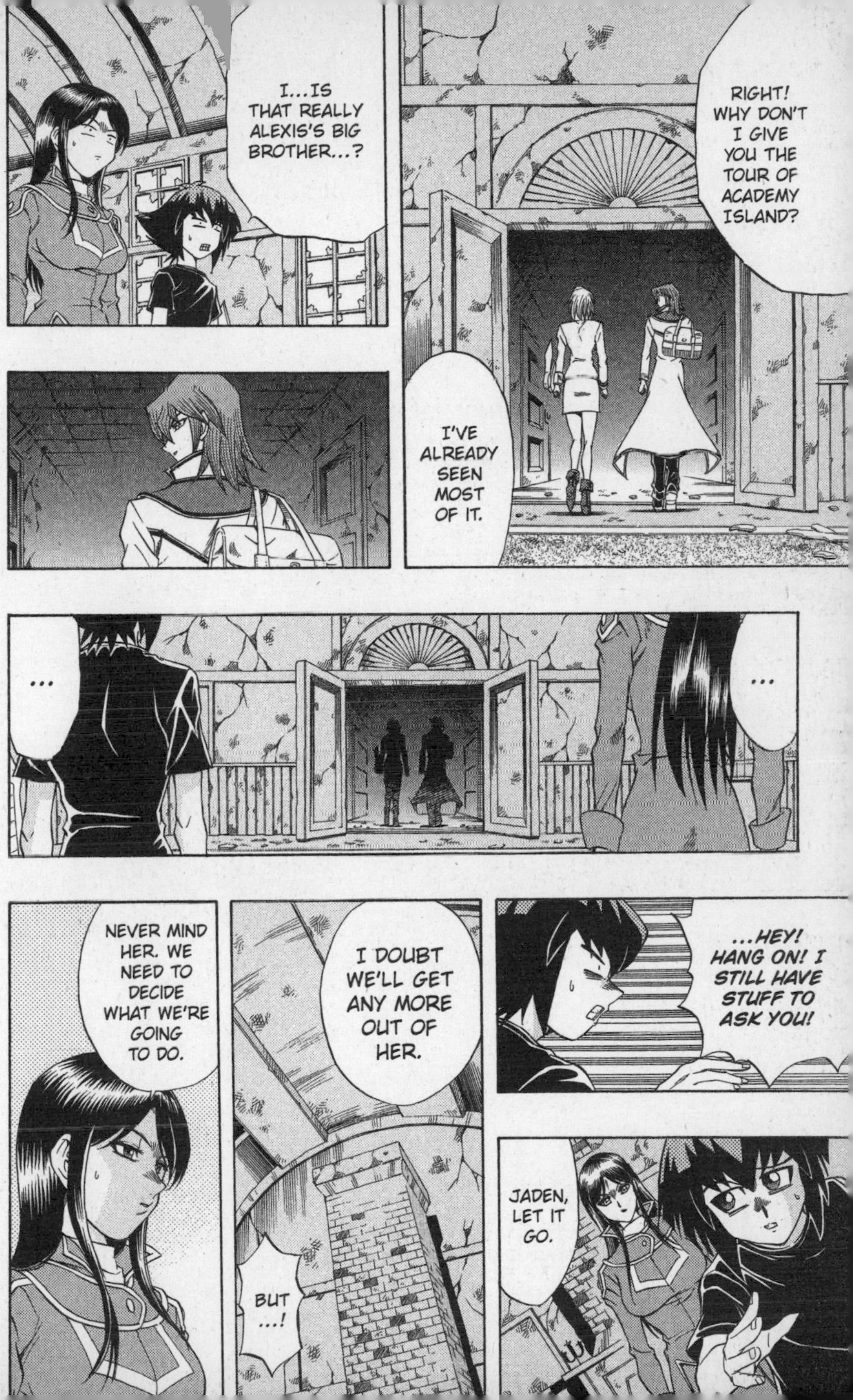
RIGHT! WHY DON'T I GIVE YOU THE TOUR OF ACADEMY ISLAND?
I'VE ALREADY SEEN MOST OF IT.
I...IS THAT REALLY ALEXIS'S BIG BROTHER...?
...
...
...HEY! HANG ON! I STILL HAVE STUFF TO ASK YOU!
JADEN, LET IT GO.
I DOUBT WE'LL GET ANY MORE OUT OF HER.
BUT ...!
NEVER MIND HER. WE NEED TO DECIDE WHAT WE'RE GOING TO DO.

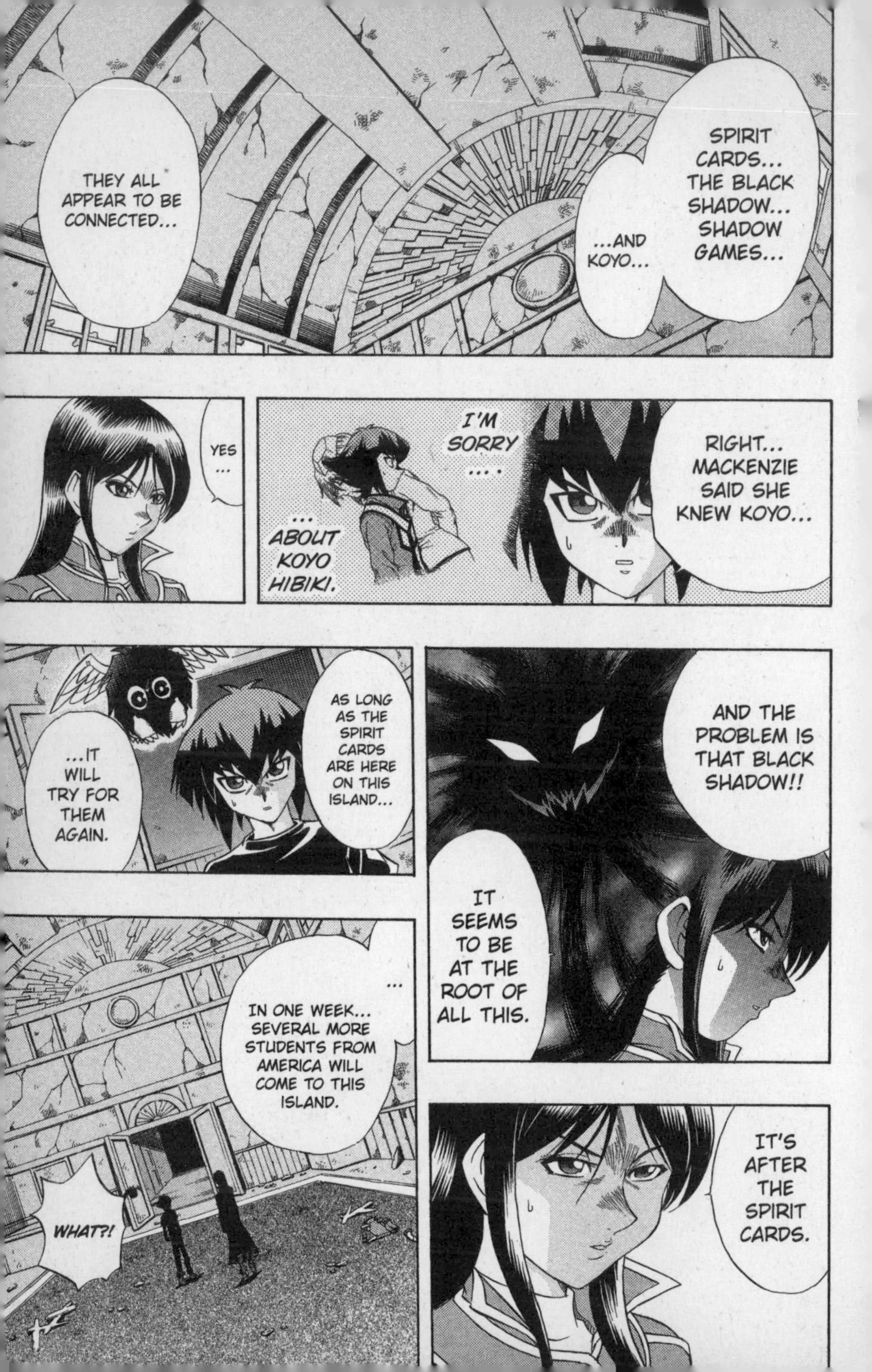
SPIRIT CARDS... THE BLACK SHADOW... SHADOW GAMES...
...AND KOYO...
THEY ALL APPEAR TO BE CONNECTED...
RIGHT... MACKENZIE SAID SHE KNEW KOYO...
I'M SORRY ....
... ABOUT KOYO HIBIKI.
YES ...
AND THE PROBLEM IS THAT BLACK SHADOW!!
IT SEEMS TO BE AT THE ROOT OF ALL THIS.
IT'S AFTER THE SPIRIT CARDS.
AS LONG AS THE SPIRIT CARDS ARE HERE ON THIS ISLAND...
...IT WILL TRY FOR THEM AGAIN.
...
IN ONE WEEK... SEVERAL MORE STUDENTS FROM AMERICA WILL COME TO THIS ISLAND.
WHAT?!

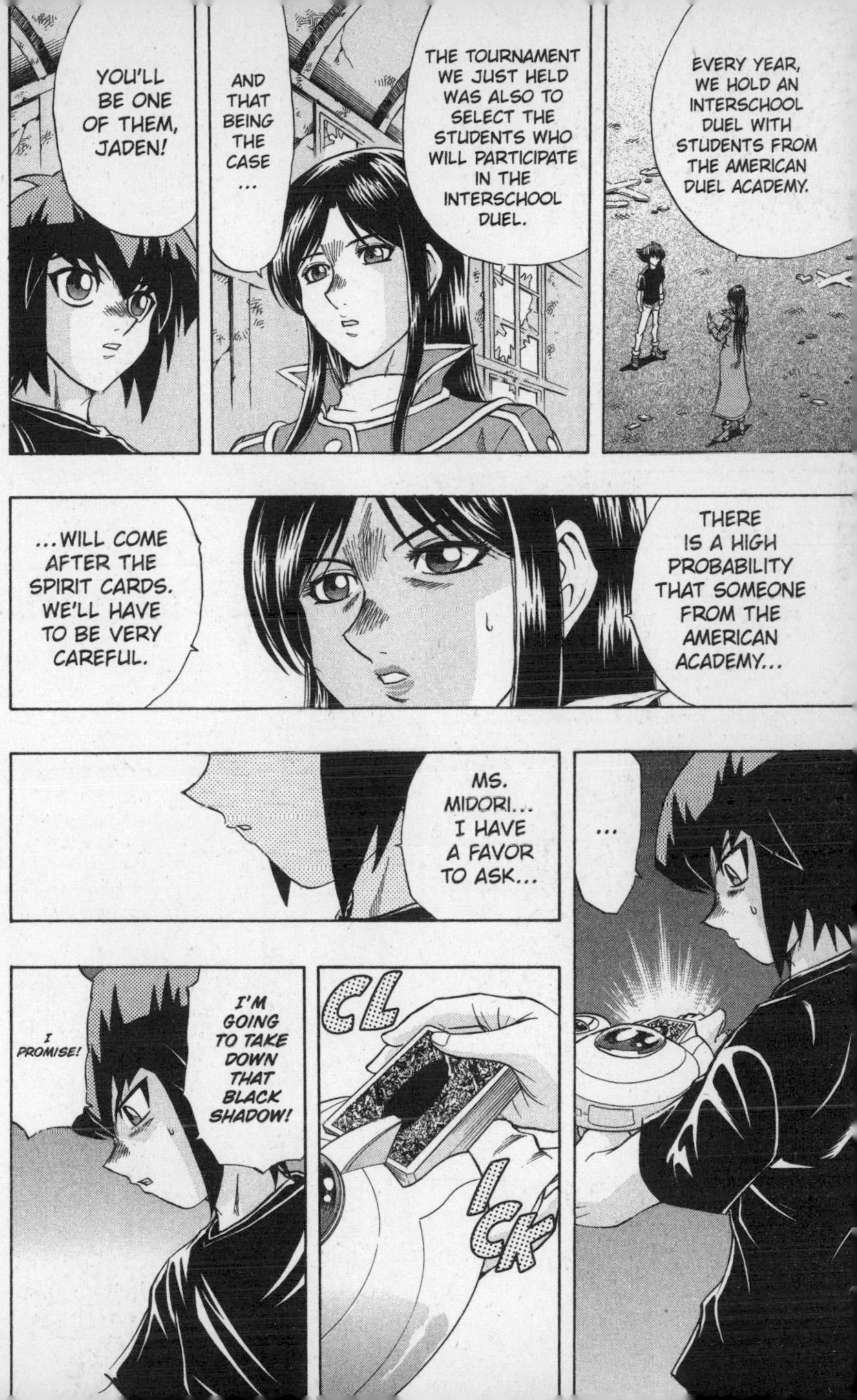
EVERY YEAR, WE HOLD AN INTERSCHOOL DUEL WITH STUDENTS FROM THE AMERICAN DUEL ACADEMY.
THE TOURNAMENT WE JUST HELD WAS ALSO TO SELECT THE STUDENTS WHO WILL PARTICIPATE IN THE INTERSCHOOL DUEL.
AND THAT BEING THE CASE ...
YOU'LL BE ONE OF THEM, JADEN!
THERE IS A HIGH PROBABILITY THAT SOMEONE FROM THE AMERICAN ACADEMY...
...WILL COME AFTER THE SPIRIT CARDS. WE'LL HAVE TO BE VERY CAREFUL.
...
MS. MIDORI... I HAVE A FAVOR TO ASK...
CLICK
I'M GOING TO TAKE DOWN THAT BLACK SHADOW!
I PROMISE!

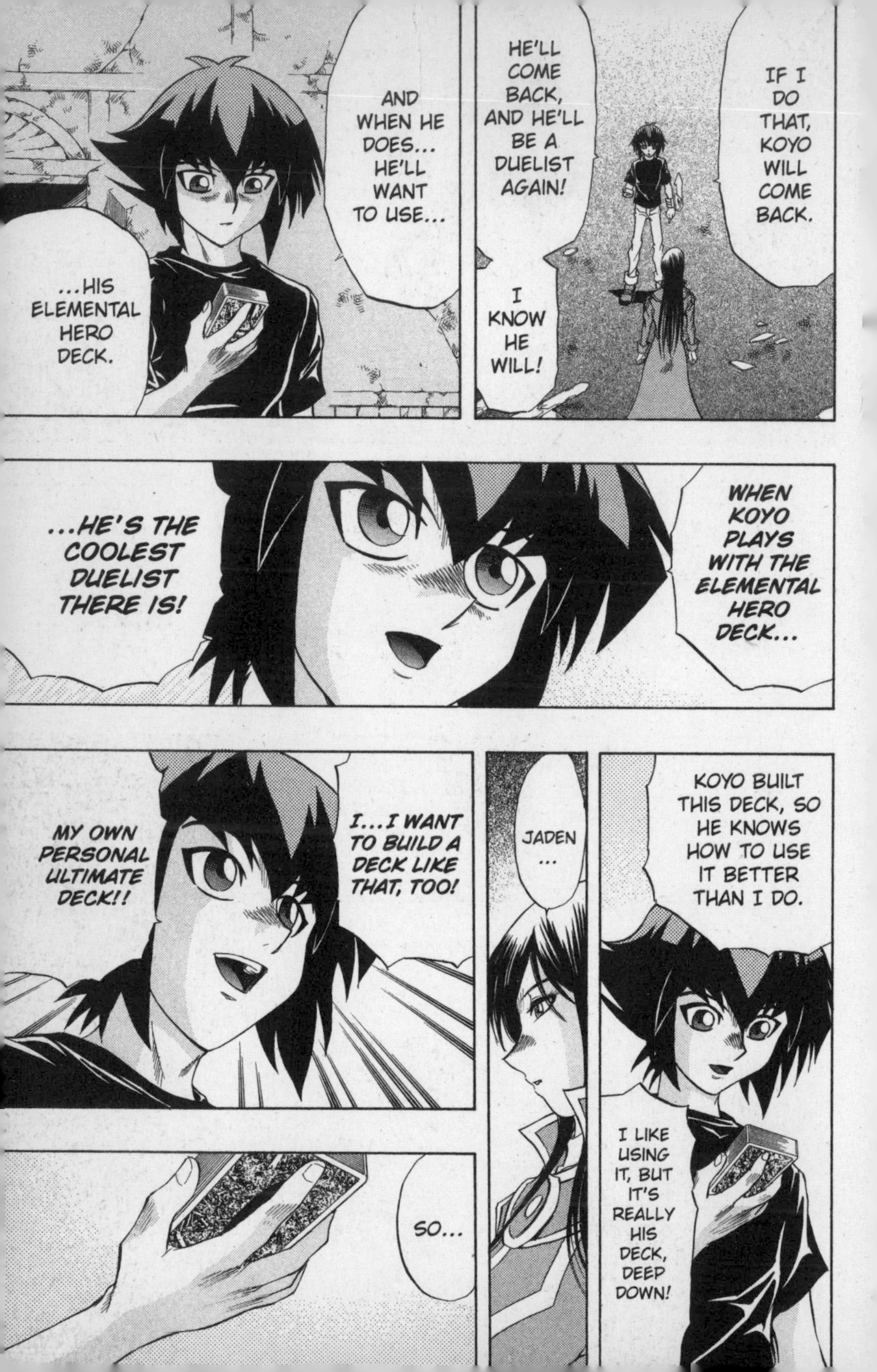
IF I DO THAT, KOYO WILL COME BACK.
HE'LL COME BACK, AND HE'LL BE A DUELIST AGAIN!
I KNOW HE WILL!
AND WHEN HE DOES... HE'LL WANT TO USE...
...HIS ELEMENTAL HERO DECK.
WHEN KOYO PLAYS WITH THE ELEMENTAL HERO DECK...
...HE'S THE COOLEST DUELIST THERE IS!
KOYO BUILT THIS DECK, SO HE KNOWS HOW TO USE IT BETTER THAN I DO.
I LIKE USING IT, BUT IT'S REALLY HIS DECK, DEEP DOWN!
JADEN...
I...I WANT TO BUILD A DECK LIKE THAT, TOO!
MY OWN PERSONAL ULTIMATE DECK!!
SO...

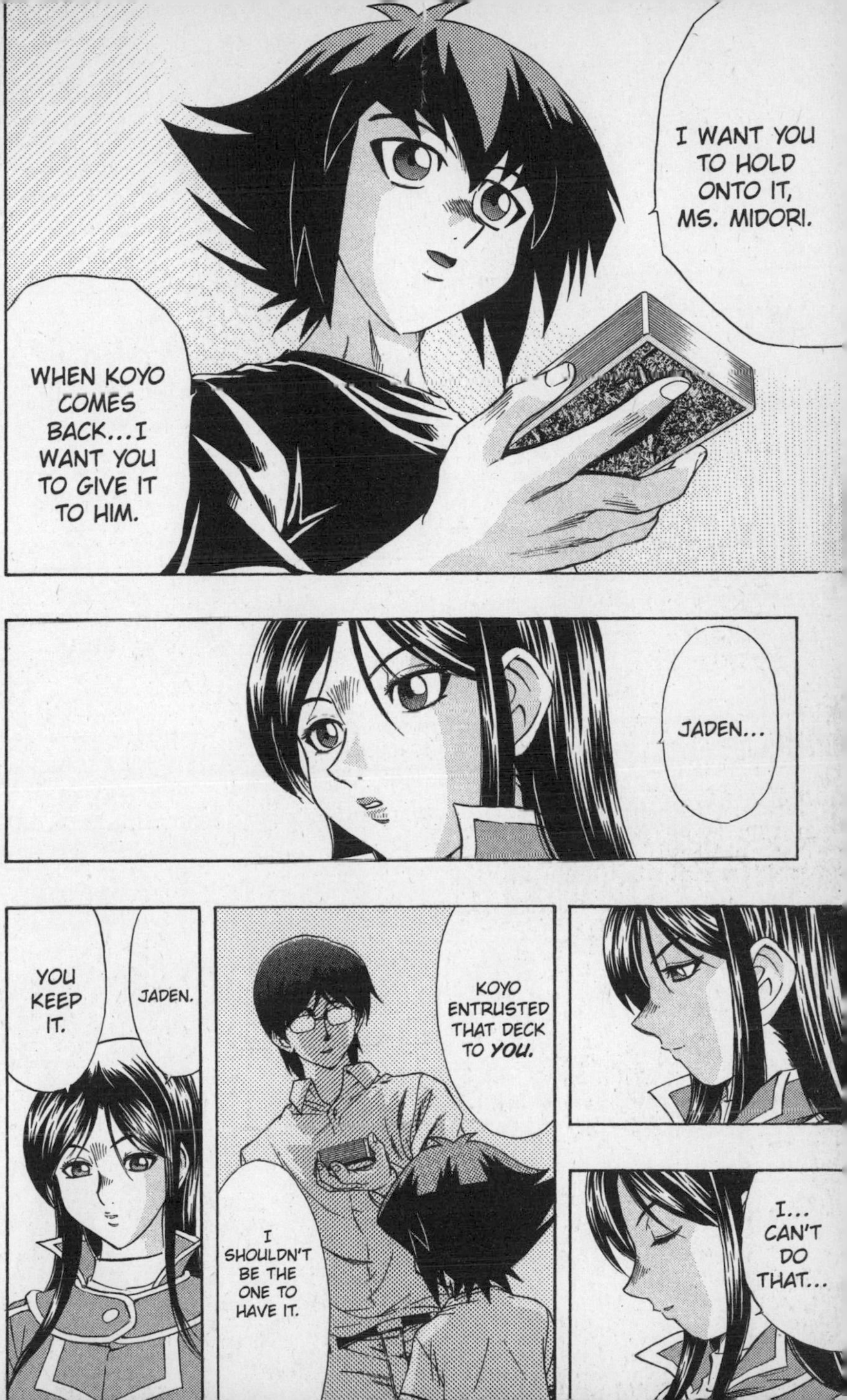
I WANT YOU TO HOLD ONTO IT, MS. MIDORI.
WHEN KOYO COMES BACK...I WANT YOU TO GIVE IT TO HIM.
JADEN...
I... CAN'T DO THAT...
KOYO ENTRUSTED THAT DECK TO *YOU.*
I SHOULDN'T BE THE ONE TO HAVE IT.
JADEN.
YOU KEEP IT.

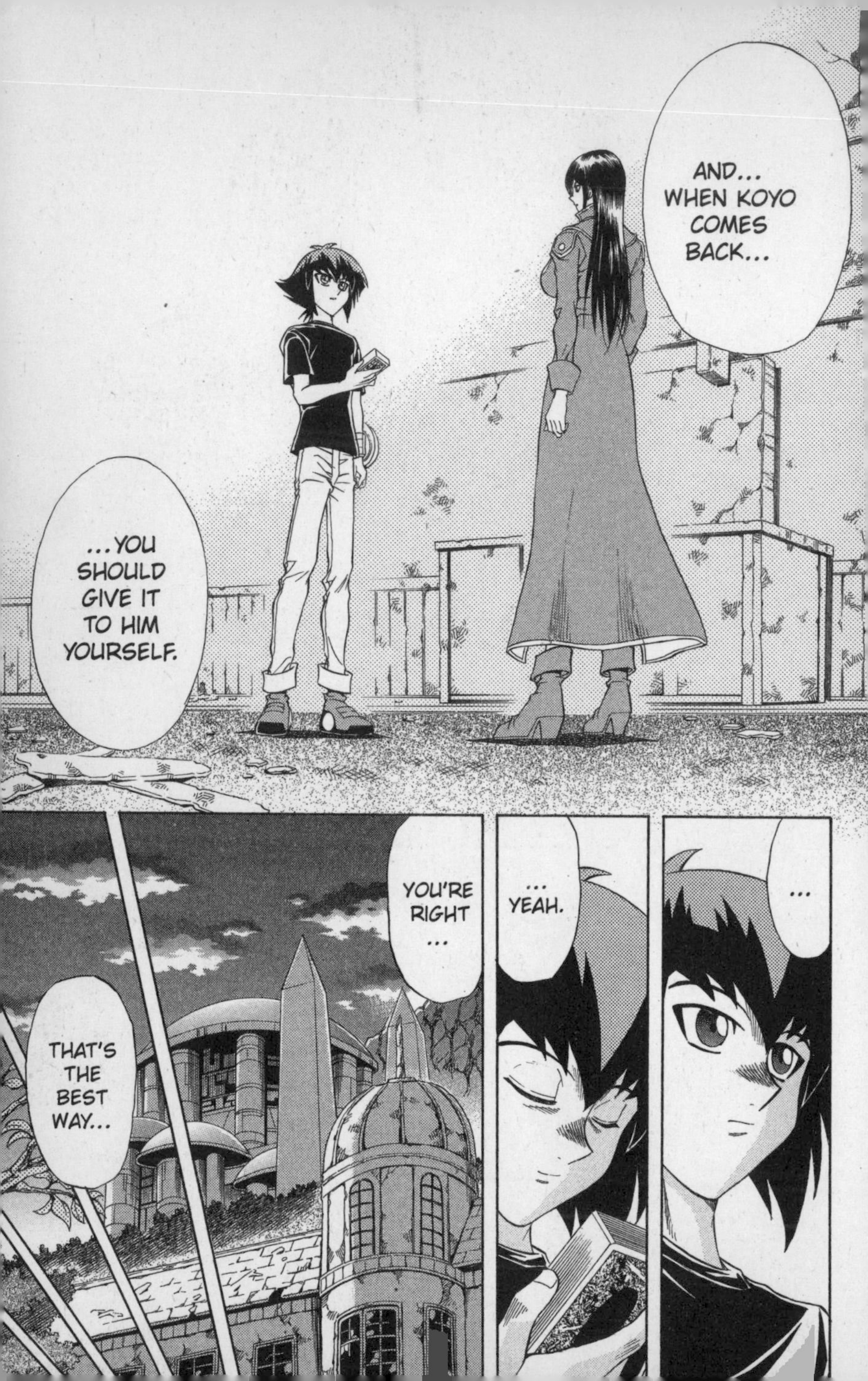
AND... WHEN KOYO COMES BACK...
...YOU SHOULD GIVE IT TO HIM YOURSELF.
...
... YEAH.
YOU'RE RIGHT ...
THAT'S THE BEST WAY...

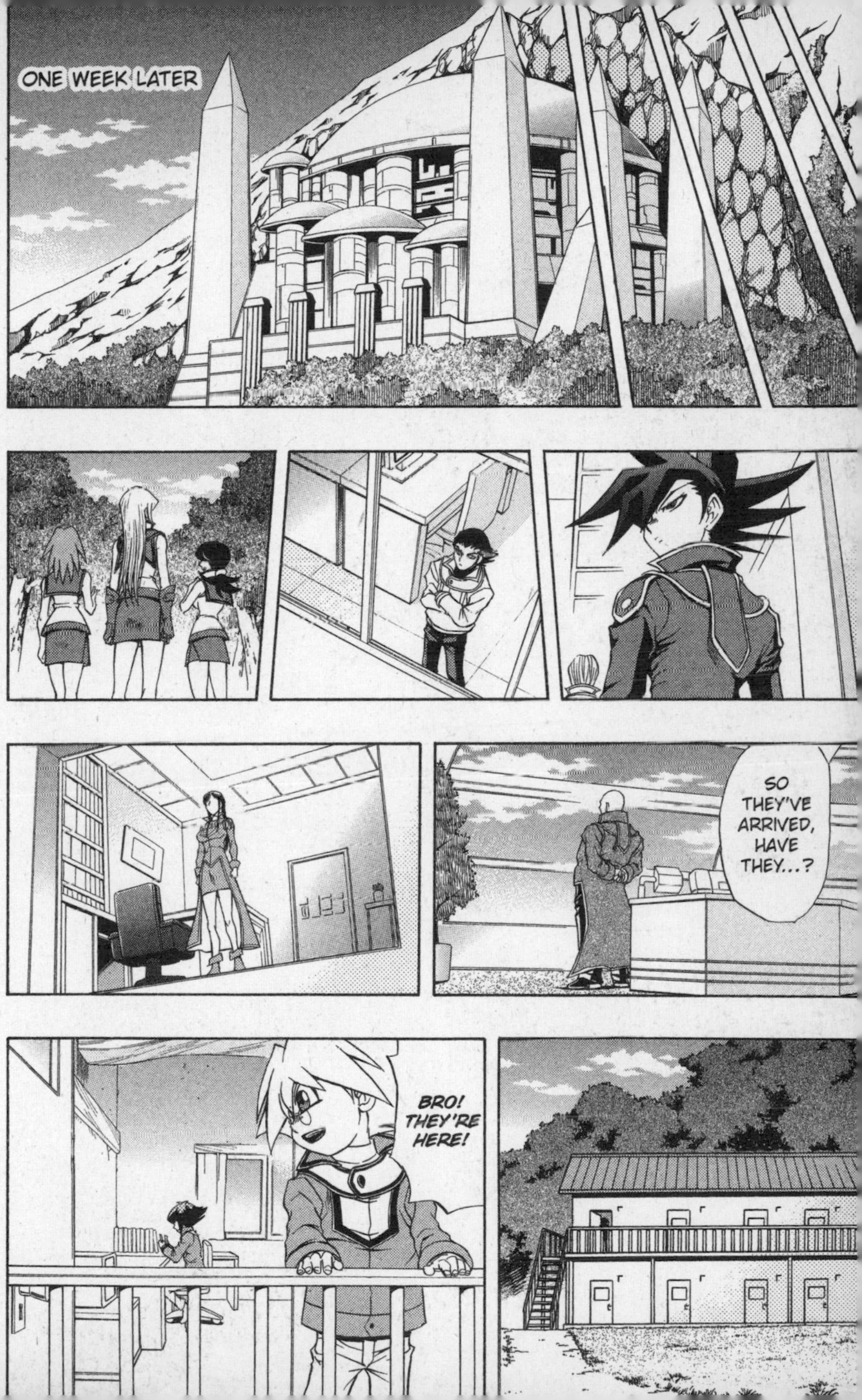
ONE WEEK LATER
SO THEY'VE ARRIVED, HAVE THEY...?
BRO! THEY'RE HERE!

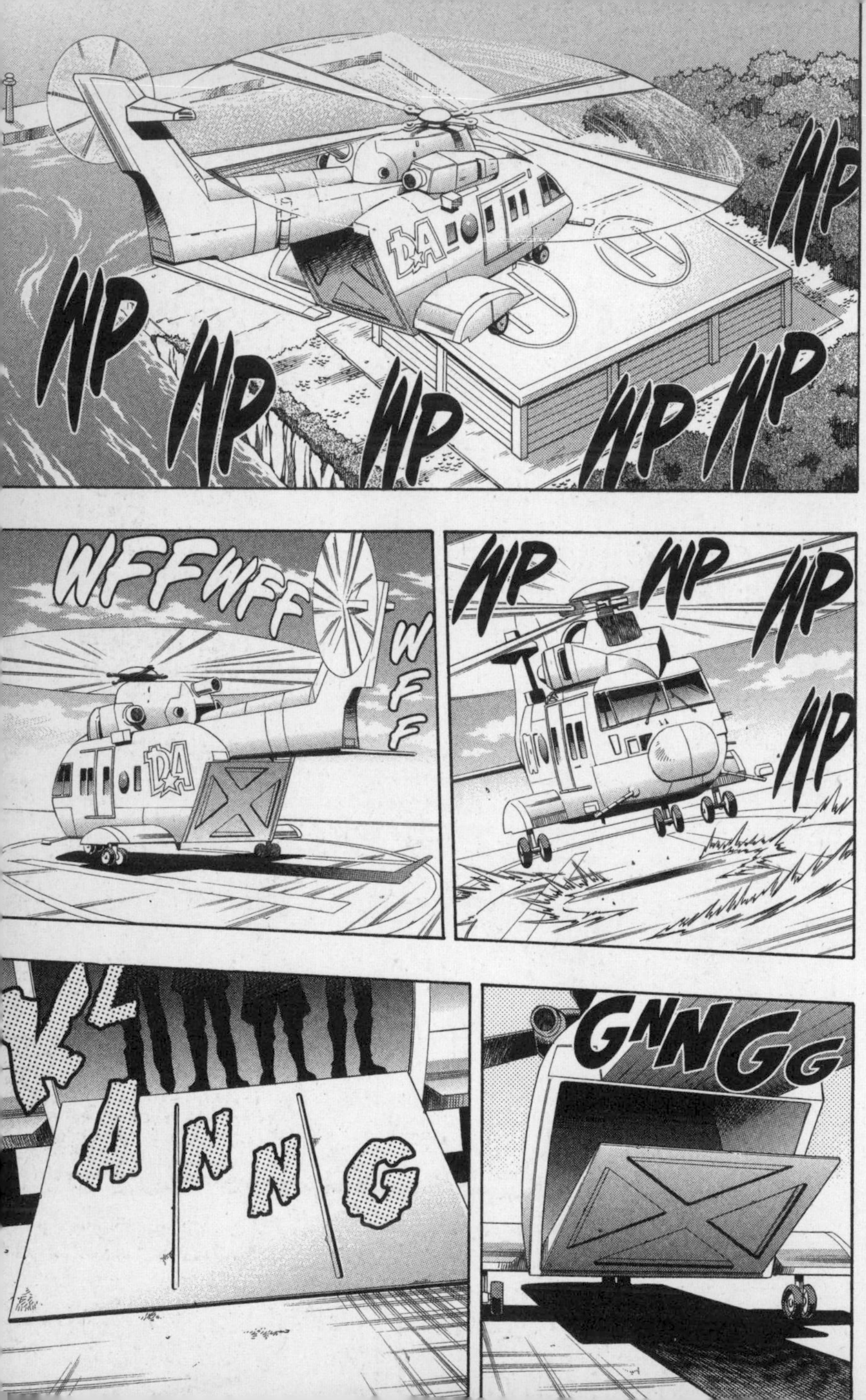
WP
WP
WP
WP
WP
WP
WP
WP
WP
WP
WFFWFF
WFF
GNNGG
KLANNG

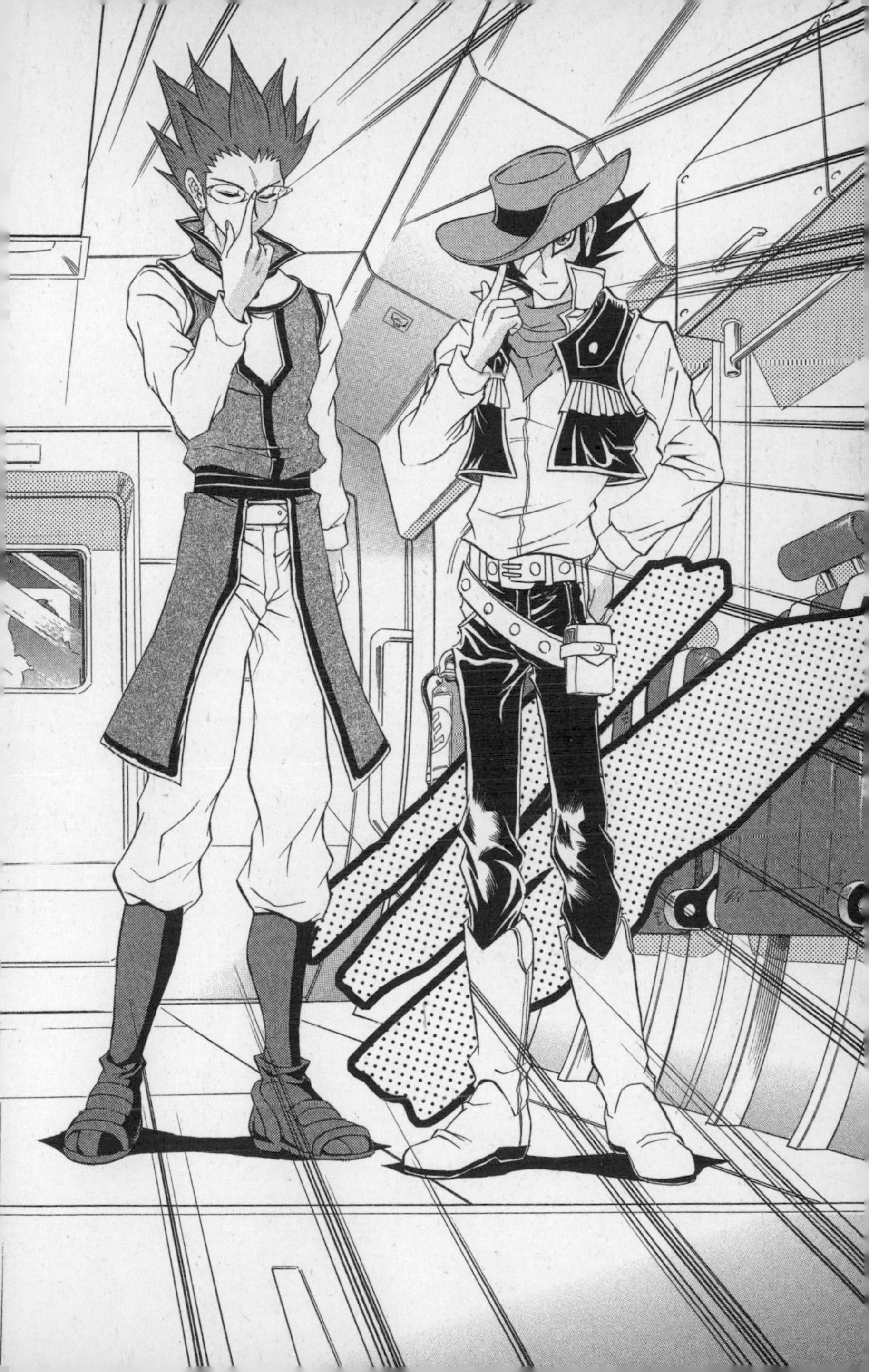

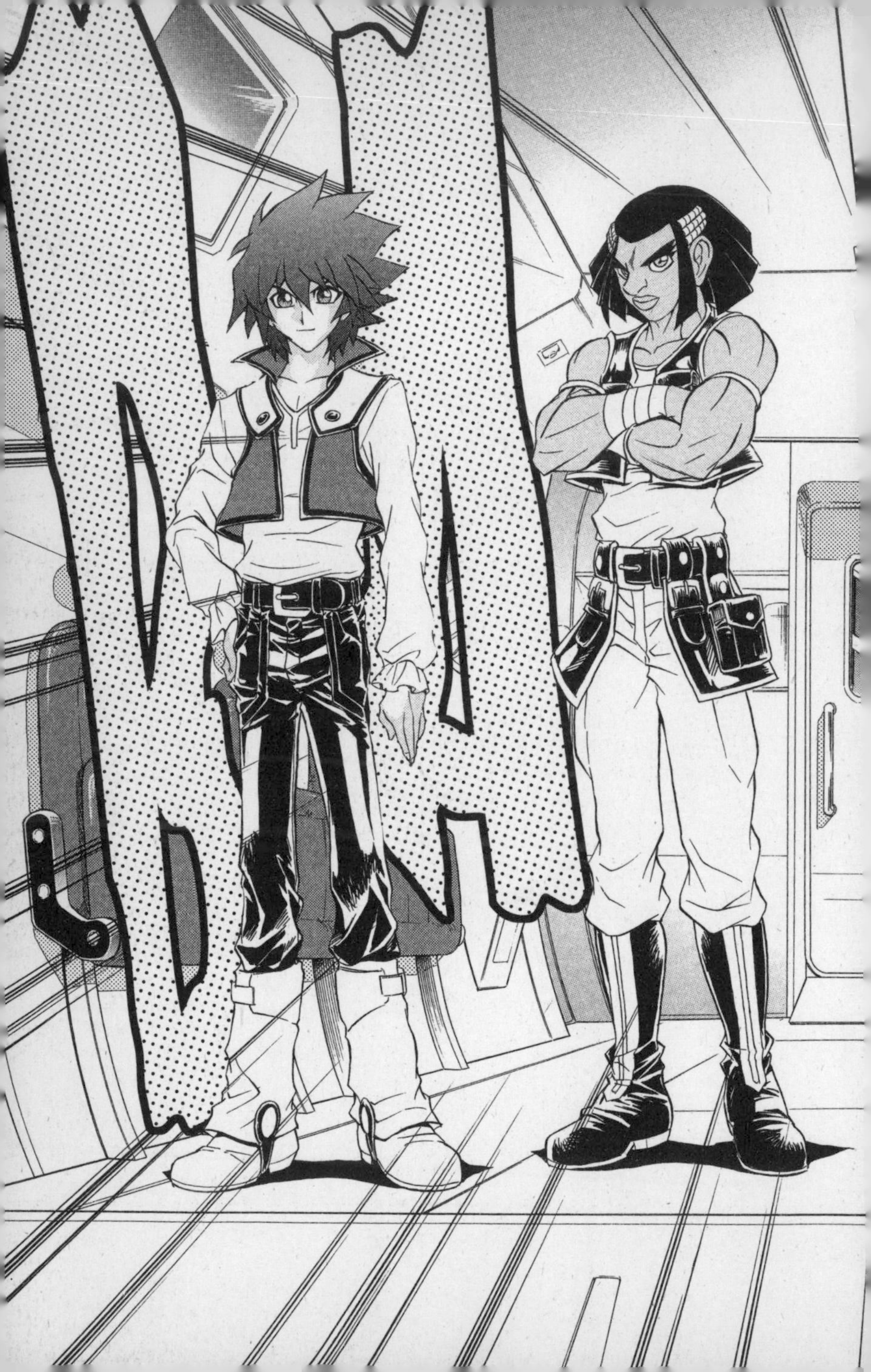

# IT'S FINALLY COME THIS FAR

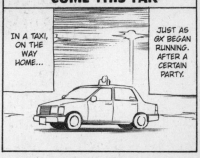

JUST AS GX BEGAN RUNNING. AFTER A CERTAIN PARTY.
IN A TAXI, ON THE WAY HOME...
IN THE ANIME, JADEN'S CARDS ARE "E-HERO" CARDS.
TO KEEP THINGS SIMPLE, WE CALLED THEM E-HEROES IN THE MANGA, TOO. BUT...
WHEN HE PICKS UP A NEW DECK...
MAKE THAT DECK *YOUR* WAY, KAGEYAMA!
THANKS...
BUT DO YOU THINK THE SERIES WILL RUN THAT LONG...?
WELL, THAT ALL DEPENDS ON HOW HARD YOU WORK!

THAT BIT ABOUT "HARD WORK" REALLY ENCOURAGED ME! HAPPILY, I CONTINUE TO DRAW.

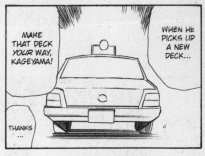

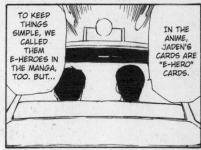

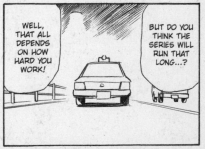

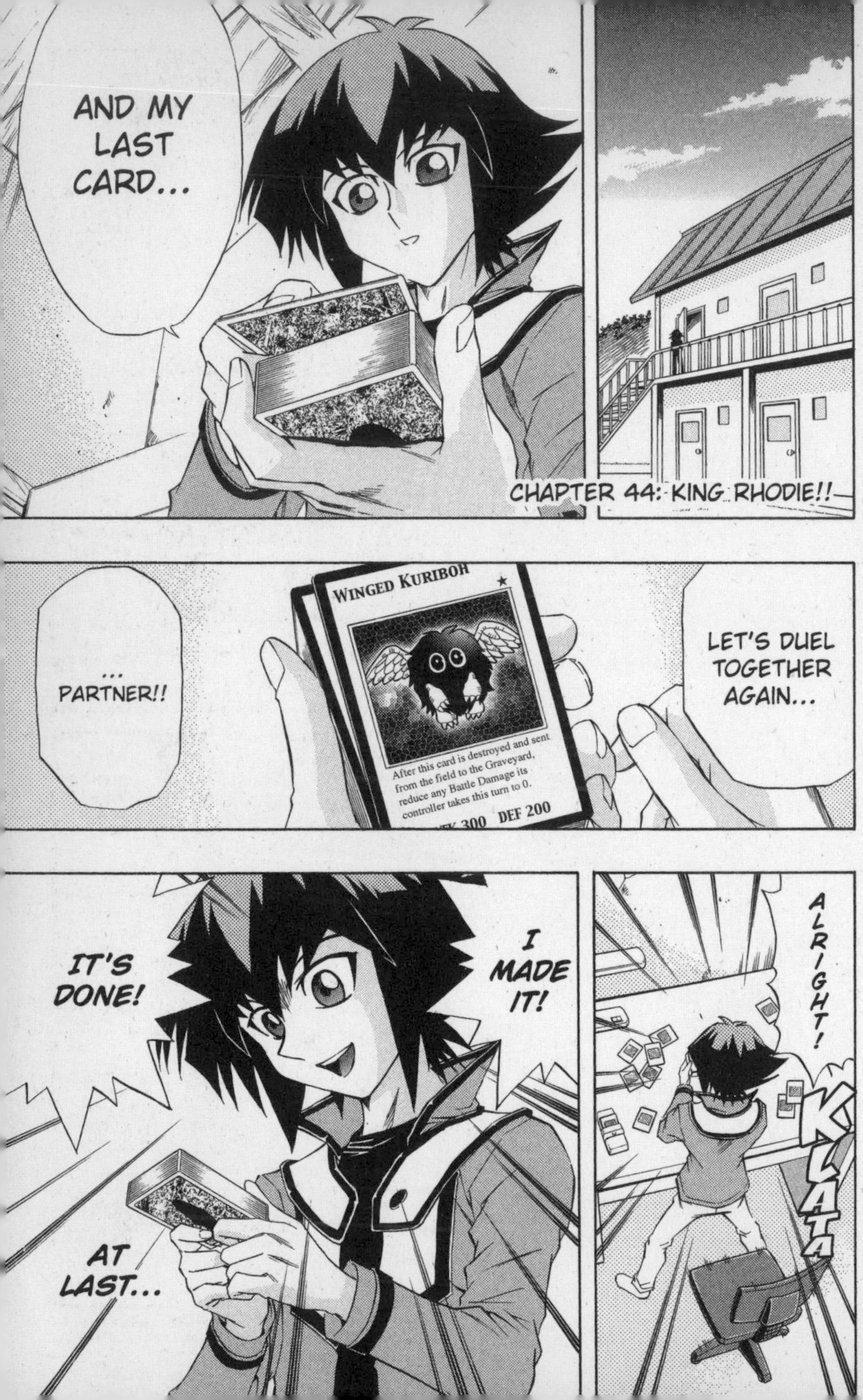
CHAPTER 44: KING RHODIE!!
AND MY LAST CARD...
LET'S DUEL TOGETHER AGAIN...
WINGED KURIBOH
After this card is destroyed and sent from the field to the Graveyard, reduce any Battle Damage its controller takes this turn to 0.
DEF 200
... PARTNER!!
ALRIGHT!
KLATA
I MADE IT!
IT'S DONE!
AT LAST...

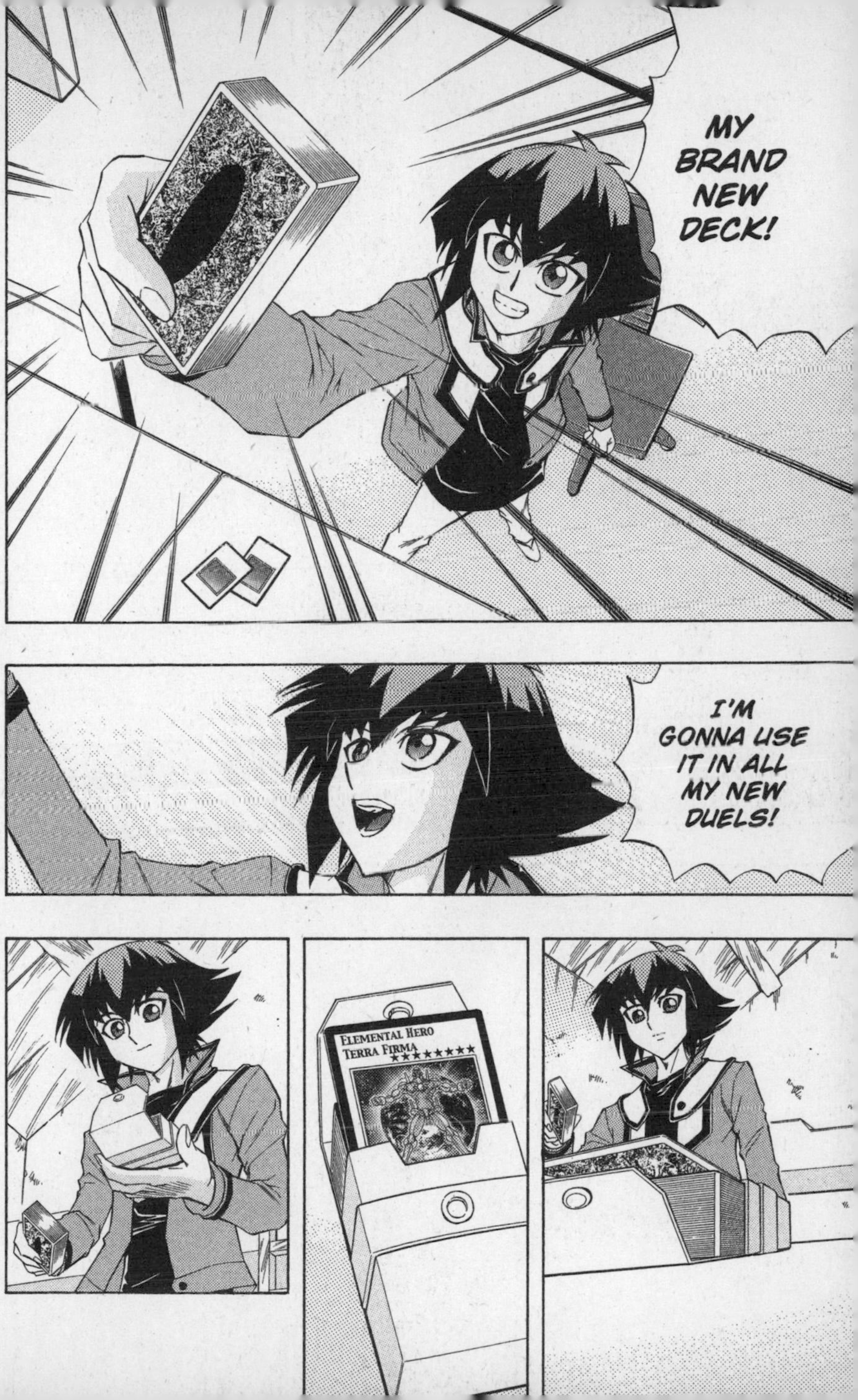
MY BRAND NEW DECK!
I'M GONNA USE IT IN ALL MY NEW DUELS!
ELEMENTAL HERO TERRA FIRMA

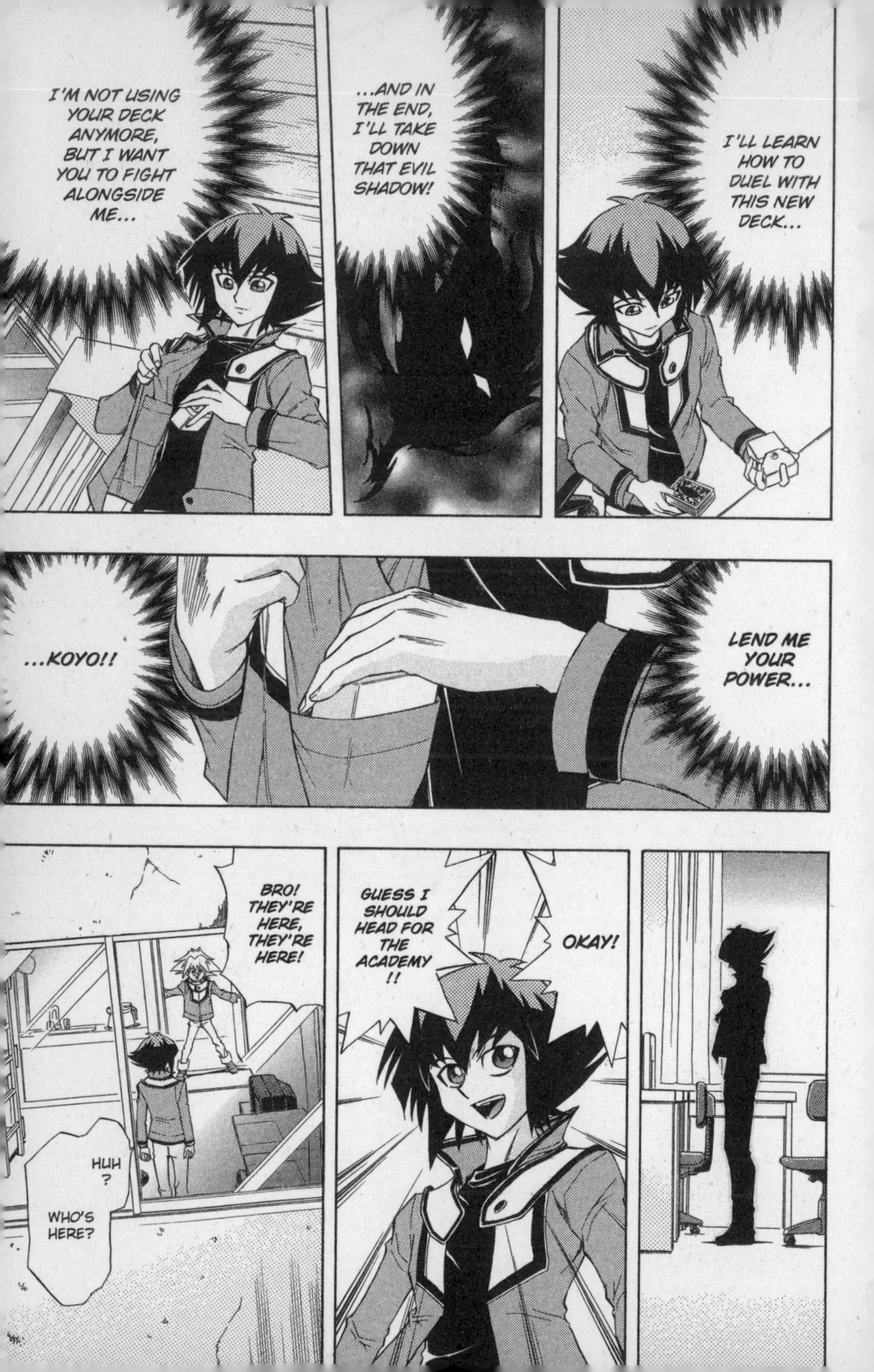
I'LL LEARN HOW TO DUEL WITH THIS NEW DECK...
...AND IN THE END, I'LL TAKE DOWN THAT EVIL SHADOW!
I'M NOT USING YOUR DECK ANYMORE, BUT I WANT YOU TO FIGHT ALONGSIDE ME...
LEND ME YOUR POWER...
...KOYO!!
OKAY!
GUESS I SHOULD HEAD FOR THE ACADEMY !!
BRO! THEY'RE HERE, THEY'RE HERE!
HUH ?
WHO'S HERE?

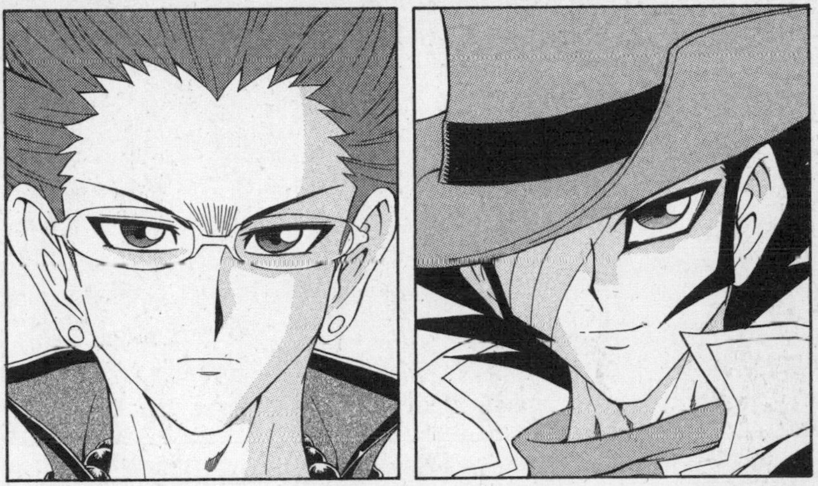

# CHAPTER 44: KING RHODIE!!

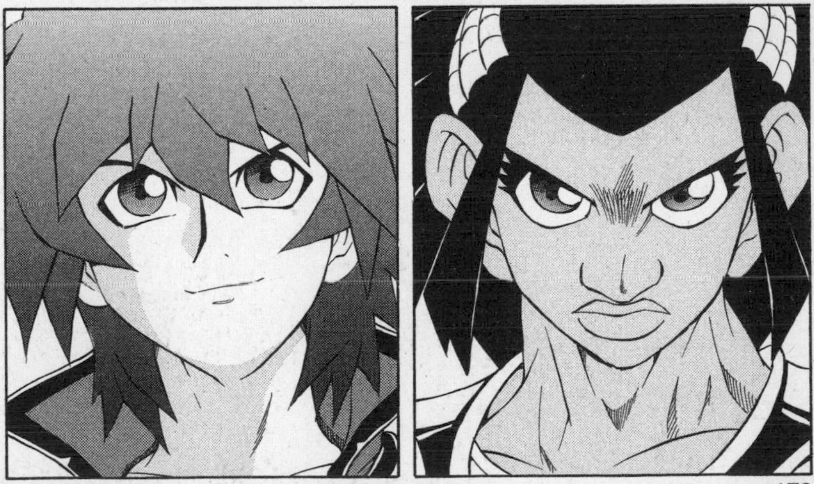

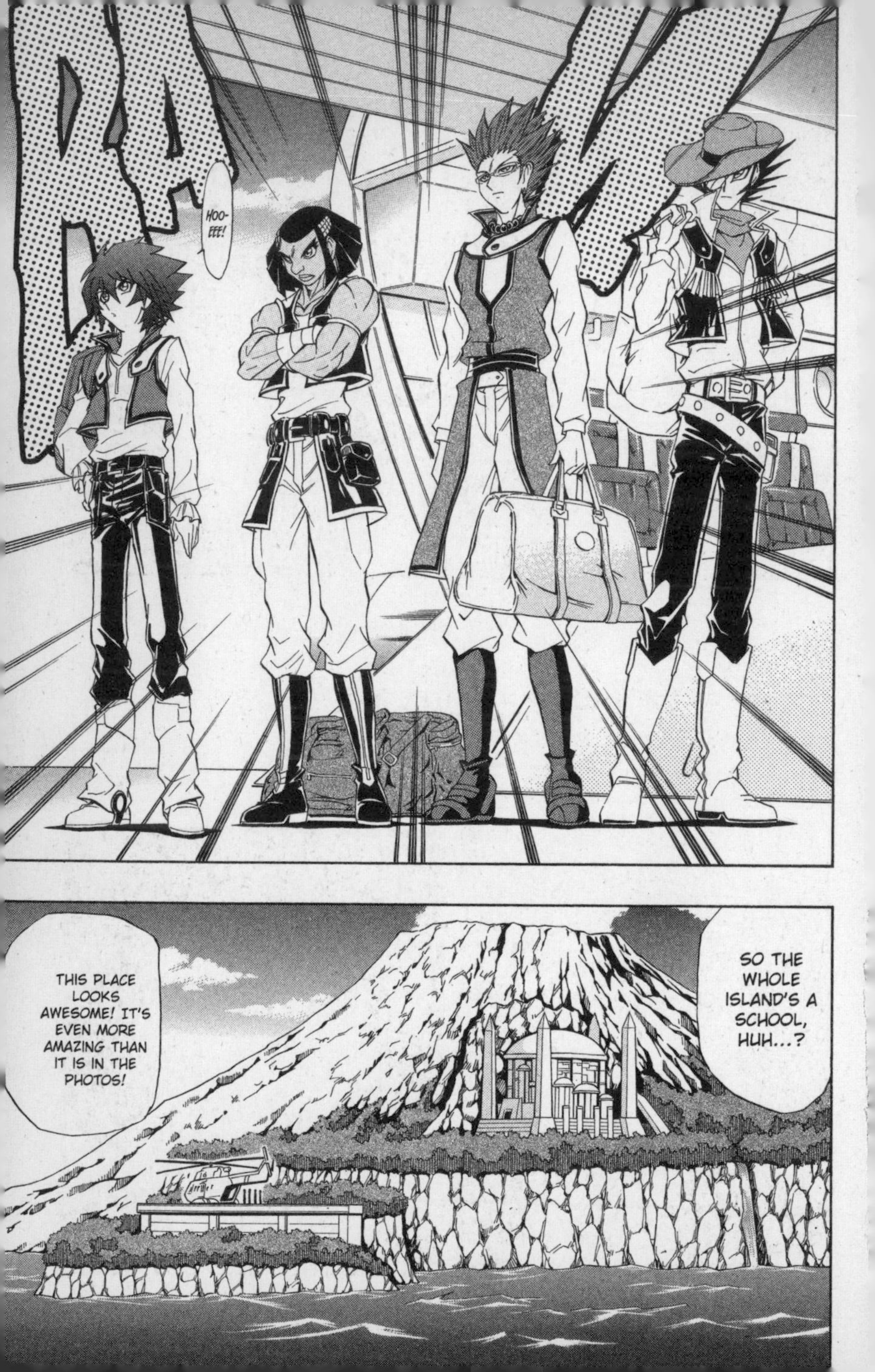
HOO-EEE!
SO THE WHOLE ISLAND'S A SCHOOL, HUH...?
THIS PLACE LOOKS AWESOME! IT'S EVEN MORE AMAZING THAN IT IS IN THE PHOTOS!

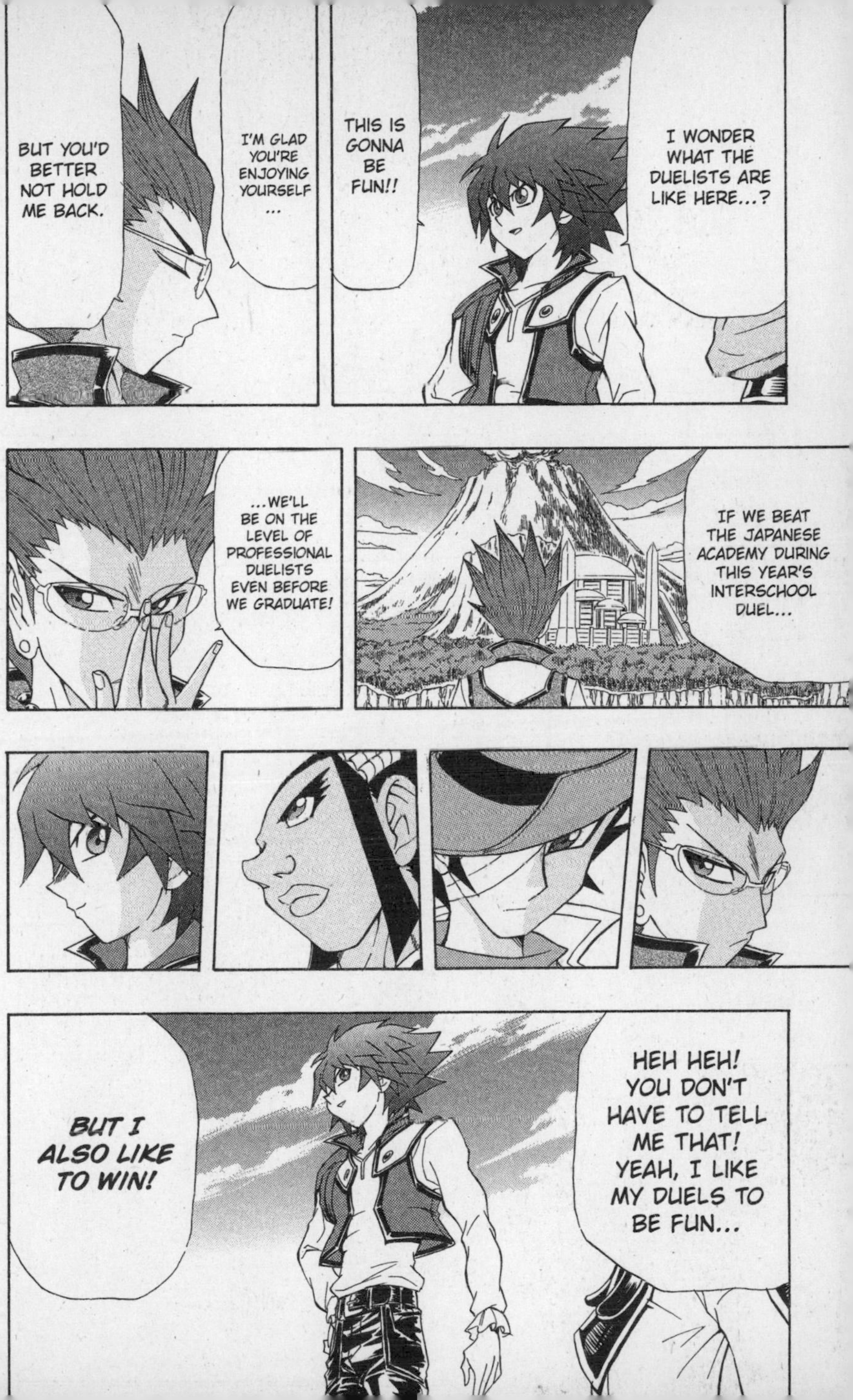
I WONDER WHAT THE DUELISTS ARE LIKE HERE...?
THIS IS GONNA BE FUN!!
I'M GLAD YOU'RE ENJOYING YOURSELF ...
BUT YOU'D BETTER NOT HOLD ME BACK.
IF WE BEAT THE JAPANESE ACADEMY DURING THIS YEAR'S INTERSCHOOL DUEL...
...WE'LL BE ON THE LEVEL OF PROFESSIONAL DUELISTS EVEN BEFORE WE GRADUATE!
HEH HEH! YOU DON'T HAVE TO TELL ME THAT! YEAH, I LIKE MY DUELS TO BE FUN...
BUT I ALSO LIKE TO WIN!

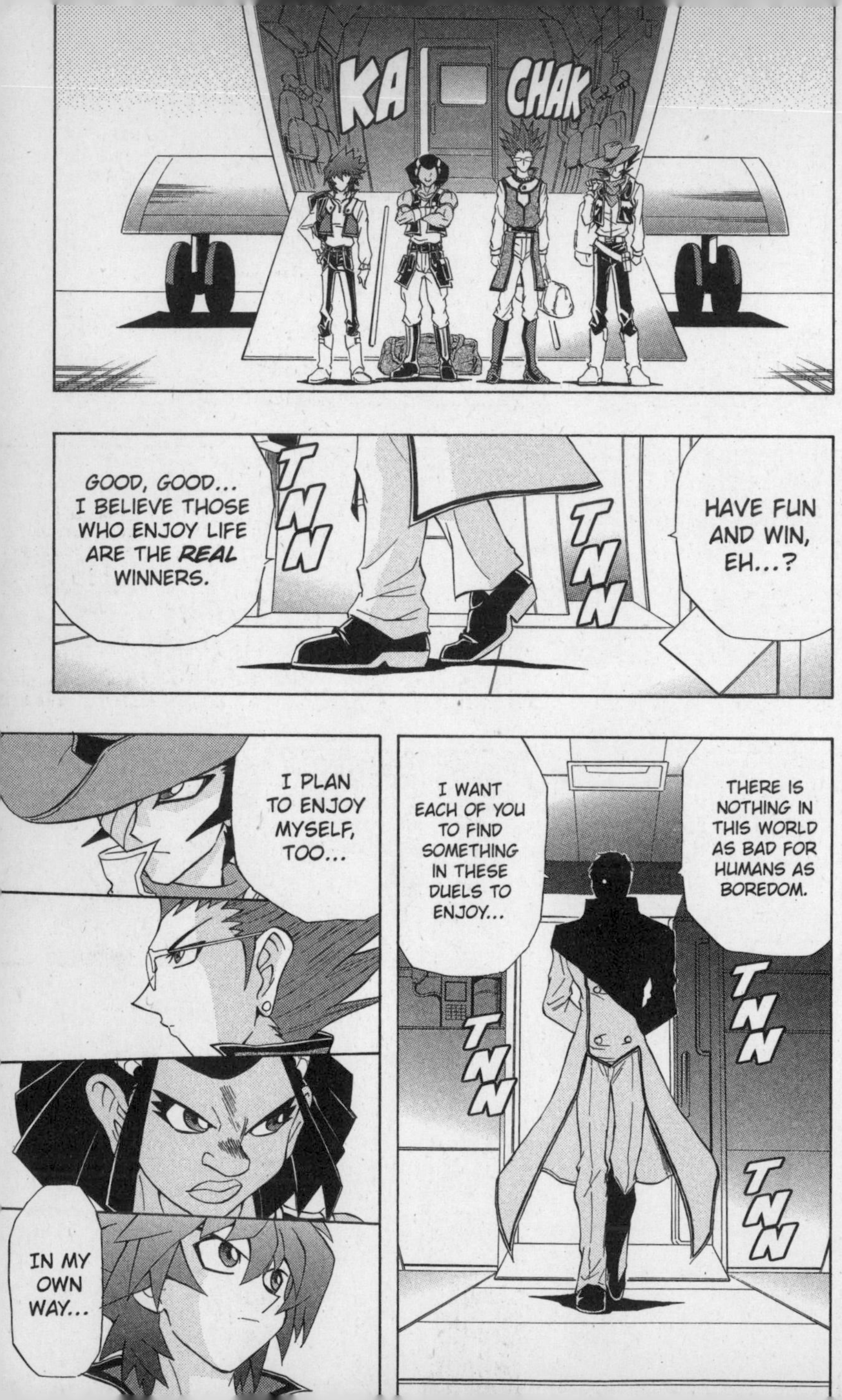
KA
CHAK
HAVE FUN AND WIN, EH...?
TNN
TNN
GOOD, GOOD... I BELIEVE THOSE WHO ENJOY LIFE ARE THE *REAL* WINNERS.
THERE IS NOTHING IN THIS WORLD AS BAD FOR HUMANS AS BOREDOM.
TNN
TNN
I WANT EACH OF YOU TO FIND SOMETHING IN THESE DUELS TO ENJOY...
TNN
I PLAN TO ENJOY MYSELF, TOO...
IN MY OWN WAY...

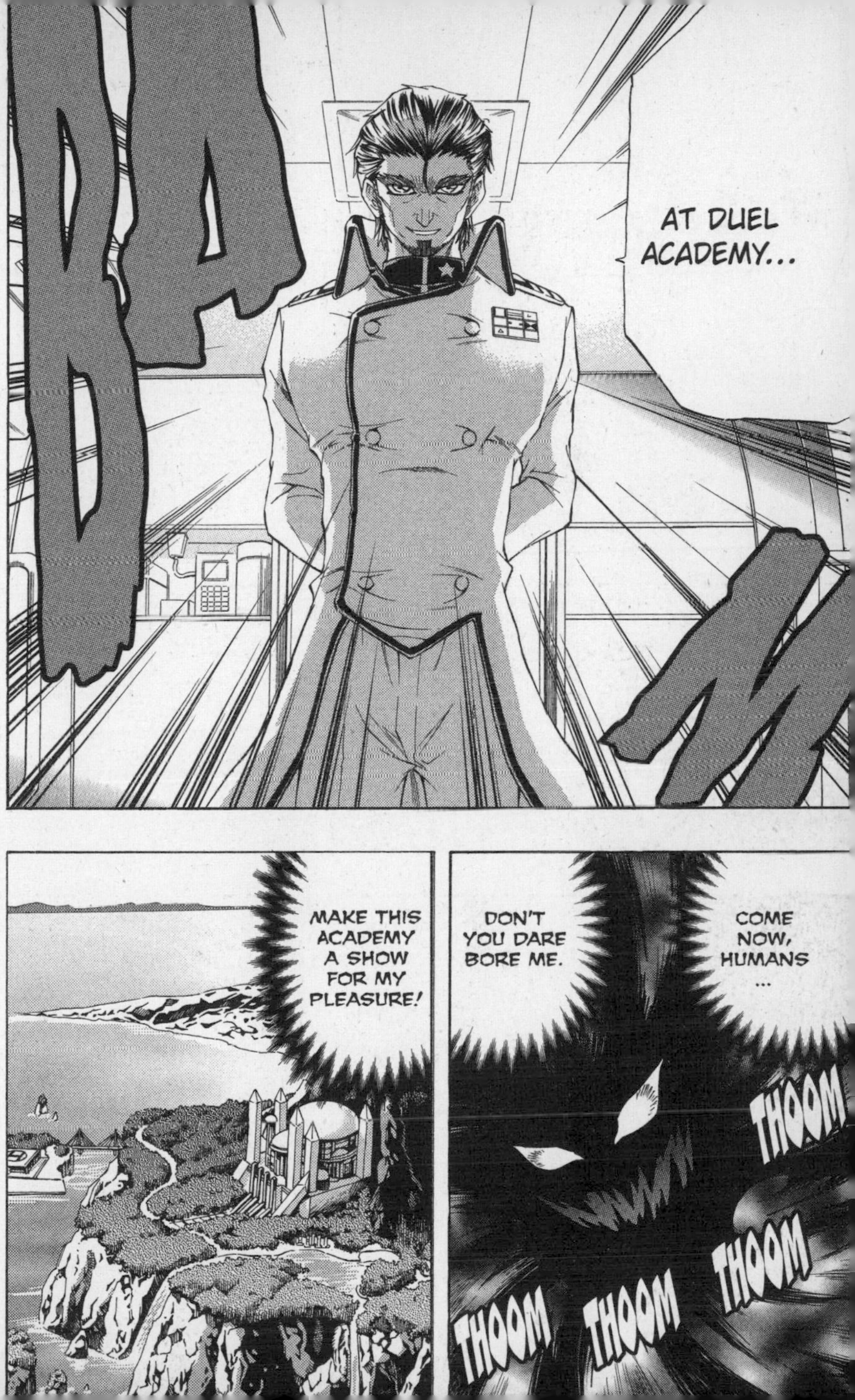
BAM
AT DUEL ACADEMY...
COME NOW, HUMANS ...
DON'T YOU DARE BORE ME.
THOOM
THOOM
THOOM
THOOM
MAKE THIS ACADEMY A SHOW FOR MY PLEASURE!

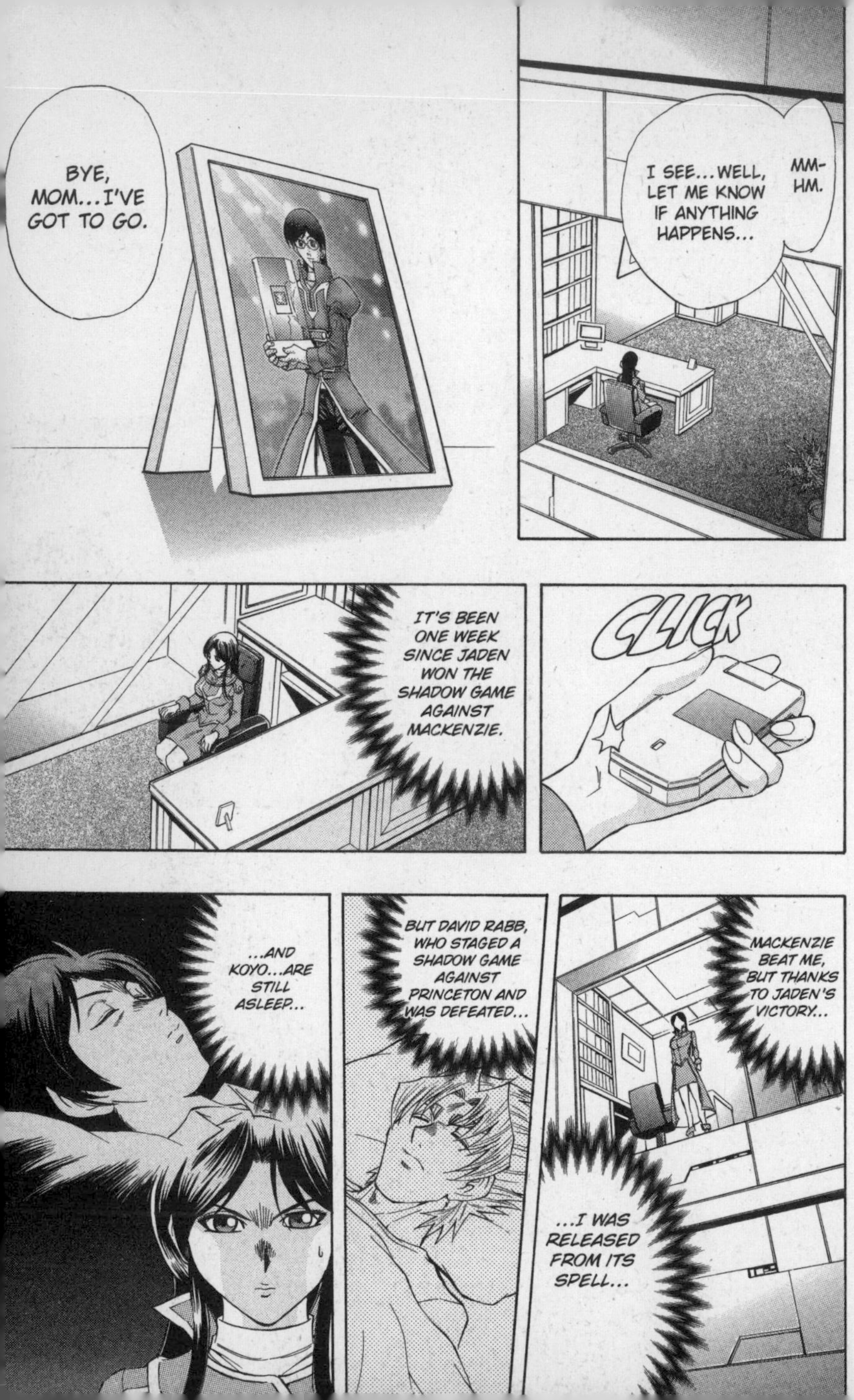
MM-HM.
I SEE...WELL, LET ME KNOW IF ANYTHING HAPPENS...
BYE, MOM...I'VE GOT TO GO.
CLICK
IT'S BEEN ONE WEEK SINCE JADEN WON THE SHADOW GAME AGAINST MACKENZIE.
MACKENZIE BEAT ME, BUT THANKS TO JADEN'S VICTORY...
...I WAS RELEASED FROM ITS SPELL...
BUT DAVID RABB, WHO STAGED A SHADOW GAME AGAINST PRINCETON AND WAS DEFEATED...
...AND KOYO...ARE STILL ASLEEP...

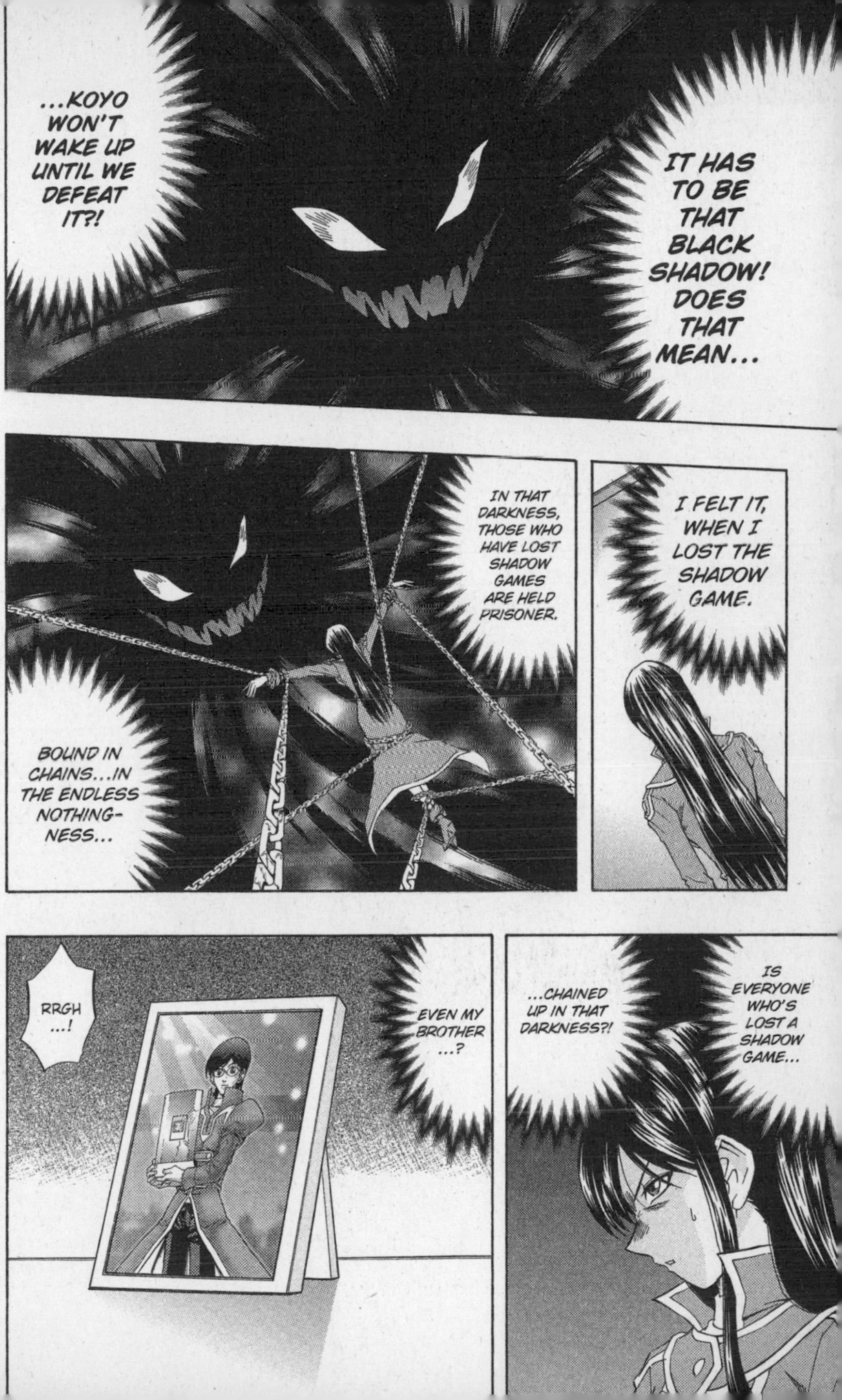
IT HAS TO BE THAT BLACK SHADOW! DOES THAT MEAN...
...KOYO WON'T WAKE UP UNTIL WE DEFEAT IT?!
I FELT IT, WHEN I LOST THE SHADOW GAME.
IN THAT DARKNESS, THOSE WHO HAVE LOST SHADOW GAMES ARE HELD PRISONER.
BOUND IN CHAINS...IN THE ENDLESS NOTHING-NESS...
IS EVERYONE WHO'S LOST A SHADOW GAME...
...CHAINED UP IN THAT DARKNESS?!
EVEN MY BROTHER ...?
RRGH ...!

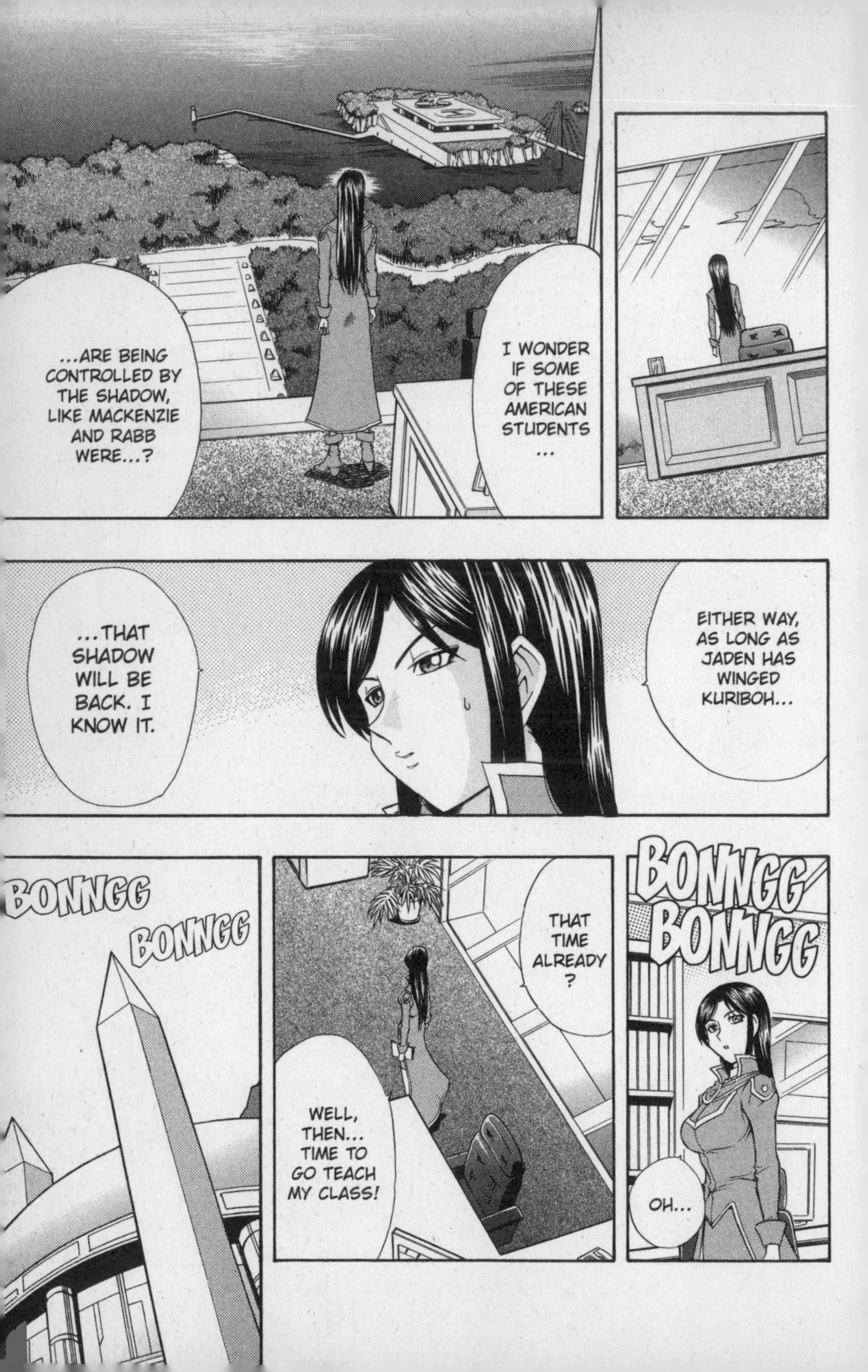
I WONDER IF SOME OF THESE AMERICAN STUDENTS...
...ARE BEING CONTROLLED BY THE SHADOW, LIKE MACKENZIE AND RABB WERE...?
EITHER WAY, AS LONG AS JADEN HAS WINGED KURIBOH...
...THAT SHADOW WILL BE BACK. I KNOW IT.
BONNGG BONNGG
OH...
THAT TIME ALREADY?
WELL, THEN... TIME TO GO TEACH MY CLASS!
BONNGG
BONNGG

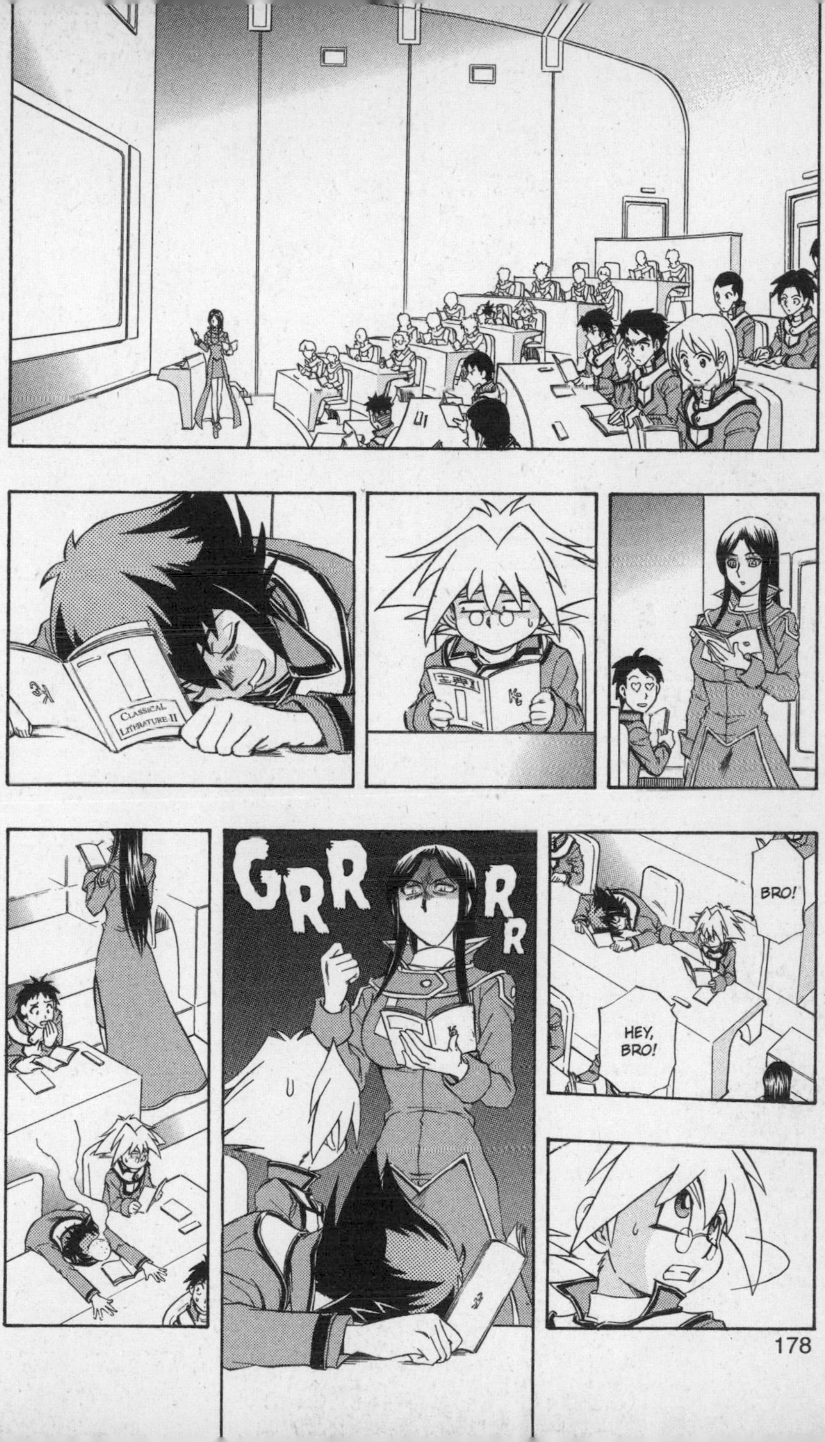
CLASSICAL LITERATURE II
BRO!
HEY, BRO!
GRR RR

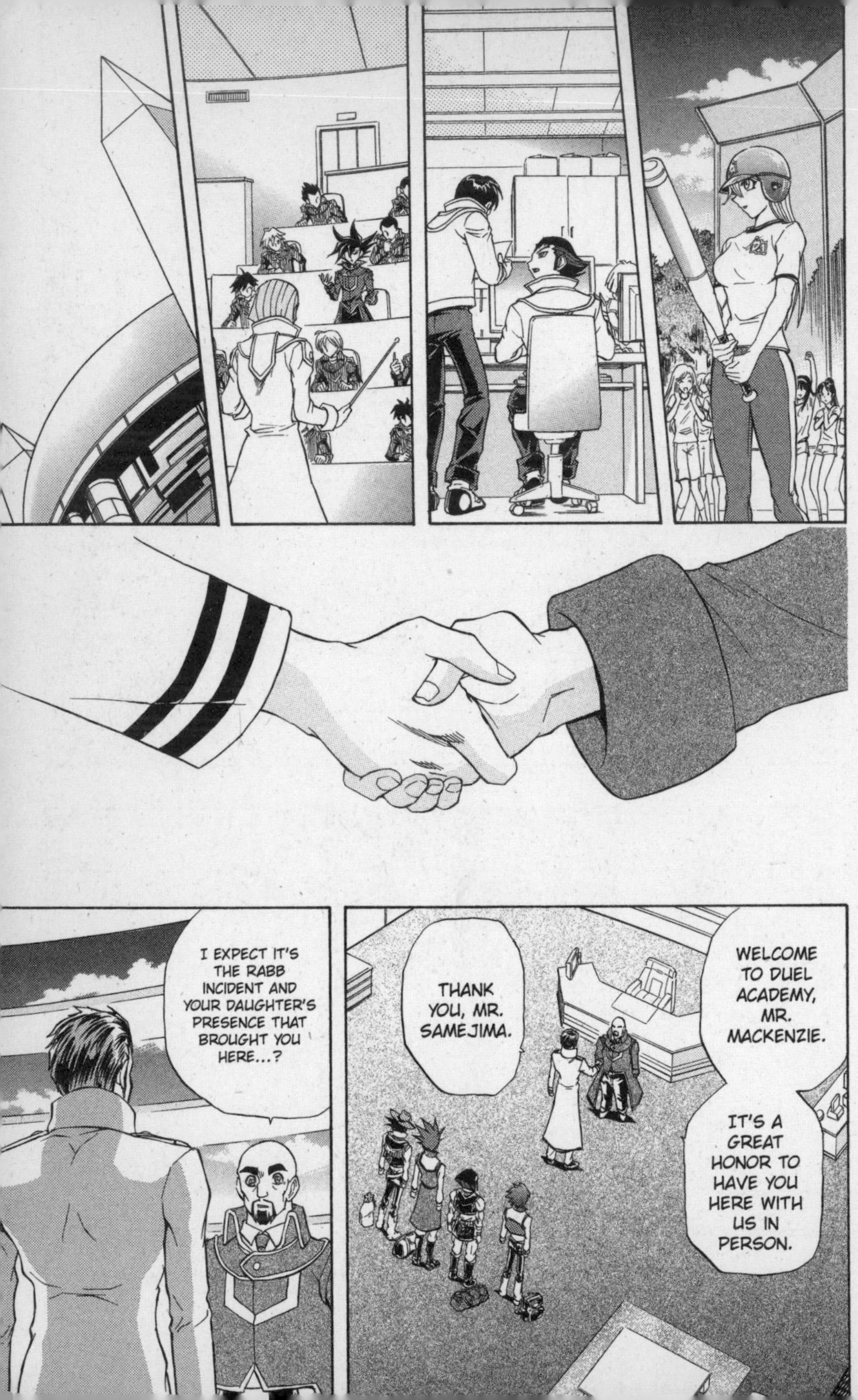
WELCOME TO DUEL ACADEMY, MR. MACKENZIE.
IT'S A GREAT HONOR TO HAVE YOU HERE WITH US IN PERSON.
THANK YOU, MR. SAMEJIMA.
I EXPECT IT'S THE RABB INCIDENT AND YOUR DAUGHTER'S PRESENCE THAT BROUGHT YOU HERE...?

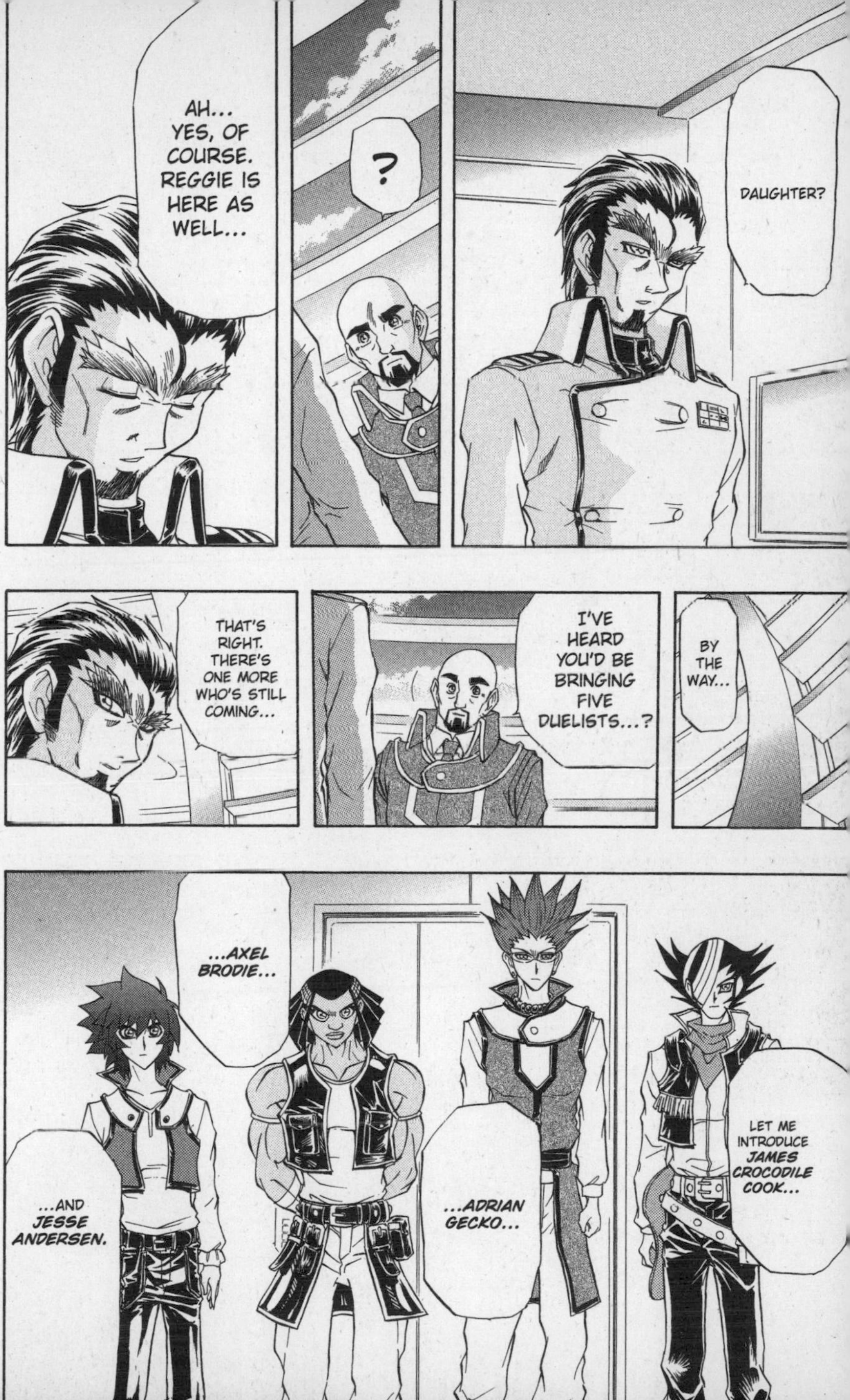
DAUGHTER?
?
AH... YES, OF COURSE. REGGIE IS HERE AS WELL...
BY THE WAY...
I'VE HEARD YOU'D BE BRINGING FIVE DUELISTS...?
THAT'S RIGHT. THERE'S ONE MORE WHO'S STILL COMING...
LET ME INTRODUCE *JAMES CROCODILE COOK*...
...*ADRIAN GECKO*...
...*AXEL BRODIE*...
...AND *JESSE ANDERSEN*.

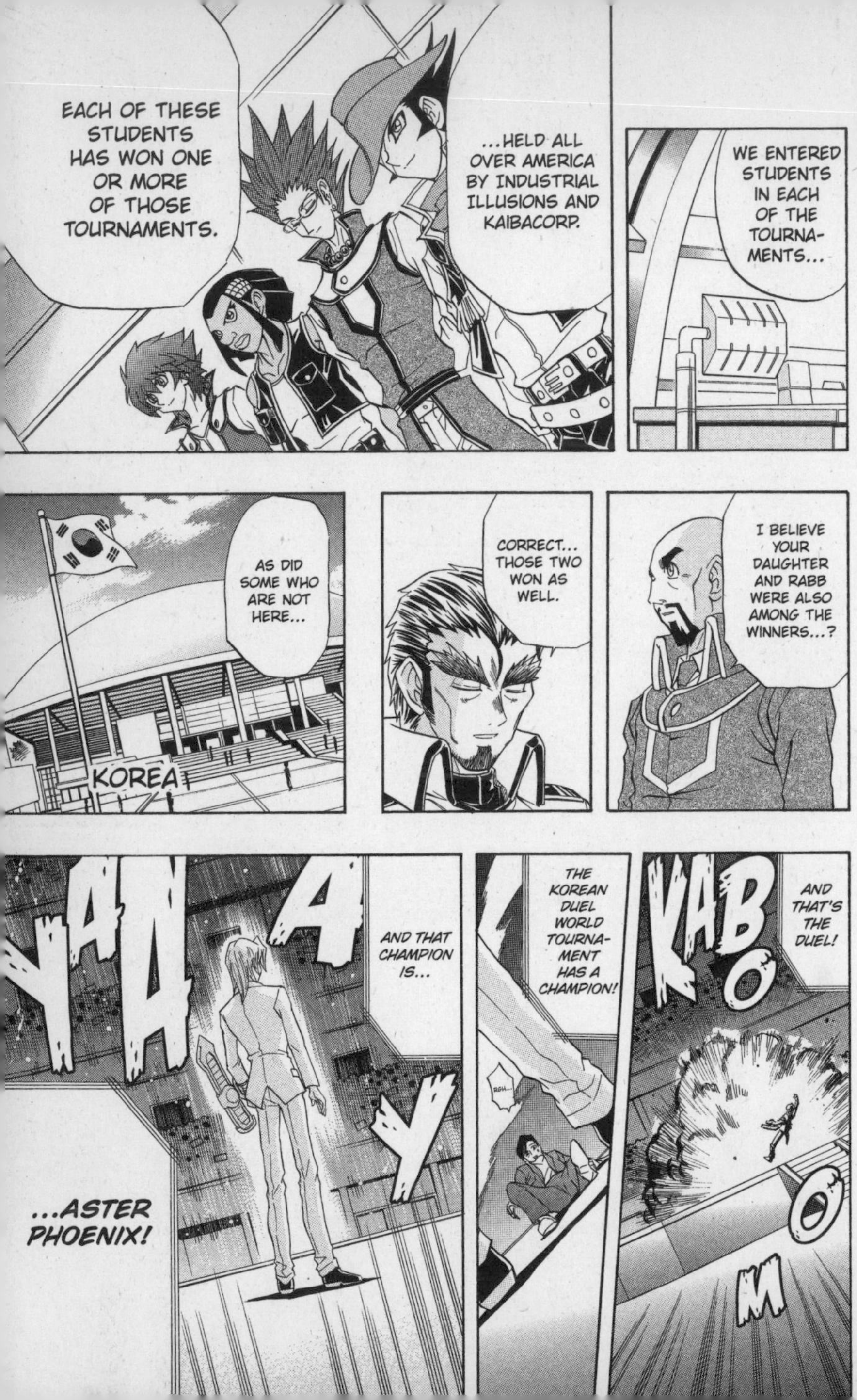
WE ENTERED STUDENTS IN EACH OF THE TOURNAMENTS...
...HELD ALL OVER AMERICA BY INDUSTRIAL ILLUSIONS AND KAIBACORP.
EACH OF THESE STUDENTS HAS WON ONE OR MORE OF THOSE TOURNAMENTS.
I BELIEVE YOUR DAUGHTER AND RABB WERE ALSO AMONG THE WINNERS...?
CORRECT... THOSE TWO WON AS WELL.
AS DID SOME WHO ARE NOT HERE...
KOREA
AND THAT'S THE DUEL!
KABOOM
THE KOREAN DUEL WORLD TOURNAMENT HAS A CHAMPION!
RGH...
AND THAT CHAMPION IS...
YAAAY
...ASTER PHOENIX!

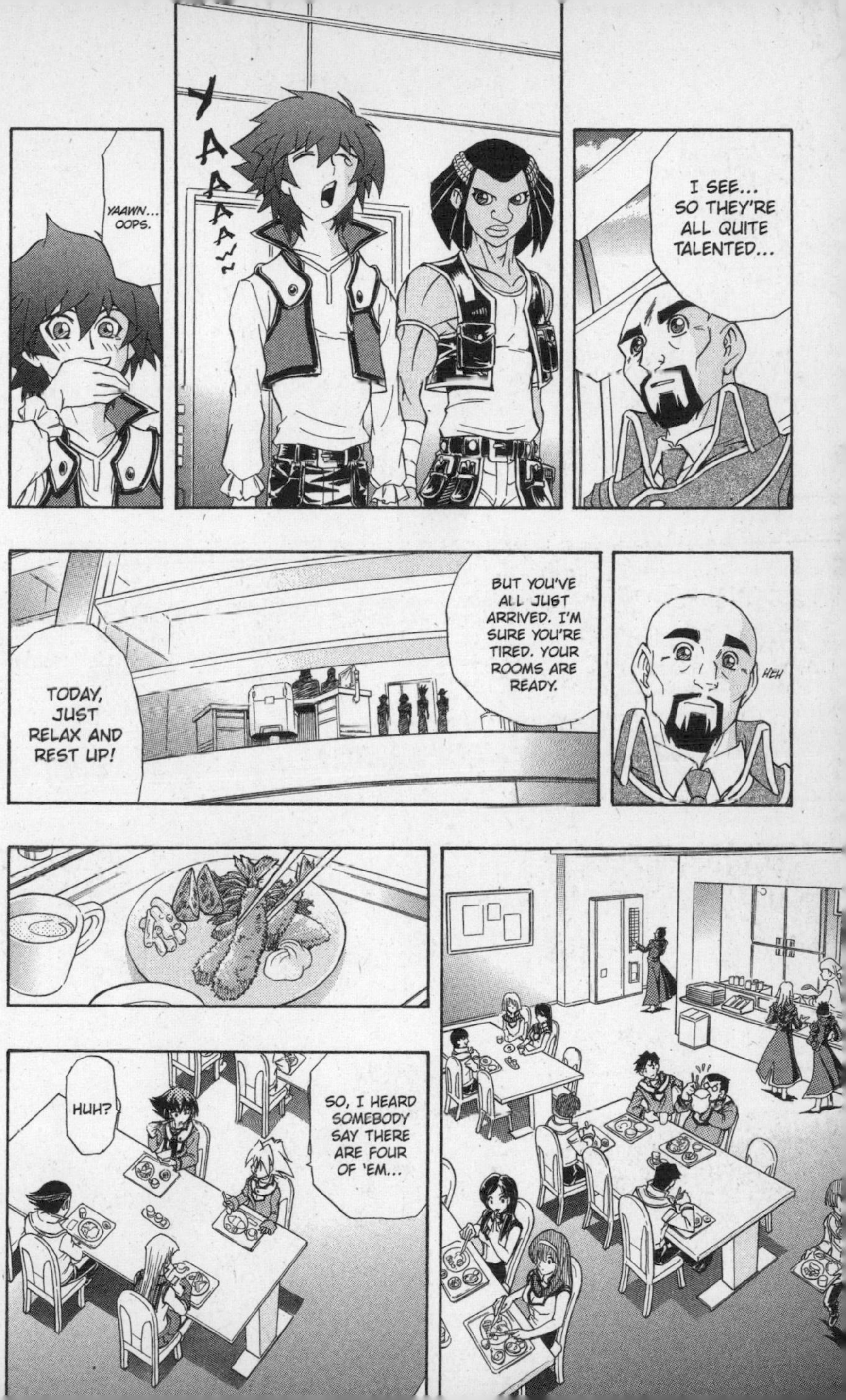
I SEE... SO THEY'RE ALL QUITE TALENTED...
YAAAAW
YAAWN... OOPS.
HEH
BUT YOU'VE ALL JUST ARRIVED. I'M SURE YOU'RE TIRED. YOUR ROOMS ARE READY.
TODAY, JUST RELAX AND REST UP!
SO, I HEARD SOMEBODY SAY THERE ARE FOUR OF 'EM...
HUH?

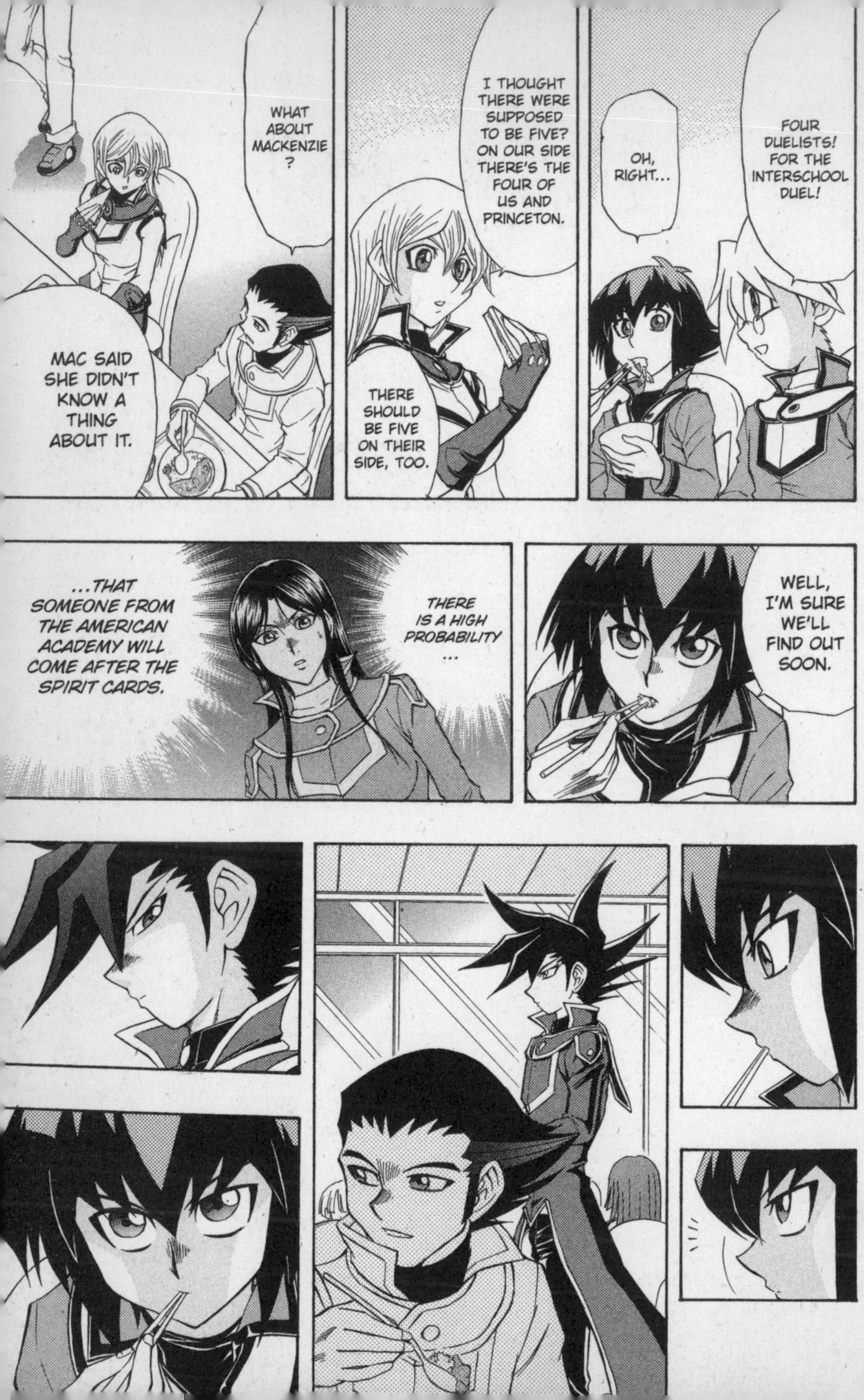
FOUR DUELISTS! FOR THE INTERSCHOOL DUEL!
OH, RIGHT...
I THOUGHT THERE WERE SUPPOSED TO BE FIVE? ON OUR SIDE THERE'S THE FOUR OF US AND PRINCETON.
THERE SHOULD BE FIVE ON THEIR SIDE, TOO.
WHAT ABOUT MACKENZIE?
MAC SAID SHE DIDN'T KNOW A THING ABOUT IT.
WELL, I'M SURE WE'LL FIND OUT SOON.
THERE IS A HIGH PROBABILITY ...
...THAT SOMEONE FROM THE AMERICAN ACADEMY WILL COME AFTER THE SPIRIT CARDS.

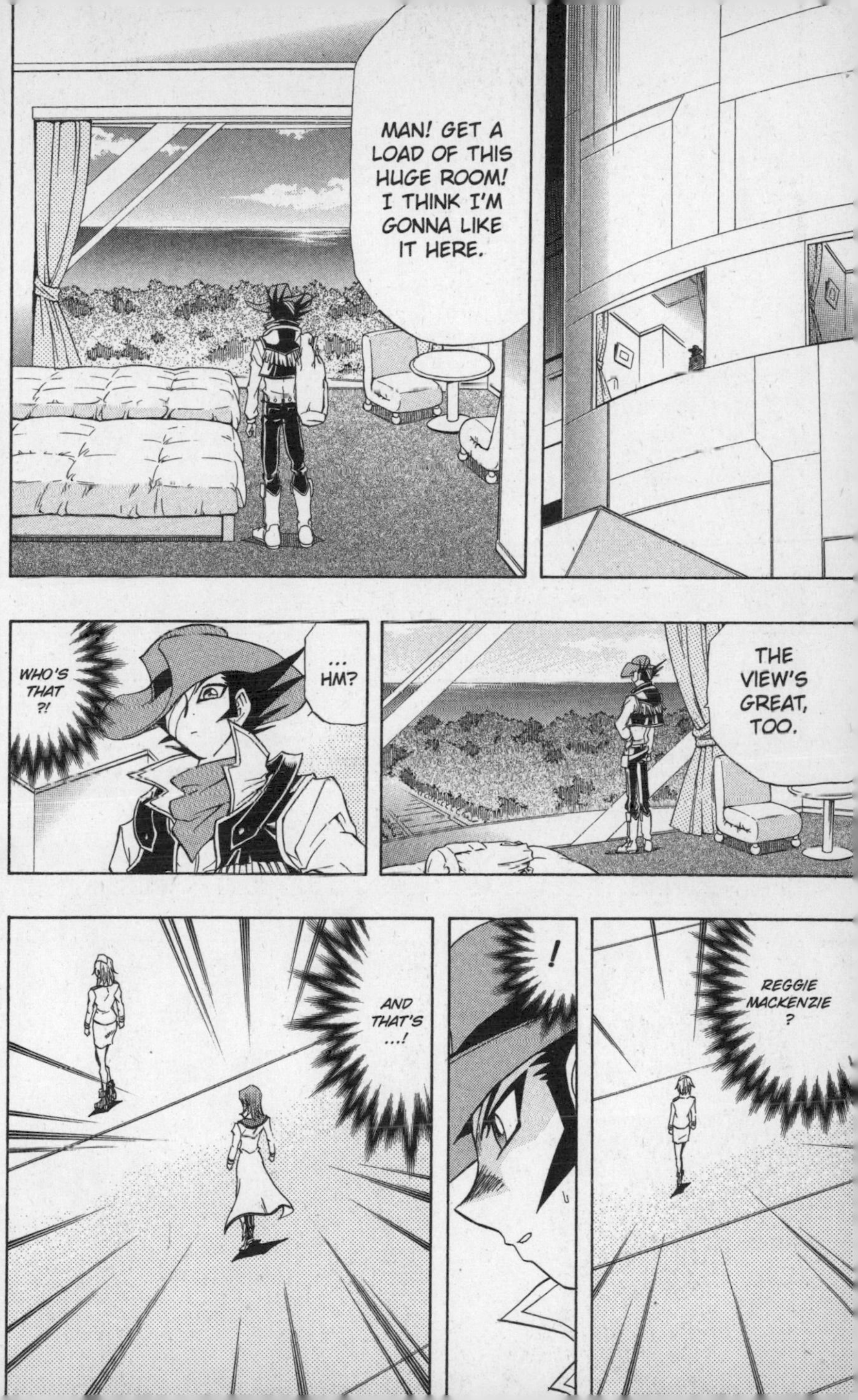
MAN! GET A LOAD OF THIS HUGE ROOM! I THINK I'M GONNA LIKE IT HERE.
THE VIEW'S GREAT, TOO.
... HM?
WHO'S THAT ?!
REGGIE MACKENZIE ?
!
AND THAT'S ...!

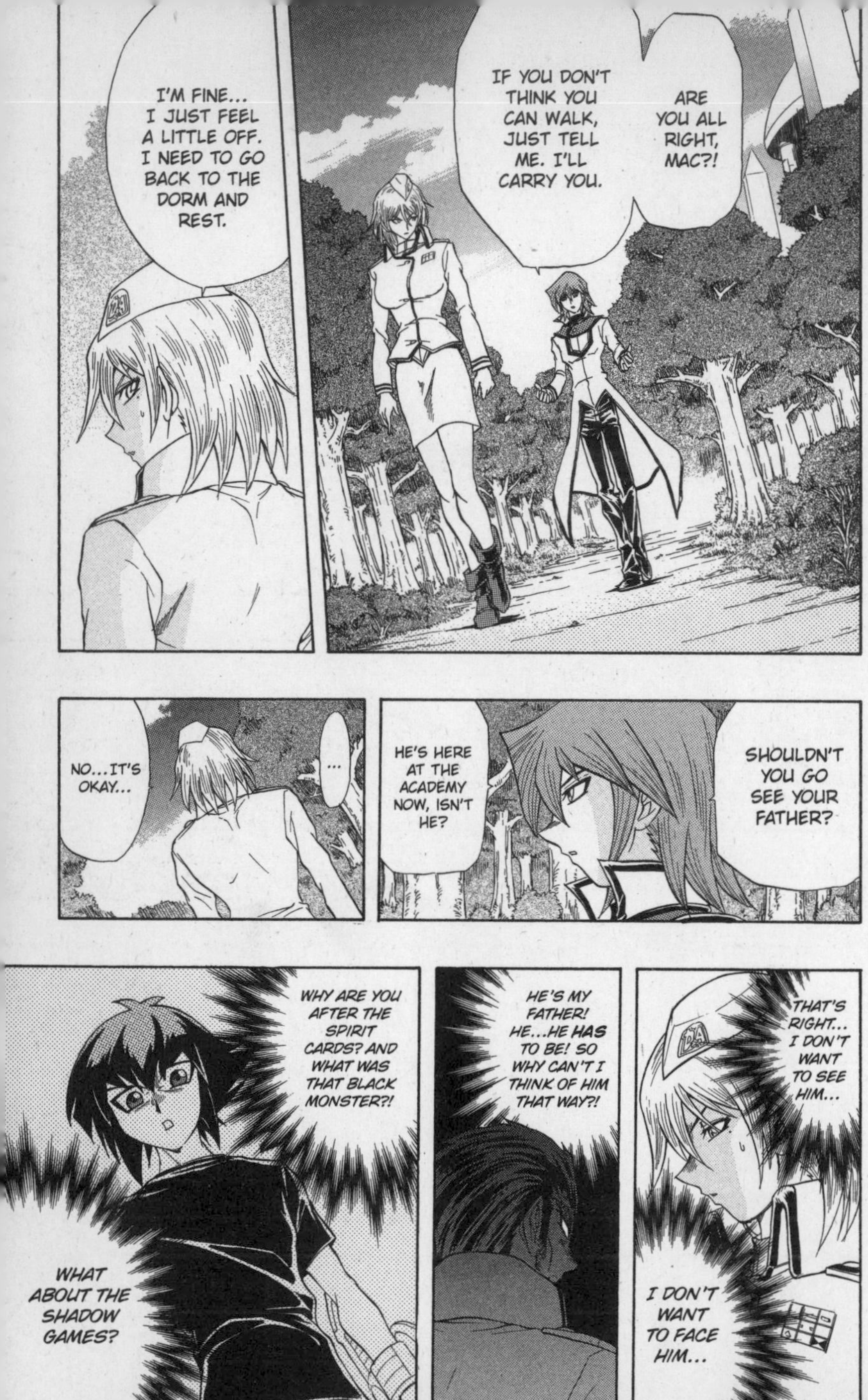
ARE YOU ALL RIGHT, MAC?!
IF YOU DON'T THINK YOU CAN WALK, JUST TELL ME. I'LL CARRY YOU.
I'M FINE... I JUST FEEL A LITTLE OFF. I NEED TO GO BACK TO THE DORM AND REST.
SHOULDN'T YOU GO SEE YOUR FATHER?
HE'S HERE AT THE ACADEMY NOW, ISN'T HE?
...
NO...IT'S OKAY...
THAT'S RIGHT... I DON'T WANT TO SEE HIM...
I DON'T WANT TO FACE HIM...
HE'S MY FATHER! HE...HE HAS TO BE! SO WHY CAN'T I THINK OF HIM THAT WAY?!
WHY ARE YOU AFTER THE SPIRIT CARDS? AND WHAT WAS THAT BLACK MONSTER?!
WHAT ABOUT THE SHADOW GAMES?

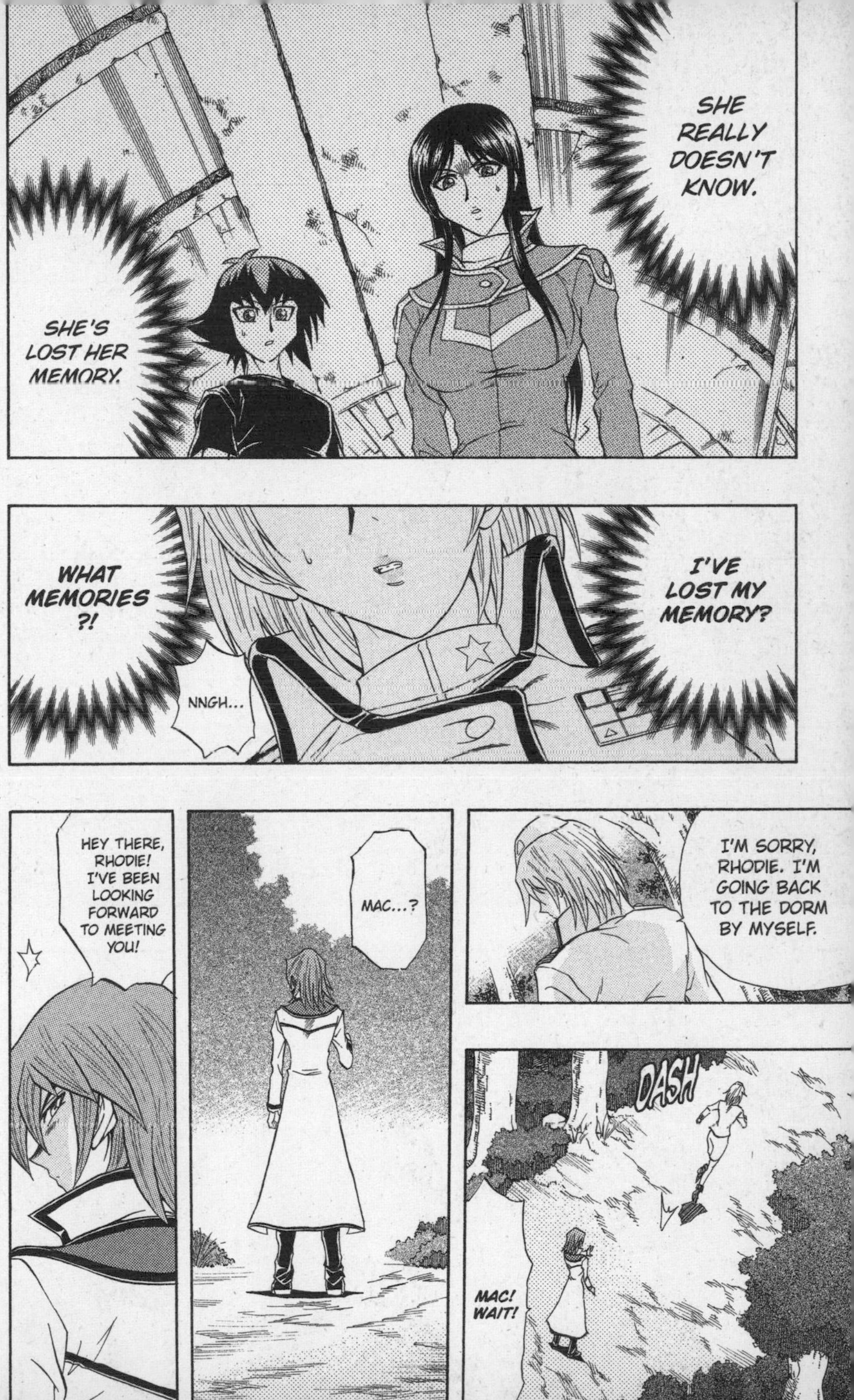
SHE REALLY DOESN'T KNOW.
SHE'S LOST HER MEMORY.
I'VE LOST MY MEMORY?
WHAT MEMORIES ?!
NNGH...
I'M SORRY, RHODIE. I'M GOING BACK TO THE DORM BY MYSELF.
DASH
MAC! WAIT!
MAC...?
HEY THERE, RHODIE! I'VE BEEN LOOKING FORWARD TO MEETING YOU!

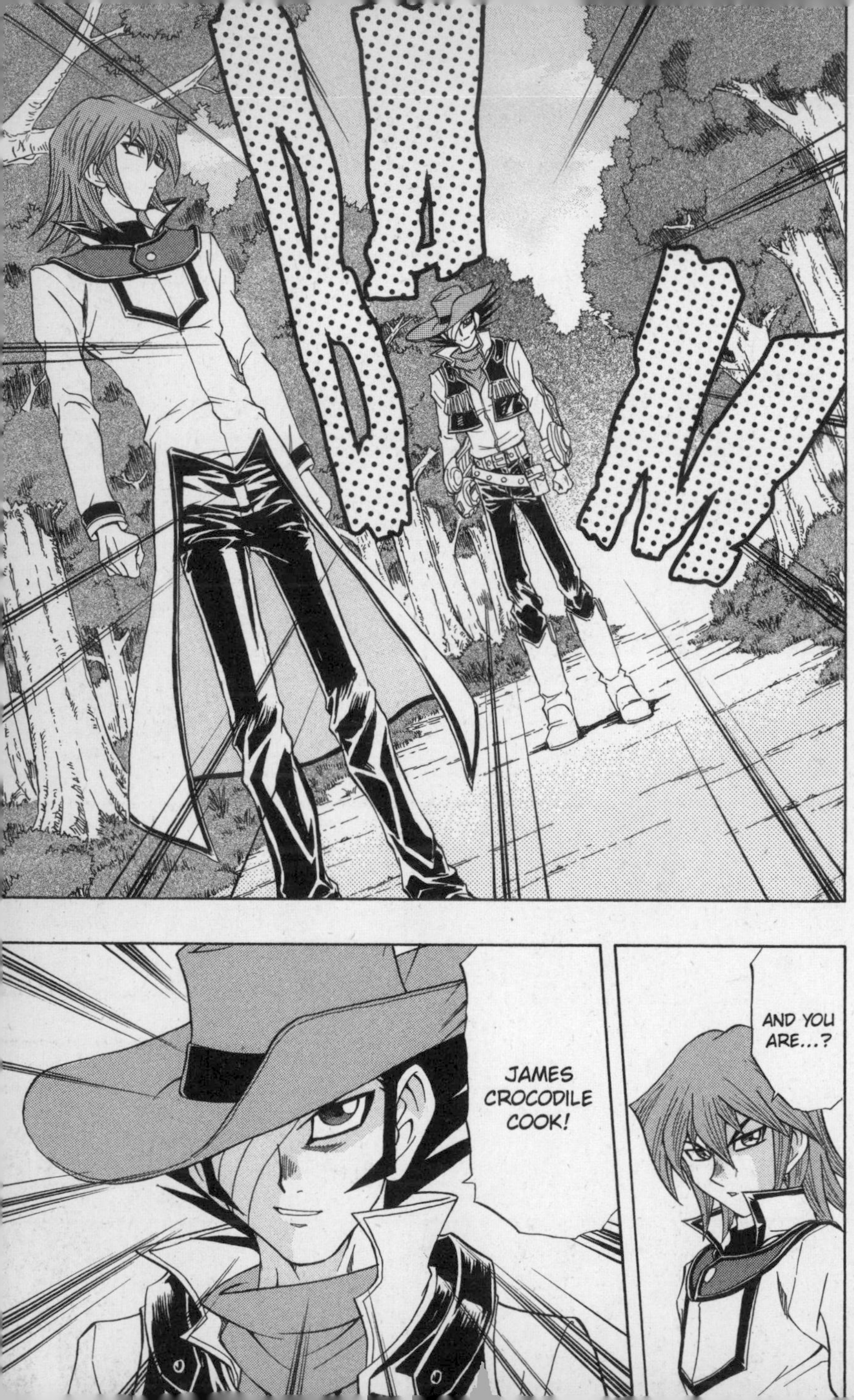
AND YOU ARE...?
JAMES CROCODILE COOK!

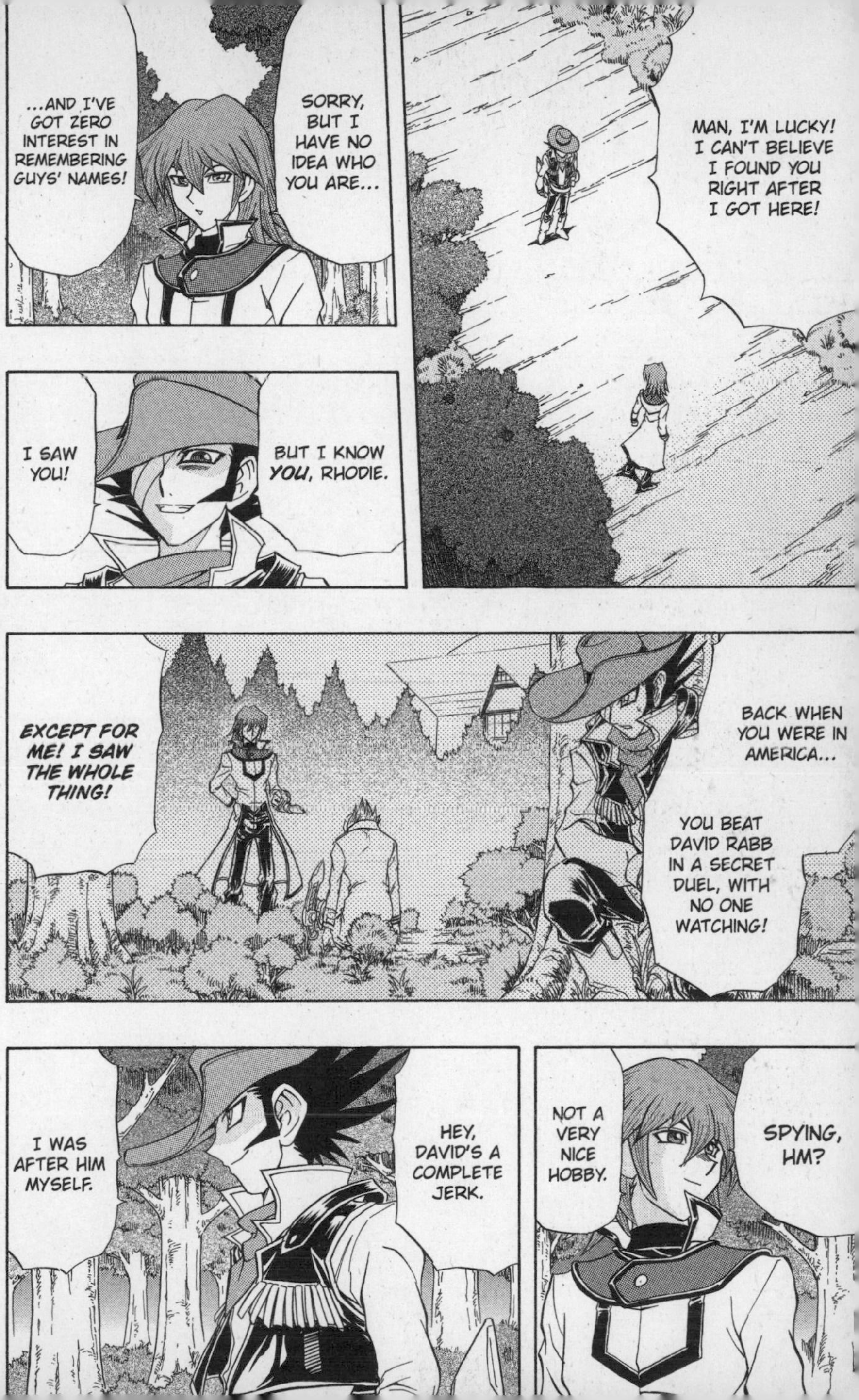
MAN, I'M LUCKY! I CAN'T BELIEVE I FOUND YOU RIGHT AFTER I GOT HERE!
SORRY, BUT I HAVE NO IDEA WHO YOU ARE...
...AND I'VE GOT ZERO INTEREST IN REMEMBERING GUYS' NAMES!
BUT I KNOW *YOU*, RHODIE.
I SAW YOU!
BACK WHEN YOU WERE IN AMERICA...
YOU BEAT DAVID RABB IN A SECRET DUEL, WITH NO ONE WATCHING!
*EXCEPT FOR ME! I SAW THE WHOLE THING!*
SPYING, HM?
NOT A VERY NICE HOBBY.
HEY, DAVID'S A COMPLETE JERK.
I WAS AFTER HIM MYSELF.

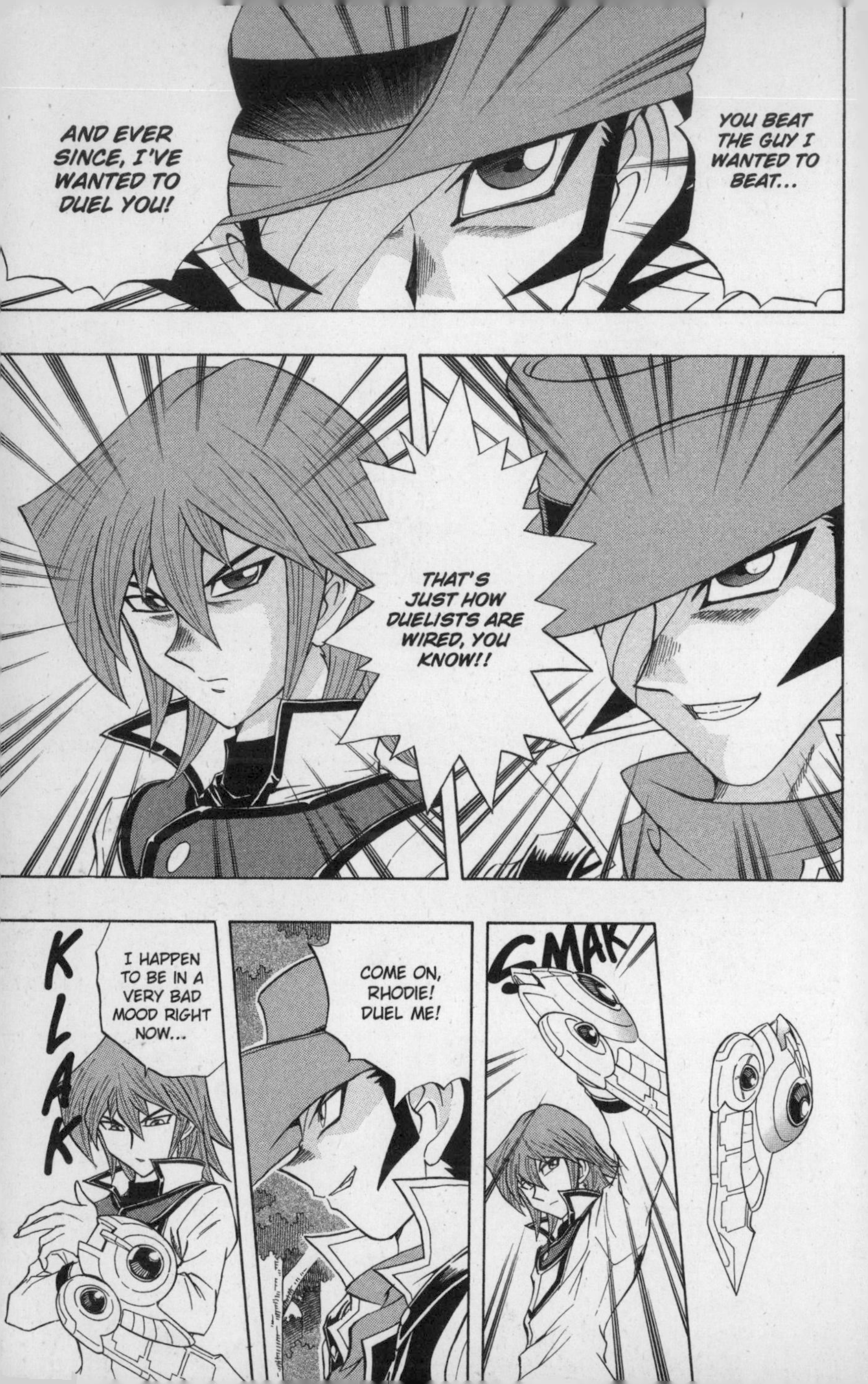
YOU BEAT THE GUY I WANTED TO BEAT...
AND EVER SINCE, I'VE WANTED TO DUEL YOU!
THAT'S JUST HOW DUELISTS ARE WIRED, YOU KNOW!!
GMAK
COME ON, RHODIE! DUEL ME!
I HAPPEN TO BE IN A VERY BAD MOOD RIGHT NOW...
KLAK

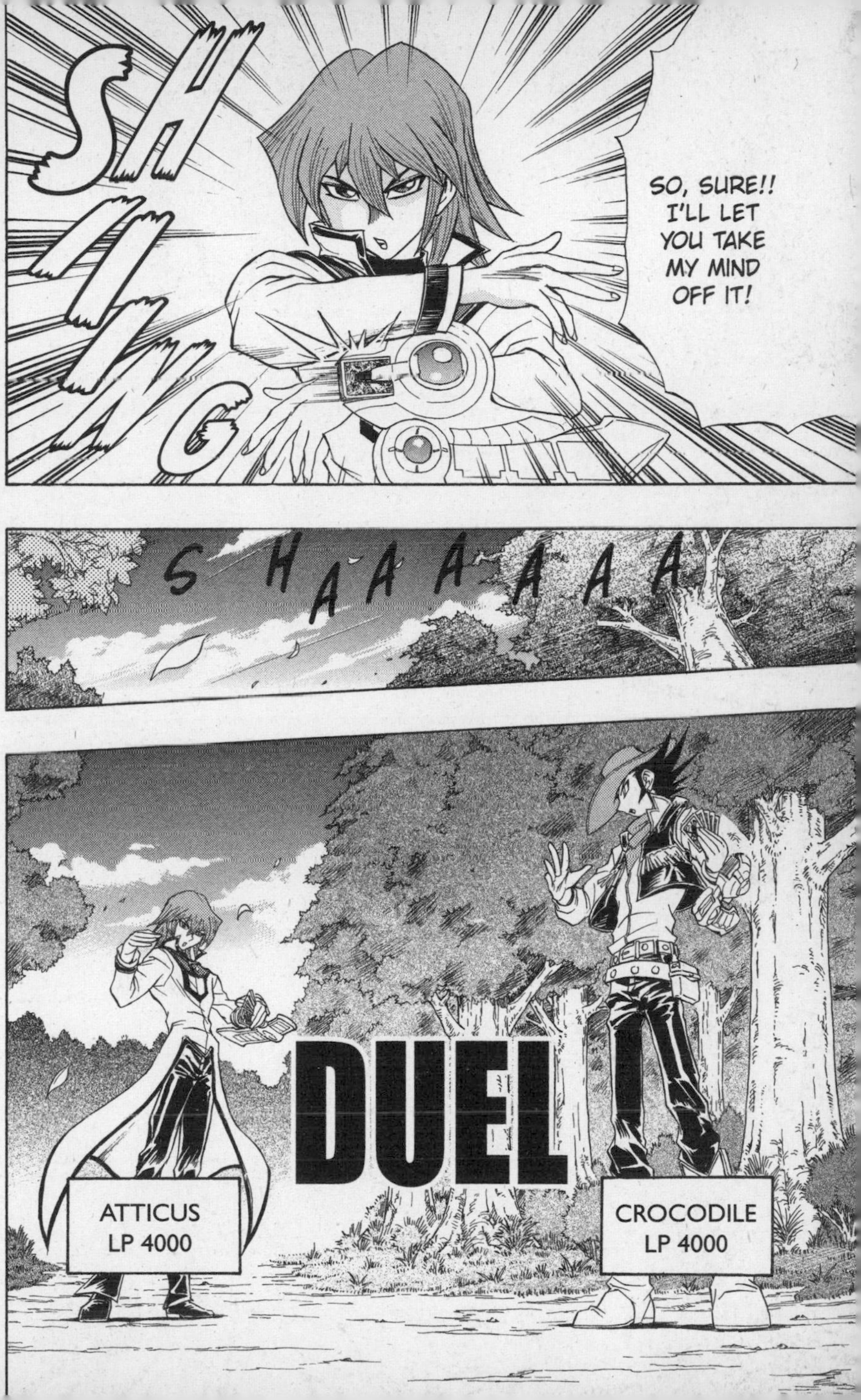
SO, SURE!! I'LL LET YOU TAKE MY MIND OFF IT!
SHING
SHAAAAAAA
DUEL
CROCODILE LP 4000
ATTICUS LP 4000

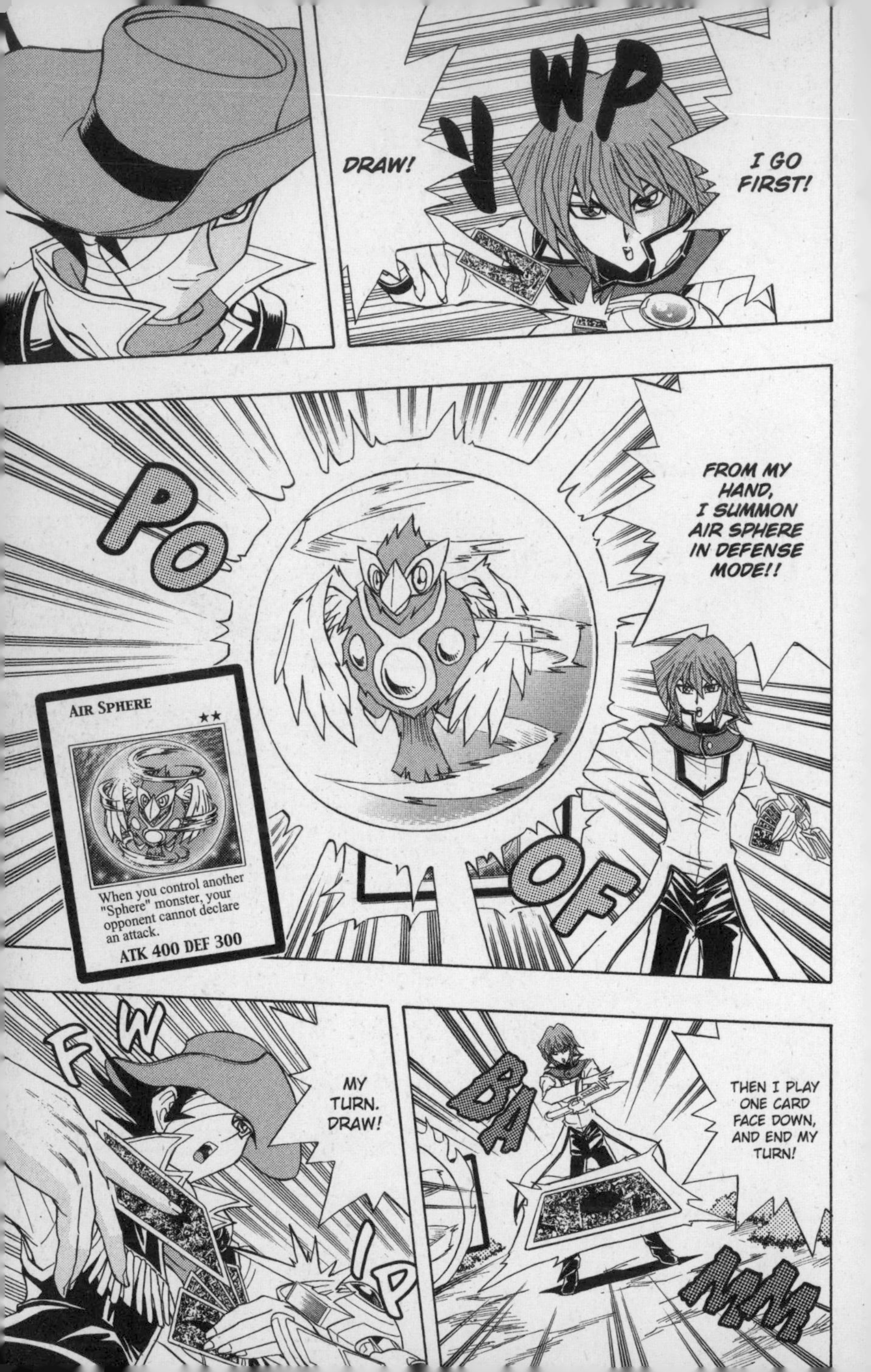
I GO FIRST!
DRAW!
FROM MY HAND, I SUMMON AIR SPHERE IN DEFENSE MODE!!
PO
OF
AIR SPHERE
When you control another "Sphere" monster, your opponent cannot declare an attack.
ATK 400 DEF 300
THEN I PLAY ONE CARD FACE DOWN, AND END MY TURN!
BA
MM
MY TURN. DRAW!
FW
IP

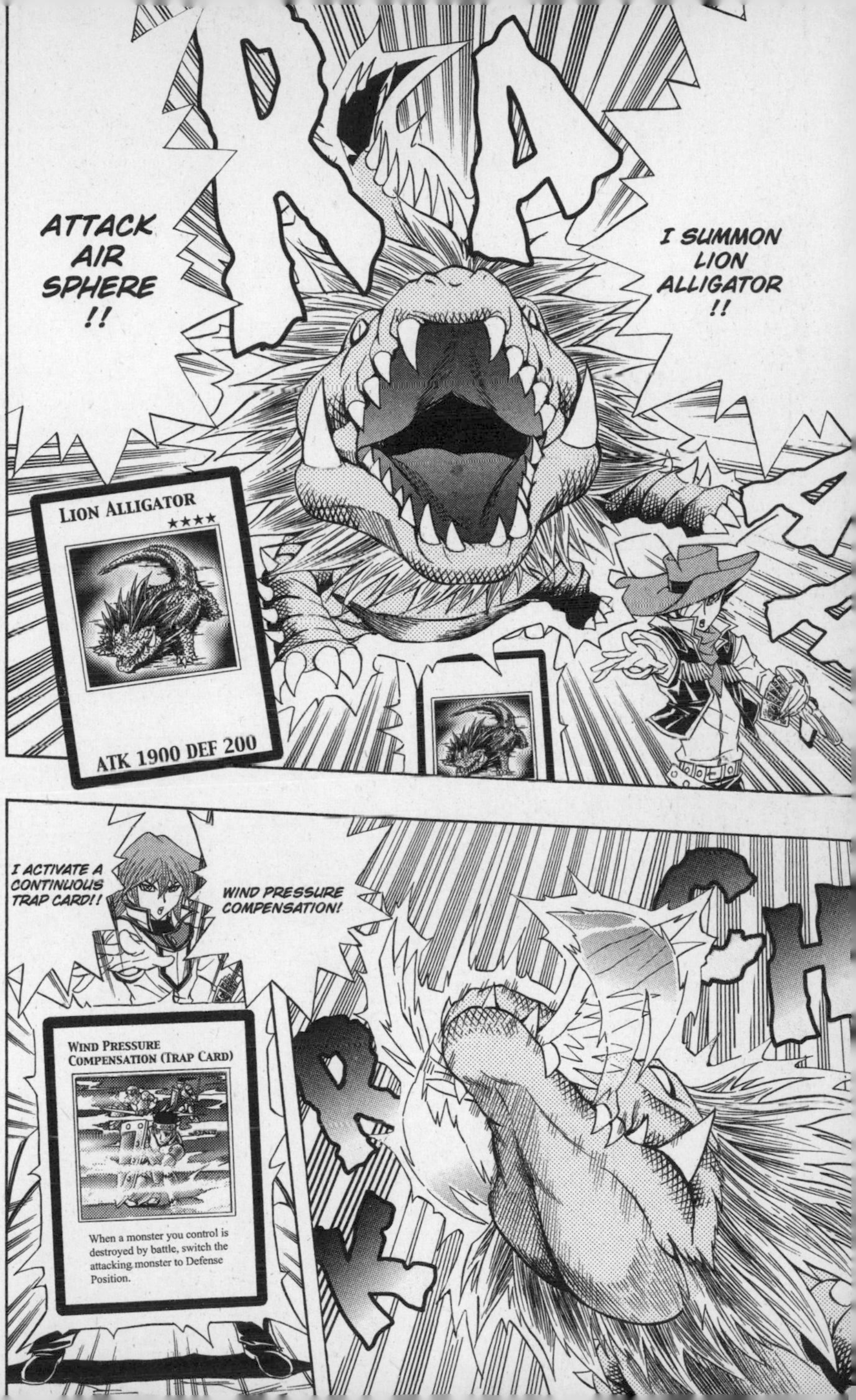
I SUMMON LION ALLIGATOR!!
ATTACK AIR SPHERE!!
LION ALLIGATOR
★★★★
ATK 1900 DEF 200
I ACTIVATE A CONTINUOUS TRAP CARD!!
WIND PRESSURE COMPENSATION!
WIND PRESSURE COMPENSATION (TRAP CARD)
When a monster you control is destroyed by battle, switch the attacking monster to Defense Position.

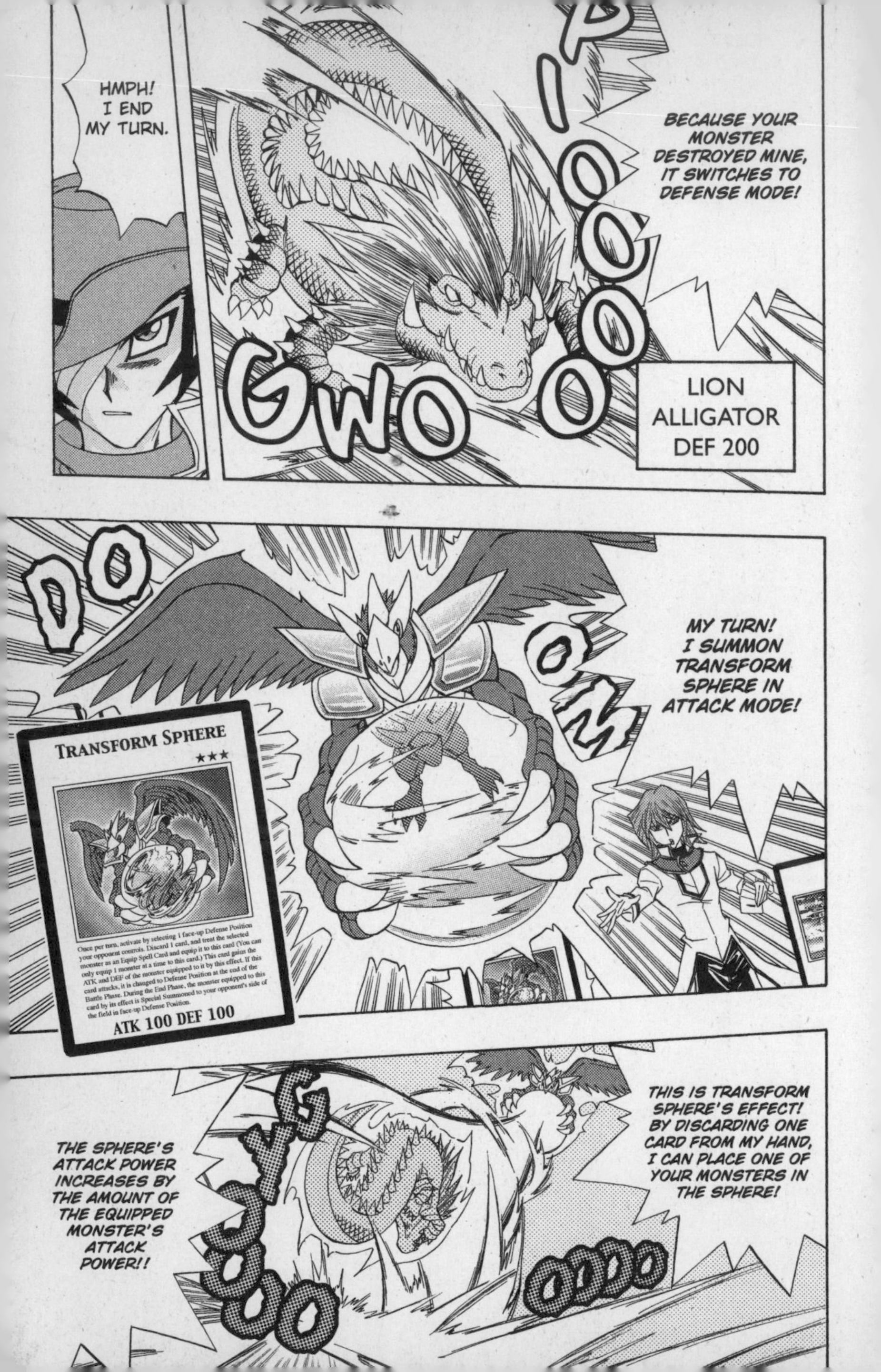
BECAUSE YOUR MONSTER DESTROYED MINE, IT SWITCHES TO DEFENSE MODE!
GWOOOOOOP
LION ALLIGATOR DEF 200
HMPH! I END MY TURN.
DOOM
MY TURN! I SUMMON TRANSFORM SPHERE IN ATTACK MODE!
TRANSFORM SPHERE
★★★
Once per turn, activate by selecting 1 face-up Defense Position your opponent controls. Discard 1 card, and treat the selected monster as an Equip Spell Card and equip it to this card (You can only equip 1 monster at a time to this card.) This card gains the ATK and DEF of the monster equipped to it by this effect. If this card attacks, it is changed to Defense Position at the end of the Battle Phase. During the End Phase, the monster equipped to this card by its effect is Special Summoned to your opponent's side of the field in face-up Defense Position.
ATK 100 DEF 100
THIS IS TRANSFORM SPHERE'S EFFECT! BY DISCARDING ONE CARD FROM MY HAND, I CAN PLACE ONE OF YOUR MONSTERS IN THE SPHERE!
THE SPHERE'S ATTACK POWER INCREASES BY THE AMOUNT OF THE EQUIPPED MONSTER'S ATTACK POWER!!
GYOOOOO
OOOOO

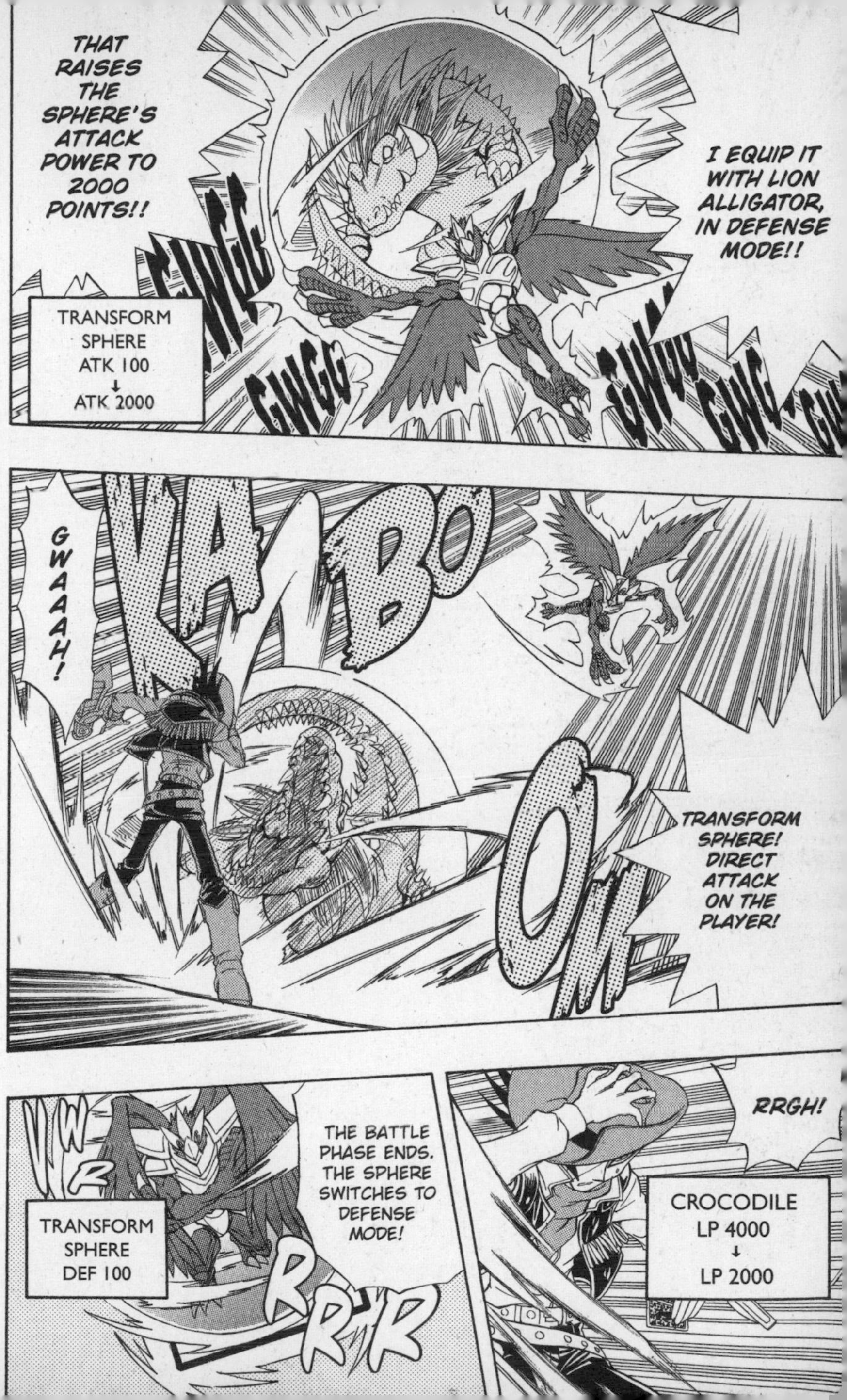
I EQUIP IT WITH LION ALLIGATOR, IN DEFENSE MODE!!
THAT RAISES THE SPHERE'S ATTACK POWER TO 2000 POINTS!!
TRANSFORM SPHERE ATK 100 ↓ ATK 2000
TRANSFORM SPHERE! DIRECT ATTACK ON THE PLAYER!
GWAAAAH!
RRGH!
CROCODILE LP 4000 ↓ LP 2000
THE BATTLE PHASE ENDS. THE SPHERE SWITCHES TO DEFENSE MODE!
TRANSFORM SPHERE DEF 100

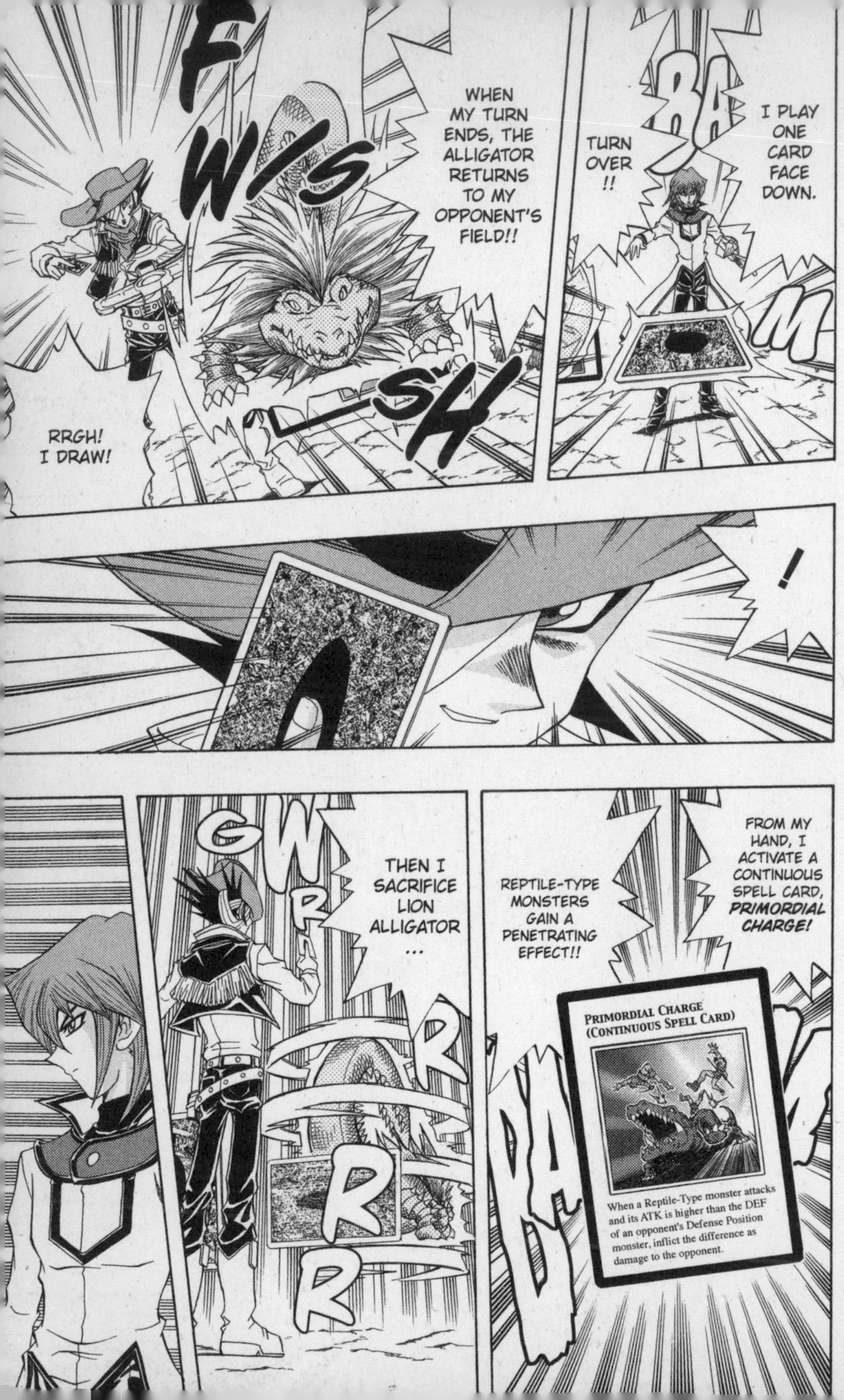
BA
I PLAY ONE CARD FACE DOWN.
TURN OVER !!
M
WHEN MY TURN ENDS, THE ALLIGATOR RETURNS TO MY OPPONENT'S FIELD!!
F
WIS
SH
RRGH! I DRAW!
!
FROM MY HAND, I ACTIVATE A CONTINUOUS SPELL CARD, ***PRIMORDIAL CHARGE!***
REPTILE-TYPE MONSTERS GAIN A PENETRATING EFFECT!!
PRIMORDIAL CHARGE (CONTINUOUS SPELL CARD)
When a Reptile-Type monster attacks and its ATK is higher than the DEF of an opponent's Defense Position monster, inflict the difference as damage to the opponent.
BA
THEN I SACRIFICE LION ALLIGATOR ...
G
W
R
R
R
R

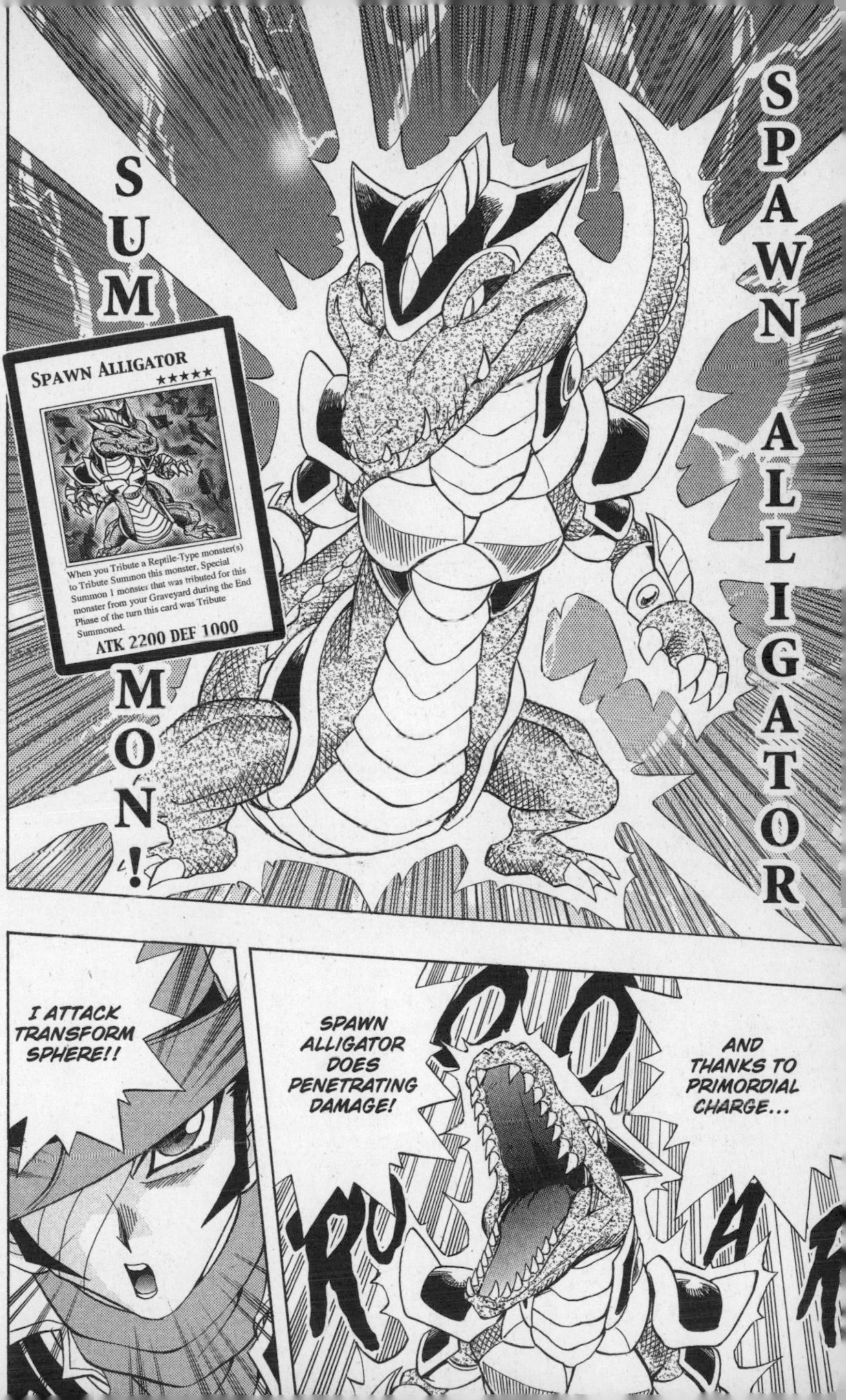
SUMMON!
SPAWN ALLIGATOR
SPAWN ALLIGATOR
★★★★★
When you Tribute a Reptile-Type monster(s) to Tribute Summon this monster, Special Summon 1 monster that was tributed for this monster from your Graveyard during the End Phase of the turn this card was Tribute Summoned.
ATK 2200 DEF 1000
I ATTACK TRANSFORM SPHERE!!
SPAWN ALLIGATOR DOES PENETRATING DAMAGE!
AND THANKS TO PRIMORDIAL CHARGE...

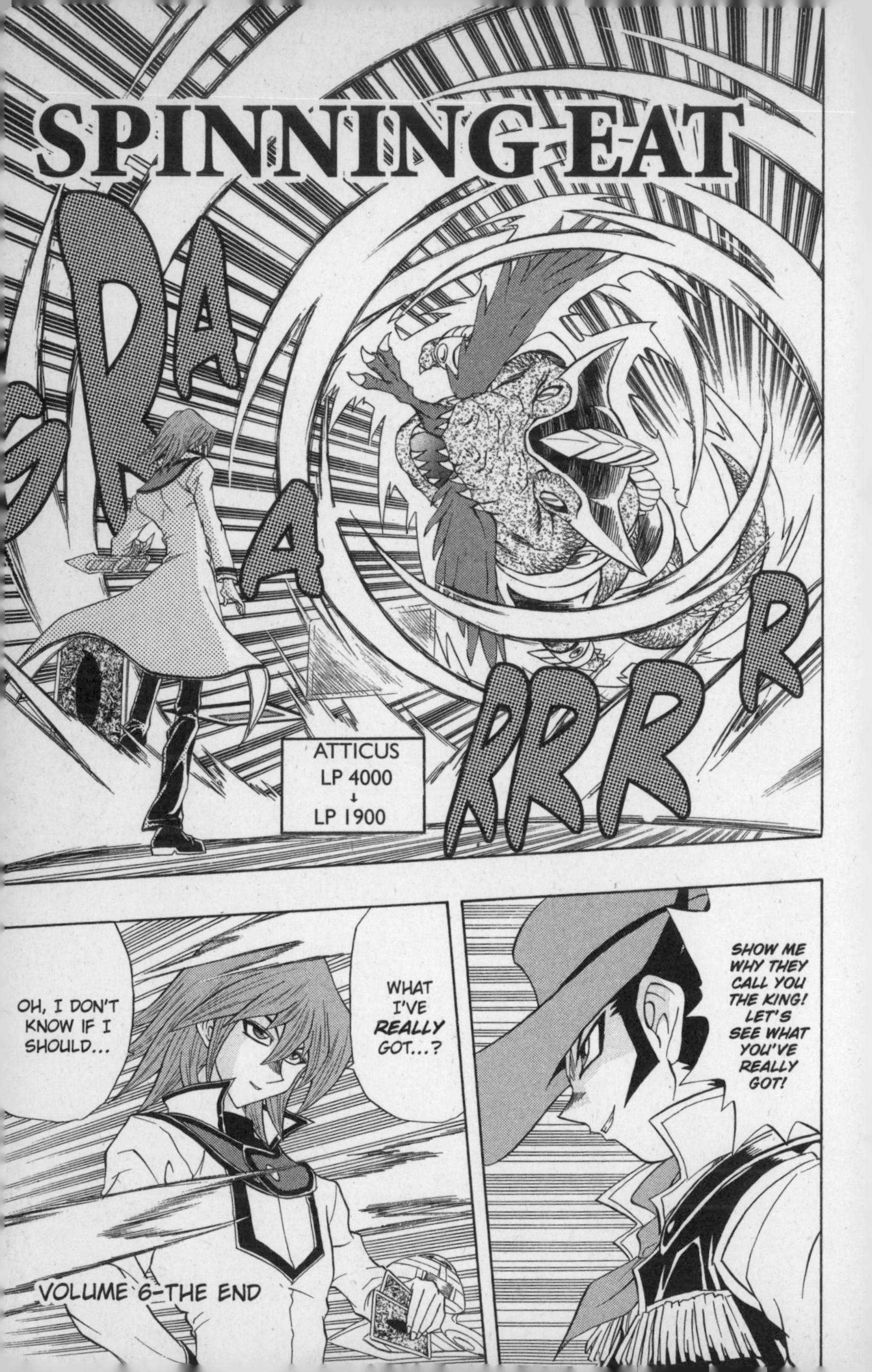
SPINNING EAT
GRAAA
RRRR
ATTICUS
LP 4000
↓
LP 1900
SHOW ME WHY THEY CALL YOU THE KING! LET'S SEE WHAT YOU'VE REALLY GOT!
WHAT I'VE *REALLY* GOT...?
OH, I DON'T KNOW IF I SHOULD...
VOLUME 6—THE END

## STAFF

MASAFUMI SATO
AKIHIRO TOMONAGA
AKIRA ITO

## DUEL COMBINATION COOPERATION

MASAHIRO UCHIDA

## COLORING

NABETARO

## EDITOR

DAISUKE TERASHI

# MASTER OF THE CARDS

Jaden Yuki and the rest of the next generation of Duelists have introduced their own cards into the *Yu-Gi-Oh!* TCG, which also make their first appearance here in the fifth volume of the *Yu-Gi-Oh: GX* manga! As with all original *Yu-Gi-Oh!* cards, names can differ slightly between the Japanese and English versions, so we're showing you both for reference. Plus, we show you the card even if the card itself doesn't show up in the manga but the monster or trap does! And some cards you may have already seen in the original *Yu-Gi-Oh!*, but we still note them the first time they appear in this volume anyway!

| First Appearance in This Volume | Japanese Card Name | English Card Name <<!>> = Not yet available in the TCG. |
|---|---|---|
| p.7 | *Dark End Dragon* ダークエンド・ドラゴン | Dark End Dragon |
| p.7 | *Light End Dragon* ライトエンド・ドラゴン | Light End Dragon |
| p.8 | *Light and Darkness Dragon* 光と闇の竜 | Light and Darkness Dragon |
| p.12 | *Shadow's Light* 陰の光 | Shadow's Light <<!>> |
| p.13 | *Cyber Dragon* サイバー・ドラゴン | Cyber Dragon |
| p.14 | *Emergency Cyber* エマージェンシー・サイバー | Cyber Emergency <<!>> |
| p.14 | *Cyber Struve* サイバー シュートルーフェ | Cyber Struve <<!>> |
| p.14 | *Cyber Alsafi* サイバー アルサーフィ | Cyber Alsafi <<!>> |
| p.14 | *Cyber Thuban* サイバー ツバーン | Cyber Thuban <<!>> |
| p.14 | *Cyber Alnair* サイバー アルナイル | Cyber Alnair <<!>> |
| p.23 | *Cyber Eltanin* サイバー・エルタニン | Cyber Eltanin |
| p.23 | *Born from Draconis* ボーン・フロム・ドラコニス | Born from Draconis <<!>> |

| | | |
|---|---|---|
| *p.45* | *Winged Kuriboh*<br>ハネクリボー | Winged Kuriboh |
| *p.58* | *Elemental Hero Voltic*<br>**E・HERO** ボルテック | Elemental Hero Voltic |
| *p.58* | *Voltic Spear*<br>ボルテック・スピア | Voltic Spear <<!>> |
| *p.58* | *Late Hero*<br>レイト・ヒーロー | Late Hero <<!>> |
| *p.58* | *Polymerization*<br>融合 | Polymerization |
| *p.58* | *Miracle Fusion*<br>ミラクル・フュージョン | Miracle Fusion |
| *p.59* | *Tiny Angel*<br>タイニィ・エンジェル | Tiny Angel <<!>> |
| *p.60* | *Elemental Hero Forestman*<br>**E・HERO** フォレストマン | Elemental Hero Woodsman |
| *p.61* | *Sei naru Tenkei*<br>聖なる天啓 | Sacred Revelation <<!>> |
| *p.61* | *Seishin Parmal*<br>聖神パーマル | Divine Spirit Parmal <<!>> |
| *p.62* | *Iofiel*<br>イオフィル | Iofiel <<!>> |
| *p.62* | *Zeriel*<br>ゼリエル | Zeriel <<!>> |
| *p.65* | *Elemental Hero Ocean*<br>**E・HERO** オーシャン | Elemental Hero Ocean |
| *p.66* | *Elemental Hero The Earth*<br>**E・HERO** ジ・アース | Elemental Hero Terra Firma |
| *p.74* | *Heaven's Judgment*<br>ヘベンズ・ジャッジメント | Heaven's Judgment <<!>> |

| | | |
|---|---|---|
| *p.75* | *The Splendid VENUS*<br>ザ　スプレンディド　ヴィーナス | Splendid Venus |
| *p.79* | *Responsibility*<br>レスポンシィビリティ | Responsibility <<!>> |
| *p.79* | *Defend Hero*<br>ディフェンド・ヒーロー | Defend Hero <<!>> |
| *p.79* | *Castle of the Gods, Valhalla*<br>神の居城　ヴァルハラー | Valhalla, Hall of the Fallen |
| *p.80* | *Angel Bow*<br>エンジェル・ボー | Angelic Bow <<!>> |
| *p.80* | *Saint Aura*<br>セイント・オーラ | *Saint Aura* <<!>> |
| *p.83* | *Megami no Kôrin*<br>女神の降臨 | Advent of the Goddess <<!>> |
| *p.88* | *Elemental Hero Flash*<br>***E・HERO*** フラッシュ | Elemental Hero Flash<<!>> |
| *p.89* | *Cyclone*<br>サイクロン | Mystical Space Typhoon |
| *p.93* | *Elemental Hero Airman*<br>***E・HERO*** エア ーマン | Elemental Hero Stratos |
| *p.94* | *Elemental Hero The Shining*<br>***E・HERO*** The シャイニング | Elemental Hero The Shining <<!>> |
| *p.109* | *Heaven's Lost Property*<br>天の落とし物 | Heaven's Lost Property <<!>> |
| *p.109* | *Shatiel*<br>シャティエル | Shatiel <<!>> |
| *p.109* | *Holy Sanctuary*<br>ホーリー・サンクチュアリ | Divine Sanctuary <<!>> |
| *p.109* | *Angel Ring*<br>エンジェル・リング | Angel's Ring <<!>> |

| | | |
|---|---|---|
| *p.109* | *Gôyoku na Tsubo* 強欲な壷 | Pot of Greed |
| *p.109* | *Earth Gravity*<br>アース・グラビティ | Terra Firma Gravity |
| *p.109* | *Hero's Bond*<br>*Hero's* ボンド | Hero's Bond |
| *p.119* | *Elemental Hero Gaia*<br>**E・HERO** ガイア | Elemental Hero Gaia |
| *p.119* | *Elemental Hero Knospe*<br>**E・HERO** クノスペ | Elemental Hero Knospe |
| *p.121* | *Weak Anger*<br>ウィーク・アンガー | Weak Anger <<!>> |
| *p.122* | *Elemental Hero Lady of Fire*<br>**E・HERO** レディ・オブ・<br>ファイア | Elemental Hero Lady Heat |
| *p.126* | *Elemental Hero Great Tornado*<br>**E・HERO** *Great Tornado* | Elemental Hero Great Tornado<br><<!>> |
| *p.191* | *Air Sphere*<br>エアースフィア | Air Sphere <<!>> |
| *p.192* | *Lion Alligator*<br>ライオ・アリゲーター | Lion Alligator <<!>> |
| *p.192* | *Daishô no Fûatsu*<br>代償の風圧 | Wind Pressure Compensation<br><<!>> |
| *p.193* | *Transform Sphere*<br>トランスフォーム・スフィア | Transforming Sphere |
| *p.195* | *Taiko no Shingeki*<br>太古の進撃 | Primordial Charge <<!>> |
| *p.196* | *Spawn Alligator*<br>スパウン・アリゲーター | Spawn Alligator <<!>> |